We hope you enjoy the Kakashi Chronicles too...

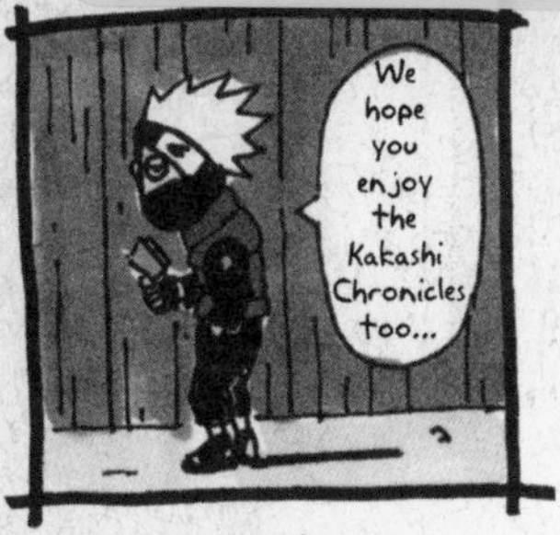

Perhaps it seems abrupt, but it felt right to end part one with this volume. The next book will begin part two. In a sense, though, I don't think *Naruto* needs to be broken up into parts... Anyway, stay with me, folks!

—*Masashi Kishimoto, 2005*

岸本斉史

Author/artist Masashi Kishimoto was born in 1974 in rural Okayama Prefecture, Japan. After spending time in art college, he won the Hop Step Award for new manga artists with his manga **Karakuri** (Mechanism). Kishimoto decided to base his next story on traditional Japanese culture. His first version of **Naruto**, drawn in 1997, was a one-shot story about fox spirits; his final version, which debuted in **Weekly Shonen Jump** in 1999, quickly became the most popular ninja manga in Japan.

ラーメン一楽

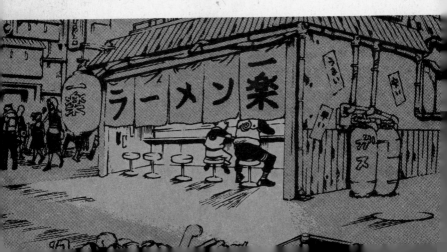

NARUTO VOL. 27
The SHONEN JUMP Manga Edition

STORY AND ART BY MASASHI KISHIMOTO

Translation & English Adaptation/Naomi Kokubo & Eric-Jon Rössel Waugh
Touch-up Art & Lettering/Annaliese Christman
Consultant/Mari Morimoto
Design/Yvonne Cai
Editor/Joel Enos

Editor in Chief, Books/Alvin Lu
Editor in Chief, Magazines/Marc Weidenbaum
VP of Publishing Licensing/Rika Inouye
VP of Sales/Gonzalo Ferreyra
Sr. VP of Marketing/Liza Coppola
Publisher/Hyoe Narita

Printed in the U.S.A.

Published by VIZ Media, LLC
P.O. Box 77010
San Francisco, CA 94107

SHONEN JUMP Manga Edition
10 9 8 7 6 5 4 3
First printing, December 2007
Third printing, December 2007

THE WORLD'S
MOST POPULAR MANGA

www.shonenjump.com

SHONEN JUMP MANGA EDITION

NARUTO

VOL. 27
DEPARTURE

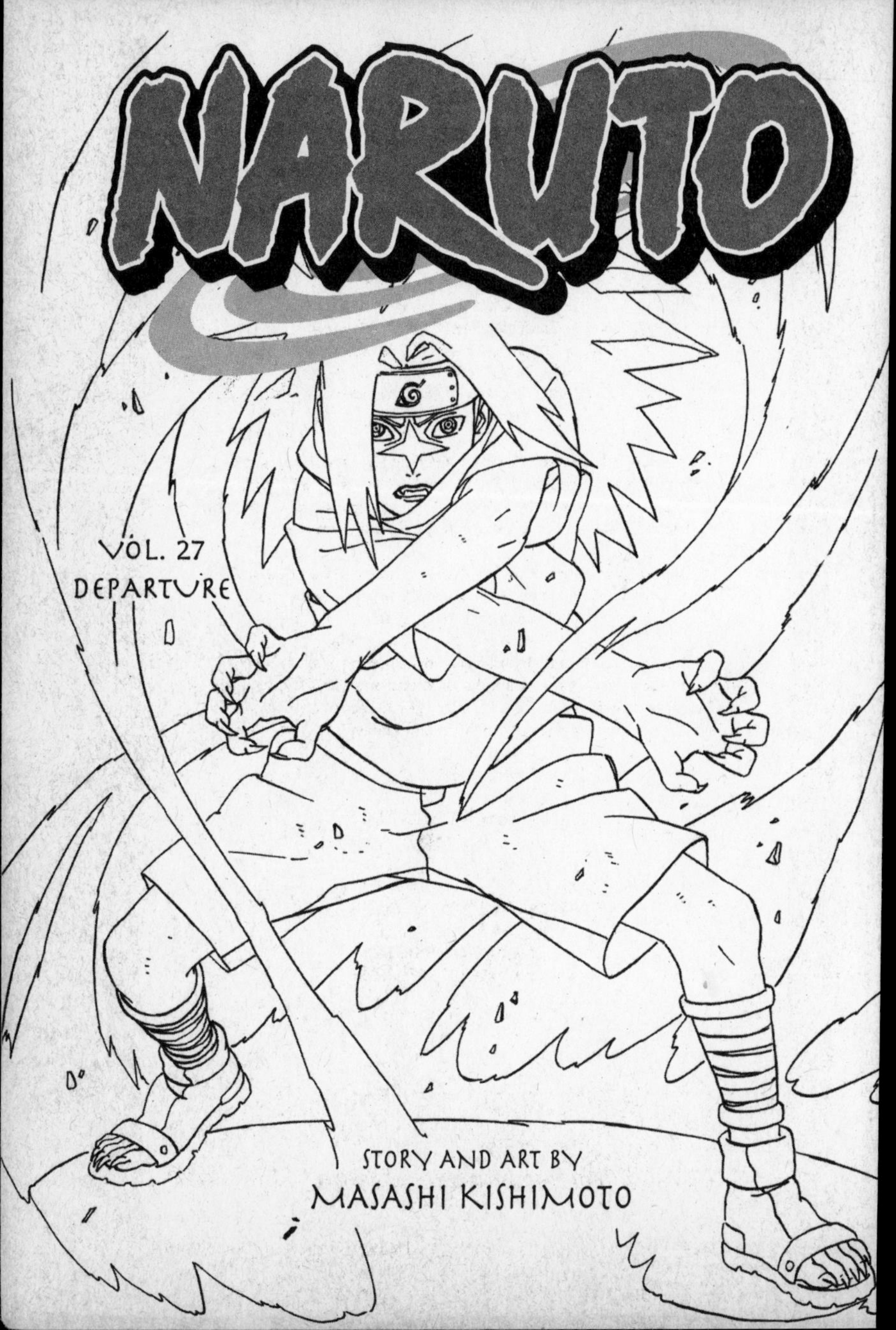

STORY AND ART BY
MASASHI KISHIMOTO

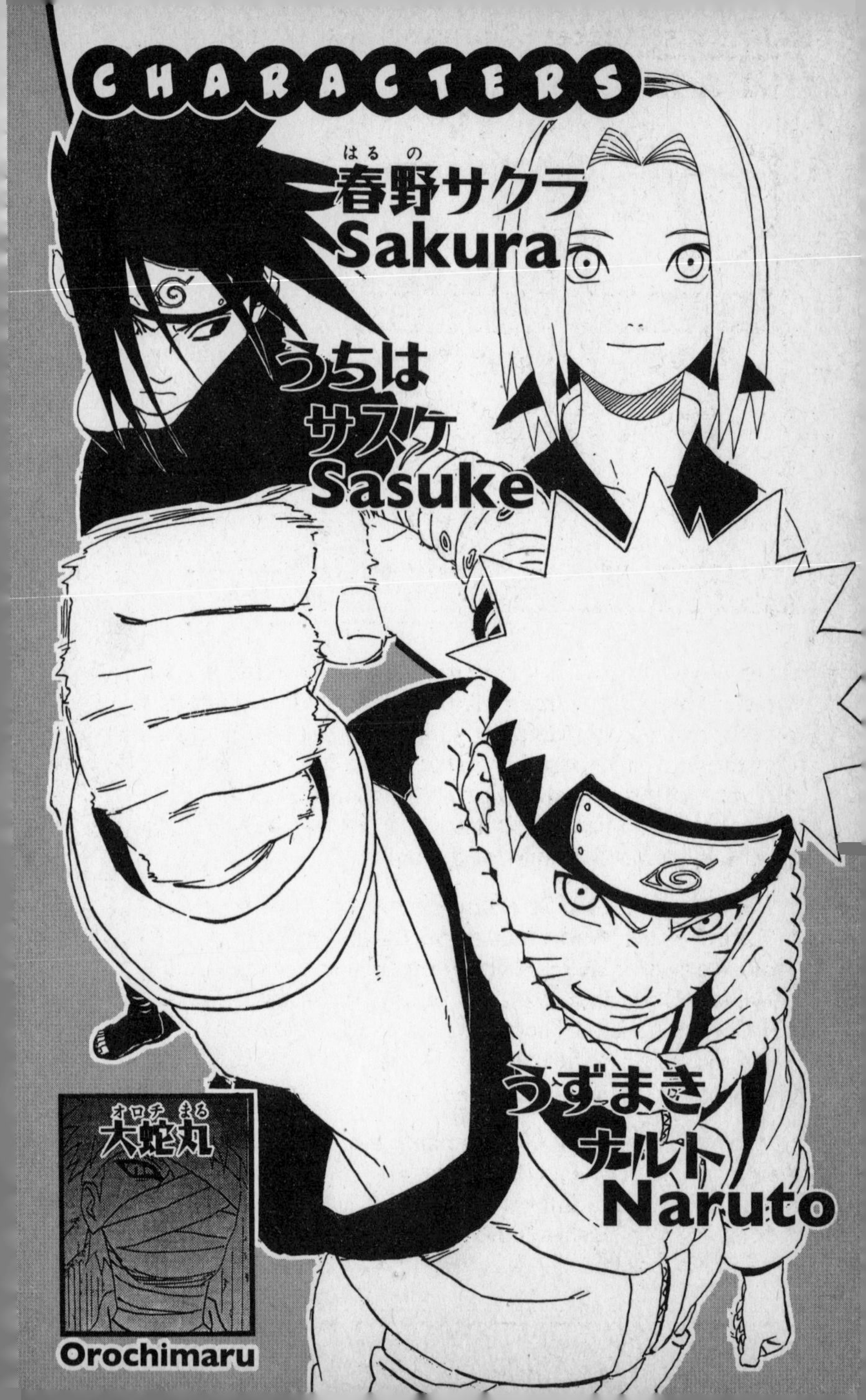
CHARACTERS
春野サクラ
Sakura
うちはサスケ
Sasuke
うずまきナルト
Naruto
大蛇丸
Orochimaru

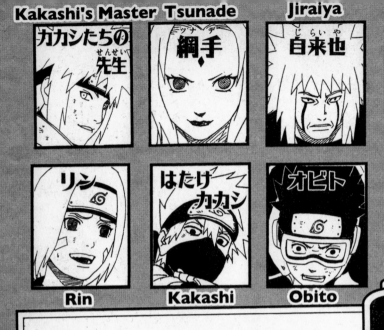

Kakashi's Master Tsunade Jiraiya

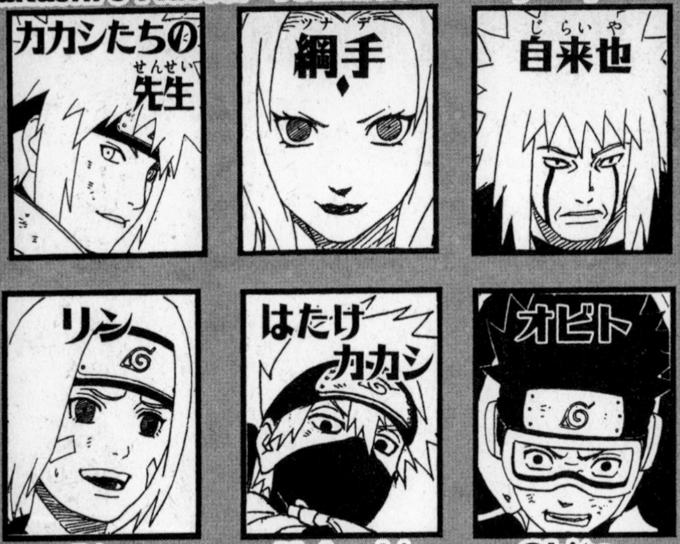
じらいや
自来也
ツナデ
網手
カカシたちの
せんせい
先生
オビト
はたけ
カカシ
リン

Rin Kakashi Obito

The Story So far...

Twelve years ago a destructive nine-tailed fox spirit attacked the ninja village of Konohagakure. The Hokage, or village champion, defeated the fox by sealing its soul into the body of a baby boy. That boy is Naruto, once the bane of the Konohagakure Ninja Academy. Despite the rough start, he and his friends, Sasuke and Sakura, successfully join the ranks of the ninja.

During the Chûnin Selection Exams, they are attacked by Orochimaru, who vanishes only after he places a curse mark on Sasuke. Halfway through the third exam, however, Orochimaru and his henchmen launch *Operation Destroy Konoha!* The attack is thwarted when the Third Hokage sacrifices his life. After a deadly battle with Orochimaru, Tsunade becomes the Fifth Hokage.

Lured by the power of Orochimaru, Sasuke departs Konoha in the company of the Sound Four. In pursuit of Sasuke, Shikamaru and his team weather desperate battles. Naruto clashes violently with Sasuke but he fails to stop his friend...

NARUTO

VOL. 27
DEPARTURE

CONTENTS

Number 236:

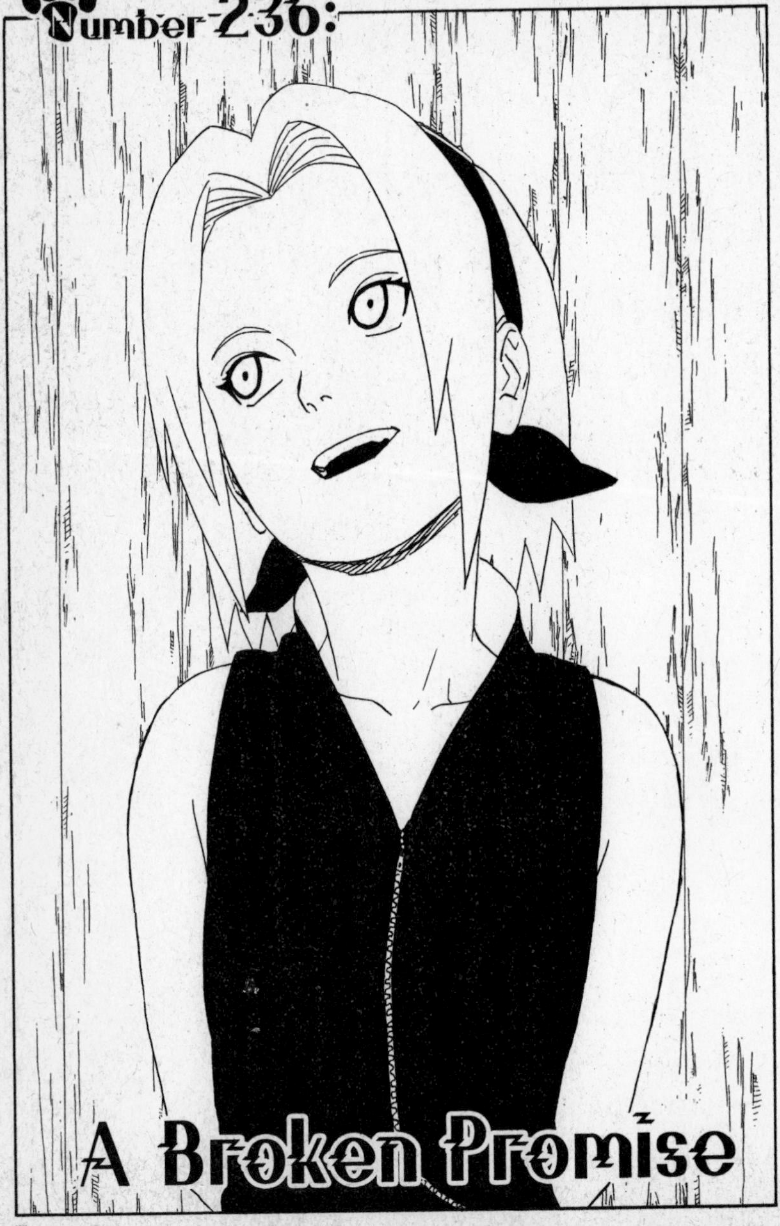

A Broken Promise

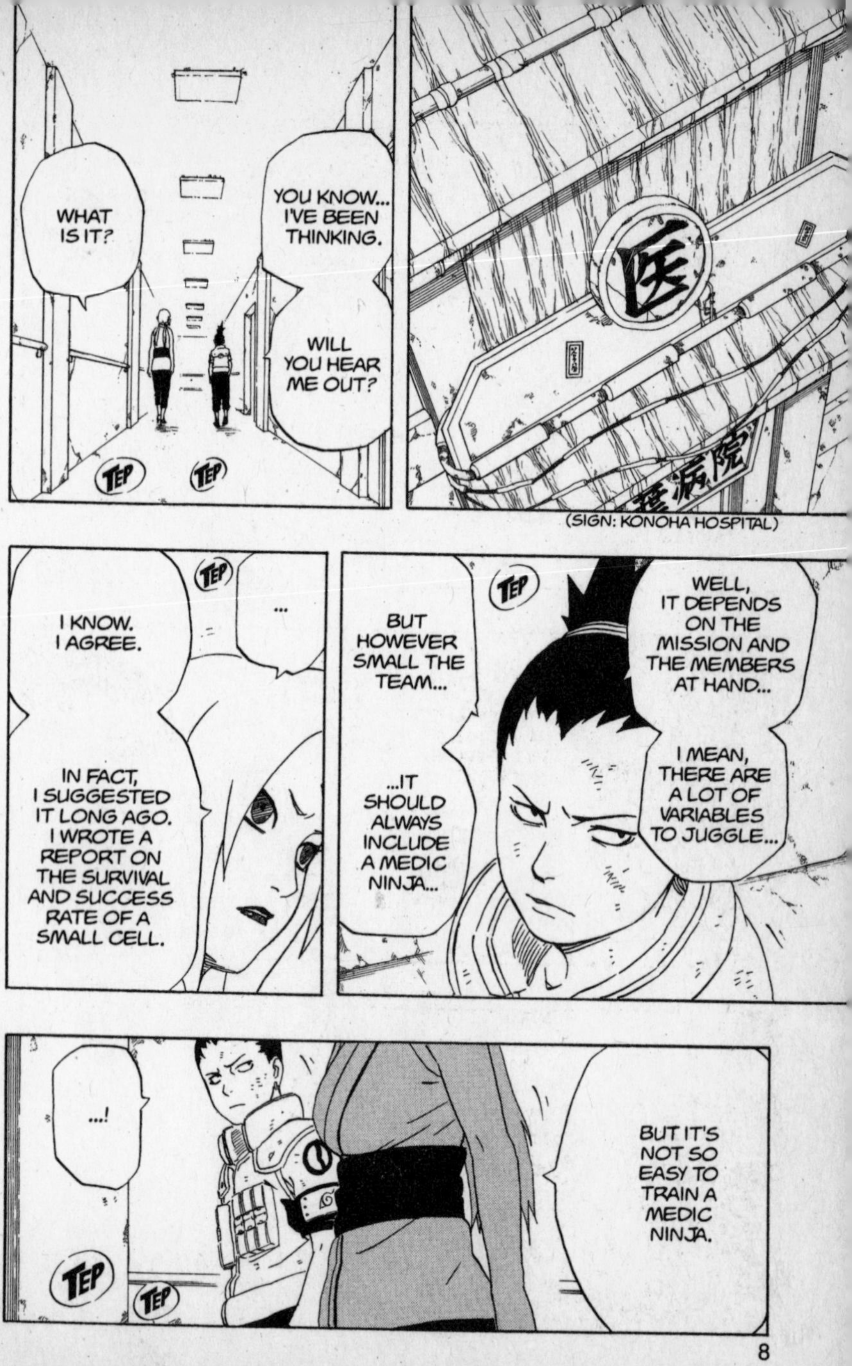
(SIGN: KONOHA HOSPITAL)
YOU KNOW... I'VE BEEN THINKING.
WILL YOU HEAR ME OUT?
WHAT IS IT?
TEP
TEP
WELL, IT DEPENDS ON THE MISSION AND THE MEMBERS AT HAND...
I MEAN, THERE ARE A LOT OF VARIABLES TO JUGGLE...
TEP
BUT HOWEVER SMALL THE TEAM...
...IT SHOULD ALWAYS INCLUDE A MEDIC NINJA...
TEP
...
I KNOW. I AGREE.
IN FACT, I SUGGESTED IT LONG AGO. I WROTE A REPORT ON THE SURVIVAL AND SUCCESS RATE OF A SMALL CELL.
BUT IT'S NOT SO EASY TO TRAIN A MEDIC NINJA.
...!
TEP
TEP

READ THIS WAY

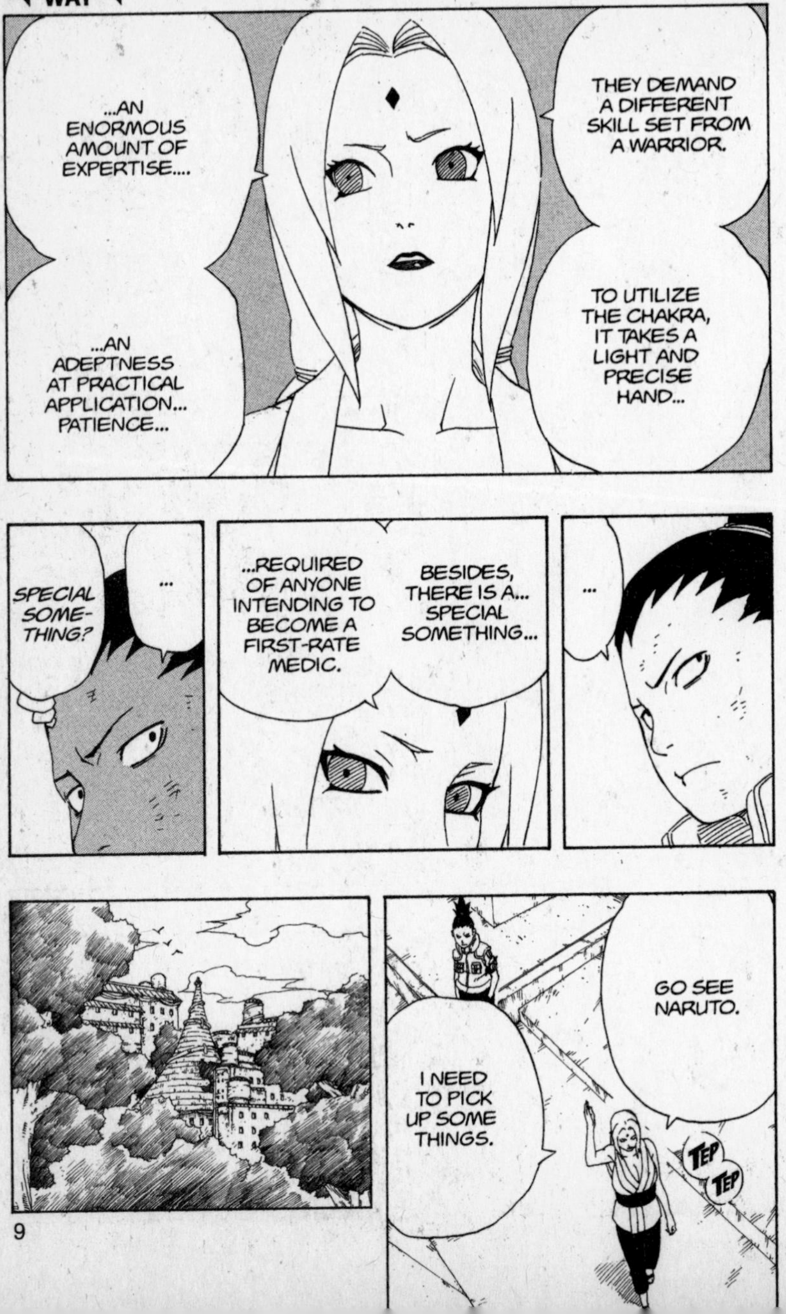

THEY DEMAND A DIFFERENT SKILL SET FROM A WARRIOR.
TO UTILIZE THE CHAKRA, IT TAKES A LIGHT AND PRECISE HAND...
...AN ENORMOUS AMOUNT OF EXPERTISE....
...AN ADEPTNESS AT PRACTICAL APPLICATION... PATIENCE...
...
BESIDES, THERE IS A... SPECIAL SOMETHING...
...REQUIRED OF ANYONE INTENDING TO BECOME A FIRST-RATE MEDIC.
...
SPECIAL SOME-THING?
GO SEE NARUTO.
I NEED TO PICK UP SOME THINGS.
TEP
TEP

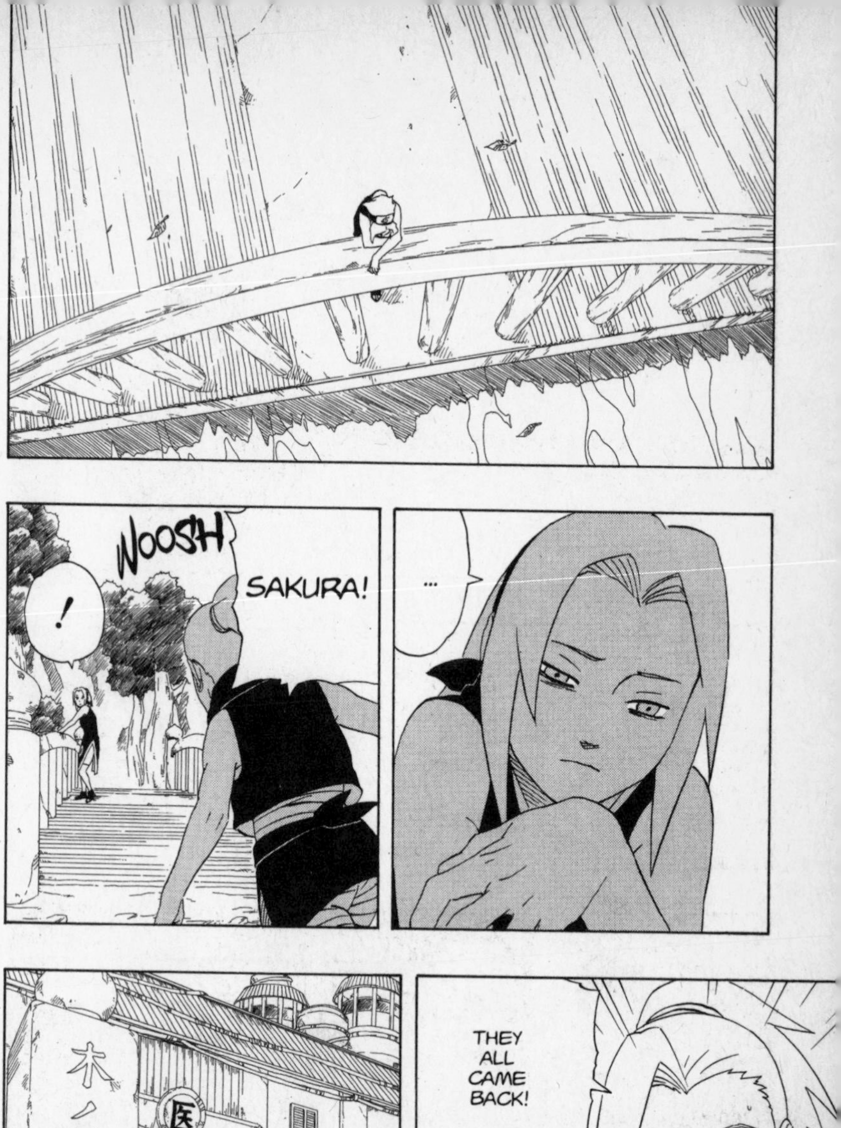
...
WOOSH
SAKURA!
!
THEY ALL CAME BACK!
C'MON, THEY'RE AT THE KONOHA HOSPITAL!
木ノ葉病院
医
木ノ葉病院

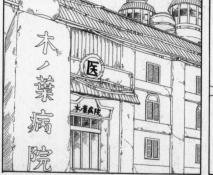

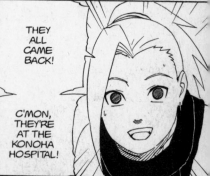

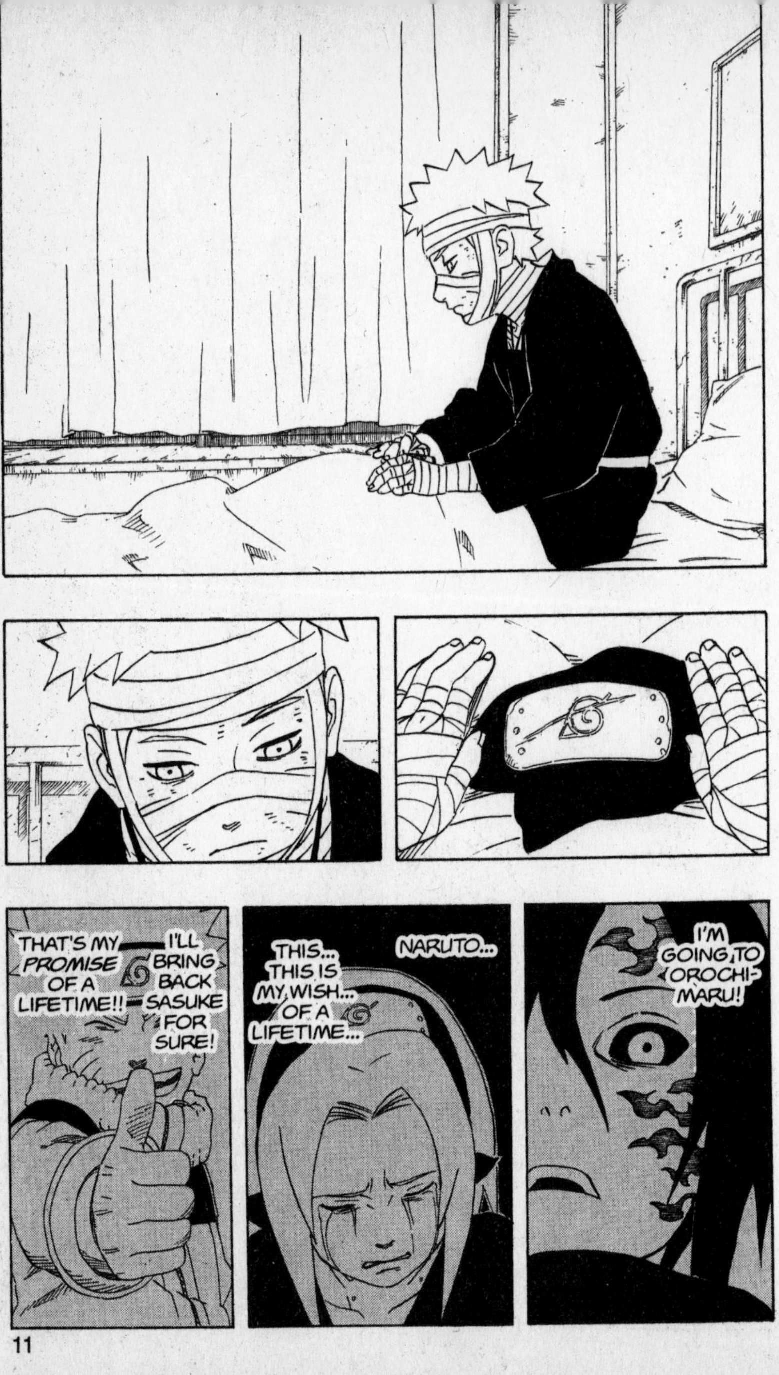
I'M GOING TO OROCHI-MARU!
NARUTO...
THIS... THIS IS MY WISH... OF A LIFETIME...
I'LL BRING BACK SASUKE FOR SURE!
THAT'S MY *PROMISE* OF A LIFETIME!!

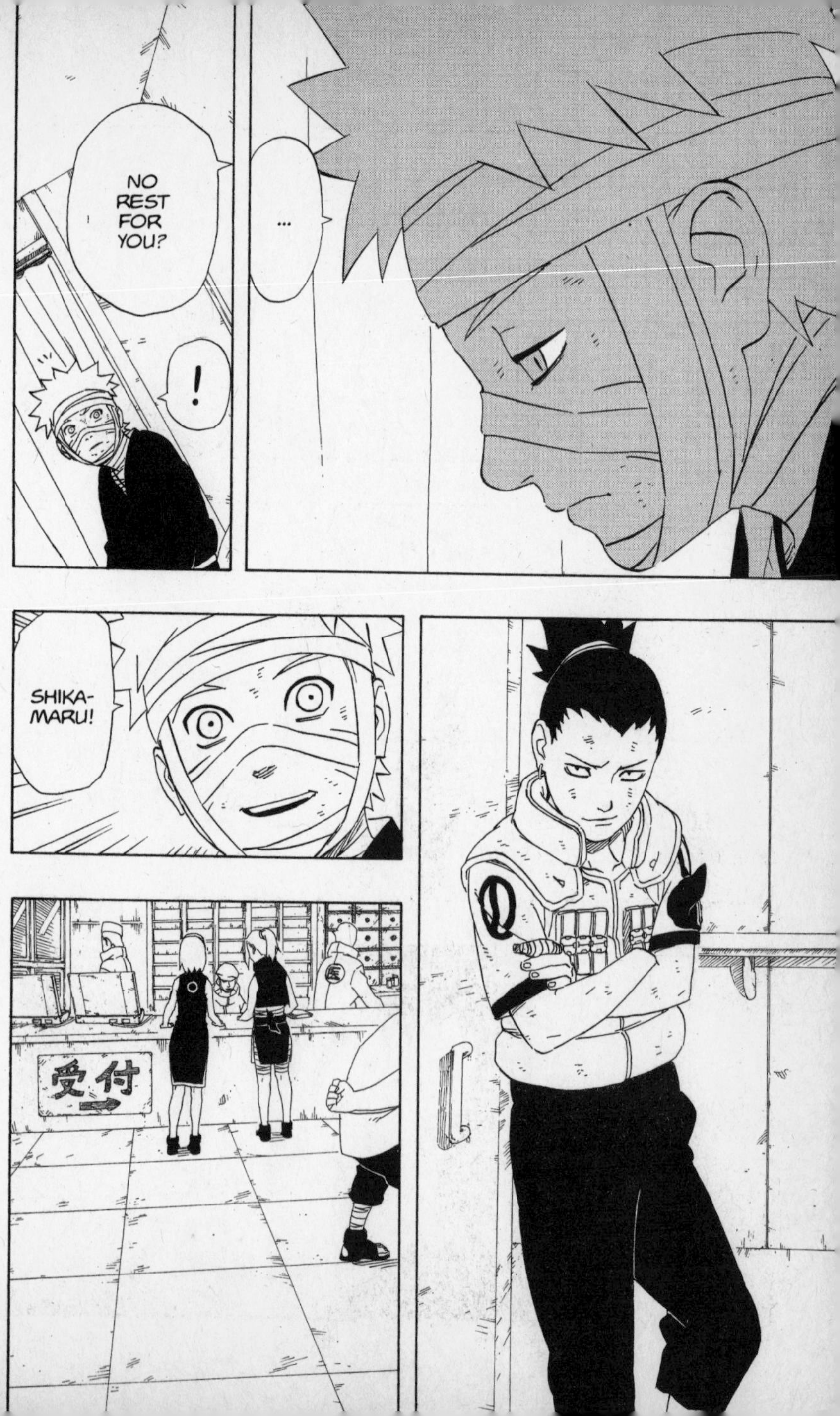
...
NO REST FOR YOU?
!
SHIKA-MARU!
受付

READ THIS WAY

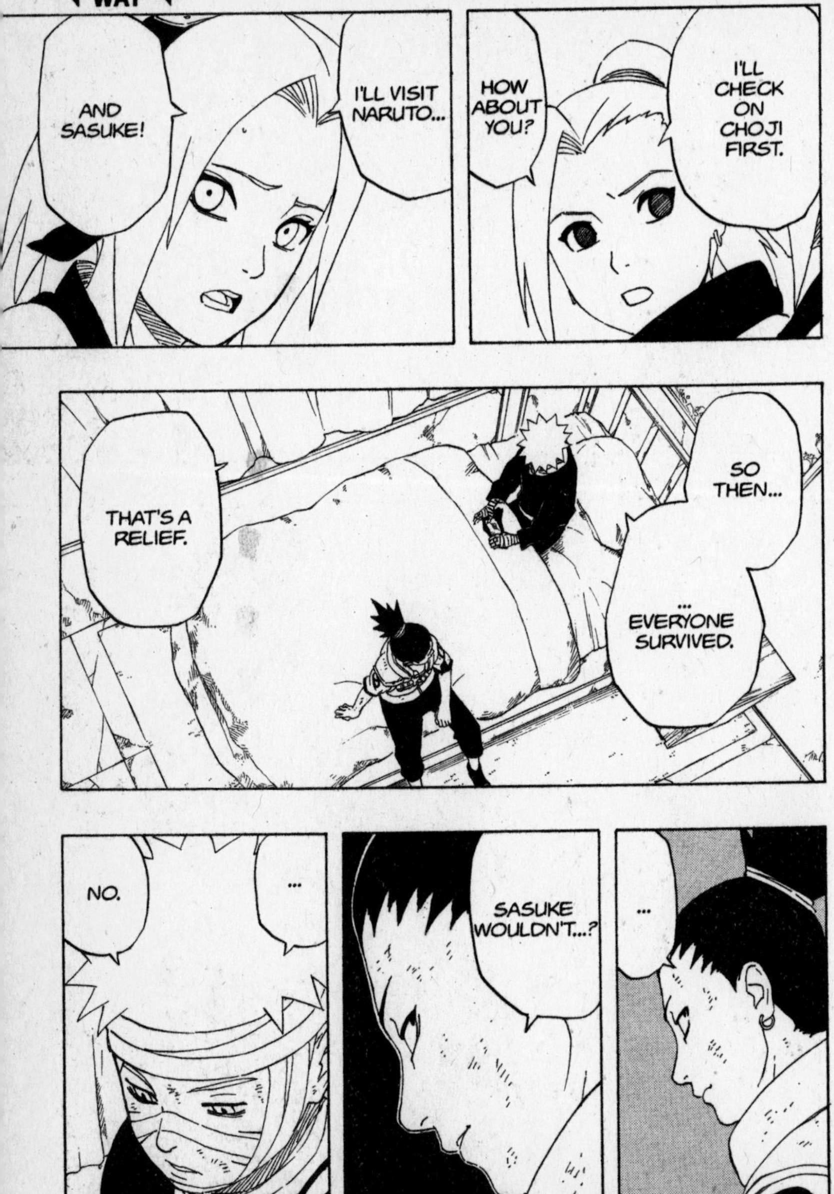
I'LL CHECK ON CHOJI FIRST.
HOW ABOUT YOU?
I'LL VISIT NARUTO...
AND SASUKE!
SO THEN...
... EVERYONE SURVIVED.
THAT'S A RELIEF.
...
SASUKE WOULDN'T...?
...
NO.

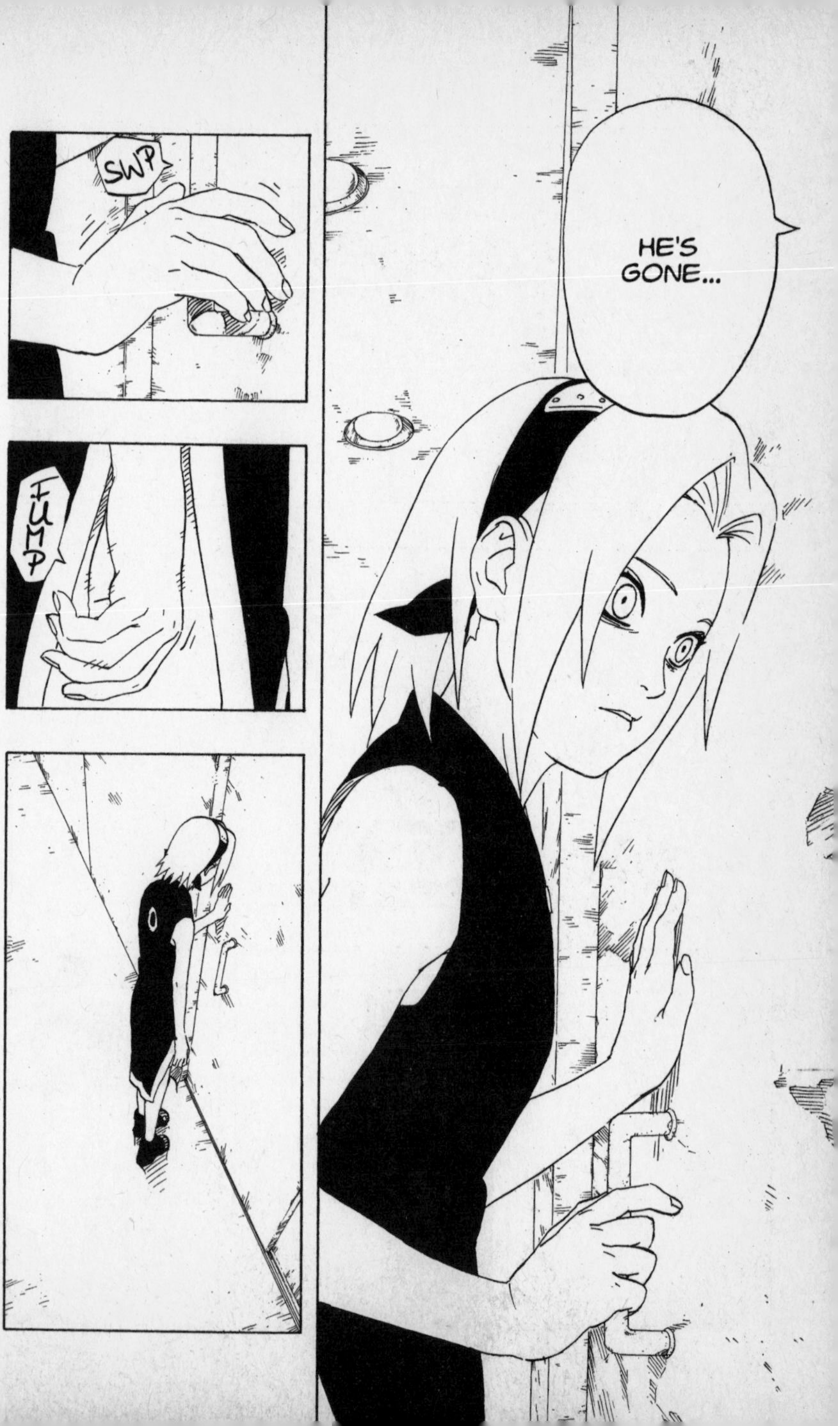
HE'S GONE...
SWP
FUMP

READ THIS WAY

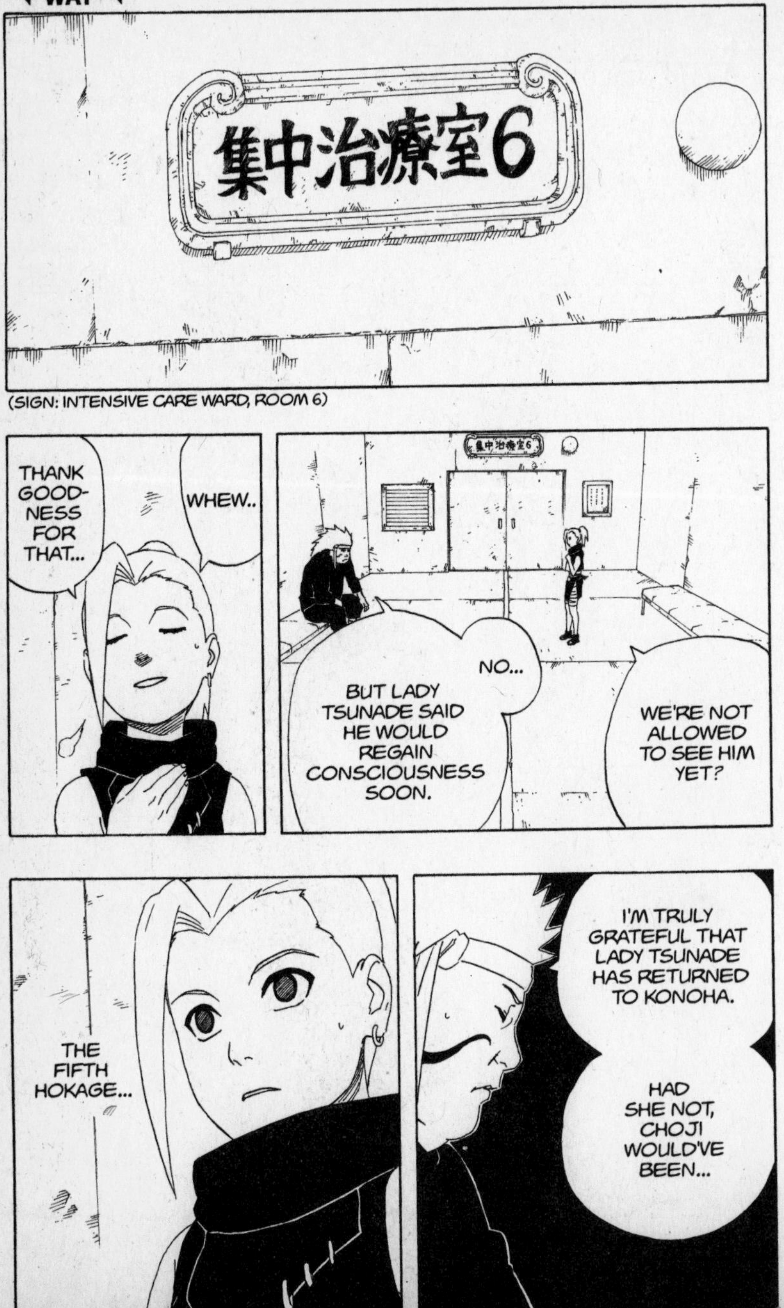
集中治療室6
(SIGN: INTENSIVE CARE WARD, ROOM 6)
集中治療室6
WE'RE NOT ALLOWED TO SEE HIM YET?
NO...
BUT LADY TSUNADE SAID HE WOULD REGAIN CONSCIOUSNESS SOON.
WHEW..
THANK GOODNESS FOR THAT...
I'M TRULY GRATEFUL THAT LADY TSUNADE HAS RETURNED TO KONOHA.
HAD SHE NOT, CHOJI WOULD'VE BEEN...
THE FIFTH HOKAGE...

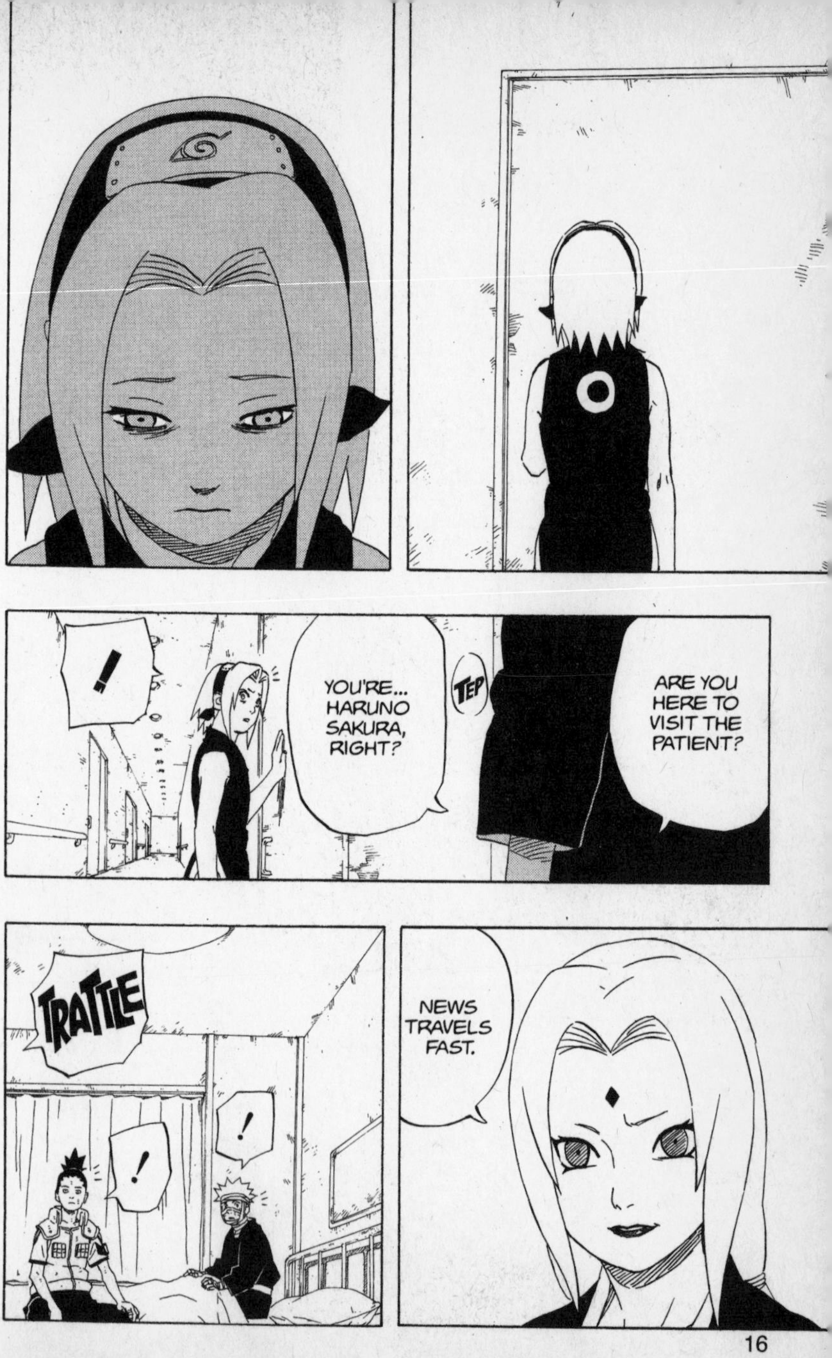
ARE YOU HERE TO VISIT THE PATIENT?
TEP
YOU'RE... HARUNO SAKURA, RIGHT?
!
NEWS TRAVELS FAST.
TRATTLE
!
!

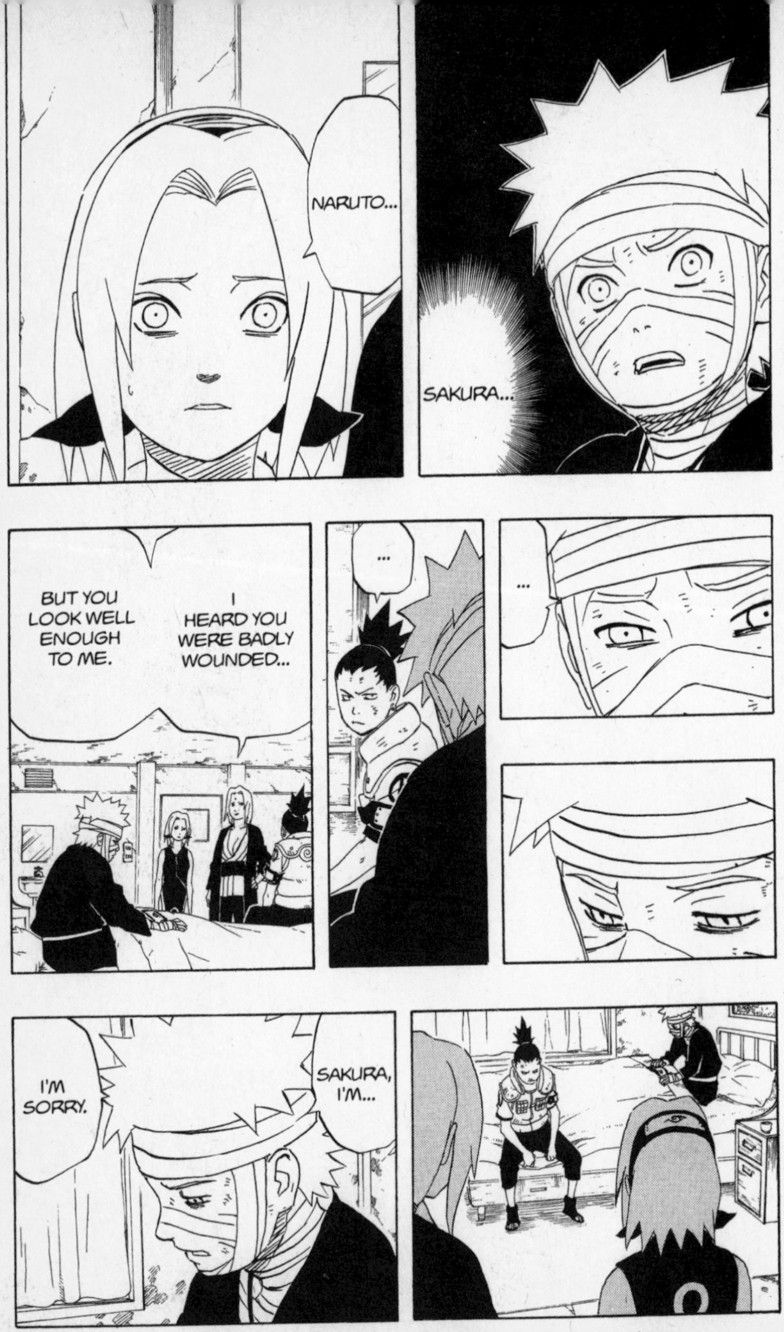
SAKURA...
NARUTO...
...
...
I HEARD YOU WERE BADLY WOUNDED...
BUT YOU LOOK WELL ENOUGH TO ME.
SAKURA, I'M...
I'M SORRY.

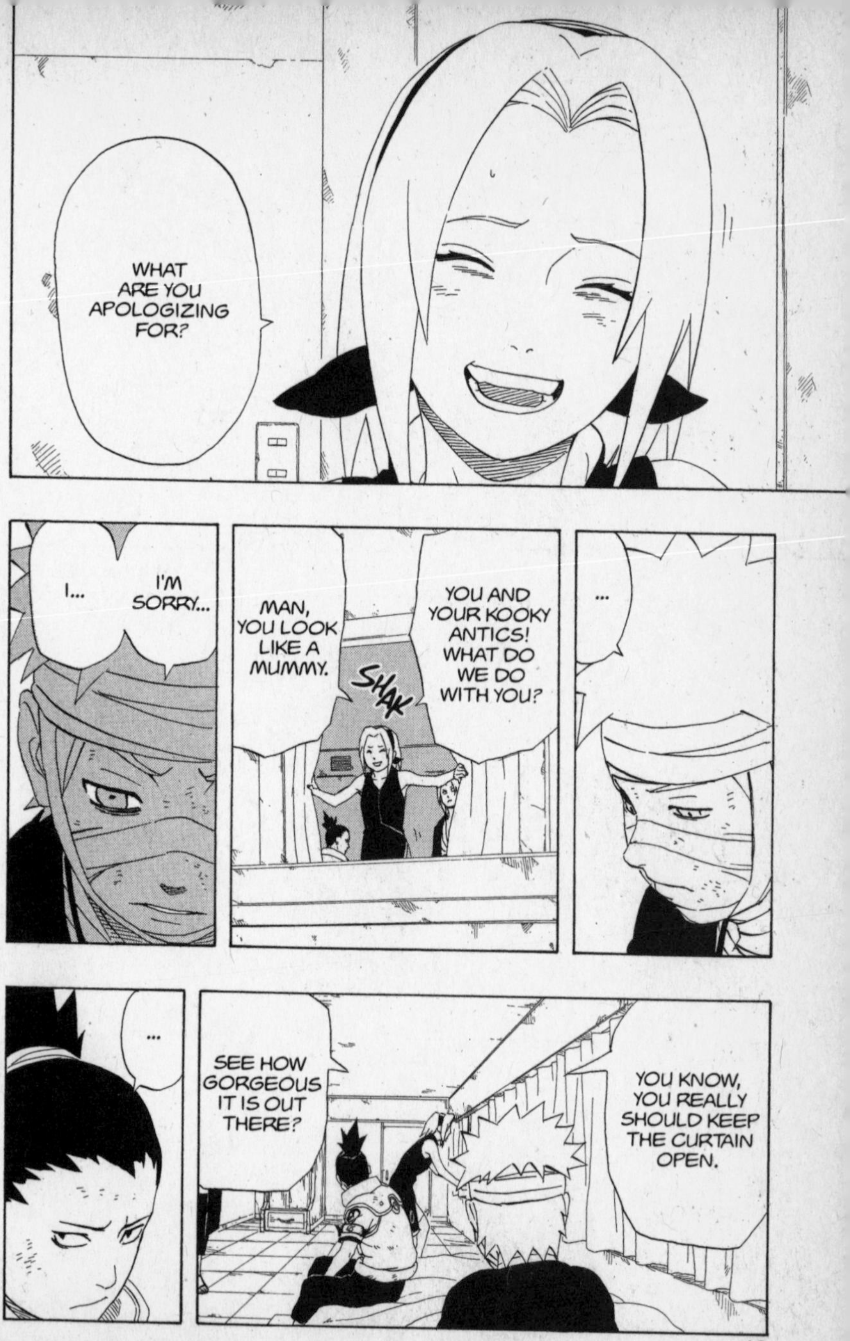
WHAT ARE YOU APOLOGIZING FOR?
...
YOU AND YOUR KOOKY ANTICS! WHAT DO WE DO WITH YOU?
MAN, YOU LOOK LIKE A MUMMY.
SHAK
I... I'M SORRY...
YOU KNOW, YOU REALLY SHOULD KEEP THE CURTAIN OPEN.
SEE HOW GORGEOUS IT IS OUT THERE?
...

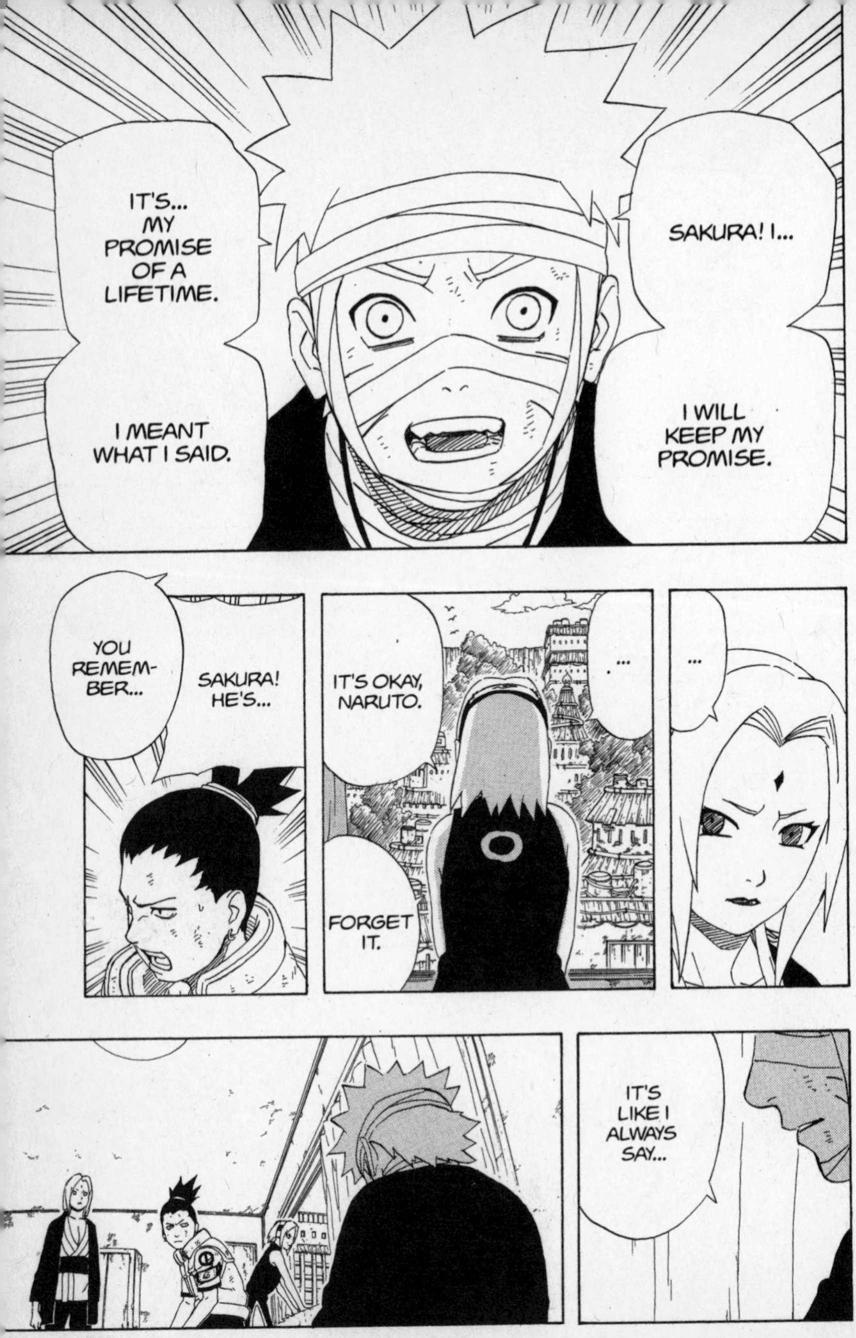
SAKURA! I...
I WILL KEEP MY PROMISE.
IT'S... MY PROMISE OF A LIFETIME.
I MEANT WHAT I SAID.
...
...
IT'S OKAY, NARUTO.
FORGET IT.
SAKURA! HE'S...
YOU REMEMBER...
IT'S LIKE I ALWAYS SAY...

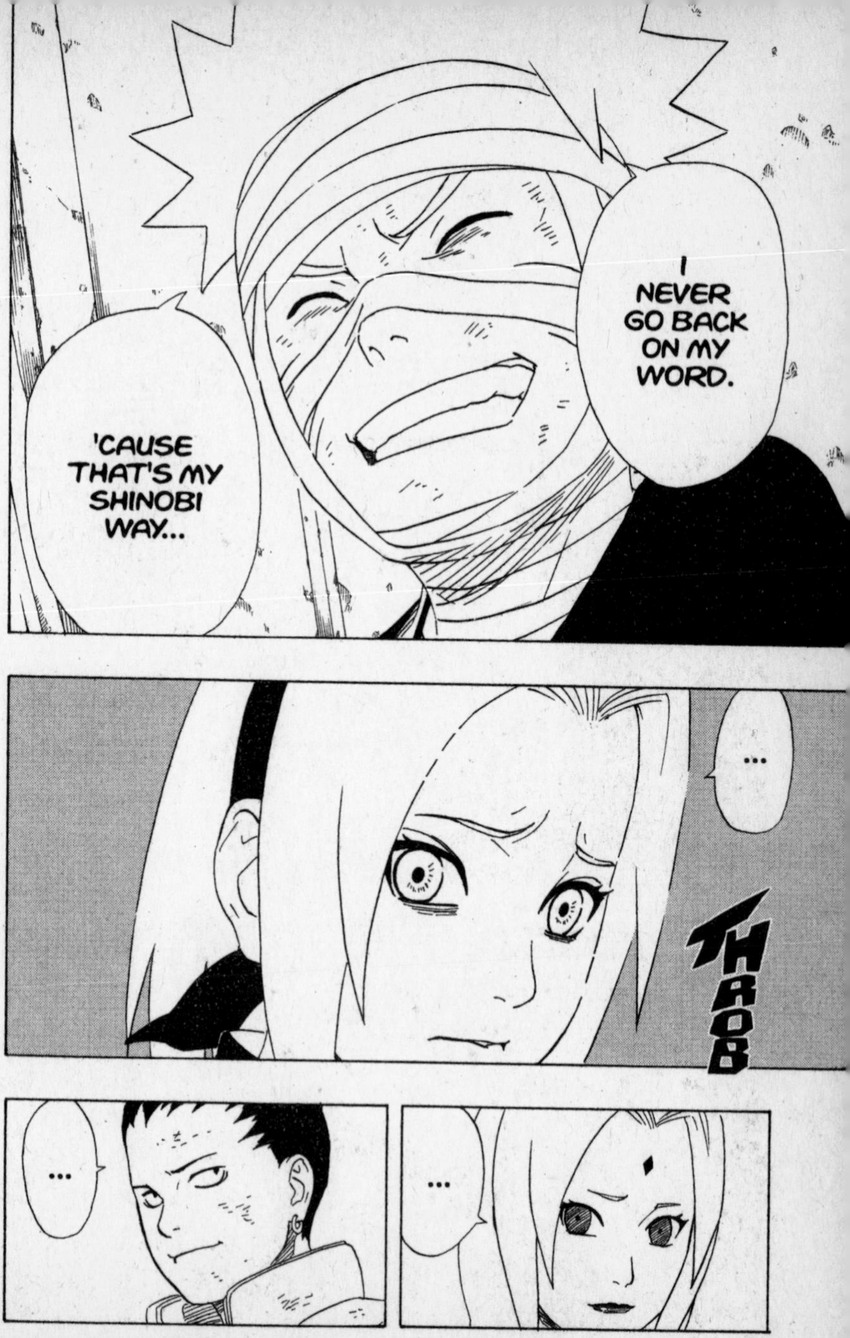
I NEVER GO BACK ON MY WORD.
'CAUSE THAT'S MY SHINOBI WAY...
...
THROB
...
...

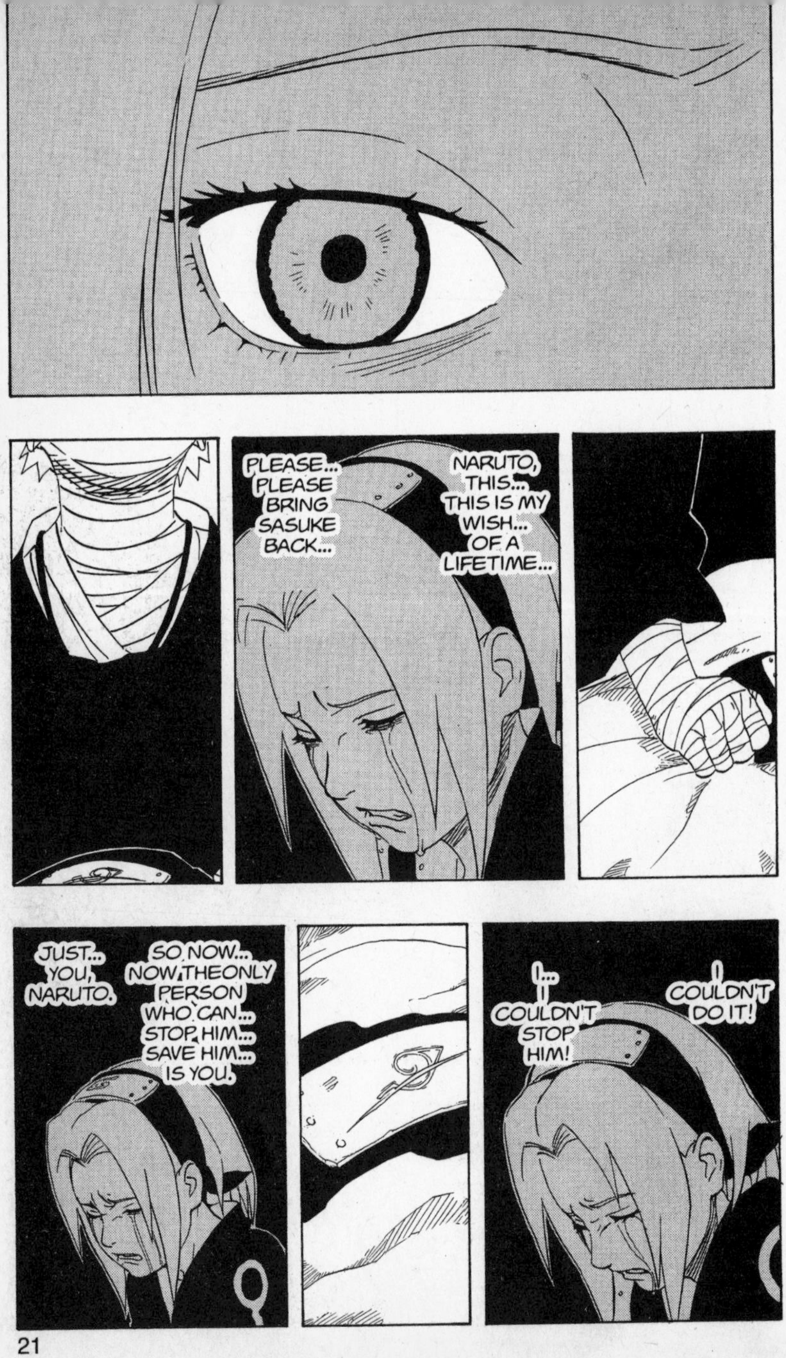
NARUTO, THIS... THIS IS MY WISH... OF A LIFETIME...
PLEASE... PLEASE BRING SASUKE BACK...
I COULDN'T DO IT!
I... I COULDN'T STOP HIM!
SO NOW... NOW THE ONLY PERSON WHO CAN... STOP HIM... SAVE HIM... IS YOU.
JUST... YOU, NARUTO.

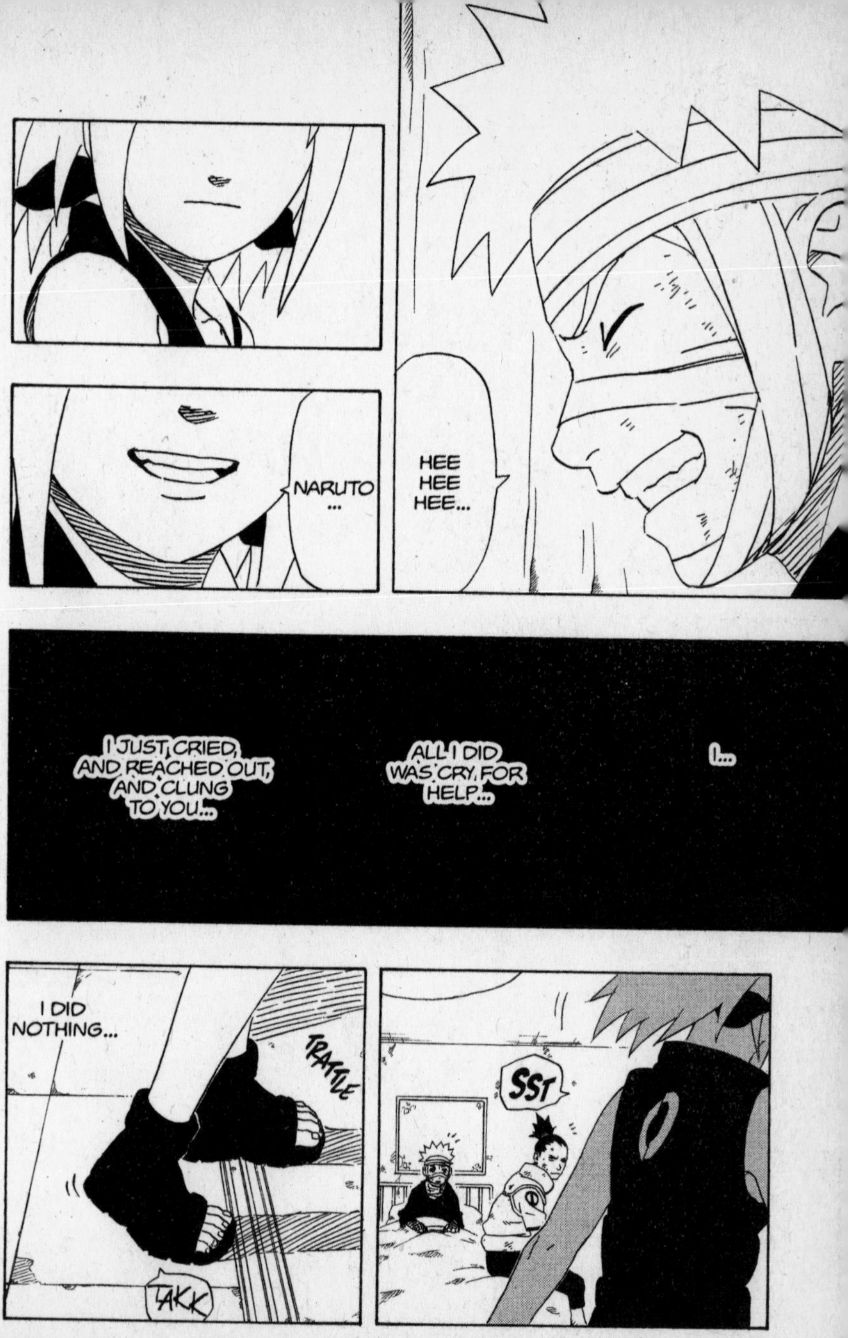

HEE HEE HEE...
NARUTO ...
I...
ALL I DID WAS CRY FOR HELP...
I JUST CRIED, AND REACHED OUT, AND CLUNG TO YOU...
SST
I DID NOTHING...
TAKK

READ THIS WAY

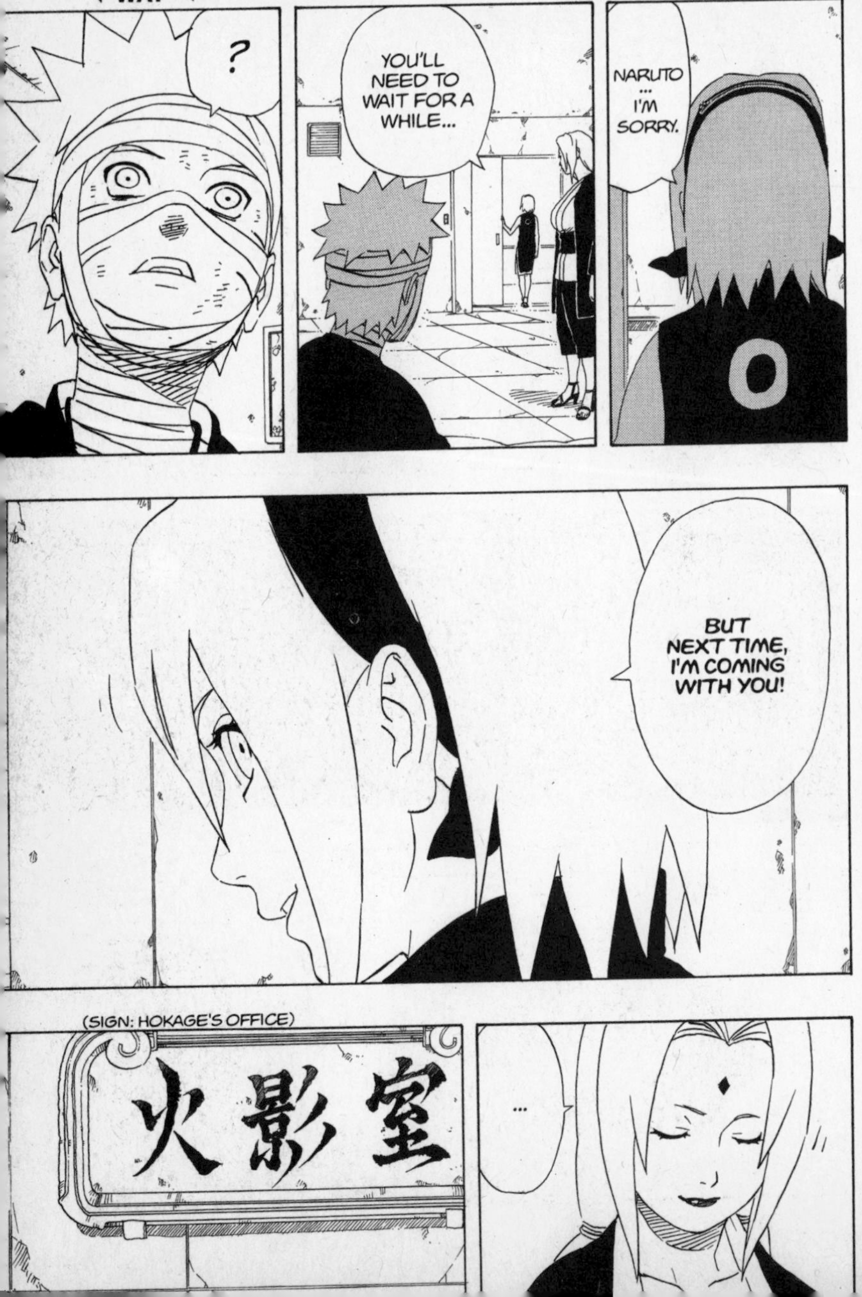
NARUTO ... I'M SORRY.
YOU'LL NEED TO WAIT FOR A WHILE...
?
BUT NEXT TIME, I'M COMING WITH YOU!
...
(SIGN: HOKAGE'S OFFICE)
火影室

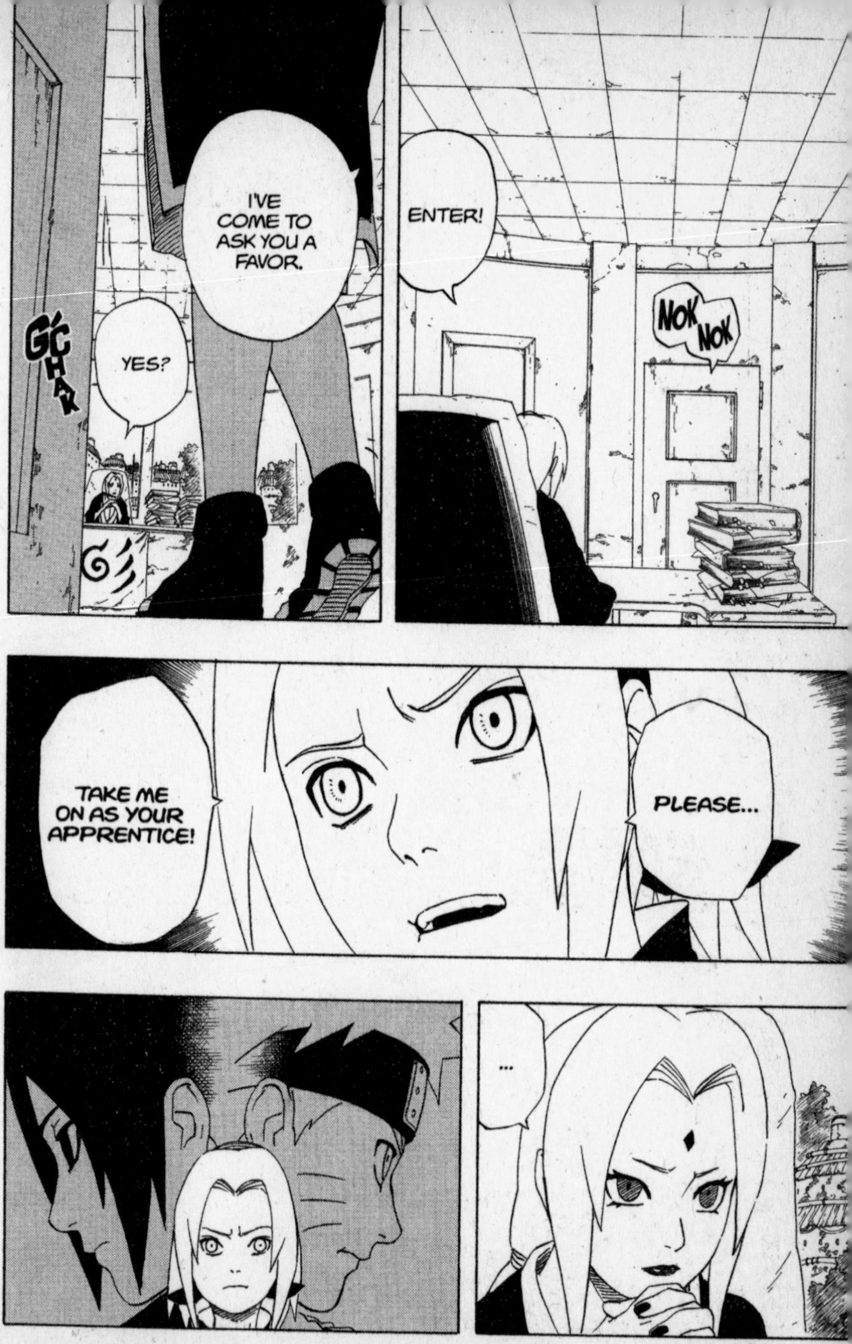
NOK NOK
ENTER!
GĆHAK
YES?
I'VE COME TO ASK YOU A FAVOR.
PLEASE...
TAKE ME ON AS YOUR APPRENTICE!
...

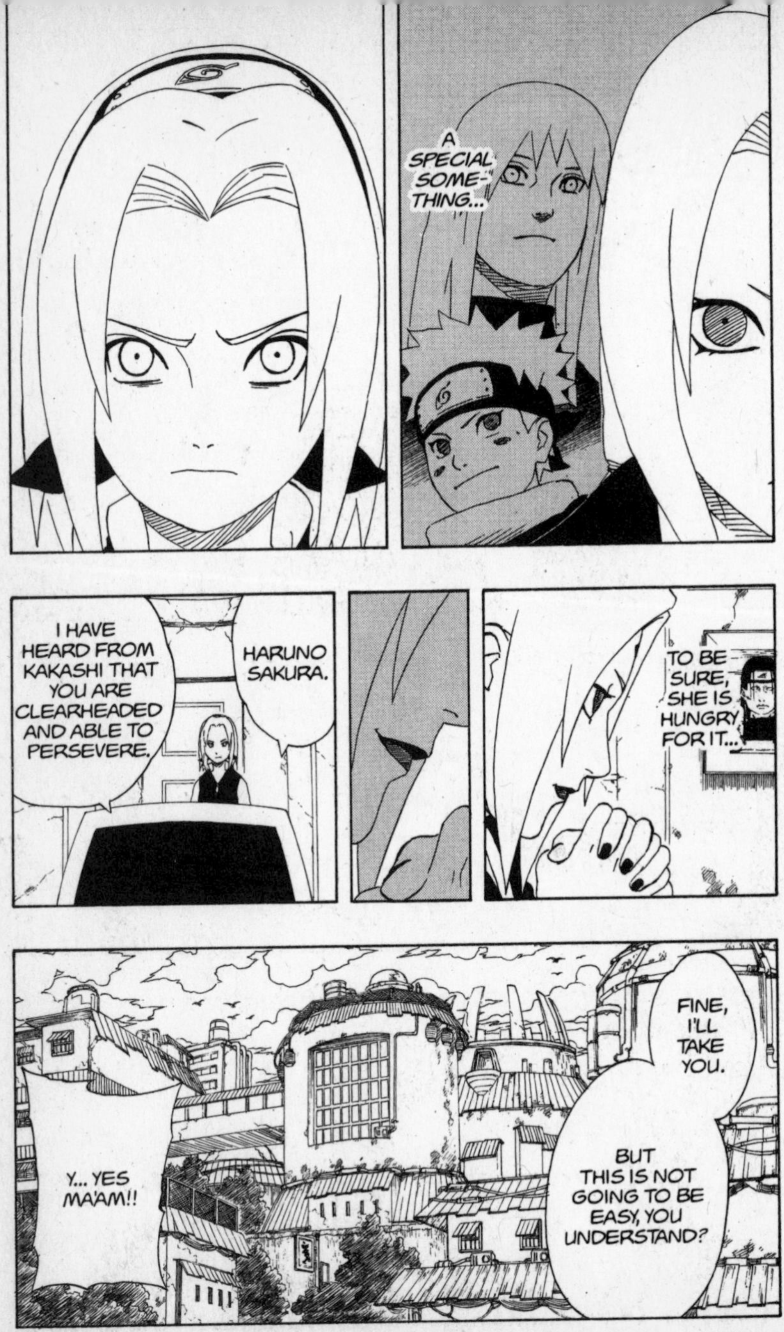
A SPECIAL SOMETHING...
TO BE SURE, SHE IS HUNGRY FOR IT...
HARUNO SAKURA.
I HAVE HEARD FROM KAKASHI THAT YOU ARE CLEARHEADED AND ABLE TO PERSEVERE.
FINE, I'LL TAKE YOU.
BUT THIS IS NOT GOING TO BE EASY, YOU UNDERSTAND?
Y... YES MA'AM!!

THE WORLD OF MASASHI KISHIMOTO
PERSONAL HISTORY: SPECIAL FRIENDS, PART I

MANGA ARTISTS HARDLY HAVE TIME TO GO OUT. THE REASON? EVERY WEEK, A NEW DEADLINE. IT'S A PRETTY DEMANDING LINE OF WORK.

THUS I KEEP DECLINING INVITATIONS. CONSEQUENTLY, I KEEP SHEDDING FRIENDS. AT THIS POINT, MY ASSISTANTS ARE PRETTY MUCH ALL I HAVE LEFT.

AS FOR MY WORK, I SPEND FOUR DAYS ALONE, CONJURING UP PLOTS (A PROCESS CALLED "NAME"). THIS PART IS DIFFERENT FROM THE DRAWING, IN THAT UNLESS I COME UP WITH AN IDEA, I CAN'T MOVE FORWARD. ONCE I DO FIND SOMETHING, I THEN SPEND THREE DAYS DRAWING IT. THING IS, SOMETIMES IT TAKES SIX DAYS TO SORT OUT A PLOT. WHEN THAT HAPPENS, I'VE GOT ONLY A DAY LEFT TO DRAW, SO I HAVE TO LEAN HEAVILY ON MY ASSISTANTS TO MAKE THE DEADLINE.

EVEN THEN I STILL HAVE TO GENERATE A WHOLE ROUGH DRAFT MYSELF, WHICH DOESN'T HELP MUCH. THE KEY TO SPEEDING THINGS ALONG IS IN FINALIZING THE DRAFT WITH PEN. THE SIMPLER CHARACTERS THAT USE FEWER LINES MY ASSISTANTS CAN CLEAN UP FOR ME. THAT SAID, I HAVE ONLY ONE ASSISTANT WHO CAN IMITATE MY STYLE OF DRAWING, SO THE TWO OF US HAVE TO HANDLE MOST OF THE "BIG" WORK.

WHERE WE REALLY RUN INTO TROUBLE, ESPECIALLY WHEN WE'RE BEHIND SCHEDULE, IS WHEN NARUTO CONJURES UP A MASS OF SHADOW DOPPELGANGERS. FOR INSTANCE, TAKE A PEEK AT VOL. 23, PAGES 64-65. NARUTO IS PLASTERED EVERYWHERE, ALL OVER A TWO-PAGE SPREAD. THE TWO OF US DIVIDED THE WORK AND DREW LIKE MADMEN. WE WERE CUTTING SO CLOSE TO THE DEADLINE, WE HAD TO PULL ALL-NIGHTERS. THE MOMENT WE FINISHED THESE TWO PAGES, MY ASSISTANT COLLAPSED AND FELL ASLEEP. THE THING IS, THOUGH, WE STILL HAD OTHER PAGES TO COMPLETE, SO HE COULD ONLY TAKE A QUICK NAP! AT TIMES LIKE THIS, I MENTALLY APOLOGIZE FOR HIS SUFFERING, AND HOPING TO SOFTEN THE TENSION, I SEARCH FOR SOMETHING TO LIVEN THE WORKPLACE... FOR INSTANCE, SHOCK THERAPY. SO THAT DAY, WHILE HE WAS NAPPING, I PHOTOCOPIED THE TWO-PAGE SPREAD AND SPLATTERED INK ALL OVER IT, AS IF BY ACCIDENT...

-- TO BE CONTINUED --

Number 237: Fool...!!

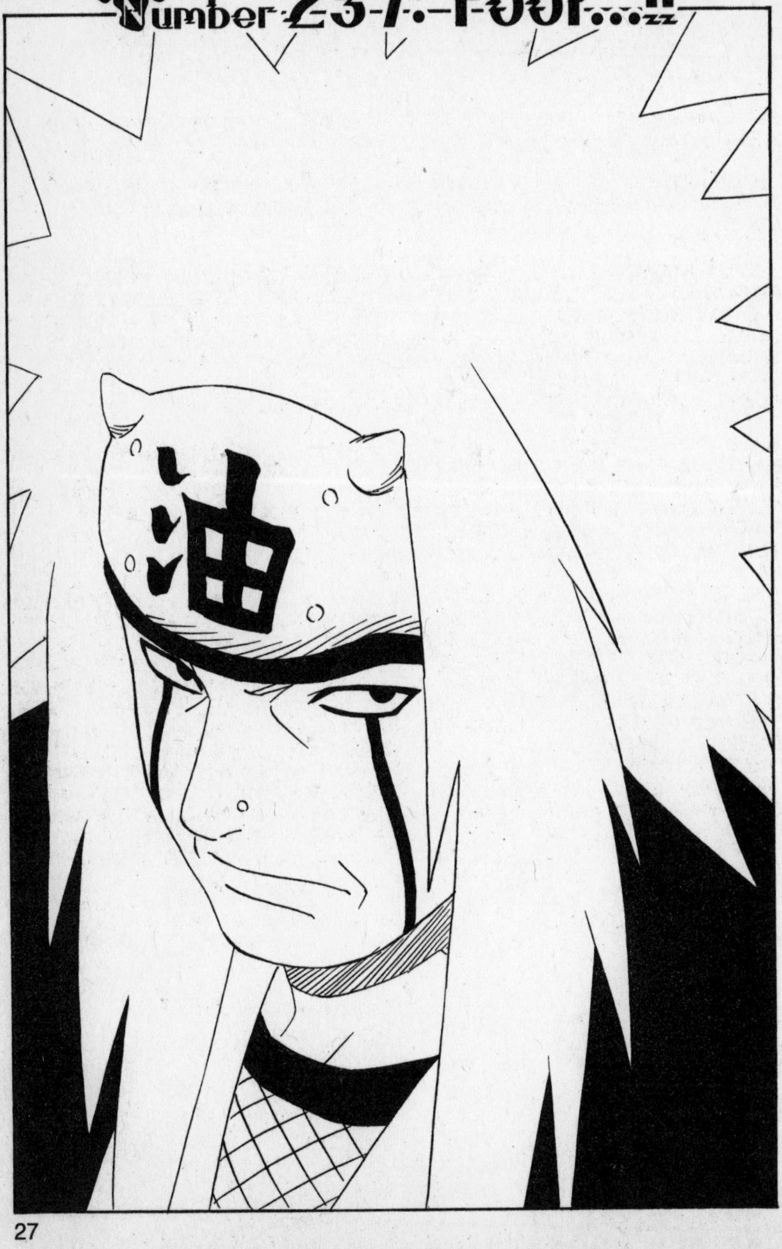
油

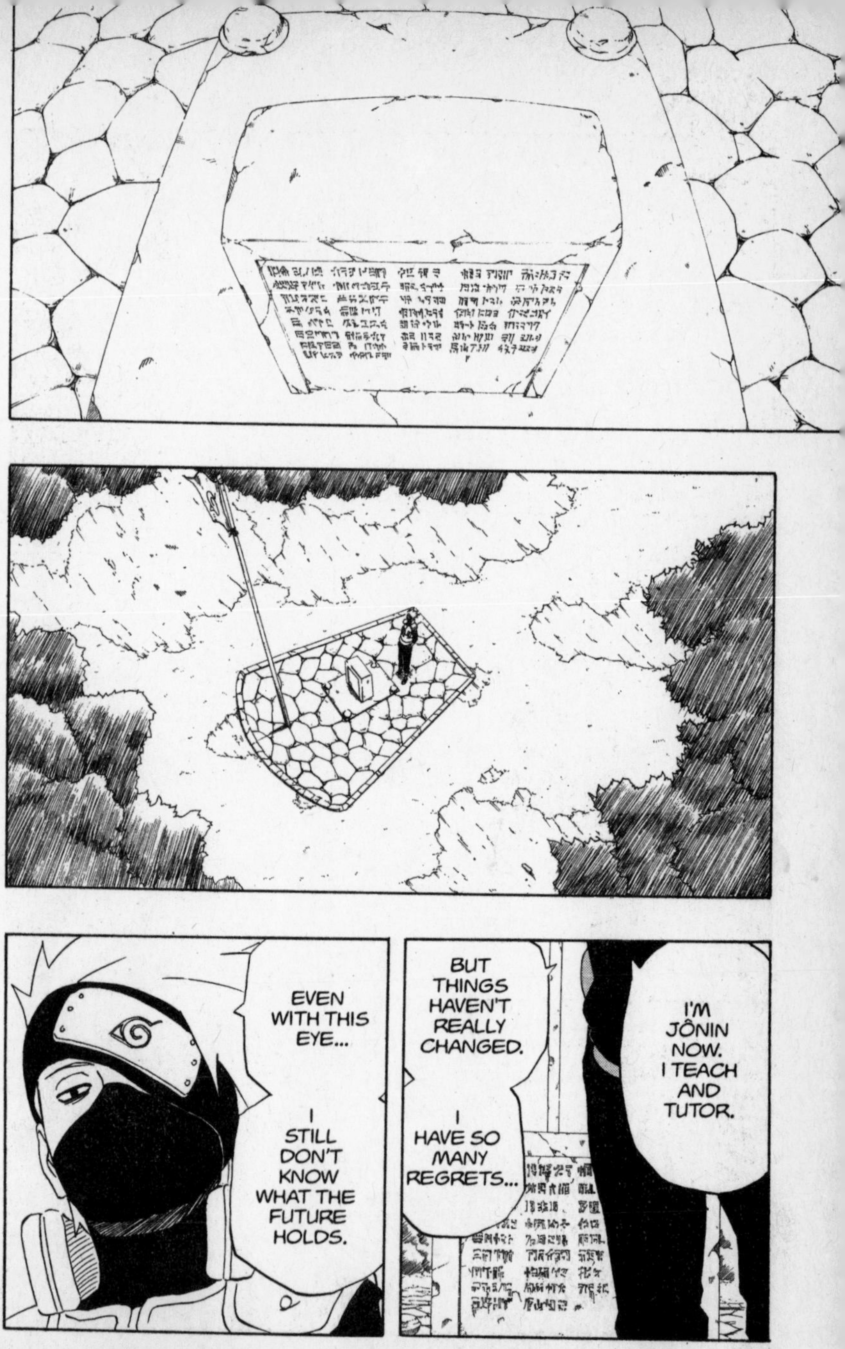
I'M JÔNIN NOW. I TEACH AND TUTOR.
BUT THINGS HAVEN'T REALLY CHANGED.
I HAVE SO MANY REGRETS...
EVEN WITH THIS EYE...
I STILL DON'T KNOW WHAT THE FUTURE HOLDS.

READ THIS WAY

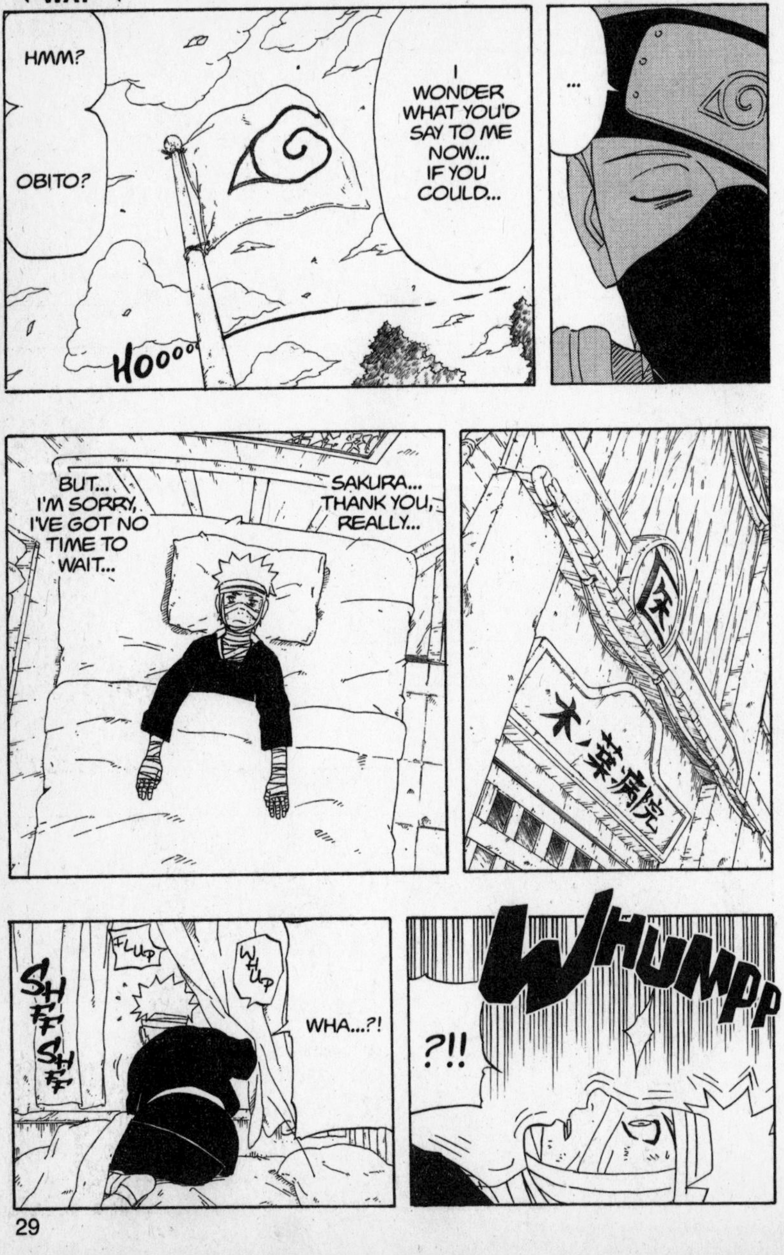
...
I WONDER WHAT YOU'D SAY TO ME NOW... IF YOU COULD...
HMM?
OBITO?
HOOOO
木ノ葉病院
SAKURA... THANK YOU, REALLY...
BUT... I'M SORRY, I'VE GOT NO TIME TO WAIT...
WHUMPP
?!!
WHA...?!
WHUP
FLUP
SHFF SHFF

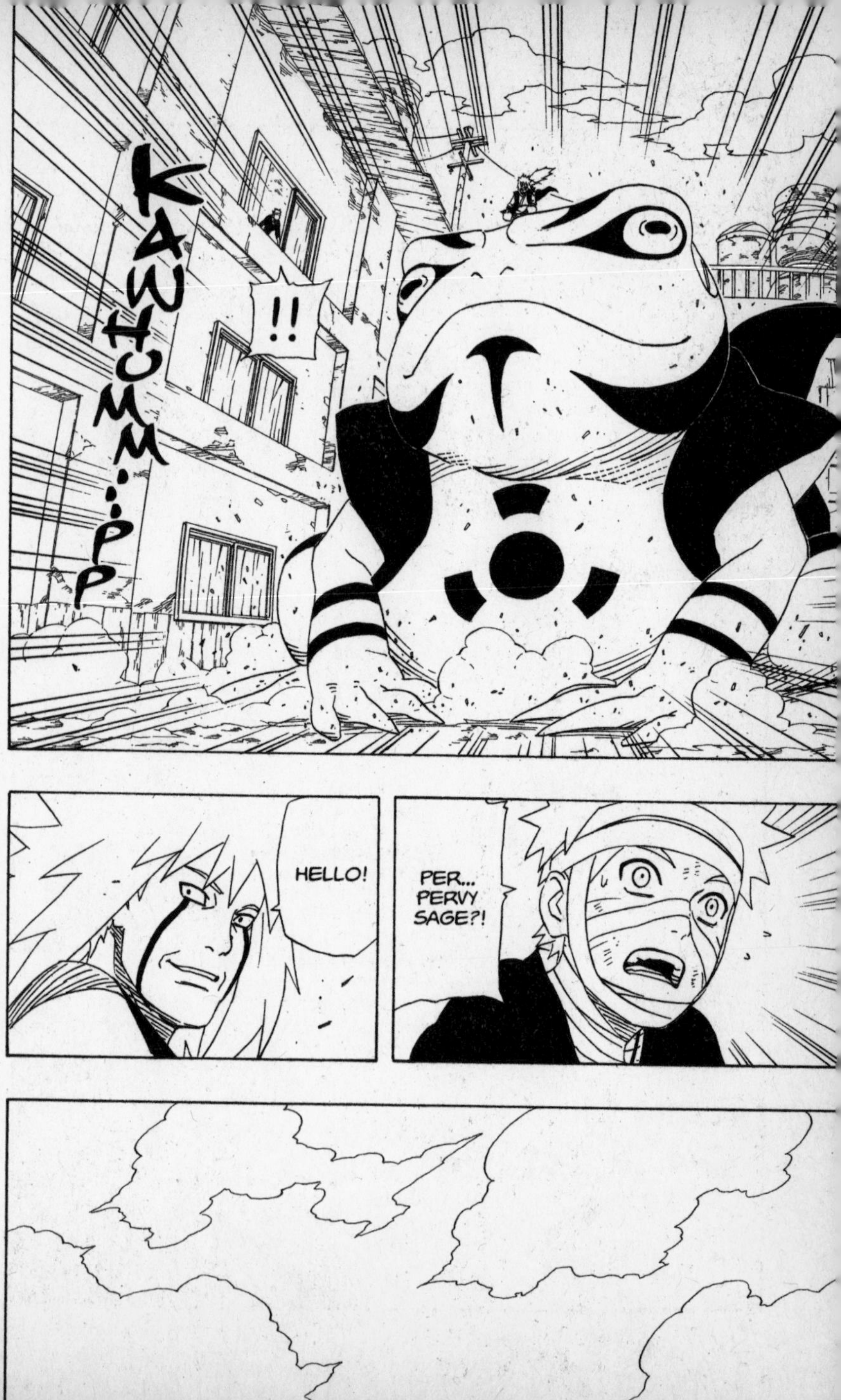
KAWHOMM...PP
!!
PER... PERVY SAGE?!
HELLO!

READ THIS WAY

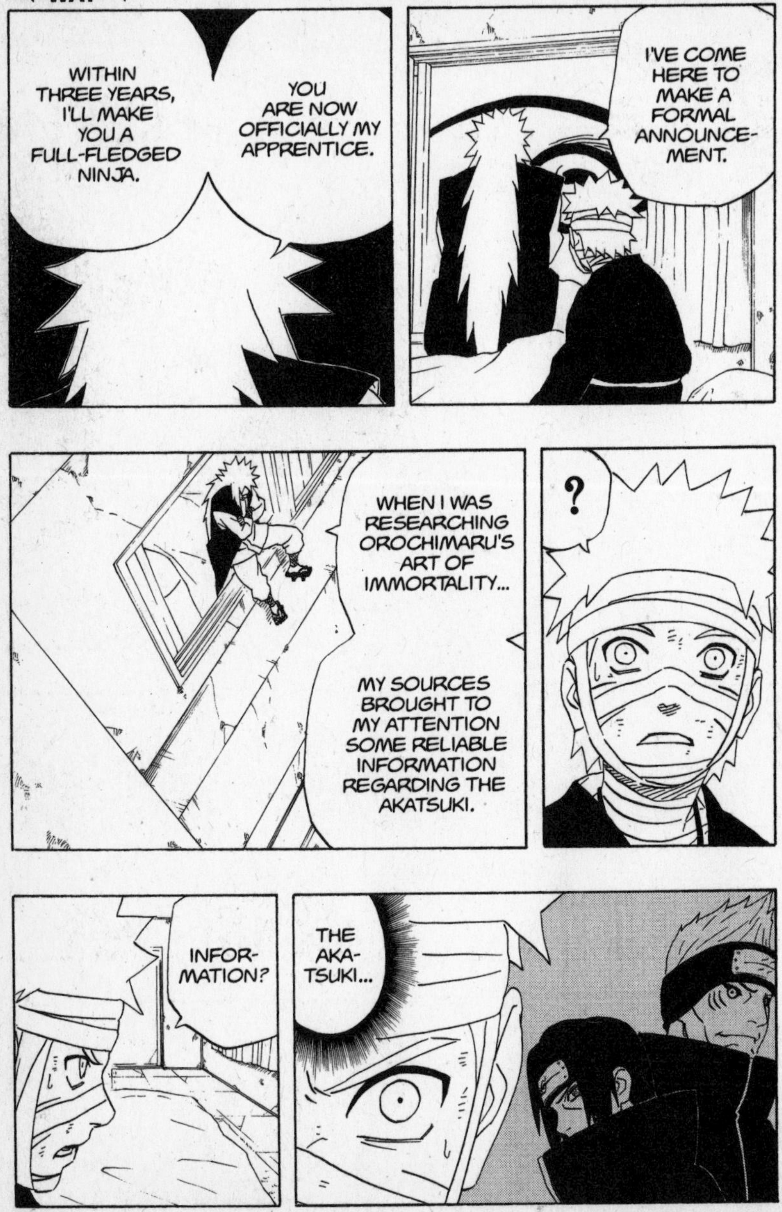

I'VE COME HERE TO MAKE A FORMAL ANNOUNCE-MENT.
YOU ARE NOW OFFICIALLY MY APPRENTICE.
WITHIN THREE YEARS, I'LL MAKE YOU A FULL-FLEDGED NINJA.
?
WHEN I WAS RESEARCHING OROCHIMARU'S ART OF IMMORTALITY...
MY SOURCES BROUGHT TO MY ATTENTION SOME RELIABLE INFORMATION REGARDING THE AKATSUKI.
THE AKA-TSUKI...
INFOR-MATION?

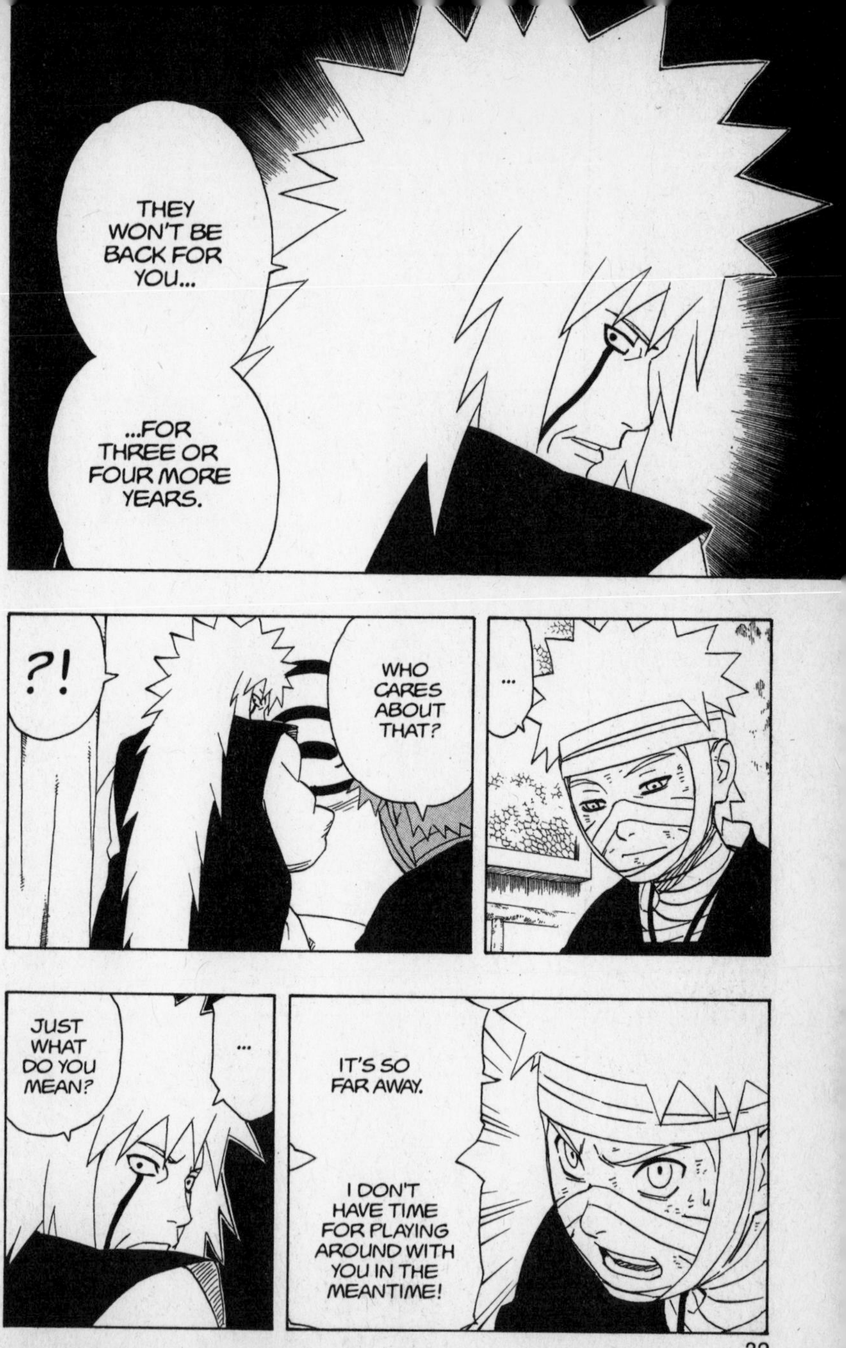
THEY WON'T BE BACK FOR YOU...
...FOR THREE OR FOUR MORE YEARS.
...
WHO CARES ABOUT THAT?
?!
IT'S SO FAR AWAY.
I DON'T HAVE TIME FOR PLAYING AROUND WITH YOU IN THE MEANTIME!
...
JUST WHAT DO YOU MEAN?

READ THIS WAY

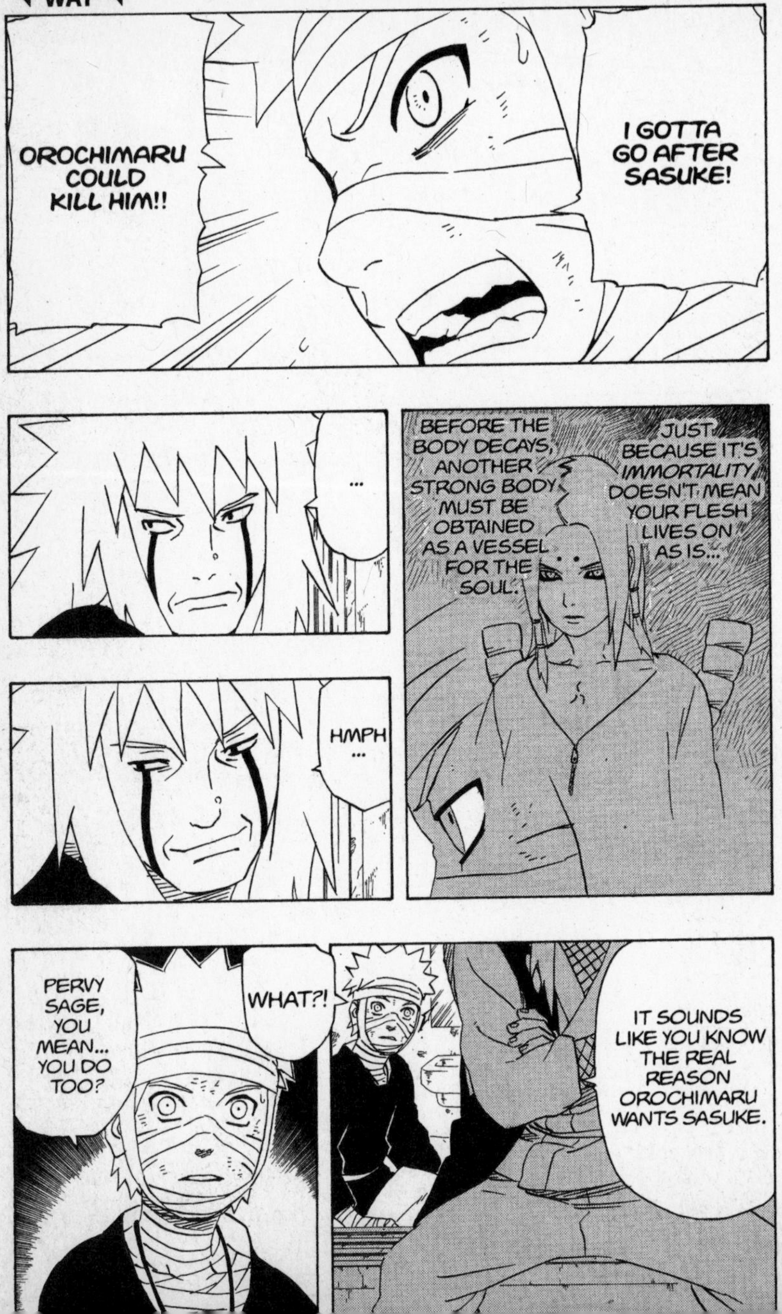
I GOTTA GO AFTER SASUKE!
OROCHIMARU COULD KILL HIM!!
JUST BECAUSE IT'S IMMORTALITY DOESN'T MEAN YOUR FLESH LIVES ON AS IS...
BEFORE THE BODY DECAYS, ANOTHER STRONG BODY MUST BE OBTAINED AS A VESSEL FOR THE SOUL.
...
HMPH ...
IT SOUNDS LIKE YOU KNOW THE REAL REASON OROCHIMARU WANTS SASUKE.
WHAT?!
PERVY SAGE, YOU MEAN... YOU DO TOO?

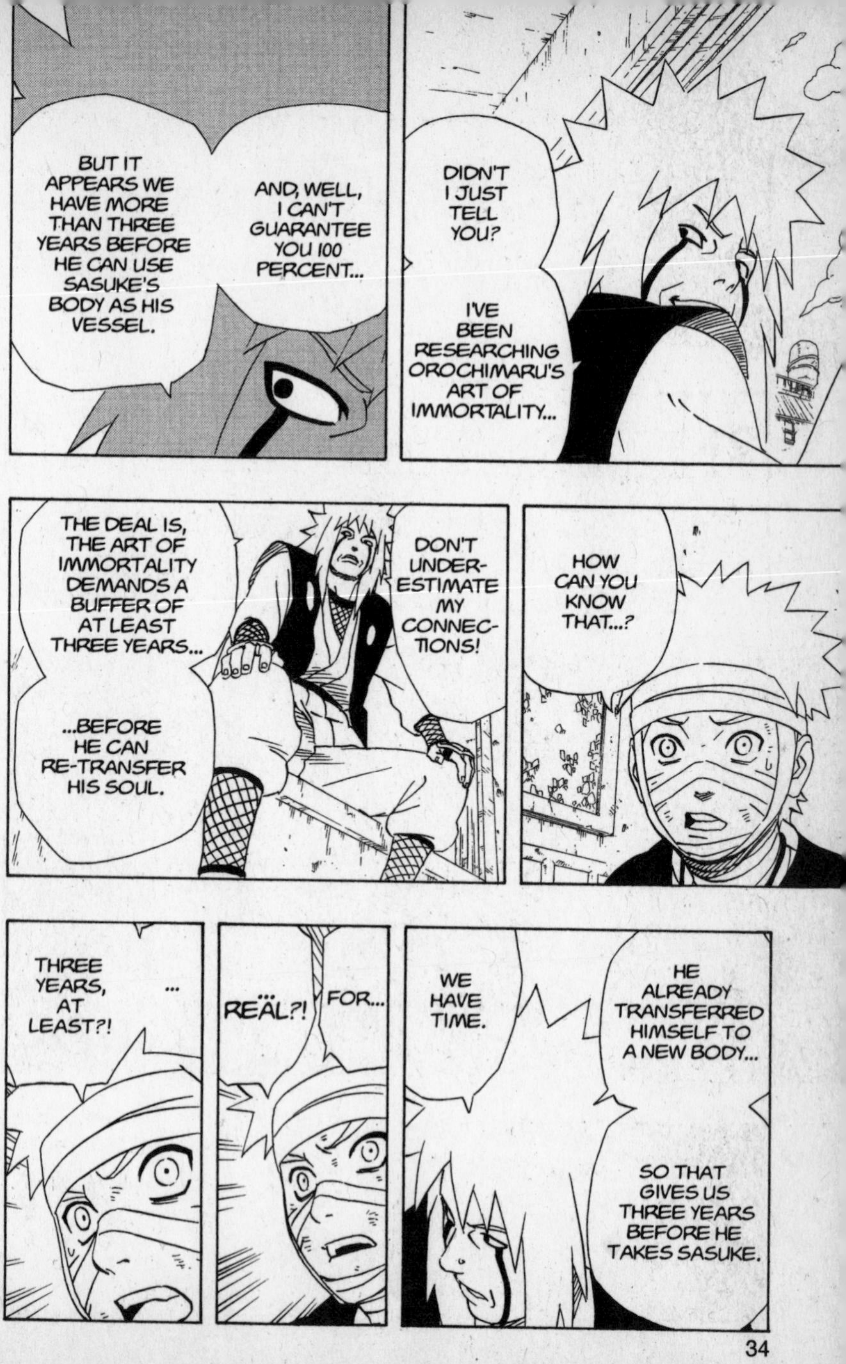
DIDN'T I JUST TELL YOU?
I'VE BEEN RESEARCHING OROCHIMARU'S ART OF IMMORTALITY...
AND, WELL, I CAN'T GUARANTEE YOU 100 PERCENT...
BUT IT APPEARS WE HAVE MORE THAN THREE YEARS BEFORE HE CAN USE SASUKE'S BODY AS HIS VESSEL.
HOW CAN YOU KNOW THAT...?
DON'T UNDER-ESTIMATE MY CONNEC-TIONS!
THE DEAL IS, THE ART OF IMMORTALITY DEMANDS A BUFFER OF AT LEAST THREE YEARS...
...BEFORE HE CAN RE-TRANSFER HIS SOUL.
HE ALREADY TRANSFERRED HIMSELF TO A NEW BODY...
SO THAT GIVES US THREE YEARS BEFORE HE TAKES SASUKE.
WE HAVE TIME.
FOR...
...REAL?!
...
THREE YEARS, AT LEAST?!

READ THIS WAY

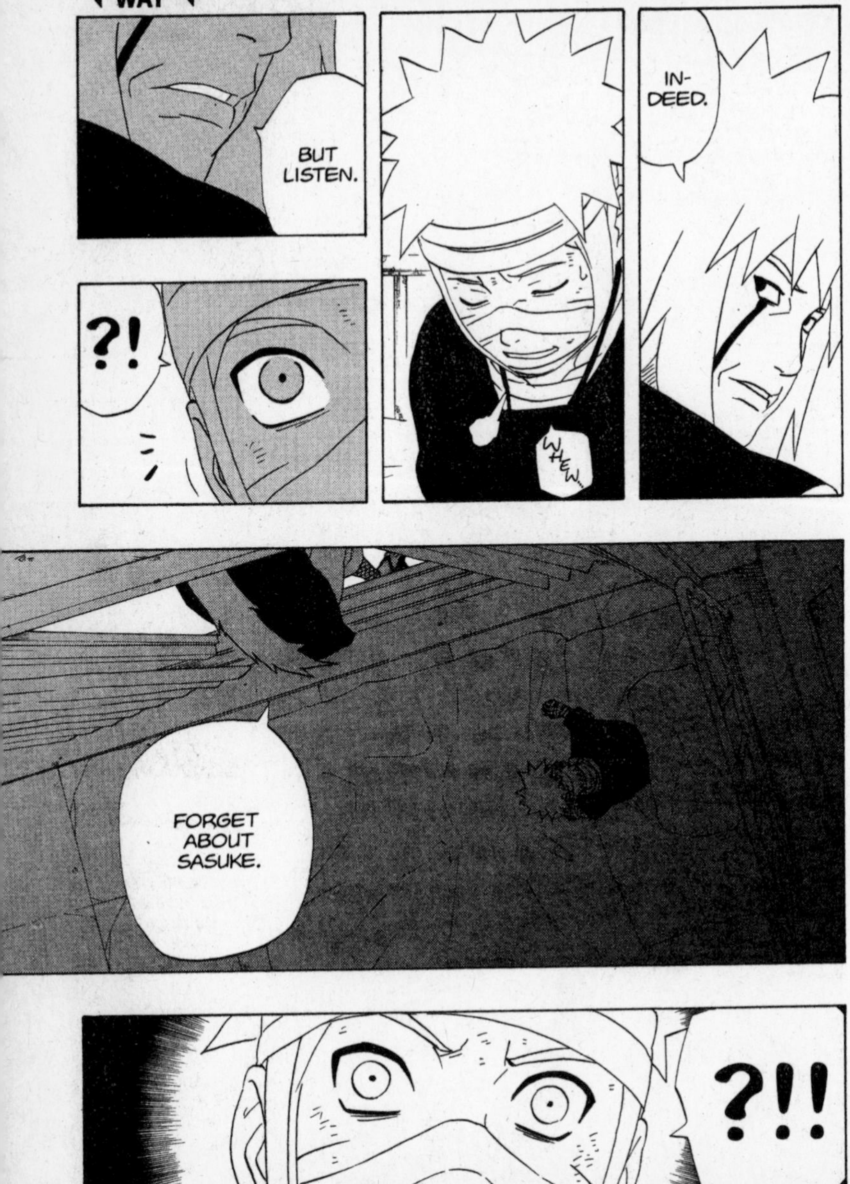
IN-DEED.
WHEW...
BUT LISTEN.
?!
FORGET ABOUT SASUKE.
?!!

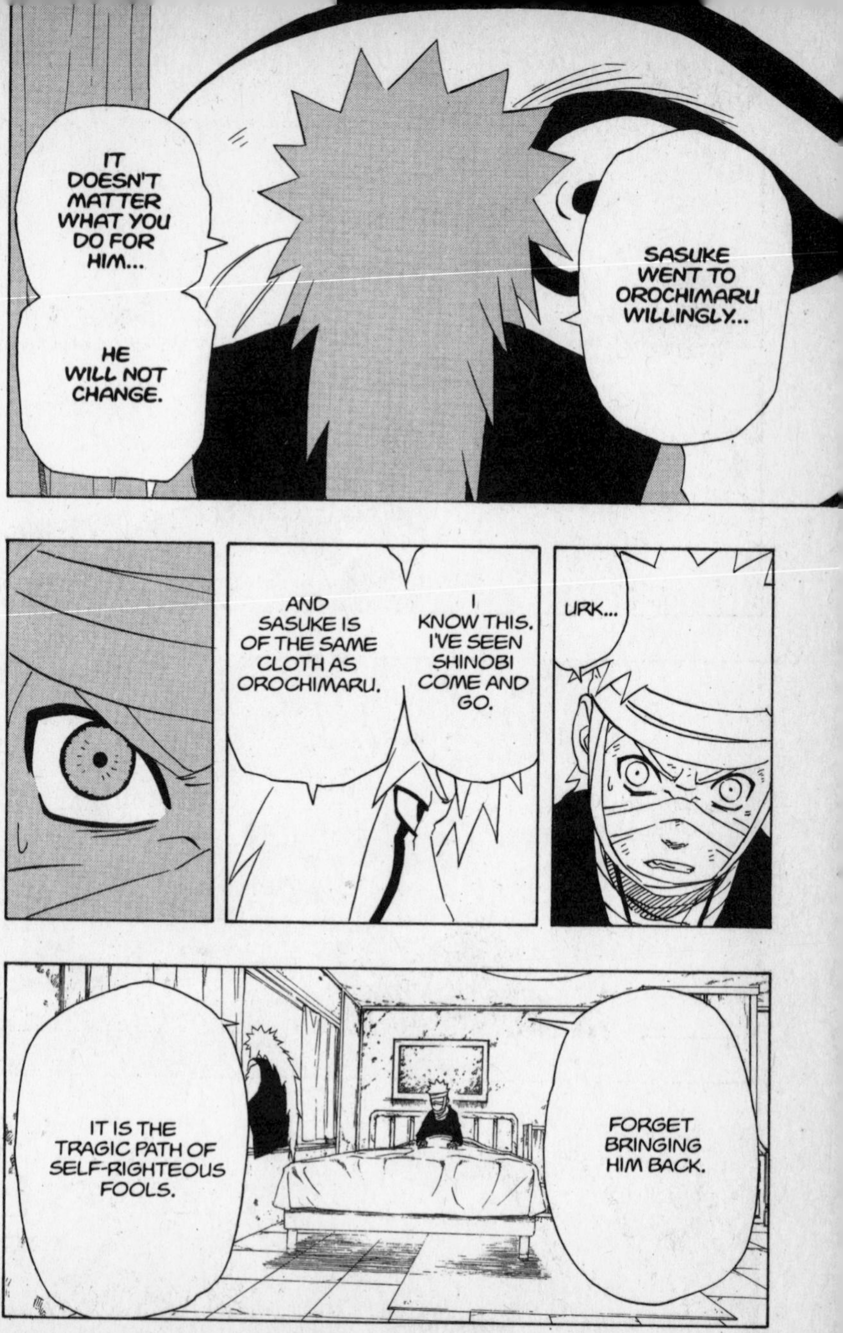
SASUKE WENT TO OROCHIMARU WILLINGLY...
IT DOESN'T MATTER WHAT YOU DO FOR HIM...
HE WILL NOT CHANGE.
URK...
I KNOW THIS. I'VE SEEN SHINOBI COME AND GO.
AND SASUKE IS OF THE SAME CLOTH AS OROCHIMARU.
FORGET BRINGING HIM BACK.
IT IS THE TRAGIC PATH OF SELF-RIGHTEOUS FOOLS.

READ THIS WAY

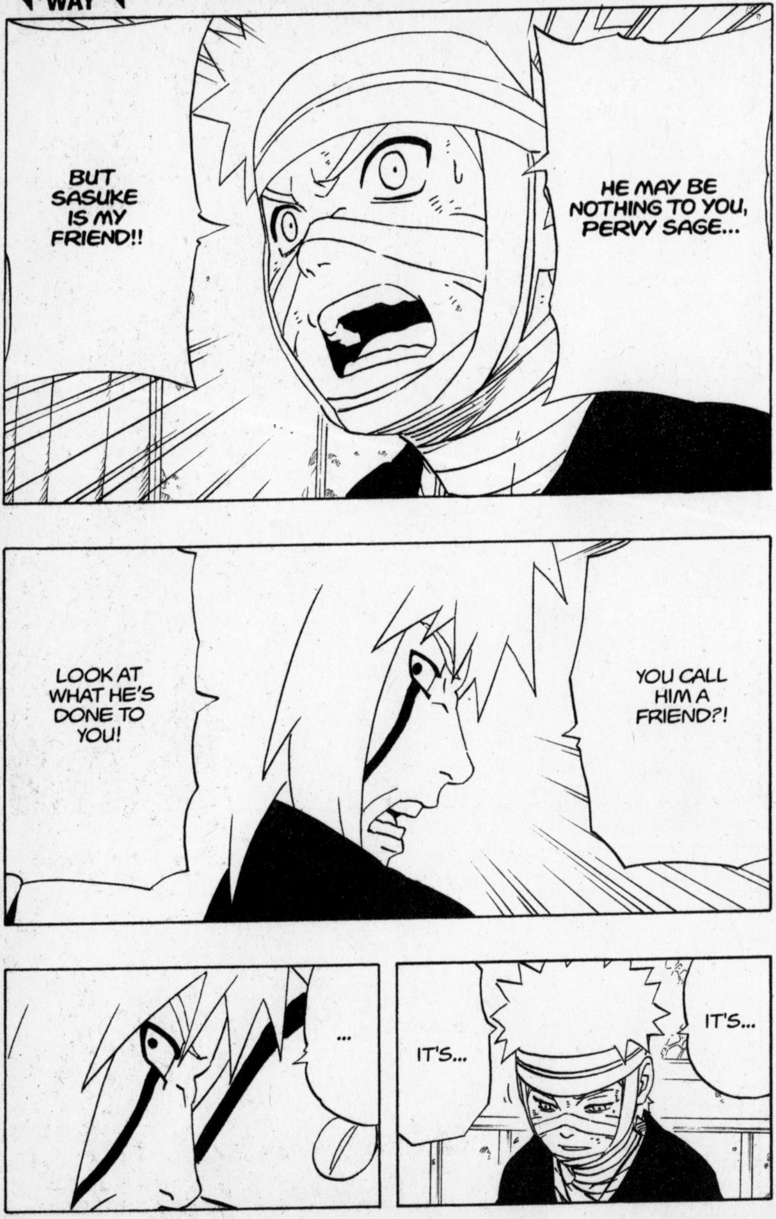
HE MAY BE NOTHING TO YOU, PERVY SAGE...
BUT SASUKE IS MY FRIEND!!
YOU CALL HIM A FRIEND?!
LOOK AT WHAT HE'S DONE TO YOU!
IT'S...
IT'S...
...

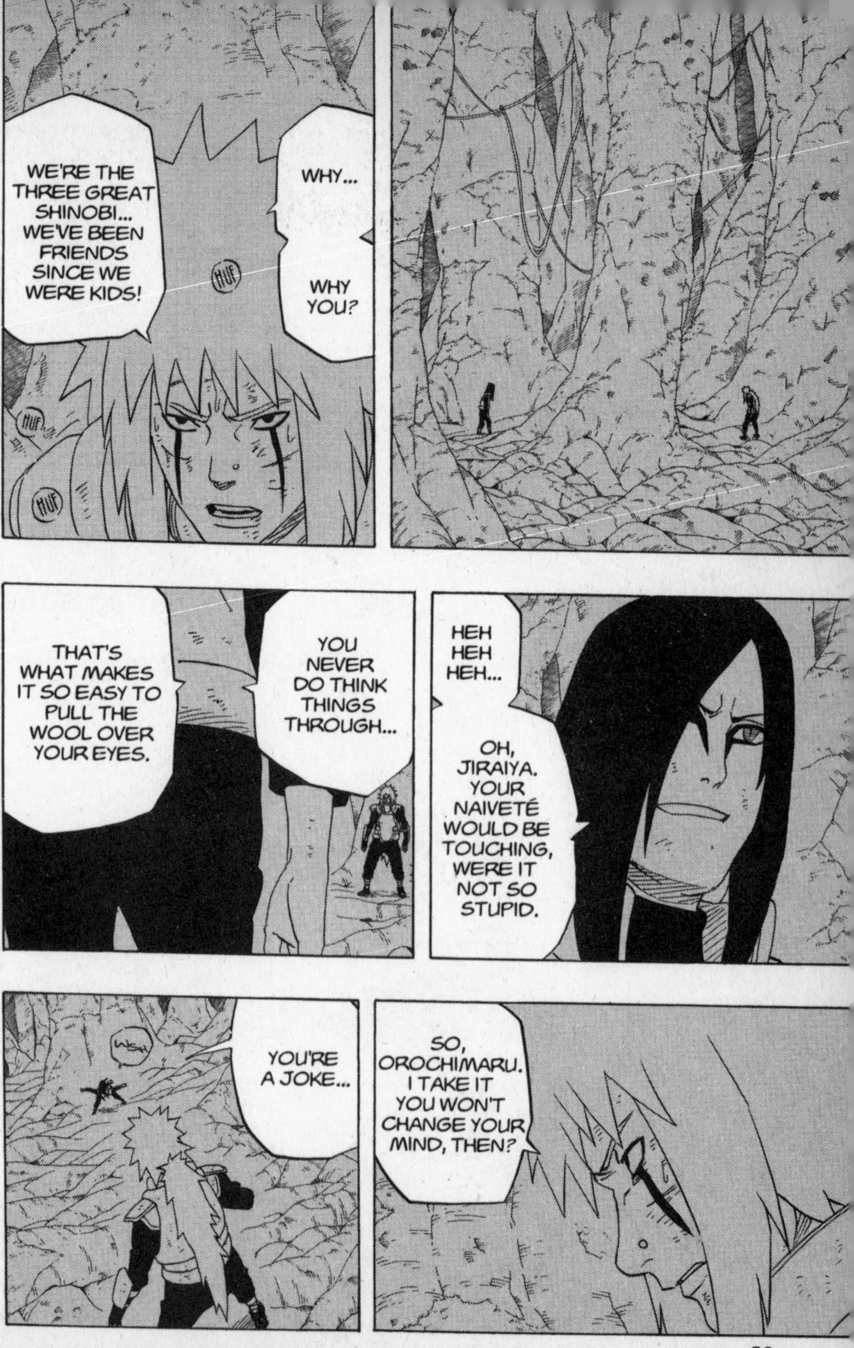
WHY... WHY YOU?
WE'RE THE THREE GREAT SHINOBI... WE'VE BEEN FRIENDS SINCE WE WERE KIDS!
HUF
HUF
HUF
HEH HEH HEH...
OH, JIRAIYA. YOUR NAIVETÉ WOULD BE TOUCHING, WERE IT NOT SO STUPID.
YOU NEVER DO THINK THINGS THROUGH...
THAT'S WHAT MAKES IT SO EASY TO PULL THE WOOL OVER YOUR EYES.
SO, OROCHIMARU. I TAKE IT YOU WON'T CHANGE YOUR MIND, THEN?
YOU'RE A JOKE...

READ THIS WAY

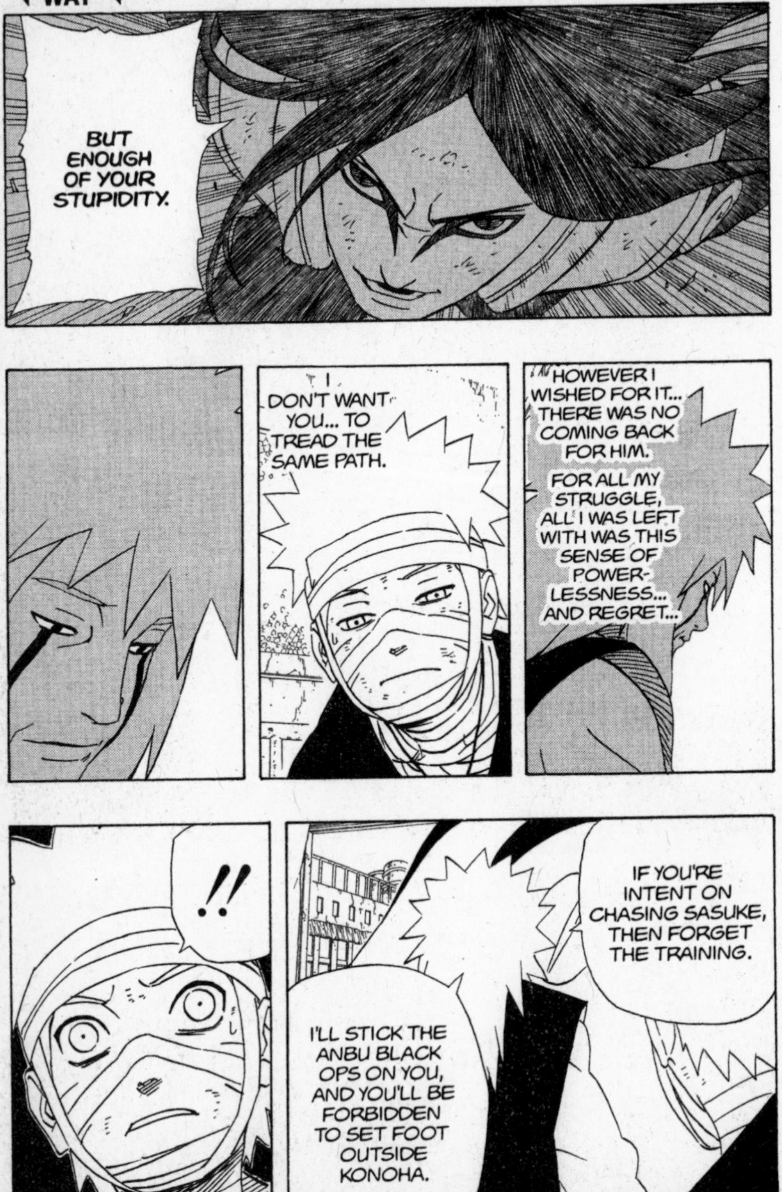
BUT ENOUGH OF YOUR STUPIDITY.
HOWEVER I WISHED FOR IT... THERE WAS NO COMING BACK FOR HIM.
FOR ALL MY STRUGGLE, ALL I WAS LEFT WITH WAS THIS SENSE OF POWER-LESSNESS... AND REGRET...
I DON'T WANT YOU... TO TREAD THE SAME PATH.
IF YOU'RE INTENT ON CHASING SASUKE, THEN FORGET THE TRAINING.
I'LL STICK THE ANBU BLACK OPS ON YOU, AND YOU'LL BE FORBIDDEN TO SET FOOT OUTSIDE KONOHA.
!!

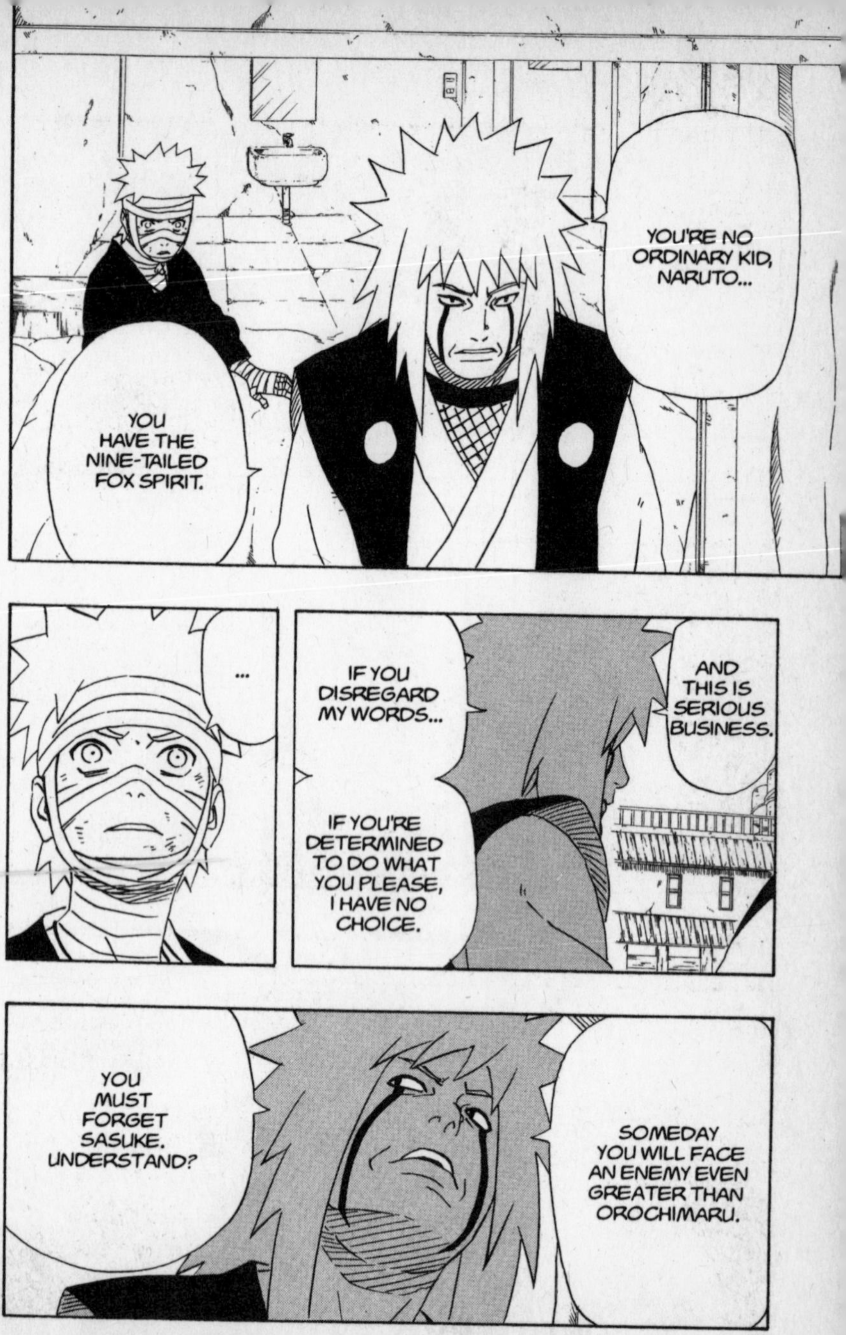
YOU'RE NO ORDINARY KID, NARUTO...
YOU HAVE THE NINE-TAILED FOX SPIRIT.
AND THIS IS SERIOUS BUSINESS.
IF YOU DISREGARD MY WORDS...
IF YOU'RE DETERMINED TO DO WHAT YOU PLEASE, I HAVE NO CHOICE.
...
SOMEDAY YOU WILL FACE AN ENEMY EVEN GREATER THAN OROCHIMARU.
YOU MUST FORGET SASUKE. UNDERSTAND?

READ THIS WAY

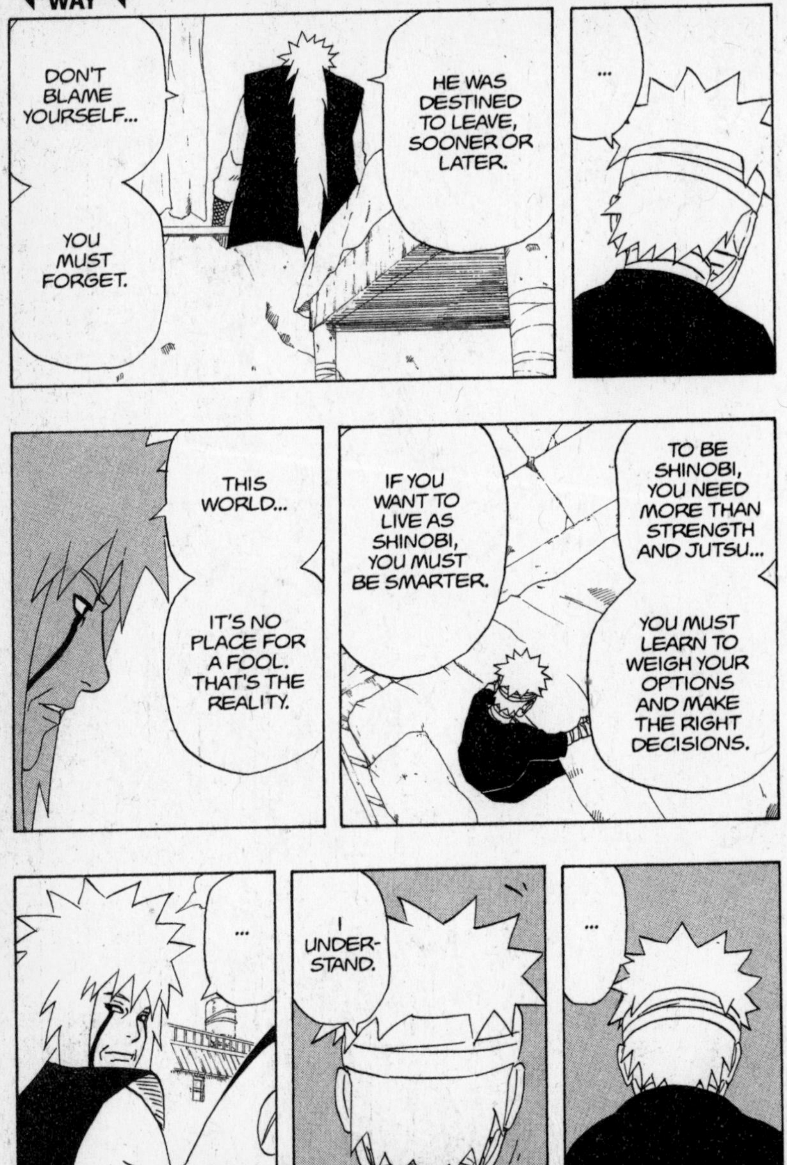
...
HE WAS DESTINED TO LEAVE, SOONER OR LATER.
DON'T BLAME YOURSELF...
YOU MUST FORGET.
TO BE SHINOBI, YOU NEED MORE THAN STRENGTH AND JUTSU...
YOU MUST LEARN TO WEIGH YOUR OPTIONS AND MAKE THE RIGHT DECISIONS.
IF YOU WANT TO LIVE AS SHINOBI, YOU MUST BE SMARTER.
THIS WORLD...
IT'S NO PLACE FOR A FOOL. THAT'S THE REALITY.
...
I UNDER-STAND.
...

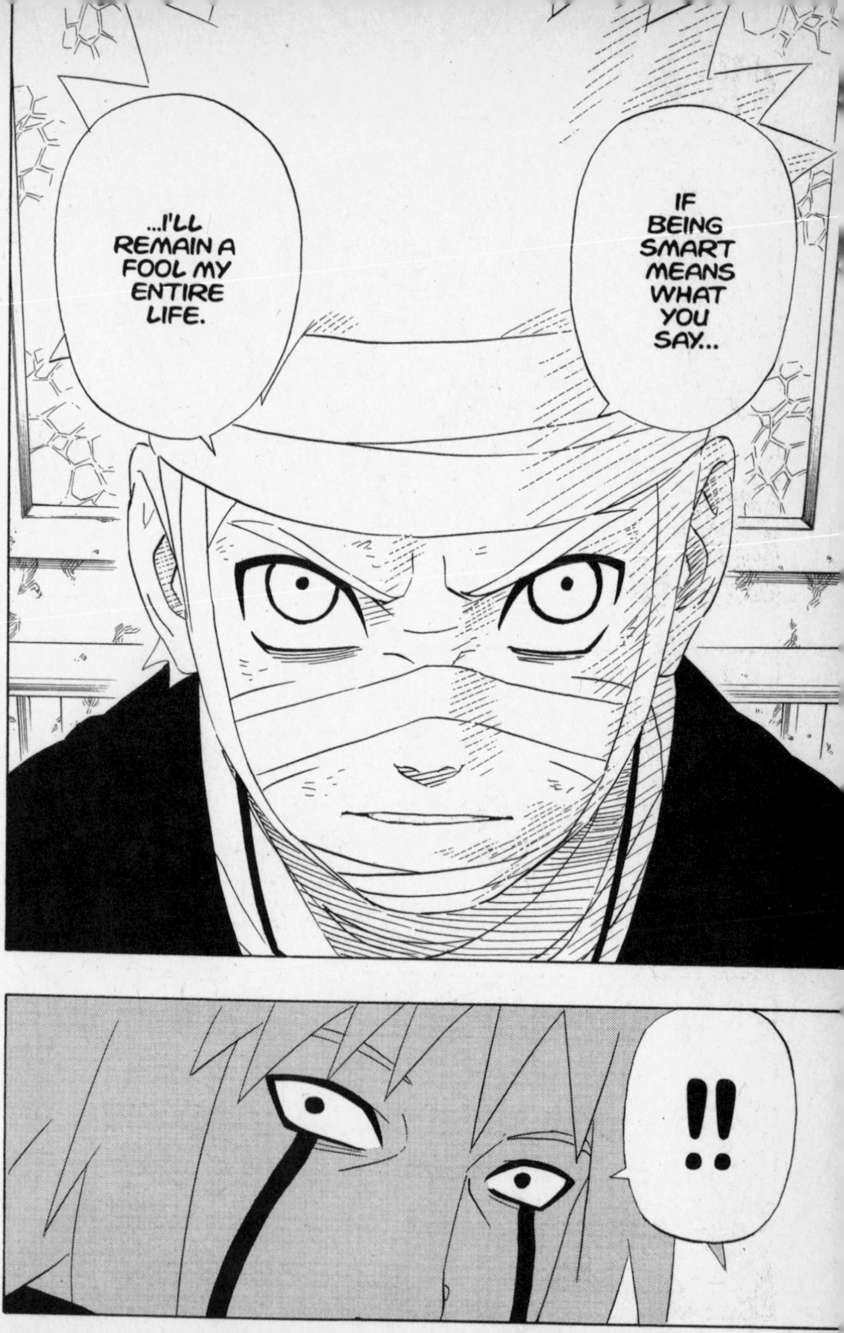
IF BEING SMART MEANS WHAT YOU SAY...
...I'LL REMAIN A FOOL MY ENTIRE LIFE.
!!

READ THIS WAY

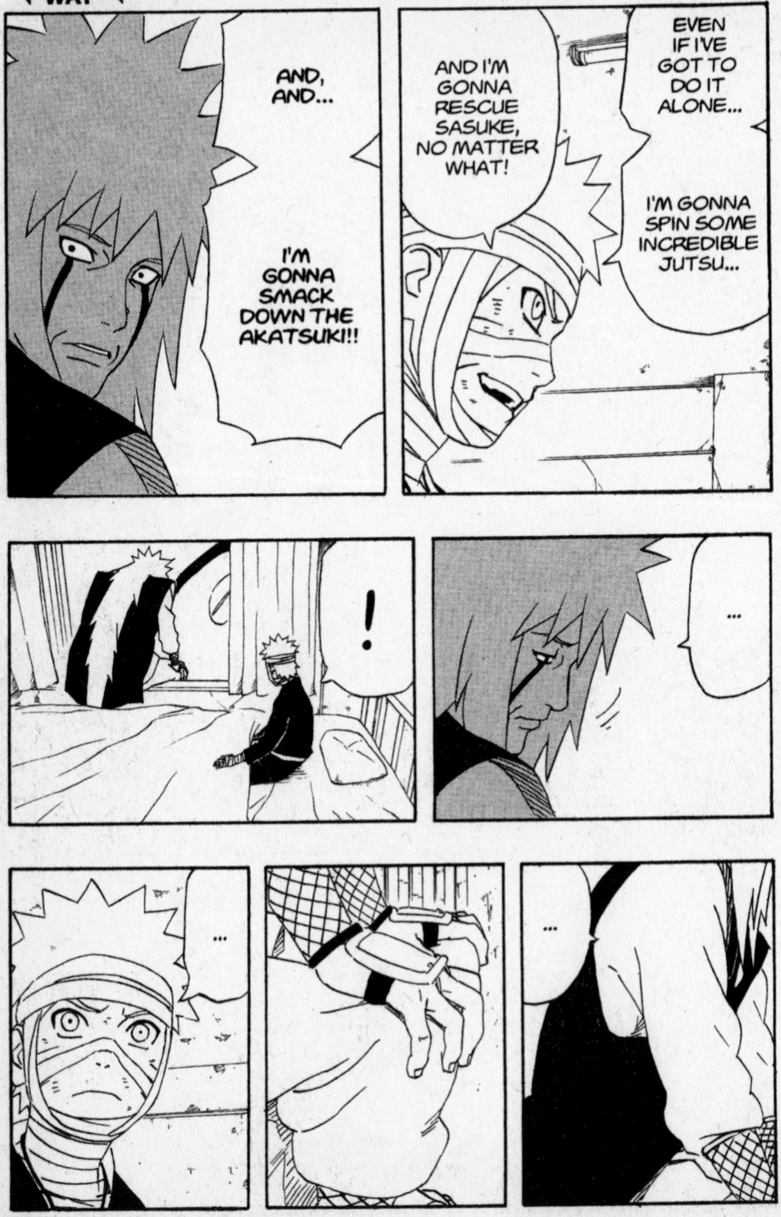
EVEN IF I'VE GOT TO DO IT ALONE...
I'M GONNA SPIN SOME INCREDIBLE JUTSU...
AND I'M GONNA RESCUE SASUKE, NO MATTER WHAT!
AND, AND...
I'M GONNA SMACK DOWN THE AKATSUKI!!
...
!
...
...

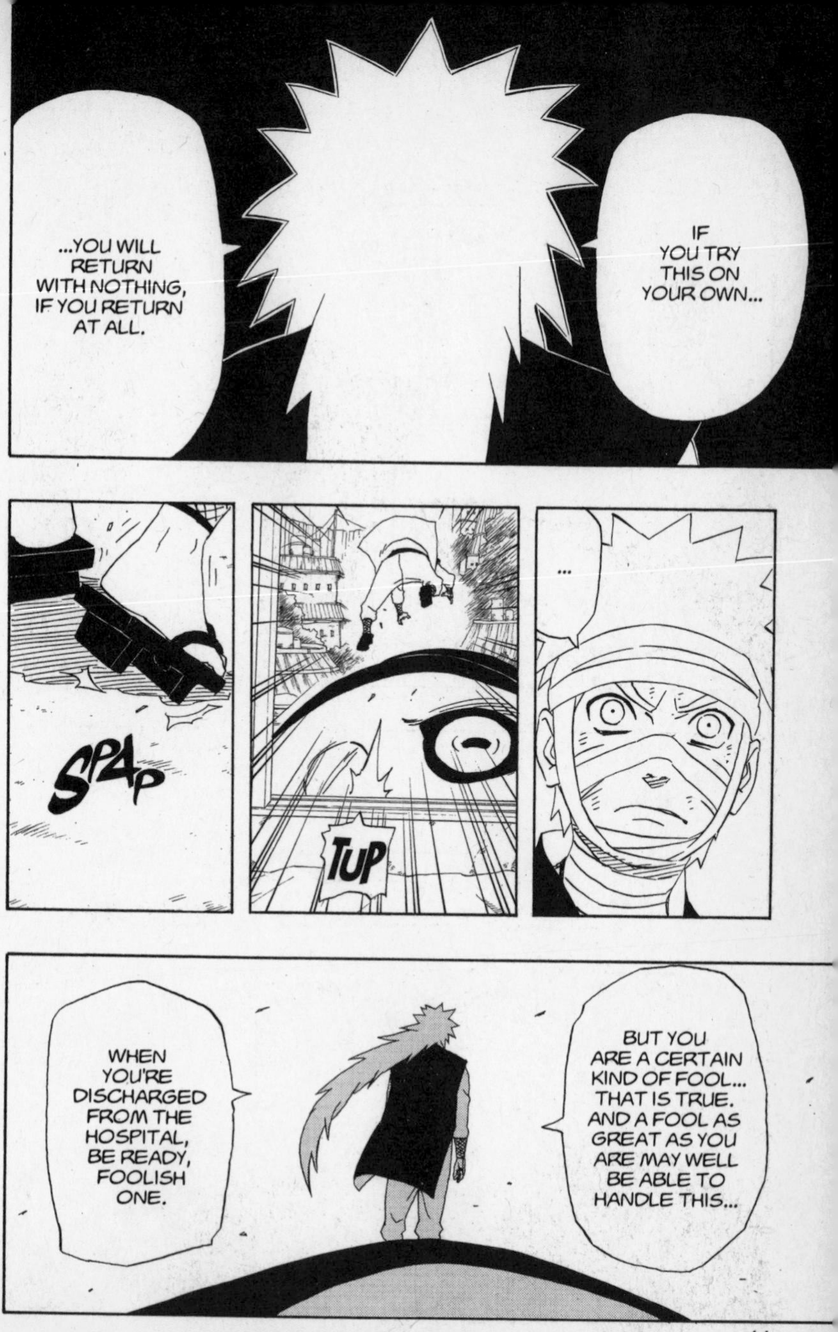
IF YOU TRY THIS ON YOUR OWN...
...YOU WILL RETURN WITH NOTHING, IF YOU RETURN AT ALL.
...
TUP
SPAP
BUT YOU ARE A CERTAIN KIND OF FOOL... THAT IS TRUE. AND A FOOL AS GREAT AS YOU ARE MAY WELL BE ABLE TO HANDLE THIS...
WHEN YOU'RE DISCHARGED FROM THE HOSPITAL, BE READY, FOOLISH ONE.

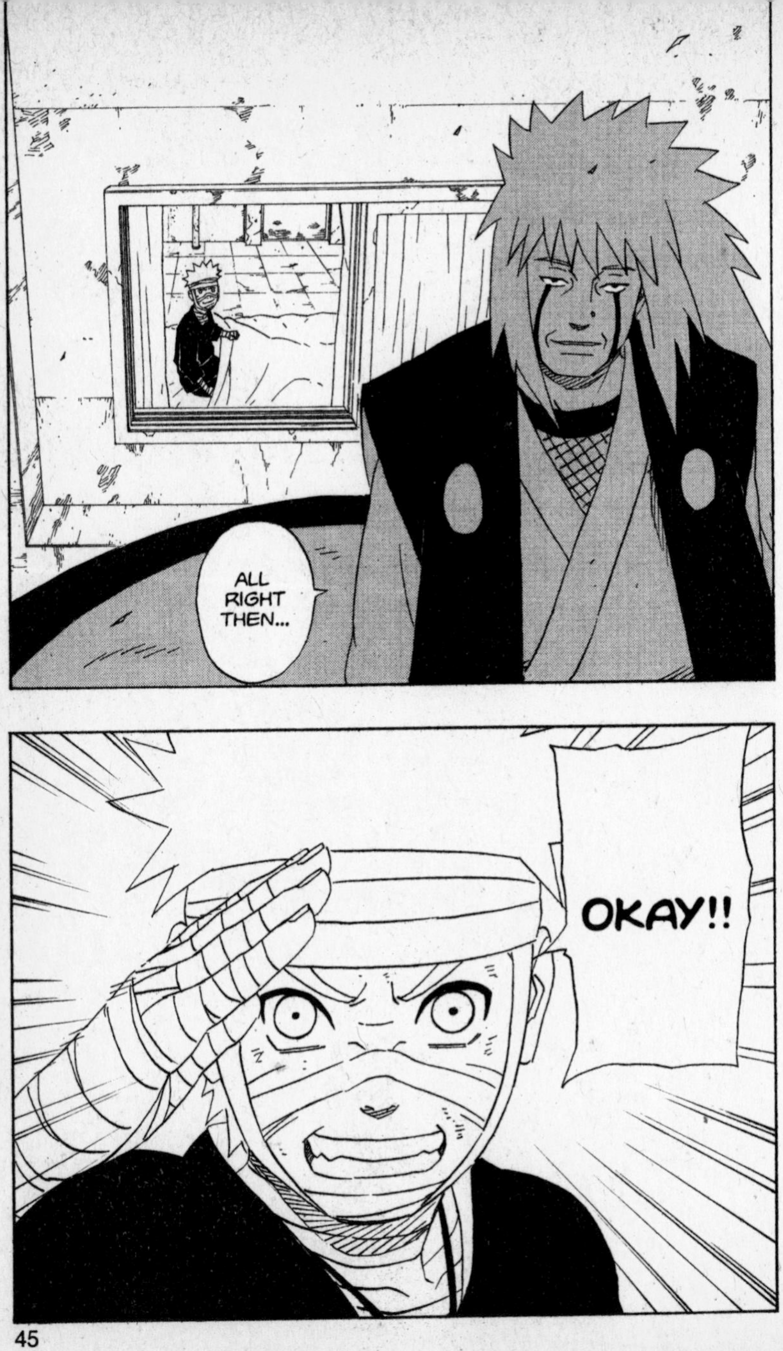
ALL RIGHT THEN...
OKAY!!

THE WORLD OF MASASHI KISHIMOTO
PERSONAL HISTORY: SPECIAL FRIENDS, PART 2

I ALSO TOOK CARE TO PERFECT THE PRESENTATION BY MAKING SURETHAT MOST ALL THE SHADOW DOPPELGANGERS WE DREW WERE RUINED BY THE JET-BLACK INK. WHEN MY ASSISTANT WOKE FROM HIS NAP, THE FIRST WORDS OUT OF HIS MOUTH WERE **"WHAT THE...?!"**

AND ME? I GUFFAWED. "AH HA HA! STUNNED, ARE YOU?! IT'S WHAT YOU CALL SHOCK THERAPY!" I ALWAYS TELL HIM THE TRUTH RIGHT OFF LIKE THAT. IT'S ALL INTENDED TO SOFTEN THE TENSION, THOUGH AT TIMES IT DOES BACKFIRE...

FOR ME, MY ASSISTANTS ARE WHAT FEW FRIENDS I HAVE LEFT.

YOU TOO SHOULD TREASURE YOUR FRIENDS.

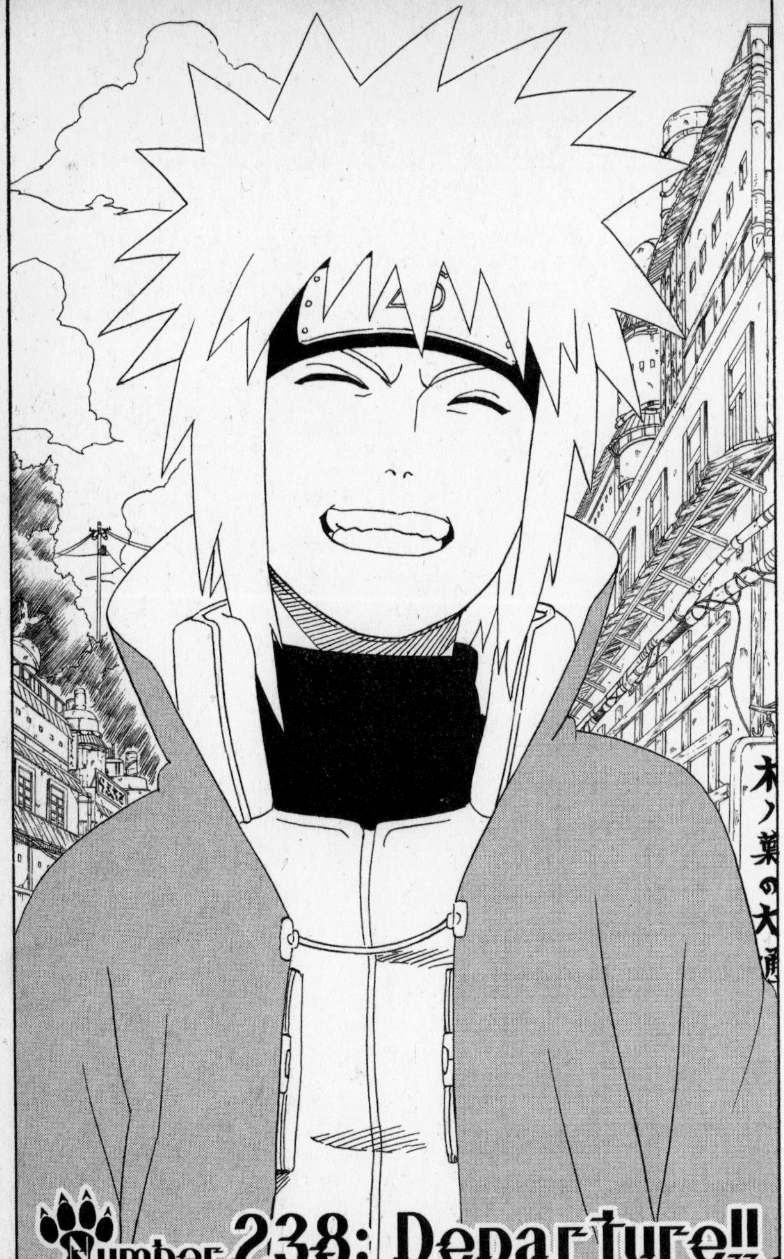

Number 238: Departure!!

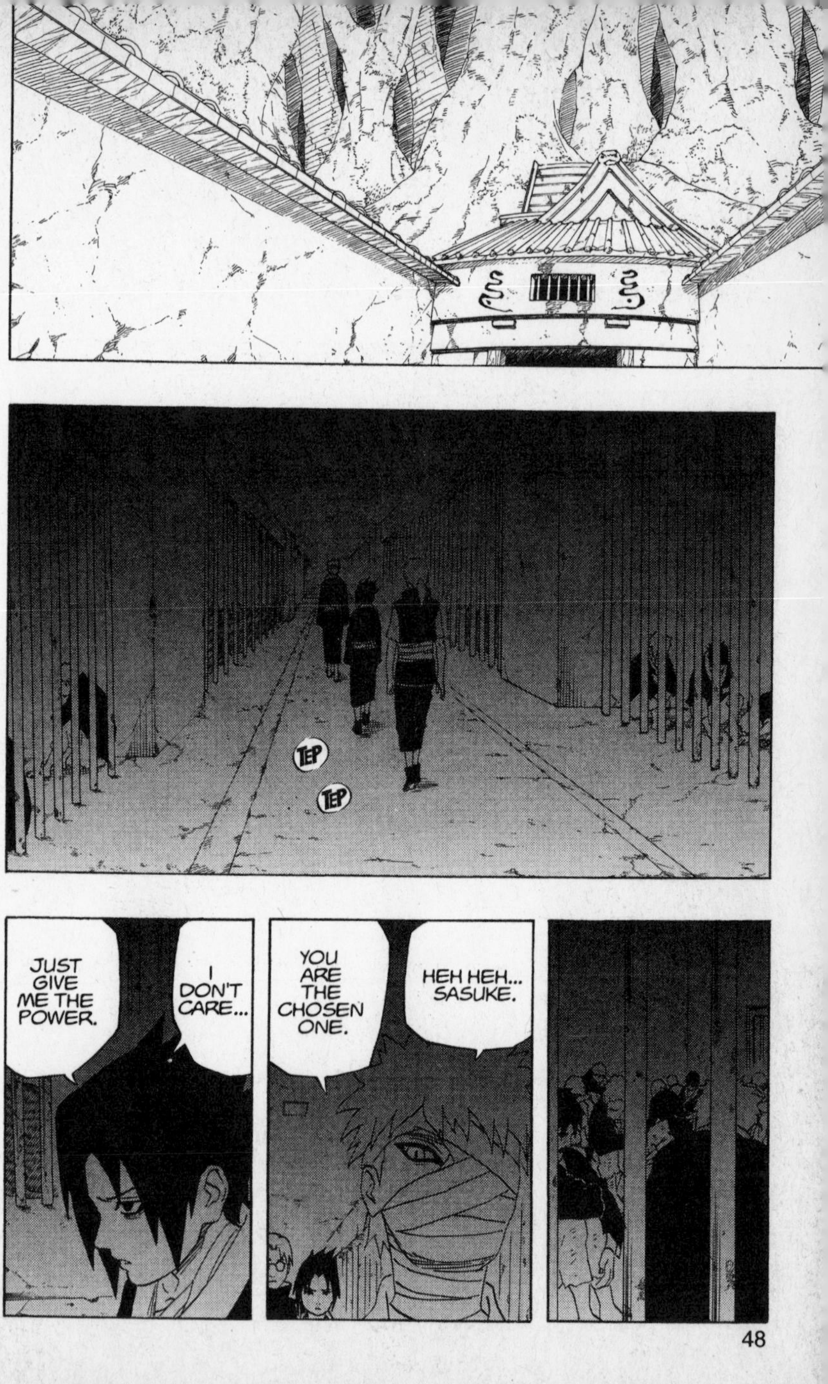
TEP
TEP
HEH HEH... SASUKE.
YOU ARE THE CHOSEN ONE.
I DON'T CARE...
JUST GIVE ME THE POWER.

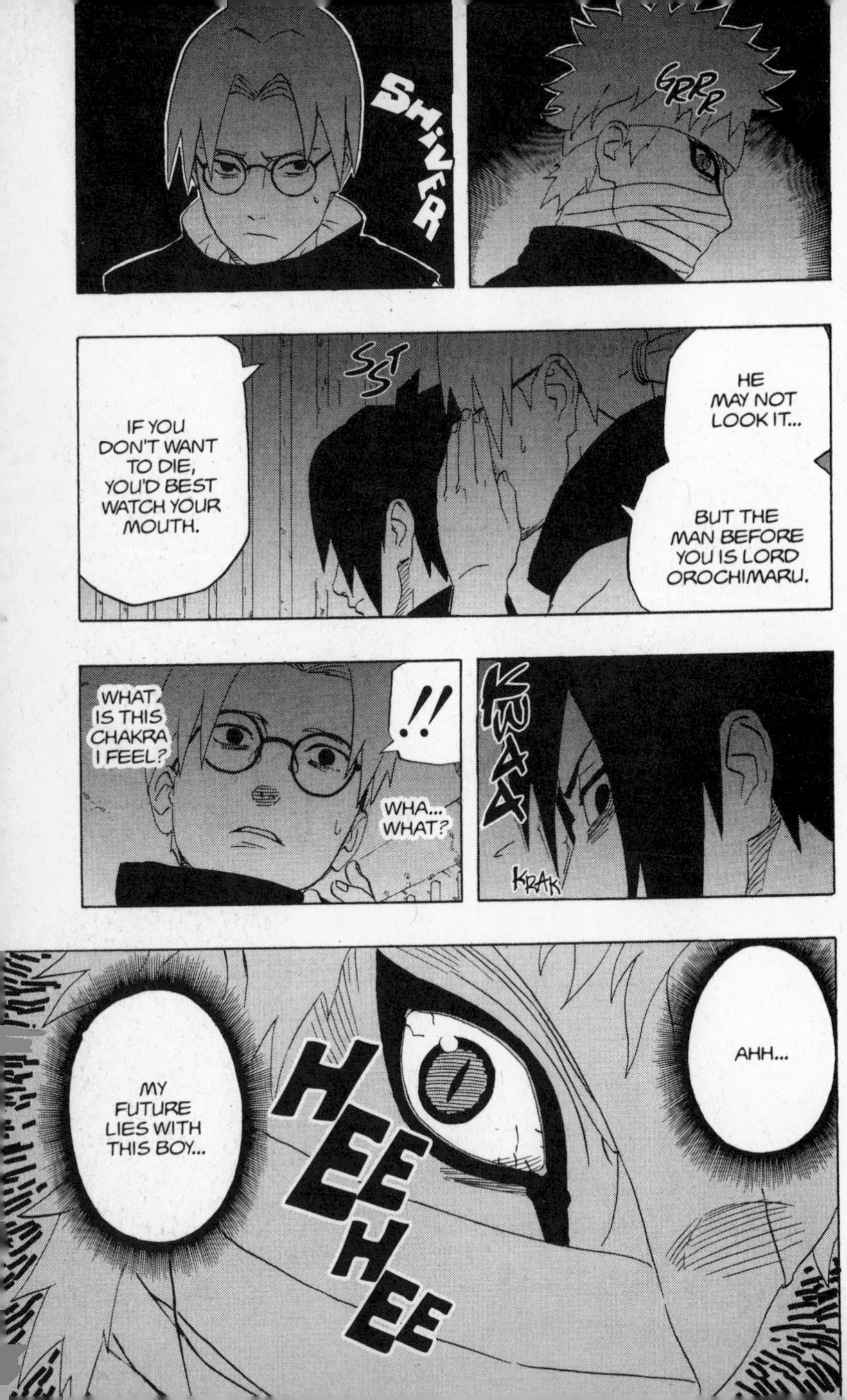
GRRR
SHIVER
HE MAY NOT LOOK IT...
BUT THE MAN BEFORE YOU IS LORD OROCHIMARU.
SST
IF YOU DON'T WANT TO DIE, YOU'D BEST WATCH YOUR MOUTH.
KRAAA
KRAK
!!
WHAT IS THIS CHAKRA I FEEL?
WHA... WHAT?
AHH...
HEE HEE
MY FUTURE LIES WITH THIS BOY...

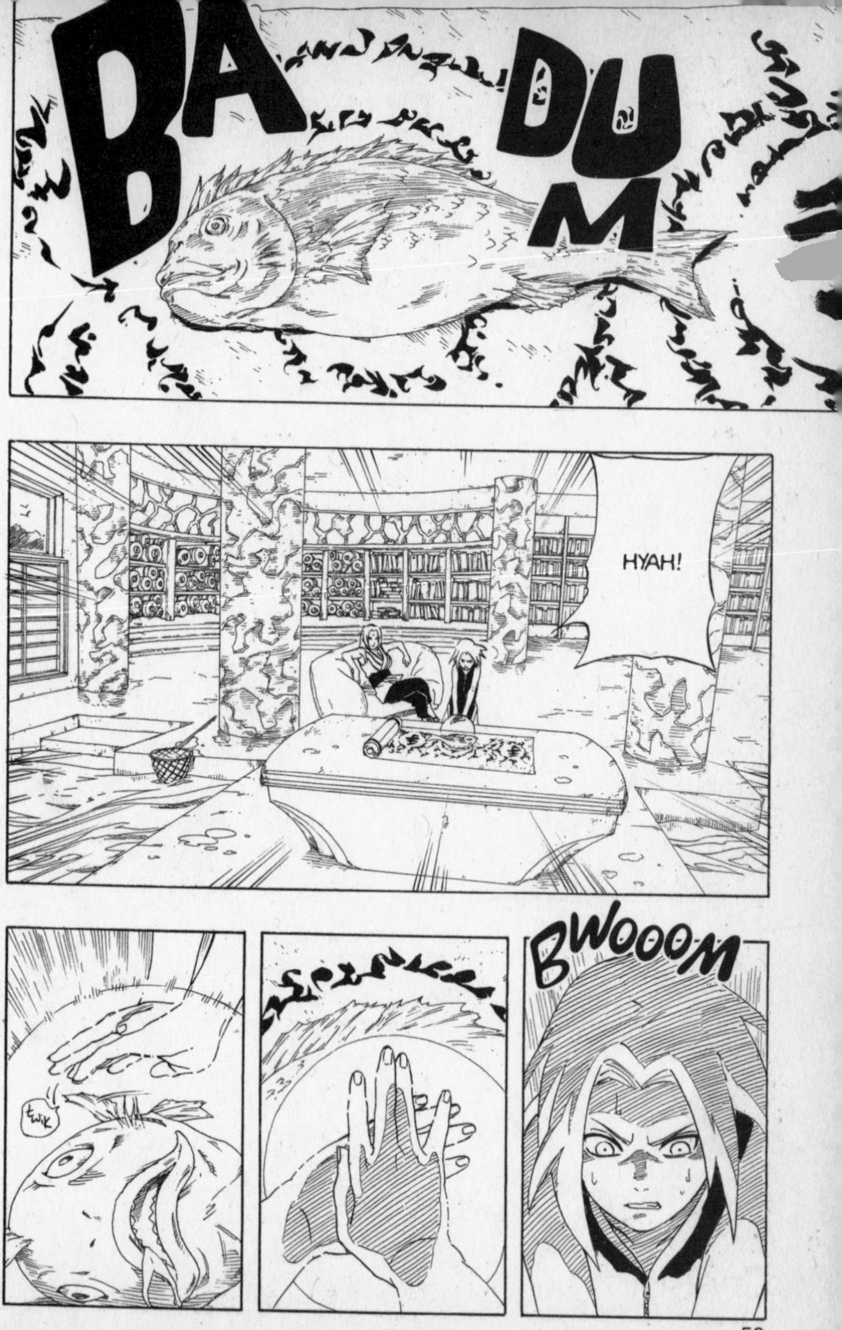
BA
DUM
HYAH!
TWIK
BWOOOM

READ THIS WAY

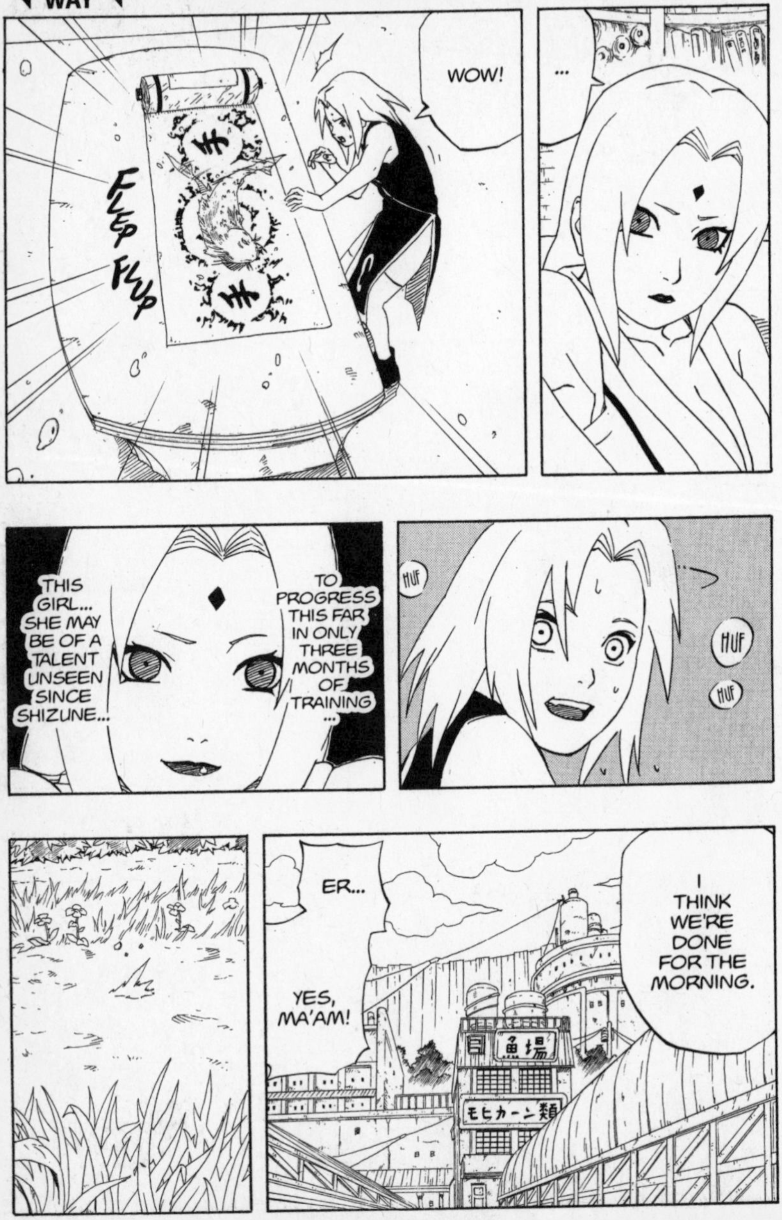
...
WOW!
FLEP FLUP
HUF
HUF
HUF
TO PROGRESS THIS FAR IN ONLY THREE MONTHS OF TRAINING ...
THIS GIRL... SHE MAY BE OF A TALENT UNSEEN SINCE SHIZUNE...
I THINK WE'RE DONE FOR THE MORNING.
ER...
YES, MA'AM!
魚場
モヒカーン類

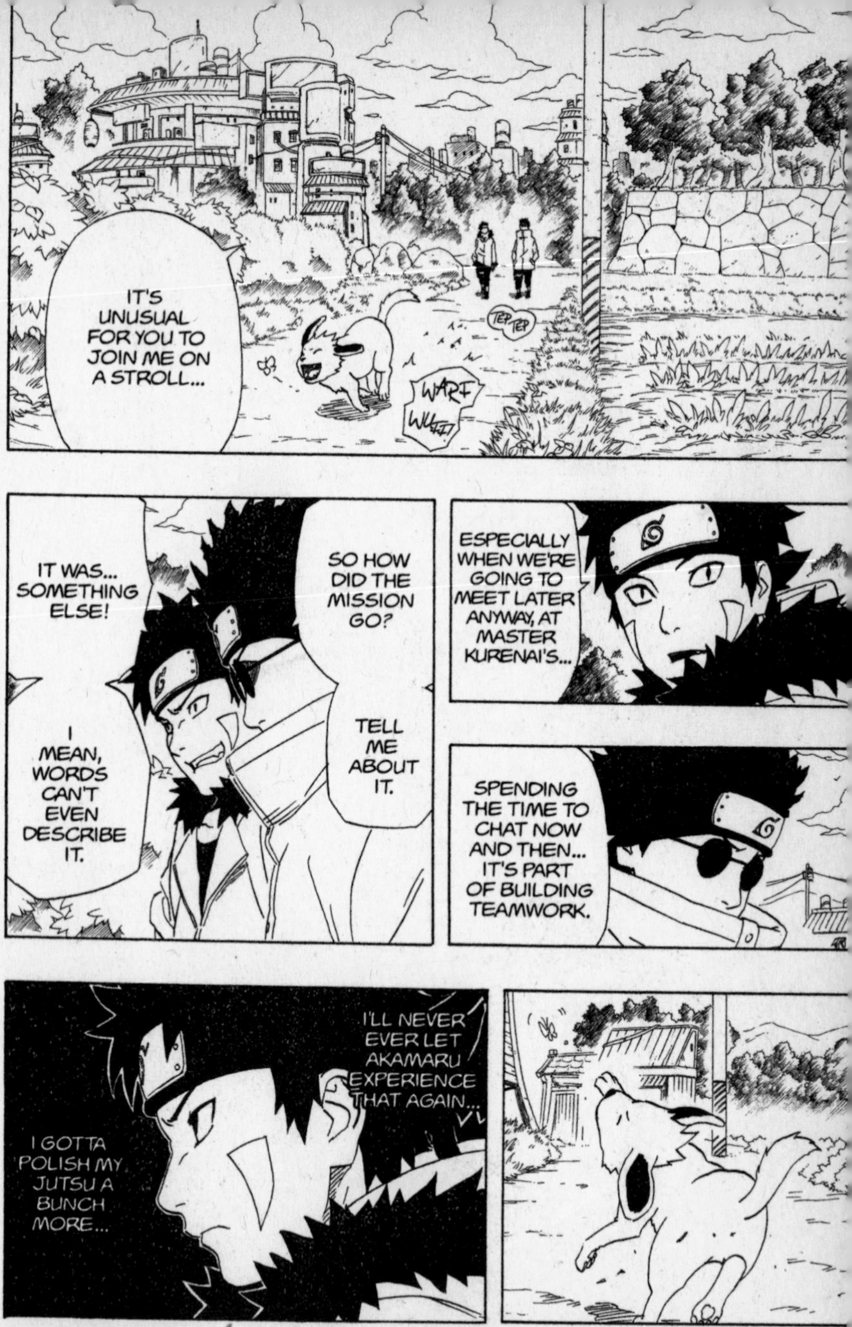
IT'S UNUSUAL FOR YOU TO JOIN ME ON A STROLL...
TEP TEP
WARF WUFF
ESPECIALLY WHEN WE'RE GOING TO MEET LATER ANYWAY, AT MASTER KURENAI'S...
SPENDING THE TIME TO CHAT NOW AND THEN... IT'S PART OF BUILDING TEAMWORK.
SO HOW DID THE MISSION GO?
TELL ME ABOUT IT.
IT WAS... SOMETHING ELSE!
I MEAN, WORDS CAN'T EVEN DESCRIBE IT.
I'LL NEVER EVER LET AKAMARU EXPERIENCE THAT AGAIN...
I GOTTA POLISH MY JUTSU A BUNCH MORE...

READ THIS WAY

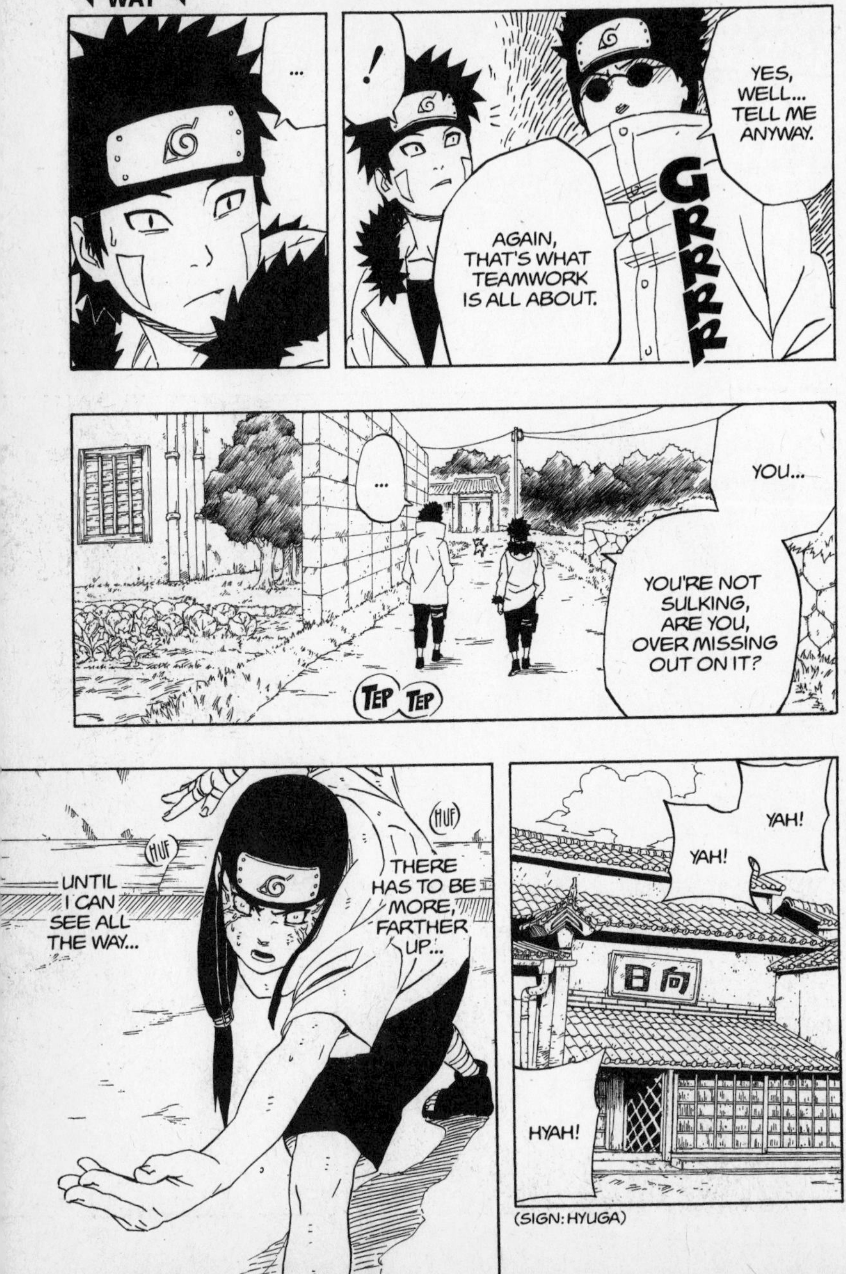
YES, WELL... TELL ME ANYWAY.
GRRRR
!
AGAIN, THAT'S WHAT TEAMWORK IS ALL ABOUT.
...
YOU...
YOU'RE NOT SULKING, ARE YOU, OVER MISSING OUT ON IT?
...
TEP TEP
YAH!
YAH!
日向
HYAH!
HUF
THERE HAS TO BE MORE, FARTHER UP...
HUF
UNTIL I CAN SEE ALL THE WAY...

(SIGN: HYUGA)

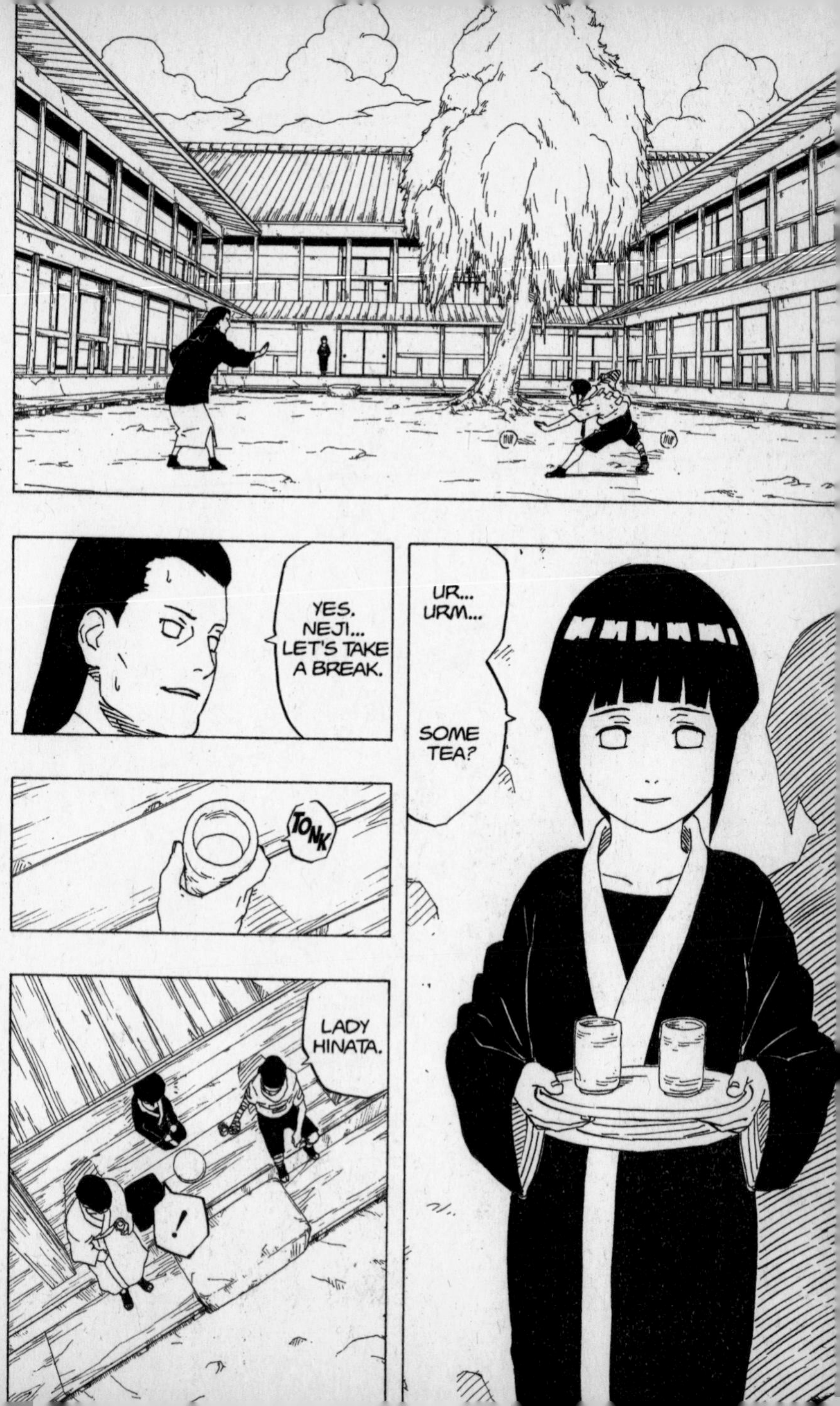
UR... URM...
SOME TEA?
YES. NEJI... LET'S TAKE A BREAK.
TONK
LADY HINATA.
!

READ THIS WAY

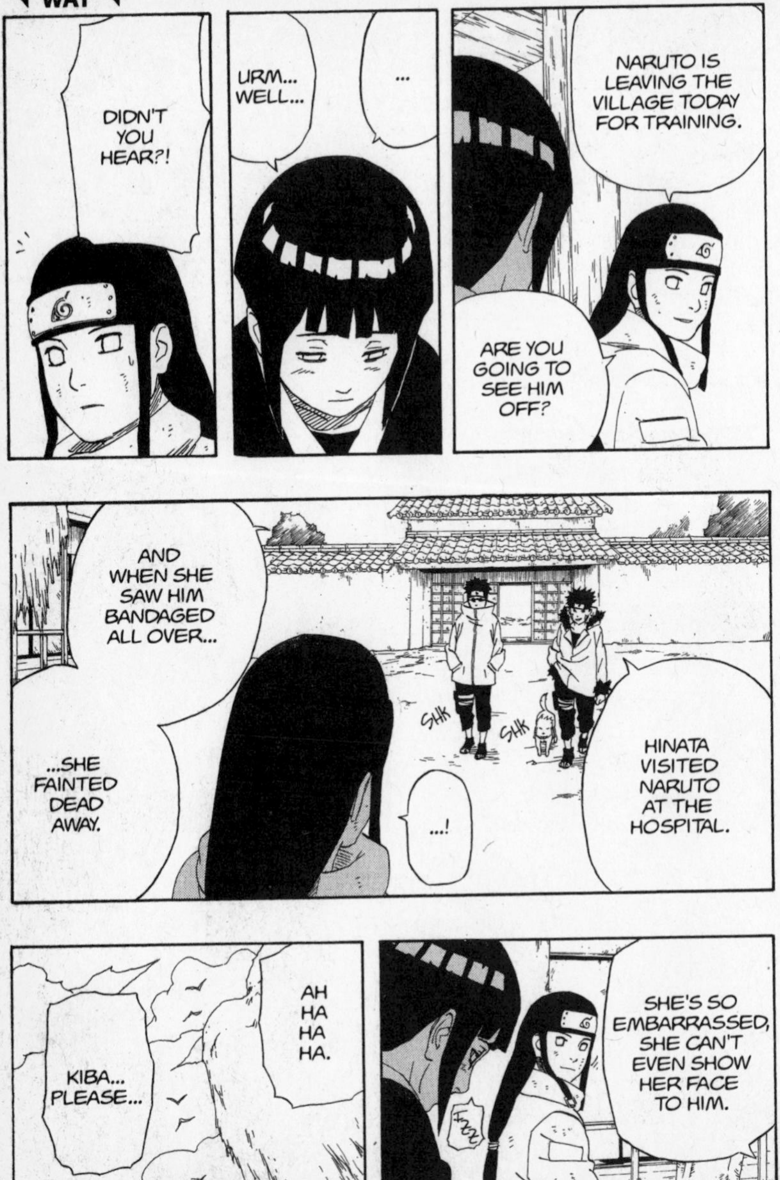
NARUTO IS LEAVING THE VILLAGE TODAY FOR TRAINING.
ARE YOU GOING TO SEE HIM OFF?
...
URM... WELL...
DIDN'T YOU HEAR?!
HINATA VISITED NARUTO AT THE HOSPITAL.
SHK
SHK
...!
AND WHEN SHE SAW HIM BANDAGED ALL OVER...
...SHE FAINTED DEAD AWAY.
SHE'S SO EMBARRASSED, SHE CAN'T EVEN SHOW HER FACE TO HIM.
AH HA HA HA.
KIBA... PLEASE...

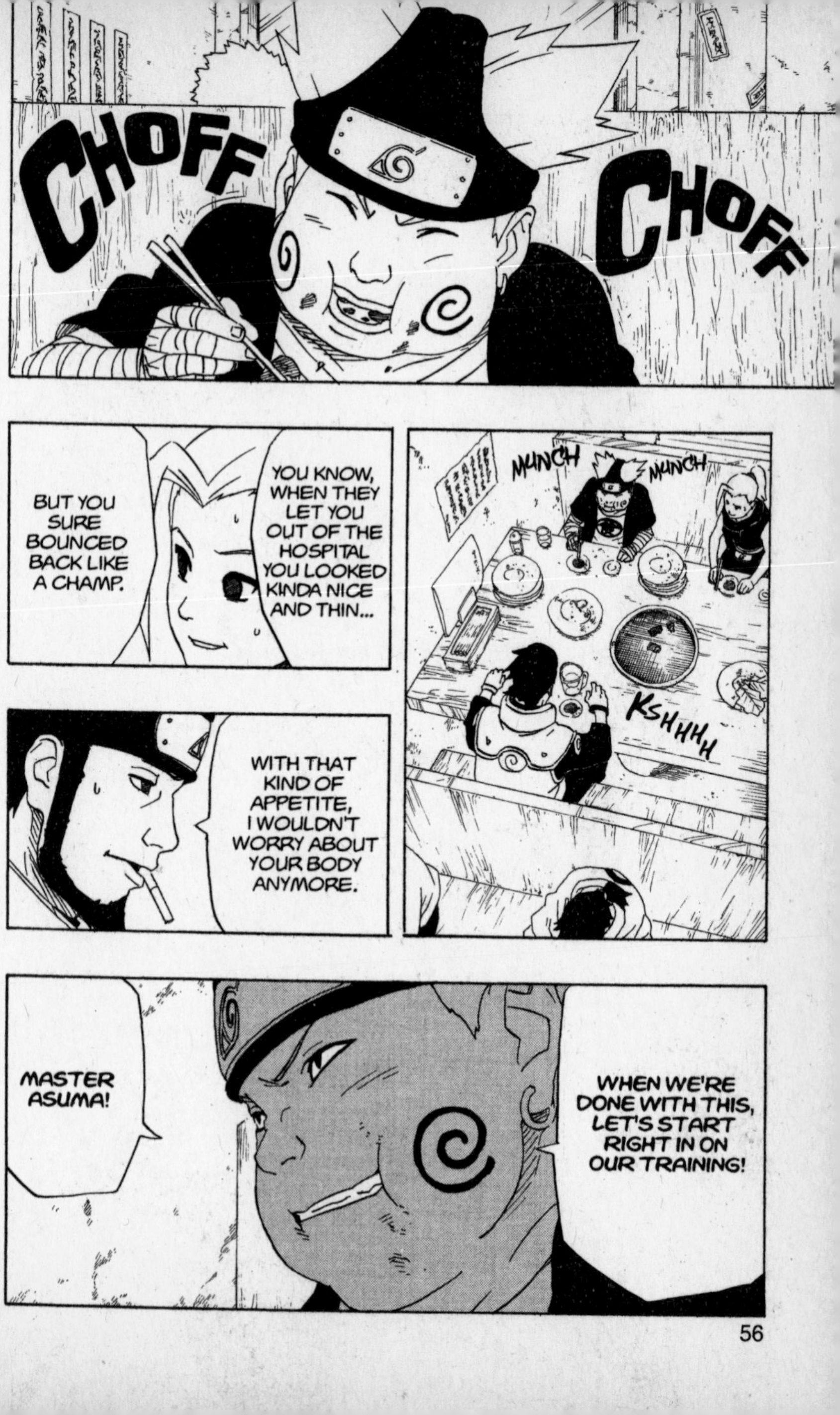
CHOFF
CHOFF
MUNCH
MUNCH
KSHHHH
YOU KNOW, WHEN THEY LET YOU OUT OF THE HOSPITAL YOU LOOKED KINDA NICE AND THIN...
BUT YOU SURE BOUNCED BACK LIKE A CHAMP.
WITH THAT KIND OF APPETITE, I WOULDN'T WORRY ABOUT YOUR BODY ANYMORE.
WHEN WE'RE DONE WITH THIS, LET'S START RIGHT IN ON OUR TRAINING!
MASTER ASUMA!

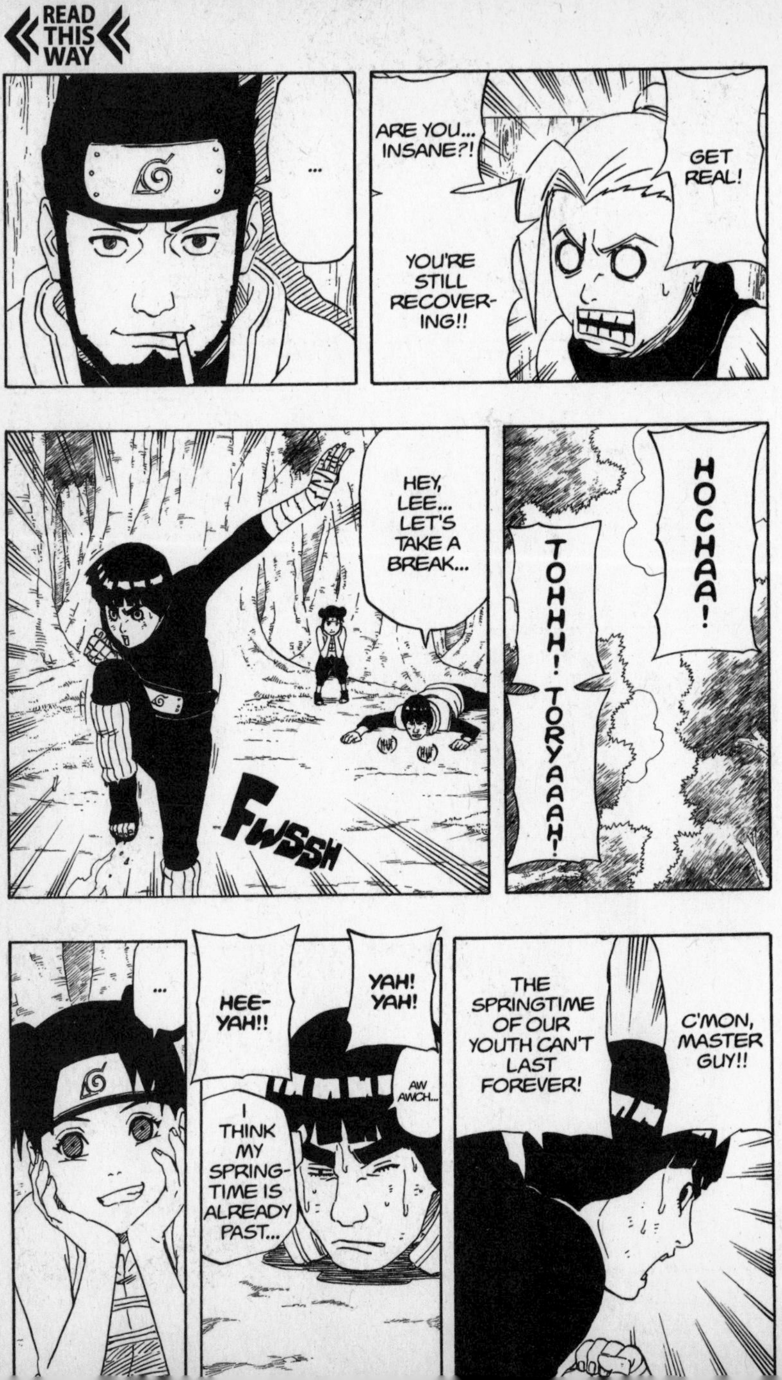
READ THIS WAY
GET REAL!
ARE YOU... INSANE?!
YOU'RE STILL RECOVER-ING!!
...
HOCHAA!
TOHHH! TORYAAAH!
HEY, LEE... LET'S TAKE A BREAK...
HUF HUF
FWSSH
C'MON, MASTER GUY!!
THE SPRINGTIME OF OUR YOUTH CAN'T LAST FOREVER!
YAH! YAH!
HEE-YAH!!
AW AWCH...
I THINK MY SPRING-TIME IS ALREADY PAST...
...

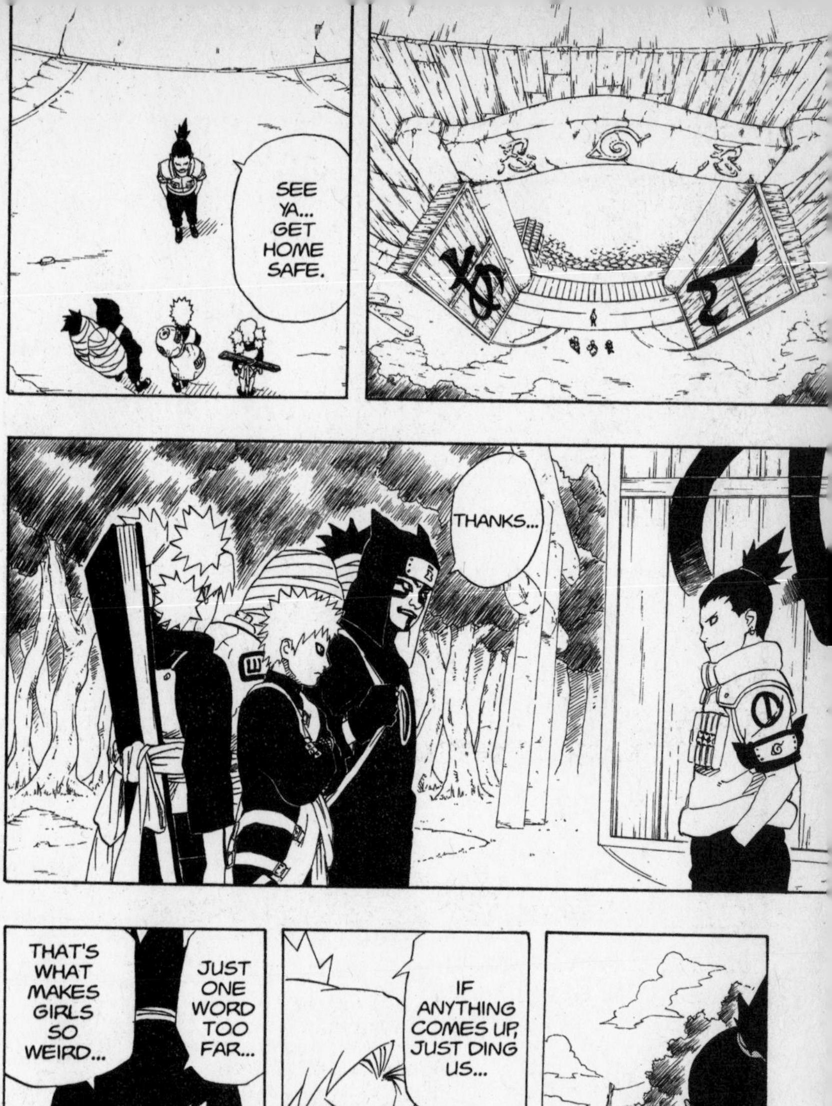
SEE YA... GET HOME SAFE.
THANKS...
IF ANYTHING COMES UP, JUST DING US...
WE'LL HELP YOU OUT. GOT IT, CRYBABY?
JUST ONE WORD TOO FAR...
THAT'S WHAT MAKES GIRLS SO WEIRD...

READ THIS WAY

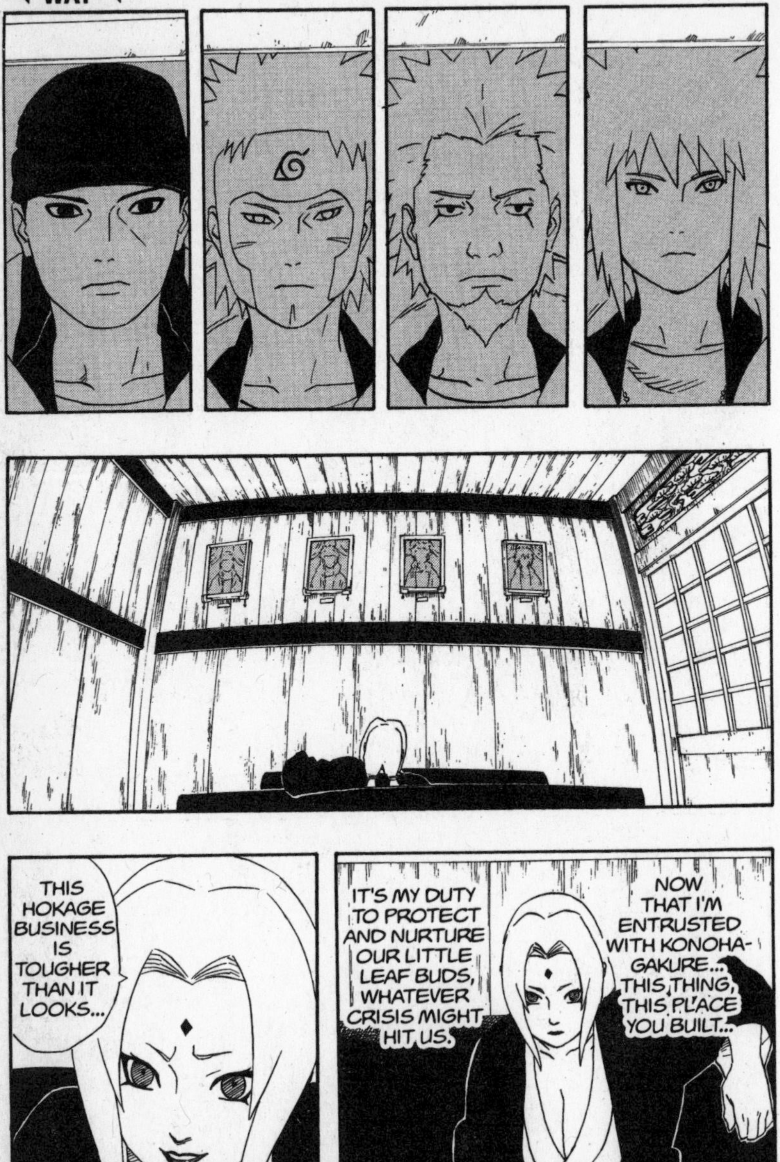
NOW THAT I'M ENTRUSTED WITH KONOHA-GAKURE... THIS THING, THIS PLACE YOU BUILT...
IT'S MY DUTY TO PROTECT AND NURTURE OUR LITTLE LEAF BUDS, WHATEVER CRISIS MIGHT HIT US.
THIS HOKAGE BUSINESS IS TOUGHER THAN IT LOOKS...

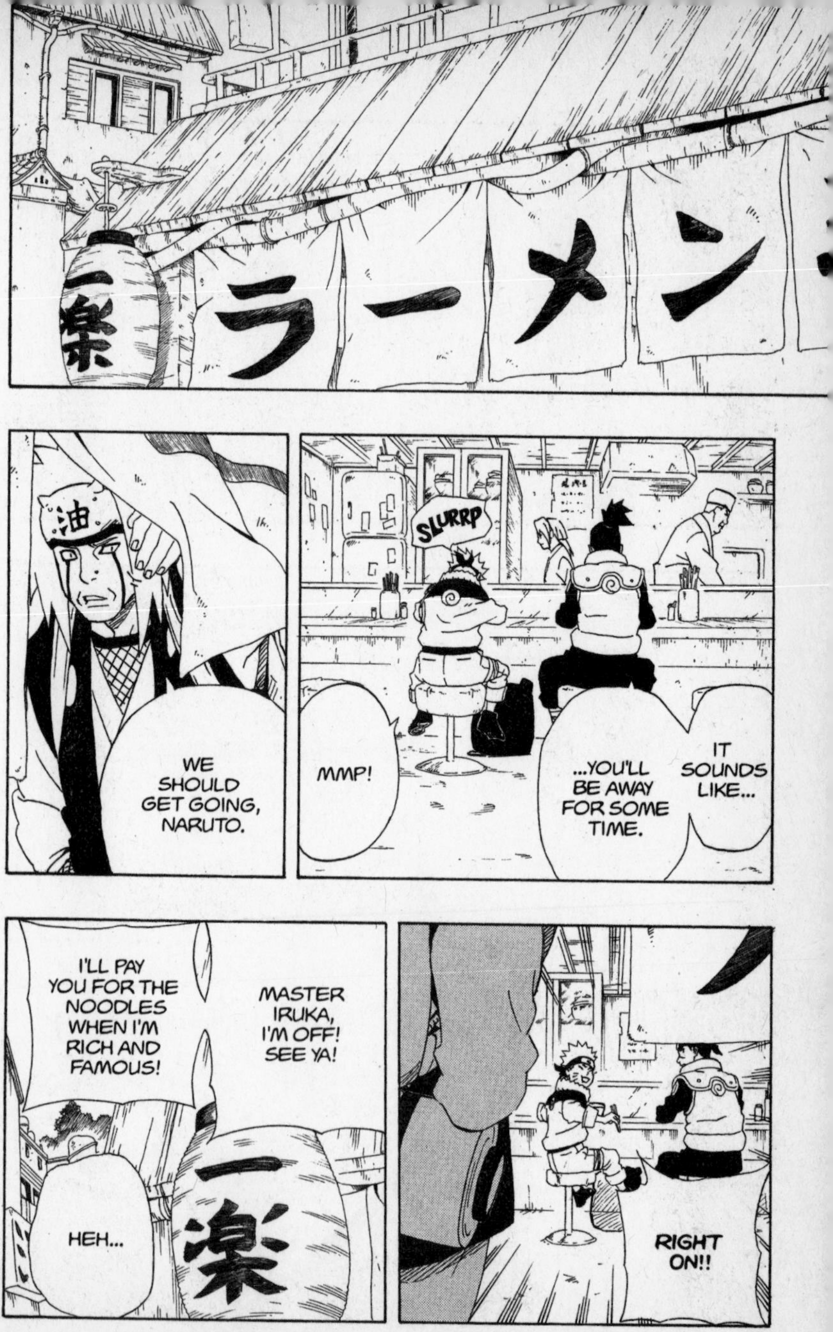
一楽
ラーメン
SLURRP
IT SOUNDS LIKE...
...YOU'LL BE AWAY FOR SOME TIME.
MMP!
WE SHOULD GET GOING, NARUTO.
RIGHT ON!!
MASTER IRUKA, I'M OFF! SEE YA!
I'LL PAY YOU FOR THE NOODLES WHEN I'M RICH AND FAMOUS!
HEH...
一楽

READ THIS WAY

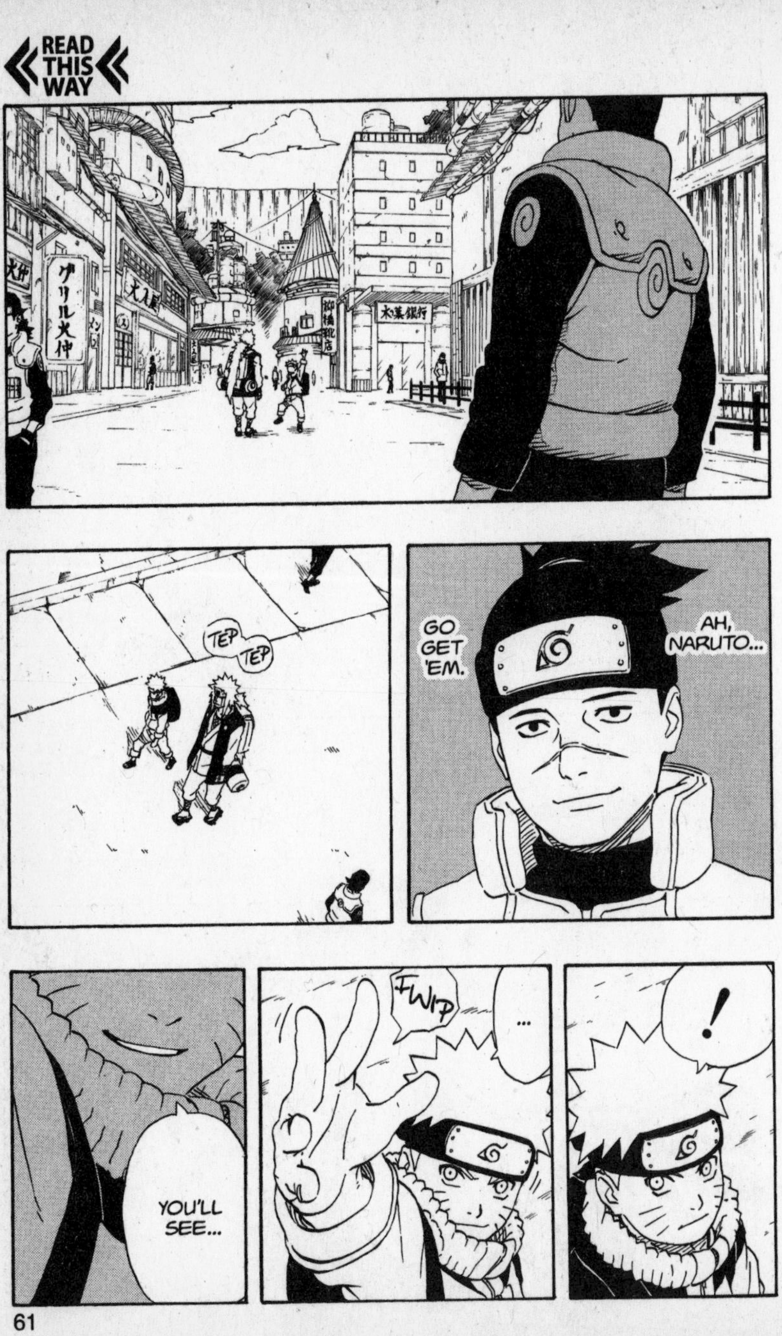

AH, NARUTO...
GO GET 'EM.
TEP
TEP
!
FWIP
...
YOU'LL SEE...

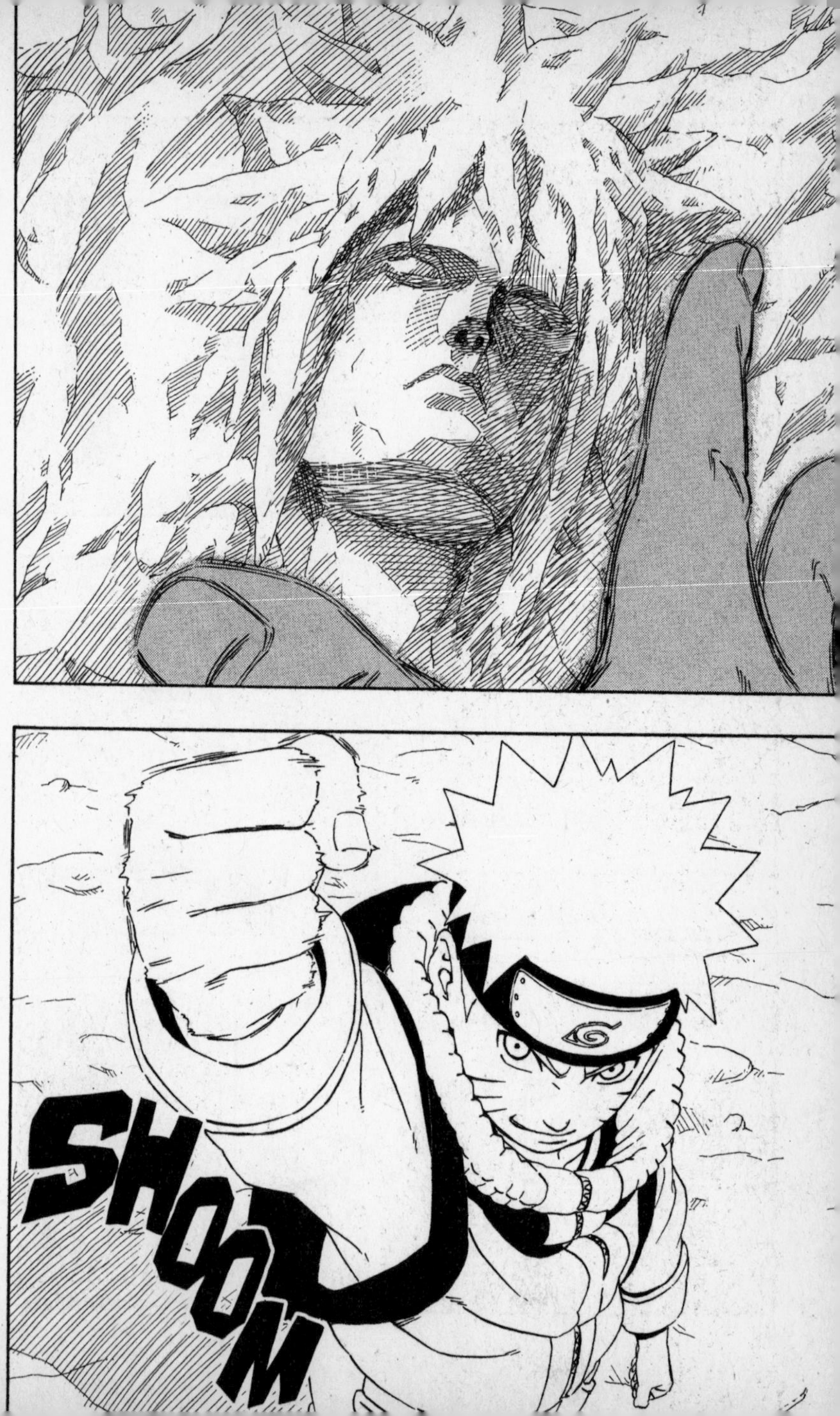
SHOOM

READ THIS WAY

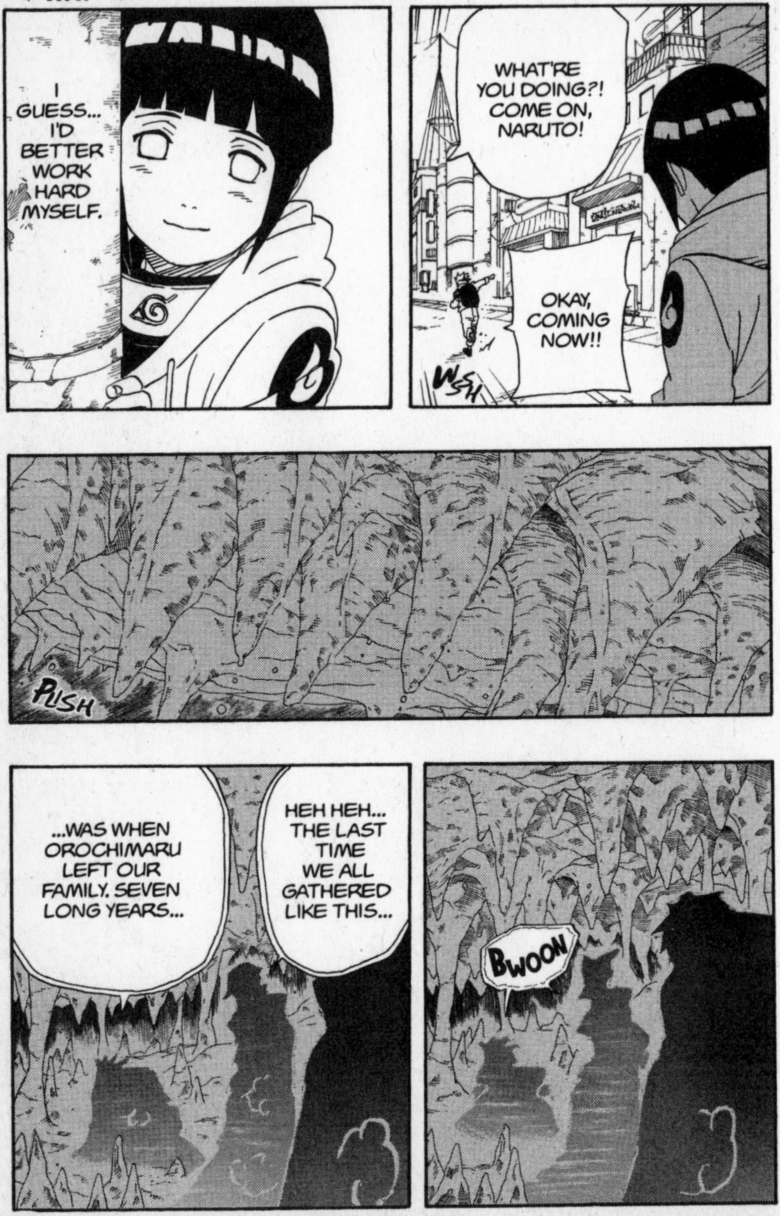
WHAT'RE YOU DOING?! COME ON, NARUTO!
OKAY, COMING NOW!!
WSH
I GUESS... I'D BETTER WORK HARD MYSELF.
PLISH
BWOON
HEH HEH... THE LAST TIME WE ALL GATHERED LIKE THIS...
...WAS WHEN OROCHIMARU LEFT OUR FAMILY. SEVEN LONG YEARS...

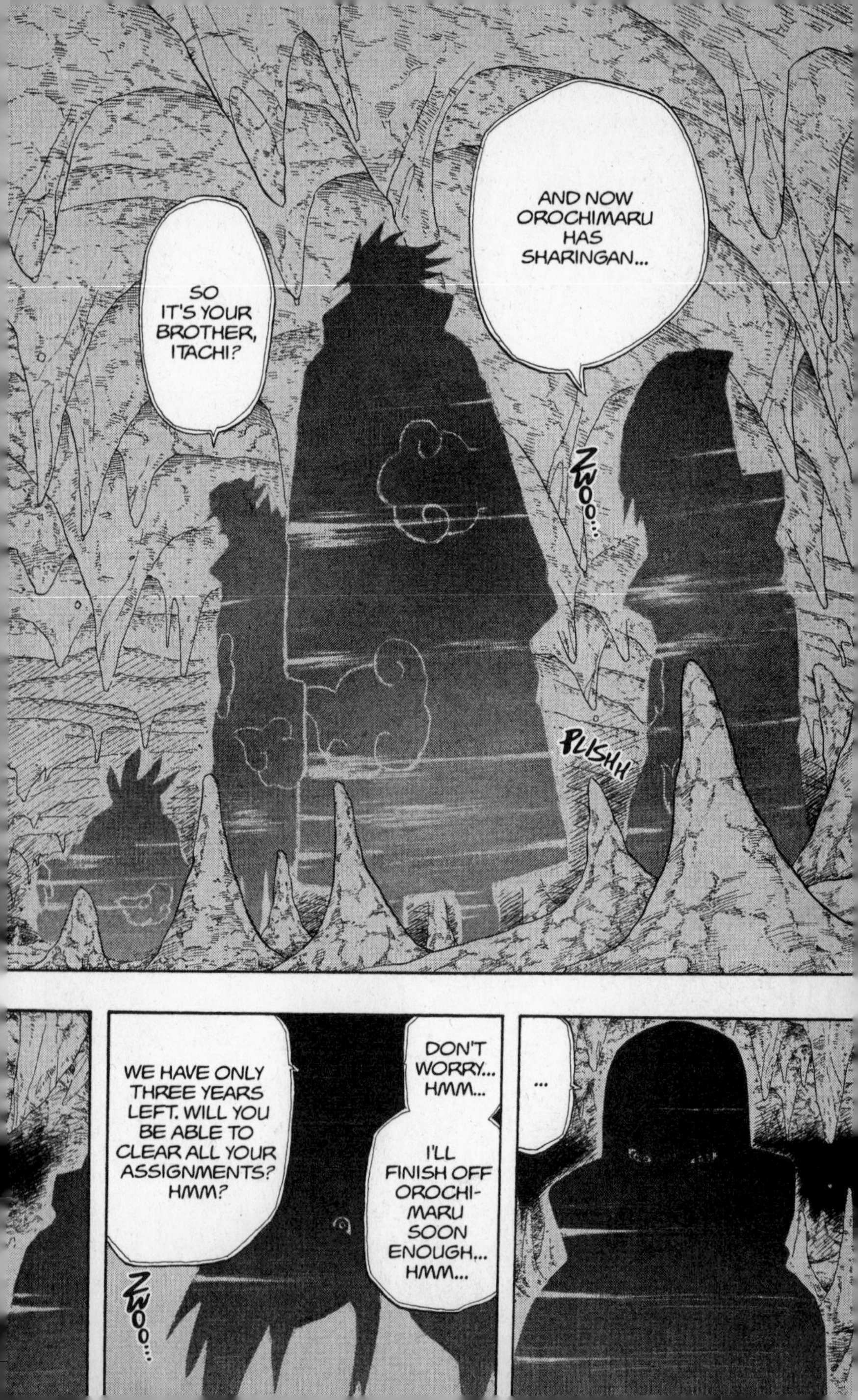
SO IT'S YOUR BROTHER, ITACHI?
AND NOW OROCHIMARU HAS SHARINGAN...
ZWOO...
PLISHH
WE HAVE ONLY THREE YEARS LEFT. WILL YOU BE ABLE TO CLEAR ALL YOUR ASSIGNMENTS? HMM?
ZWOO...
DON'T WORRY... HMM...
I'LL FINISH OFF OROCHIMARU SOON ENOUGH... HMM...
...

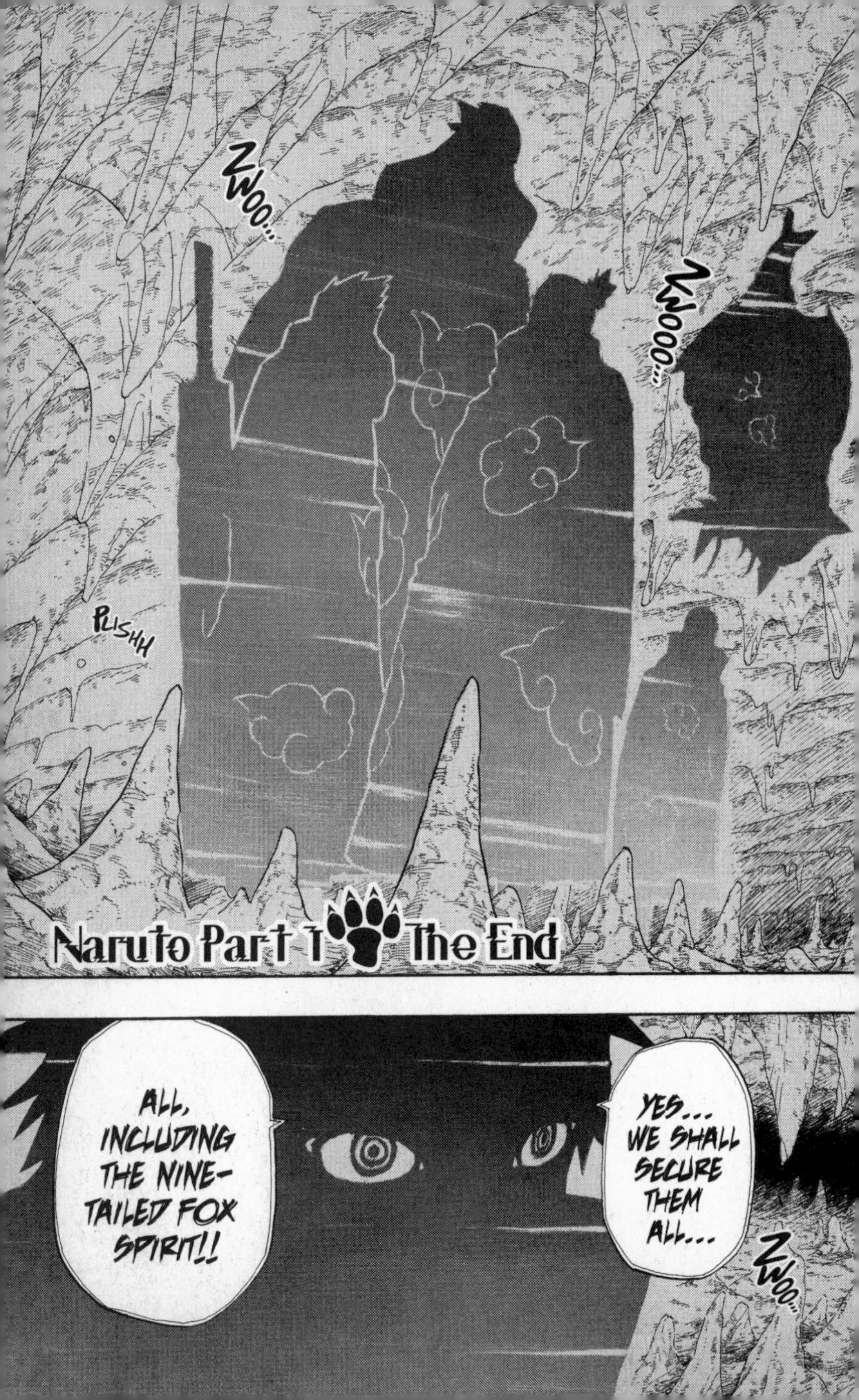
ZWOO...
ZWOOOO...
PLISHH
Naruto Part I The End
YES... WE SHALL SECURE THEM ALL...
ALL, INCLUDING THE NINE-TAILED FOX SPIRIT!!
ZWOO...

KAKASHI CHRONICLES ~ BOYS' LIFE ON THE BATTLEFIELD ~

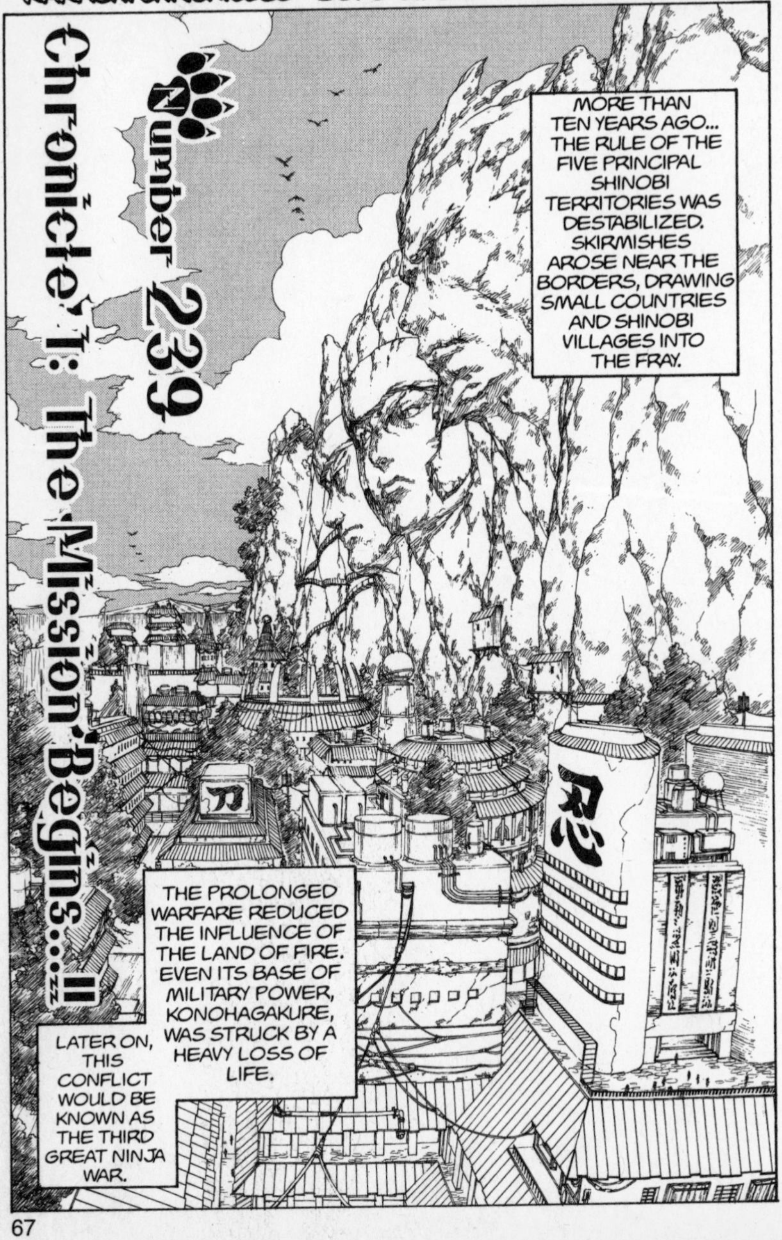
Number 239
Chronicle 1: The Mission Begins...!!
MORE THAN TEN YEARS AGO... THE RULE OF THE FIVE PRINCIPAL SHINOBI TERRITORIES WAS DESTABILIZED. SKIRMISHES AROSE NEAR THE BORDERS, DRAWING SMALL COUNTRIES AND SHINOBI VILLAGES INTO THE FRAY.
THE PROLONGED WARFARE REDUCED THE INFLUENCE OF THE LAND OF FIRE. EVEN ITS BASE OF MILITARY POWER, KONOHAGAKURE, WAS STRUCK BY A HEAVY LOSS OF LIFE.
LATER ON, THIS CONFLICT WOULD BE KNOWN AS THE THIRD GREAT NINJA WAR.

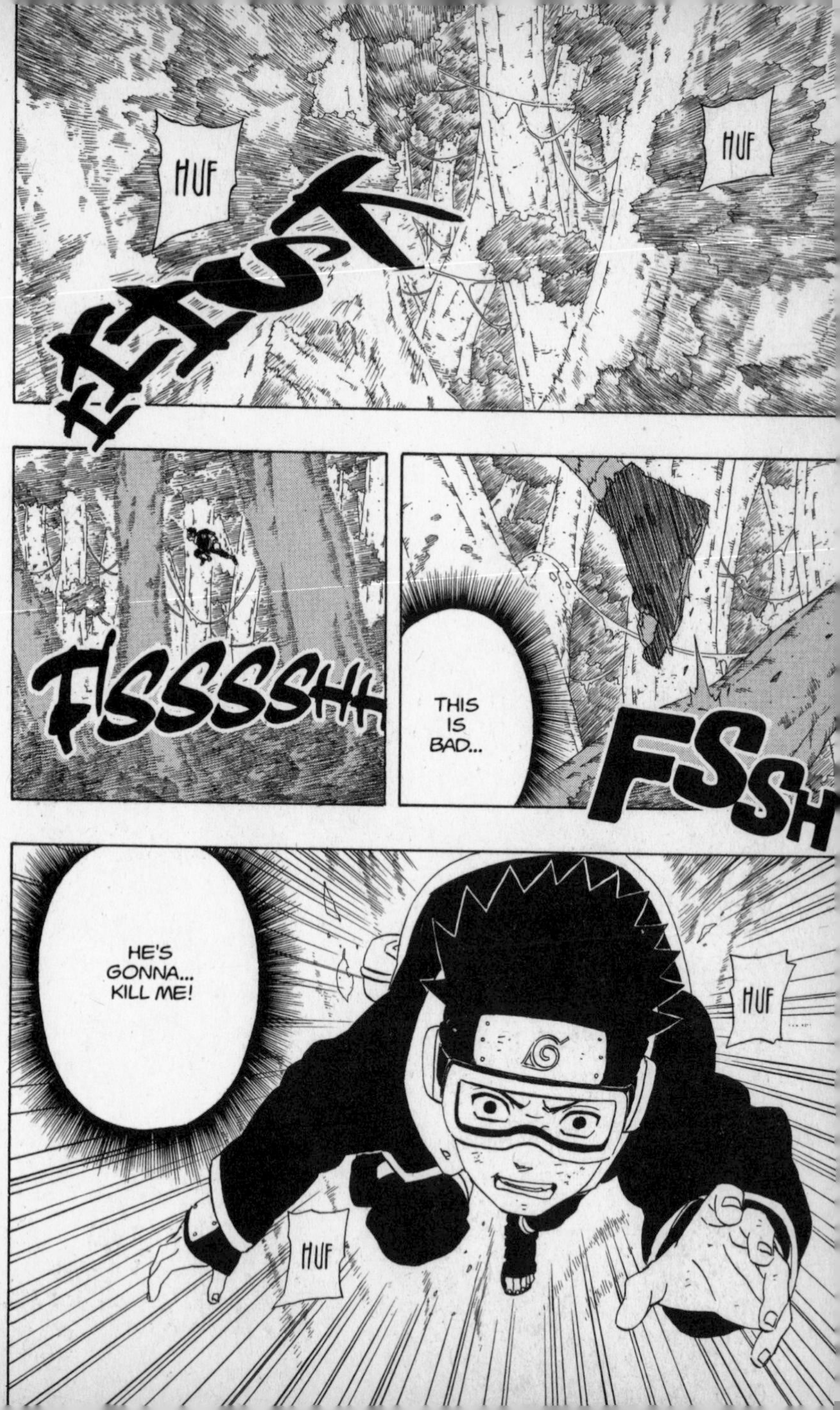
HUF
HUF
THIS IS BAD...
FSSH
FISSSSH
HE'S GONNA... KILL ME!
HUF
HUF

READ THIS WAY

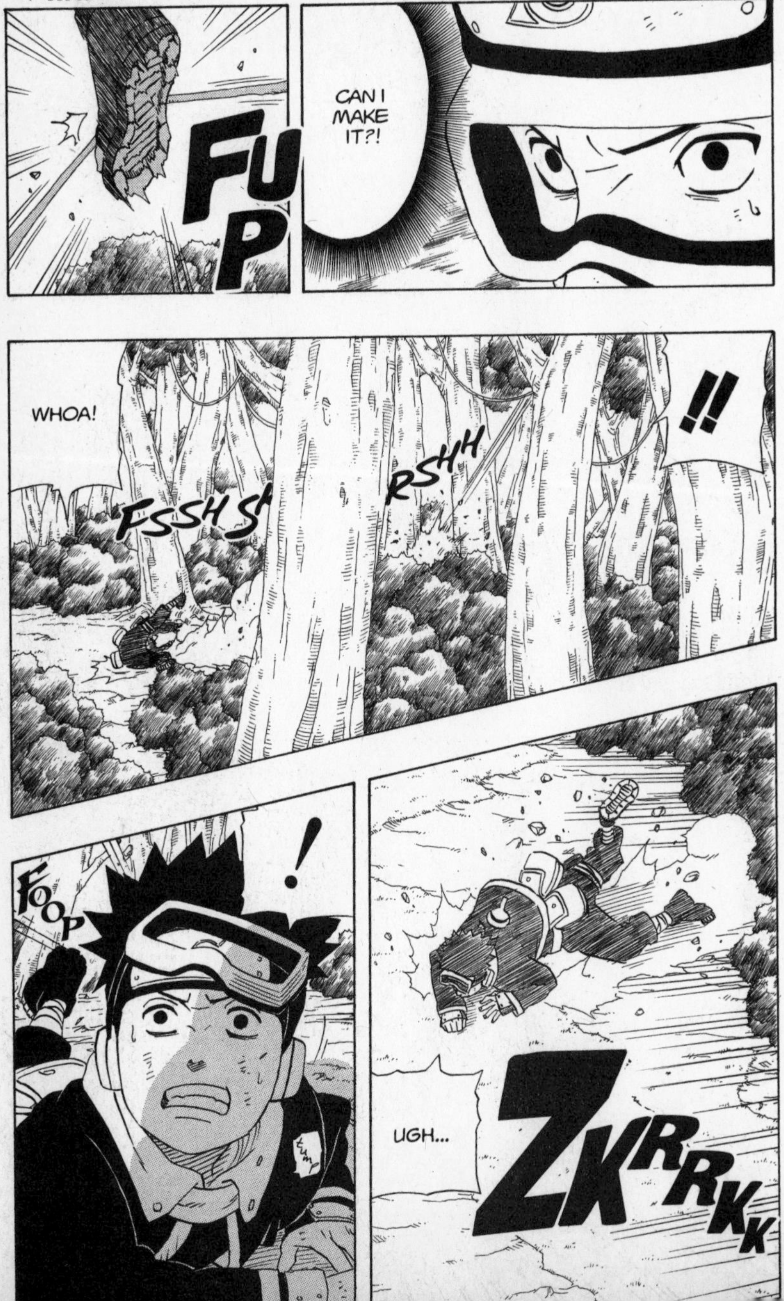
CAN I MAKE IT?!
FUP
!!
WHOA!
RSHH
FSSH SH
UGH...
ZKRRKK
!
FOOP

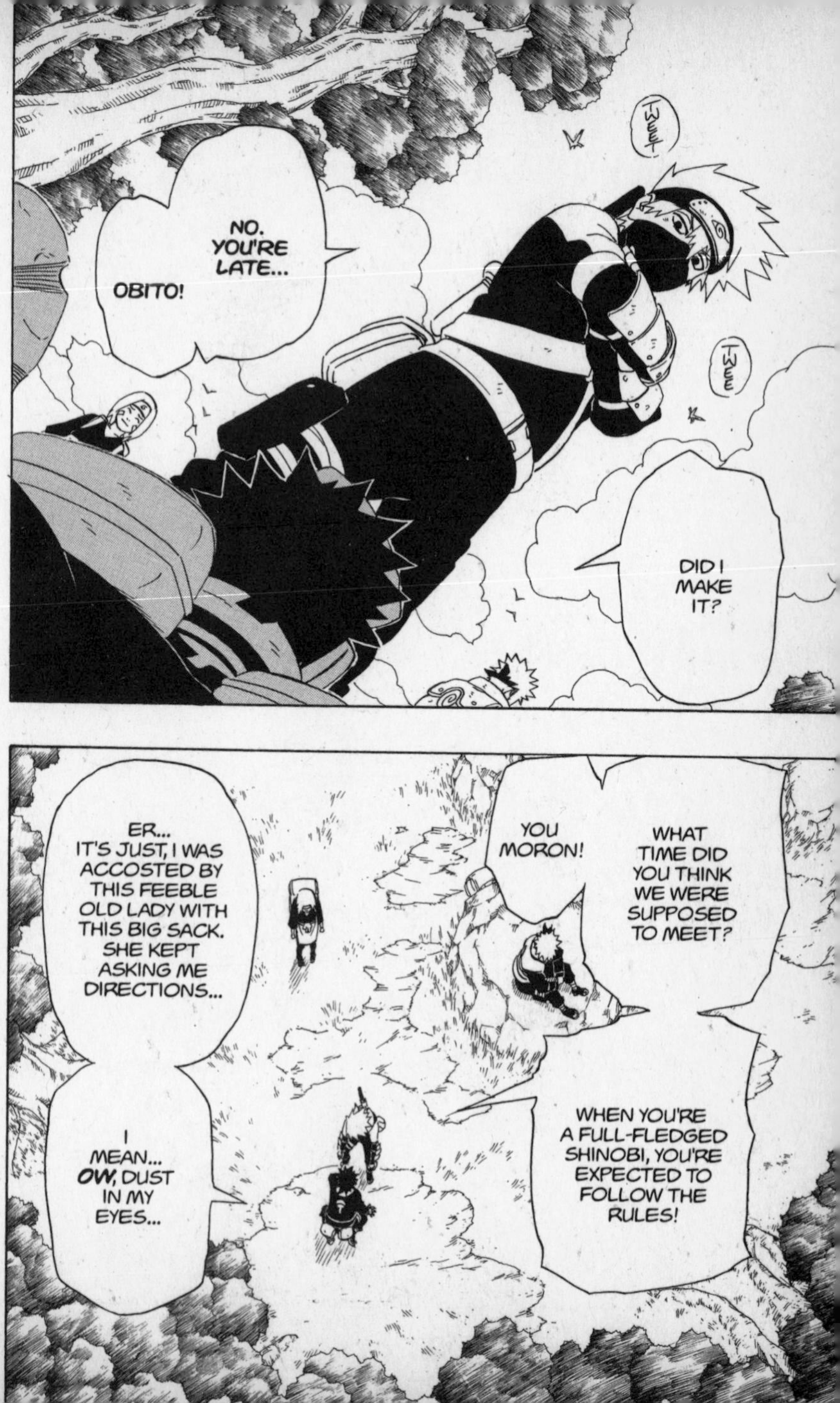
TWEET
TWEE
DID I MAKE IT?
NO. YOU'RE LATE... OBITO!
YOU MORON!
WHAT TIME DID YOU THINK WE WERE SUPPOSED TO MEET?
WHEN YOU'RE A FULL-FLEDGED SHINOBI, YOU'RE EXPECTED TO FOLLOW THE RULES!
ER... IT'S JUST, I WAS ACCOSTED BY THIS FEEBLE OLD LADY WITH THIS BIG SACK. SHE KEPT ASKING ME DIRECTIONS...
I MEAN... **OW**, DUST IN MY EYES...

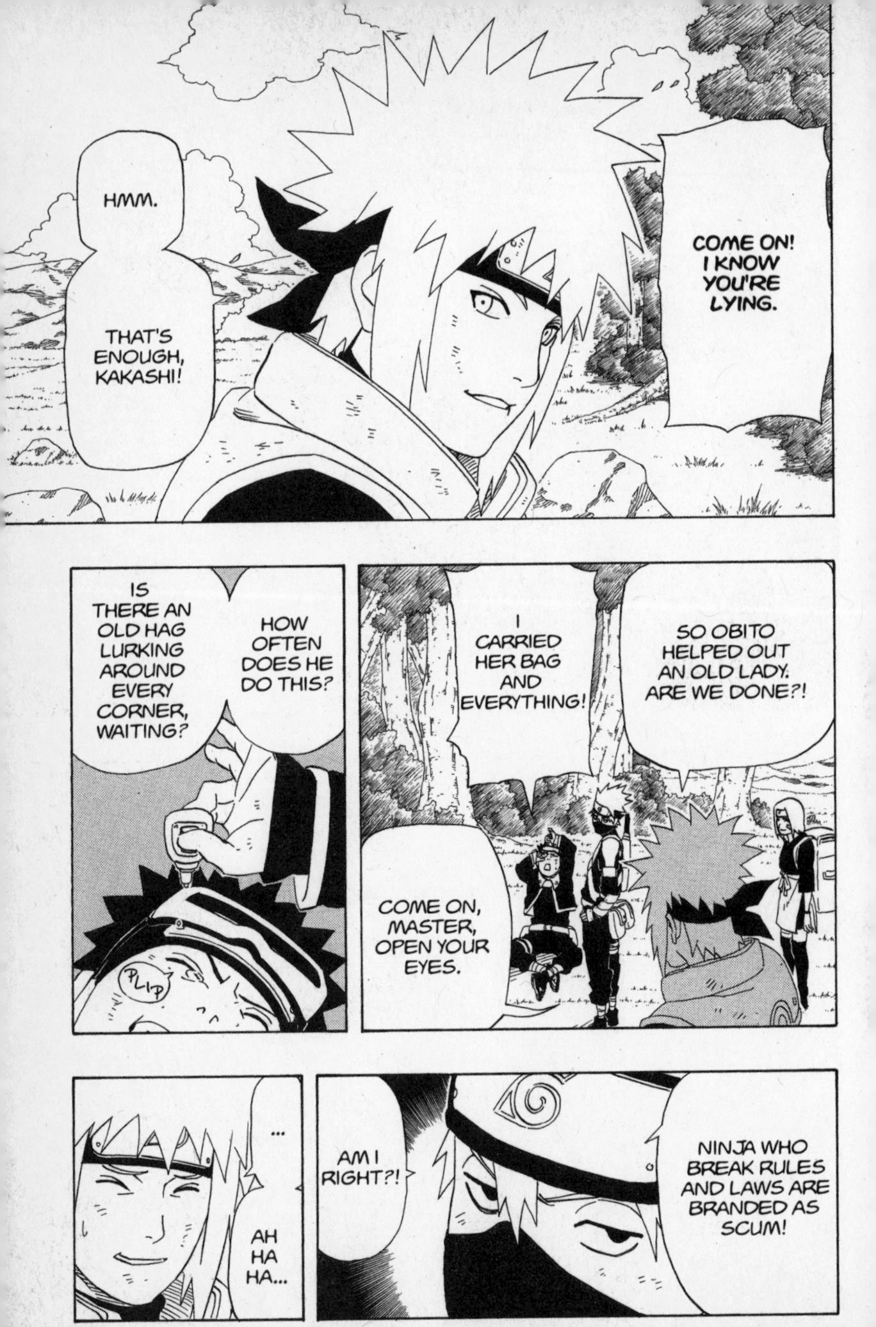

COME ON! I KNOW YOU'RE LYING.
HMM.
THAT'S ENOUGH, KAKASHI!
SO OBITO HELPED OUT AN OLD LADY. ARE WE DONE?!
I CARRIED HER BAG AND EVERYTHING!
COME ON, MASTER, OPEN YOUR EYES.
HOW OFTEN DOES HE DO THIS?
IS THERE AN OLD HAG LURKING AROUND EVERY CORNER, WAITING?
PLIP
NINJA WHO BREAK RULES AND LAWS ARE BRANDED AS SCUM!
AM I RIGHT?!
...
AH HA HA...

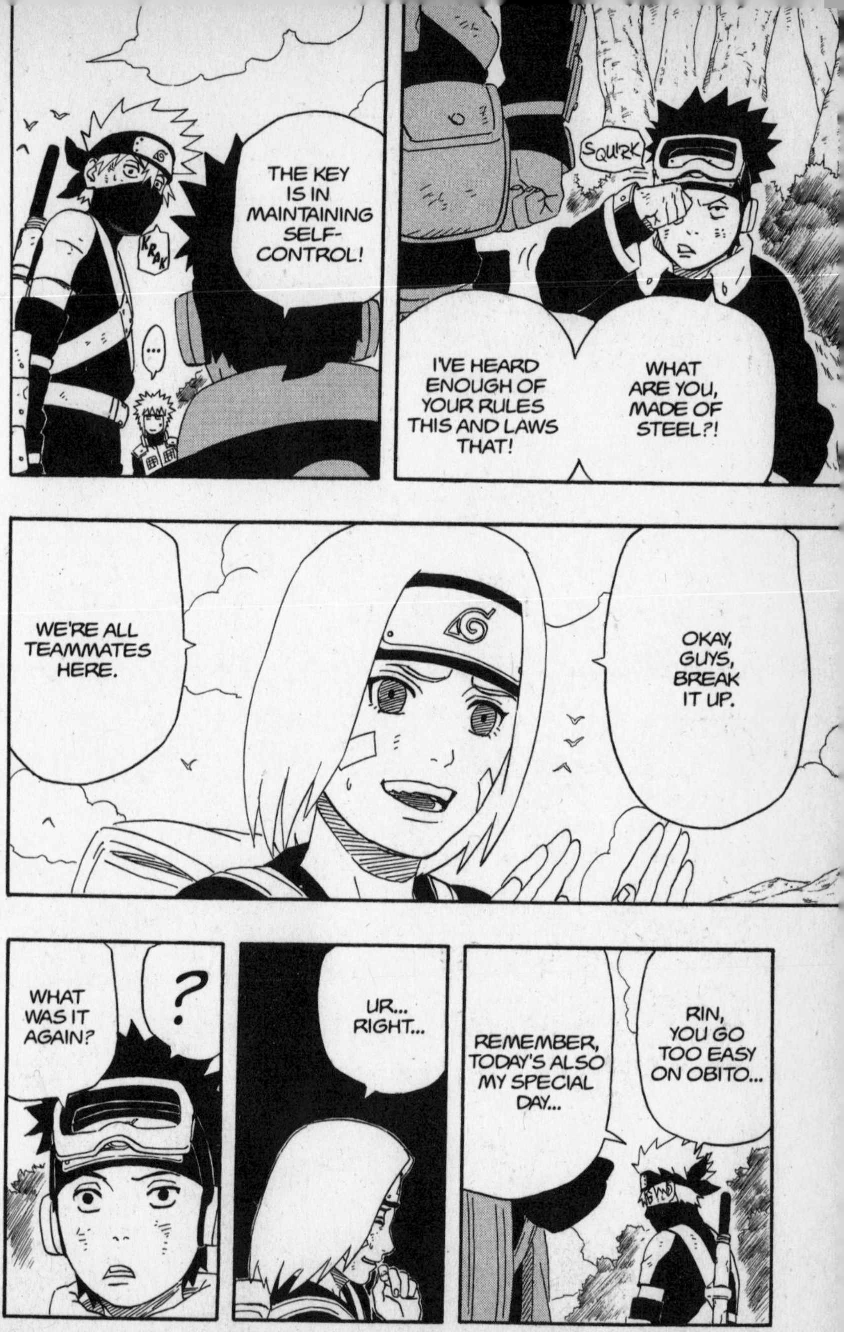
SQU'RK
WHAT ARE YOU, MADE OF STEEL?!
I'VE HEARD ENOUGH OF YOUR RULES THIS AND LAWS THAT!
THE KEY IS IN MAINTAINING SELF-CONTROL!
KRAK
...
OKAY, GUYS, BREAK IT UP.
WE'RE ALL TEAMMATES HERE.
RIN, YOU GO TOO EASY ON OBITO...
REMEMBER, TODAY'S ALSO MY SPECIAL DAY...
UR... RIGHT...
?
WHAT WAS IT AGAIN?

READ THIS WAY

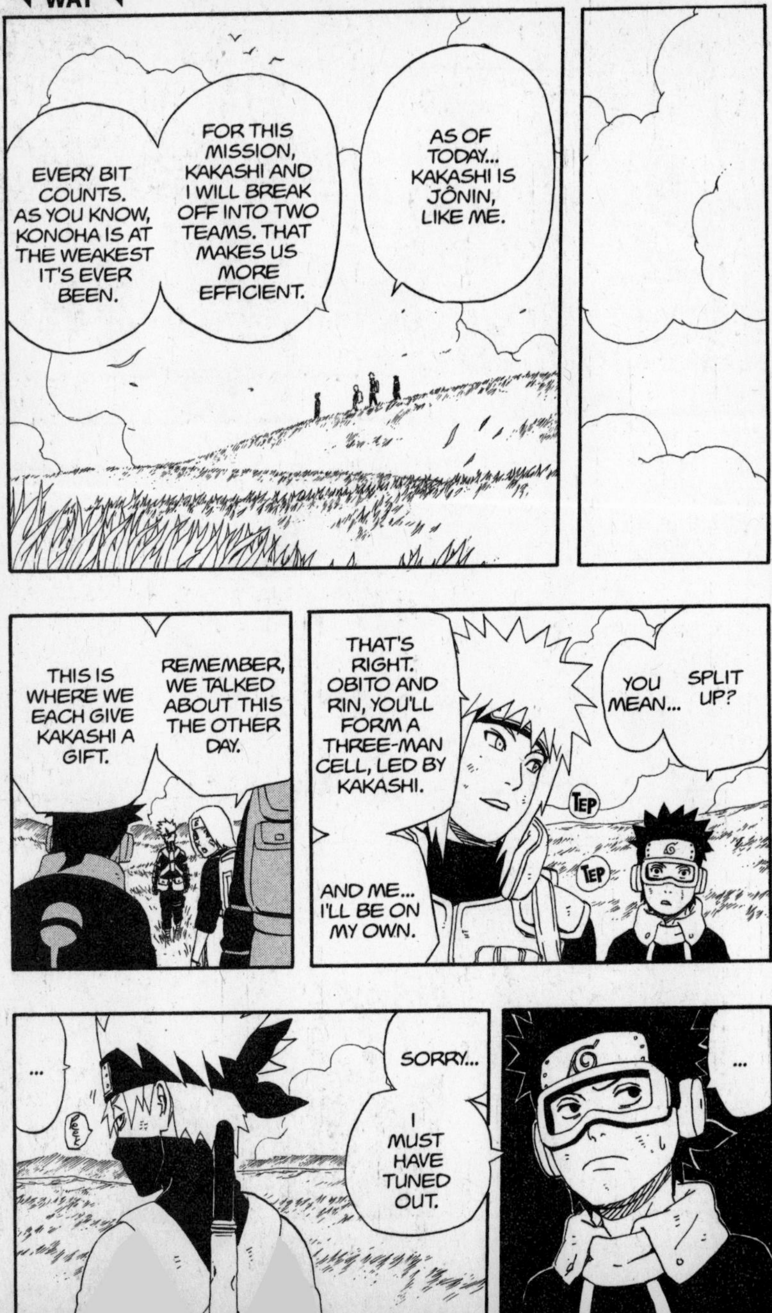
AS OF TODAY... KAKASHI IS JÔNIN, LIKE ME.
FOR THIS MISSION, KAKASHI AND I WILL BREAK OFF INTO TWO TEAMS. THAT MAKES US MORE EFFICIENT.
EVERY BIT COUNTS. AS YOU KNOW, KONOHA IS AT THE WEAKEST IT'S EVER BEEN.
YOU MEAN... SPLIT UP?
THAT'S RIGHT. OBITO AND RIN, YOU'LL FORM A THREE-MAN CELL, LED BY KAKASHI.
TEP
TEP
AND ME... I'LL BE ON MY OWN.
REMEMBER, WE TALKED ABOUT THIS THE OTHER DAY.
THIS IS WHERE WE EACH GIVE KAKASHI A GIFT.
...
SORRY...
I MUST HAVE TUNED OUT.
...

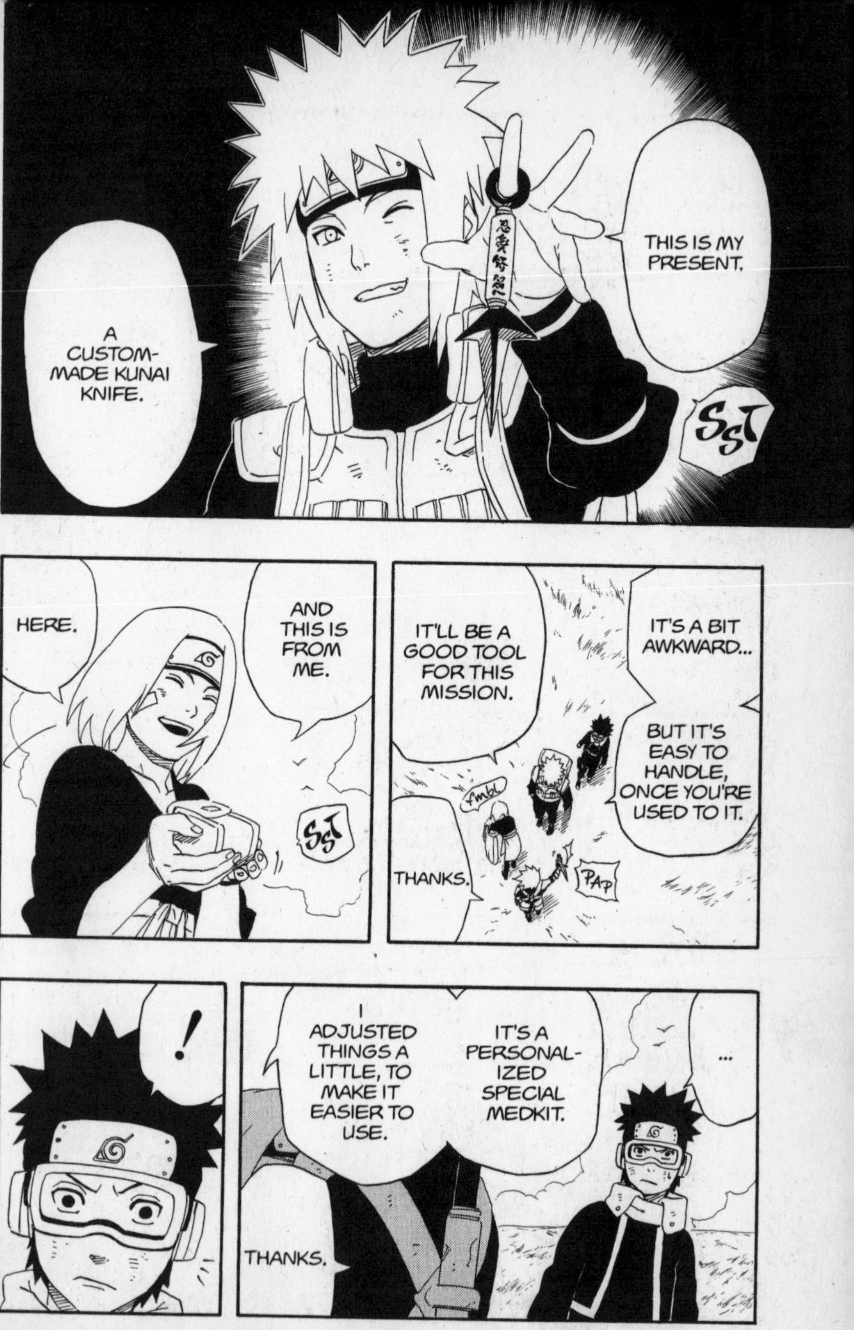
THIS IS MY PRESENT.
SST
A CUSTOM-MADE KUNAI KNIFE.
IT'S A BIT AWKWARD...
BUT IT'S EASY TO HANDLE, ONCE YOU'RE USED TO IT.
IT'LL BE A GOOD TOOL FOR THIS MISSION.
PAP
fmbl
THANKS.
AND THIS IS FROM ME.
HERE.
SST
...
IT'S A PERSONAL-IZED SPECIAL MEDKIT.
I ADJUSTED THINGS A LITTLE, TO MAKE IT EASIER TO USE.
THANKS.
!

READ THIS WAY

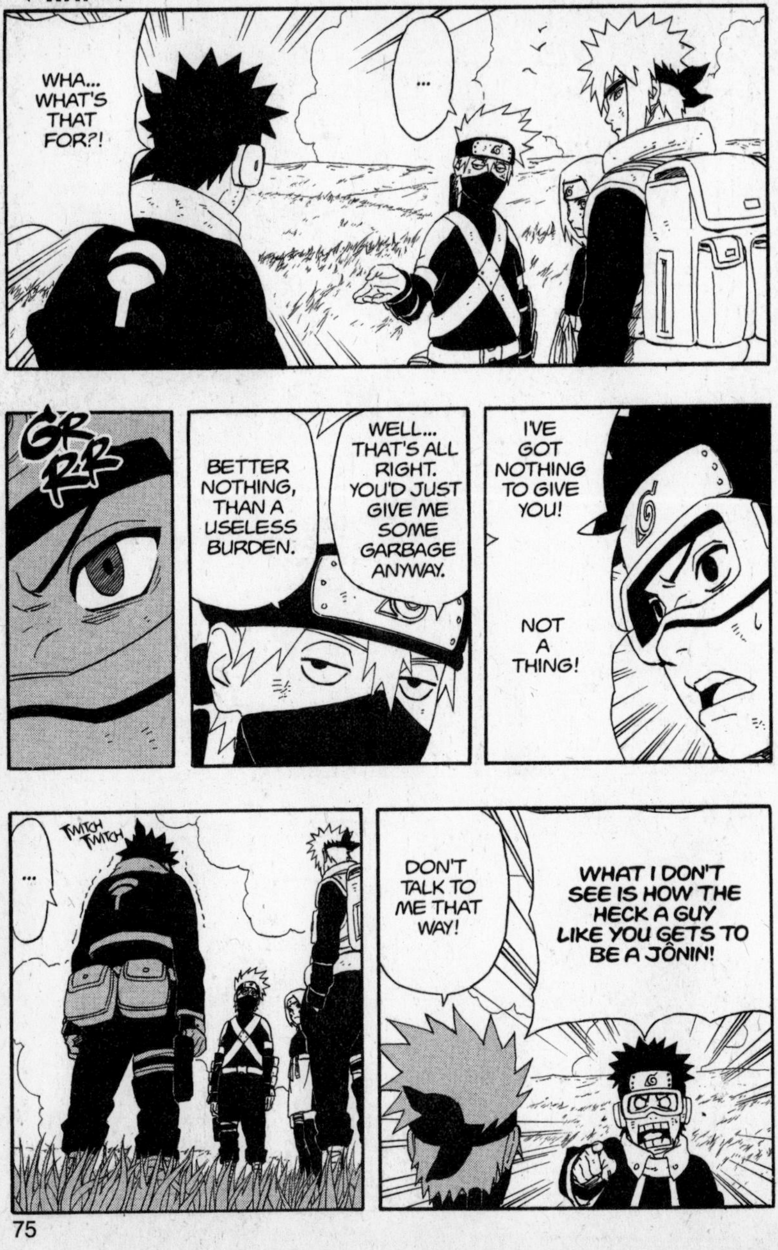

...
WHA... WHAT'S THAT FOR?!
I'VE GOT NOTHING TO GIVE YOU!
NOT A THING!
WELL... THAT'S ALL RIGHT. YOU'D JUST GIVE ME SOME GARBAGE ANYWAY.
BETTER NOTHING, THAN A USELESS BURDEN.
GRRR
WHAT I DON'T SEE IS HOW THE HECK A GUY LIKE YOU GETS TO BE A JÔNIN!
DON'T TALK TO ME THAT WAY!
TWITCH TWITCH
...

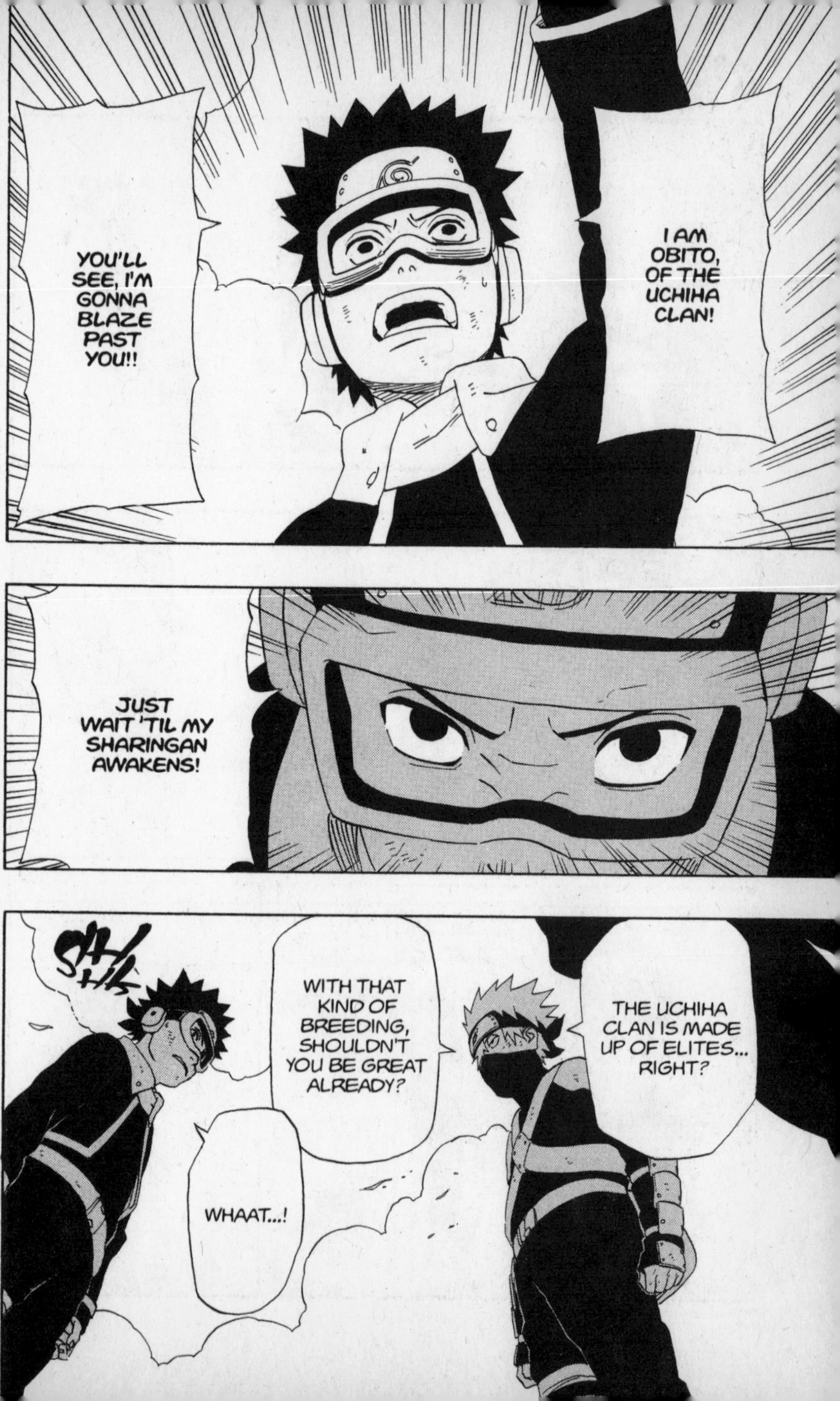
I AM OBITO, OF THE UCHIHA CLAN!
YOU'LL SEE, I'M GONNA BLAZE PAST YOU!!
JUST WAIT 'TIL MY SHARINGAN AWAKENS!
THE UCHIHA CLAN IS MADE UP OF ELITES... RIGHT?
WITH THAT KIND OF BREEDING, SHOULDN'T YOU BE GREAT ALREADY?
WHAAT...!

READ THIS WAY

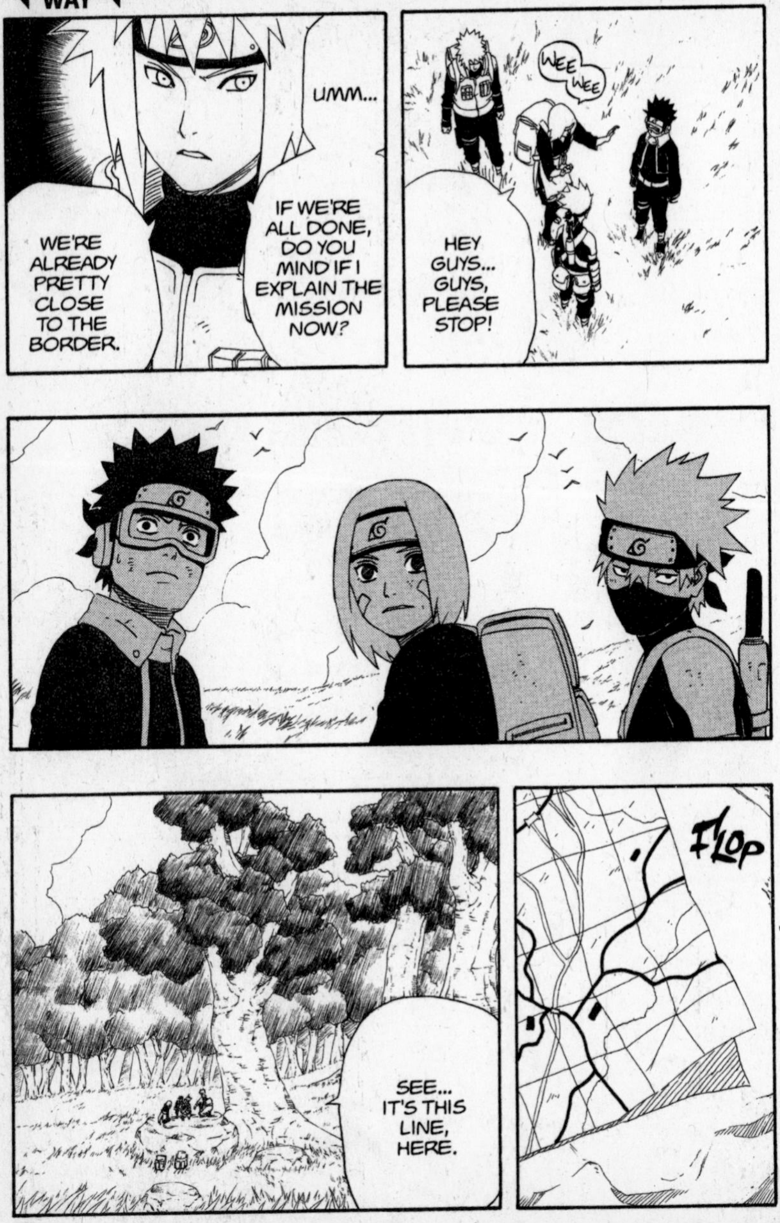

WEE WEE
HEY GUYS... GUYS, PLEASE STOP!
UMM...
IF WE'RE ALL DONE, DO YOU MIND IF I EXPLAIN THE MISSION NOW?
WE'RE ALREADY PRETTY CLOSE TO THE BORDER.
FLOP
SEE... IT'S THIS LINE, HERE.

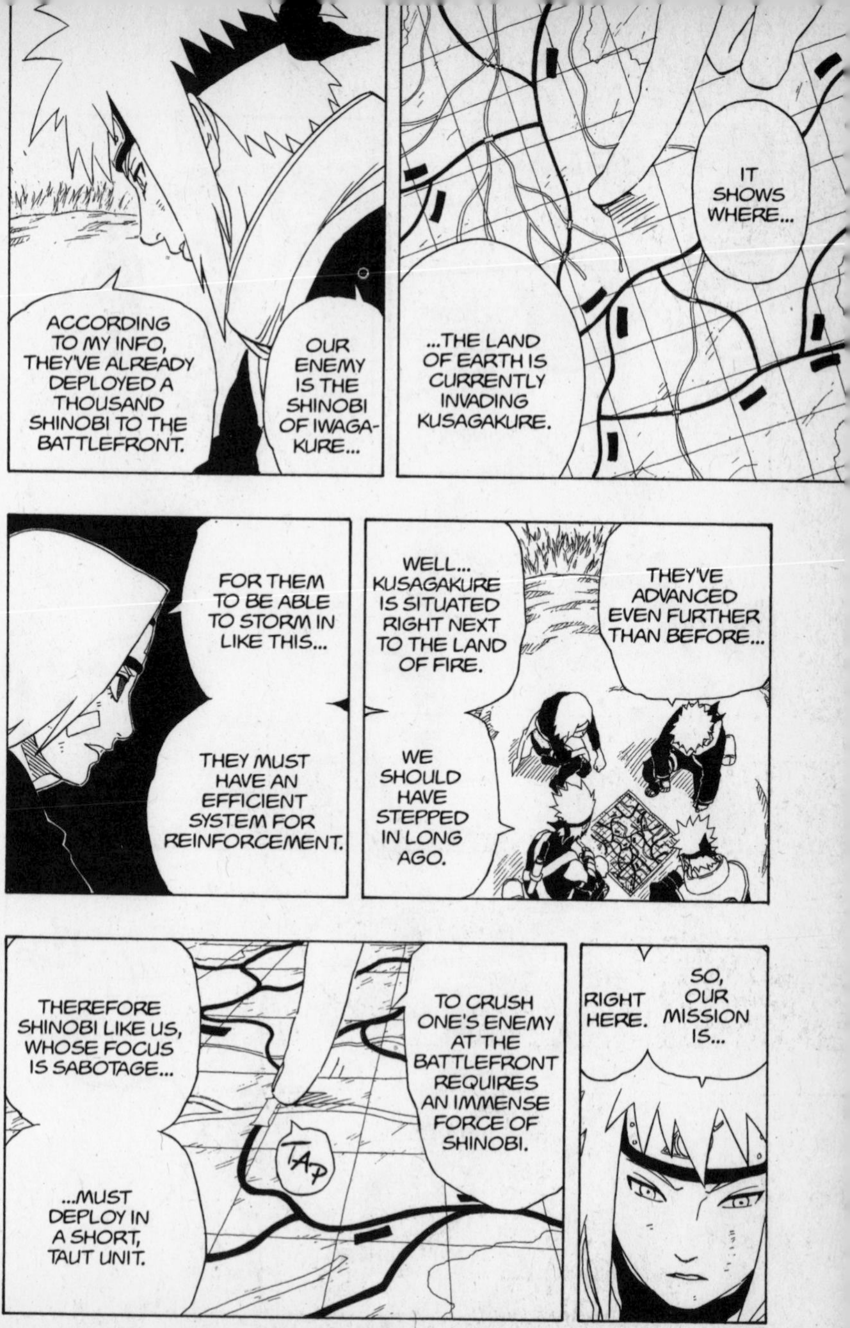
IT SHOWS WHERE...
...THE LAND OF EARTH IS CURRENTLY INVADING KUSAGAKURE.
OUR ENEMY IS THE SHINOBI OF IWAGA-KURE...
ACCORDING TO MY INFO, THEY'VE ALREADY DEPLOYED A THOUSAND SHINOBI TO THE BATTLEFRONT.
THEY'VE ADVANCED EVEN FURTHER THAN BEFORE...
WELL... KUSAGAKURE IS SITUATED RIGHT NEXT TO THE LAND OF FIRE.
WE SHOULD HAVE STEPPED IN LONG AGO.
FOR THEM TO BE ABLE TO STORM IN LIKE THIS...
THEY MUST HAVE AN EFFICIENT SYSTEM FOR REINFORCEMENT.
SO, OUR MISSION IS...
RIGHT HERE.
TAP
TO CRUSH ONE'S ENEMY AT THE BATTLEFRONT REQUIRES AN IMMENSE FORCE OF SHINOBI.
THEREFORE SHINOBI LIKE US, WHOSE FOCUS IS SABOTAGE...
...MUST DEPLOY IN A SHORT, TAUT UNIT.

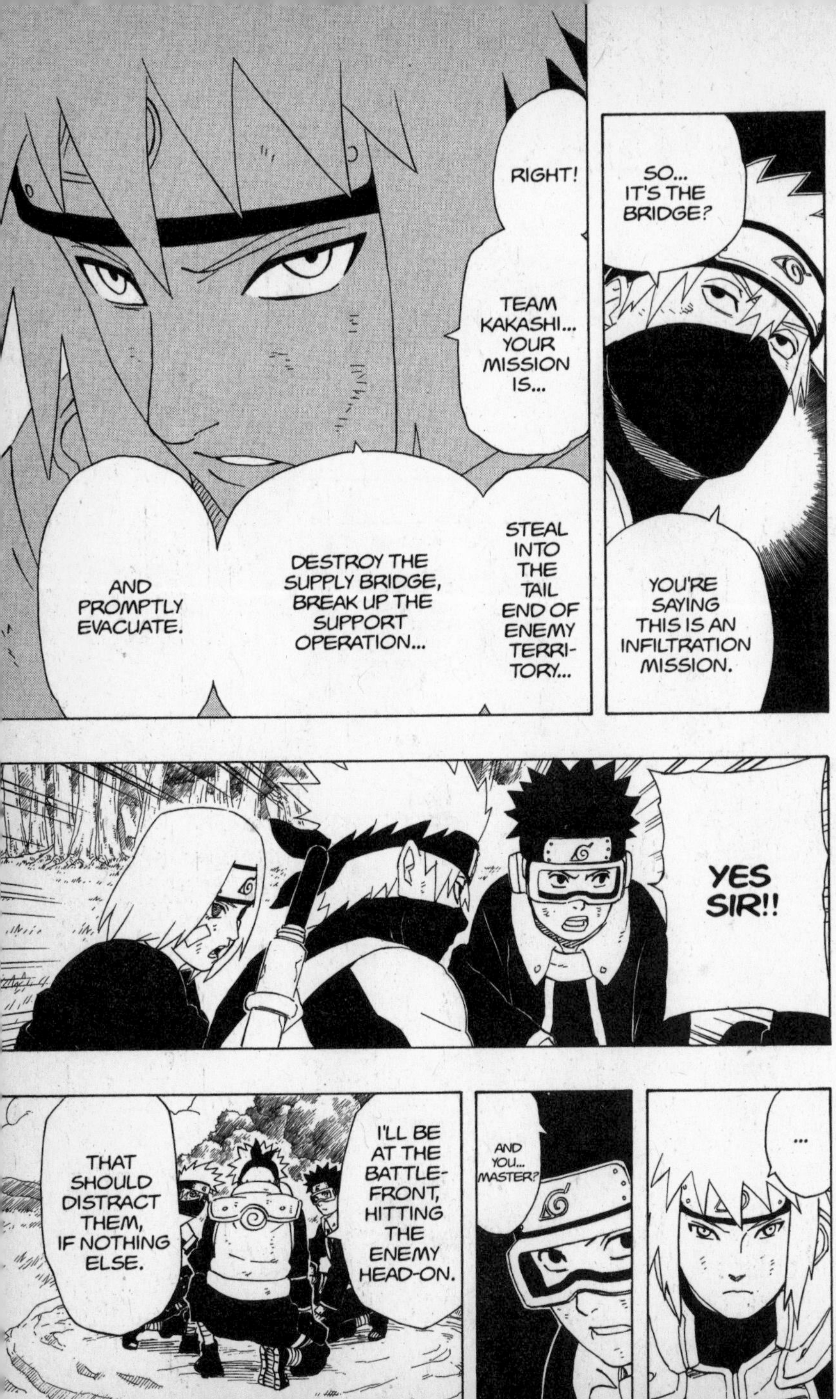
SO... IT'S THE BRIDGE?
YOU'RE SAYING THIS IS AN INFILTRATION MISSION.
RIGHT!
TEAM KAKASHI... YOUR MISSION IS...
STEAL INTO THE TAIL END OF ENEMY TERRI-TORY...
DESTROY THE SUPPLY BRIDGE, BREAK UP THE SUPPORT OPERATION...
AND PROMPTLY EVACUATE.
YES SIR!!
...
AND YOU... MASTER?
I'LL BE AT THE BATTLE-FRONT, HITTING THE ENEMY HEAD-ON.
THAT SHOULD DISTRACT THEM, IF NOTHING ELSE.

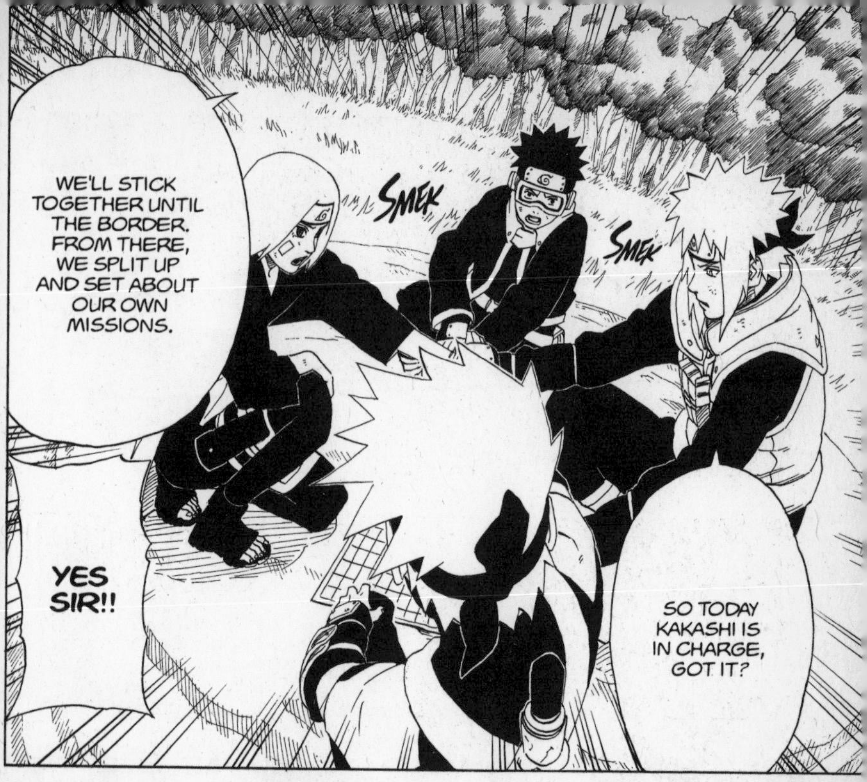
SMEK
SMEK
SO TODAY KAKASHI IS IN CHARGE, GOT IT?
WE'LL STICK TOGETHER UNTIL THE BORDER. FROM THERE, WE SPLIT UP AND SET ABOUT OUR OWN MISSIONS.
YES SIR!!
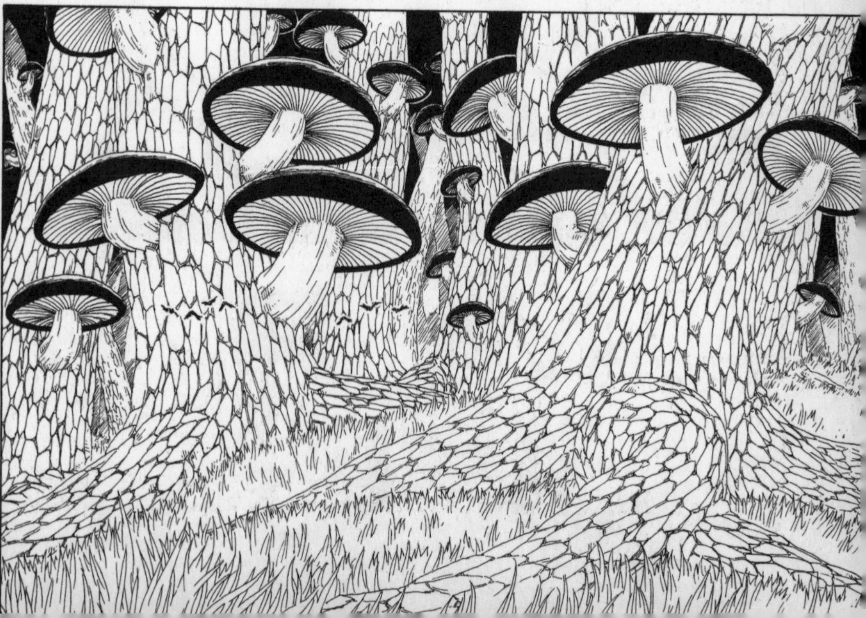

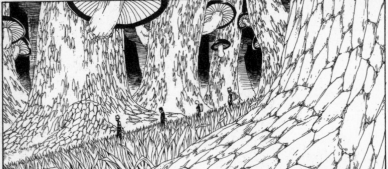

SSST

!

TWHK

SFT

NICE...
KAKASHI.

!

!

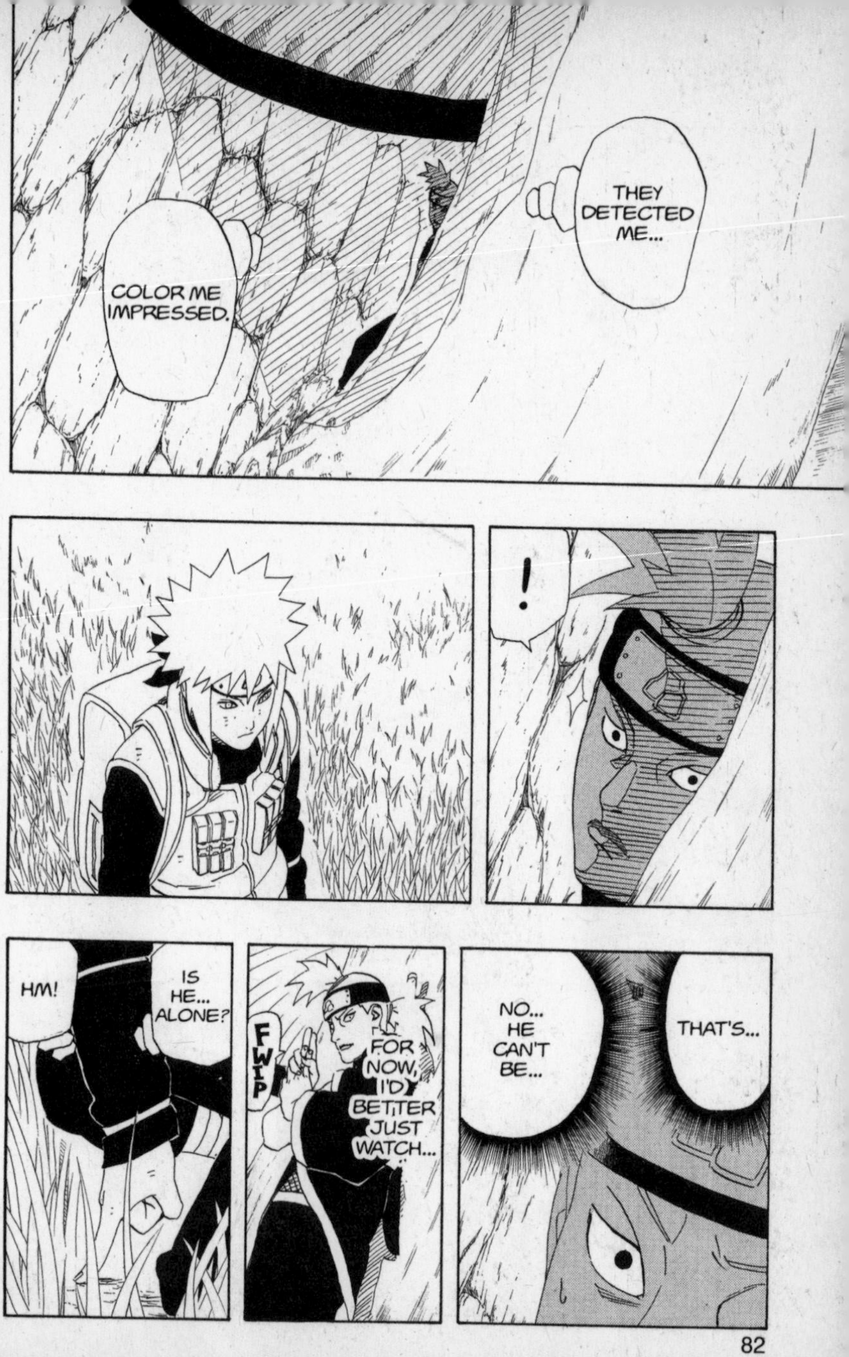
THEY DETECTED ME...
COLOR ME IMPRESSED.
!
THAT'S...
NO... HE CAN'T BE...
FWIP
FOR NOW, I'D BETTER JUST WATCH...
IS HE... ALONE?
HM!

READ THIS WAY

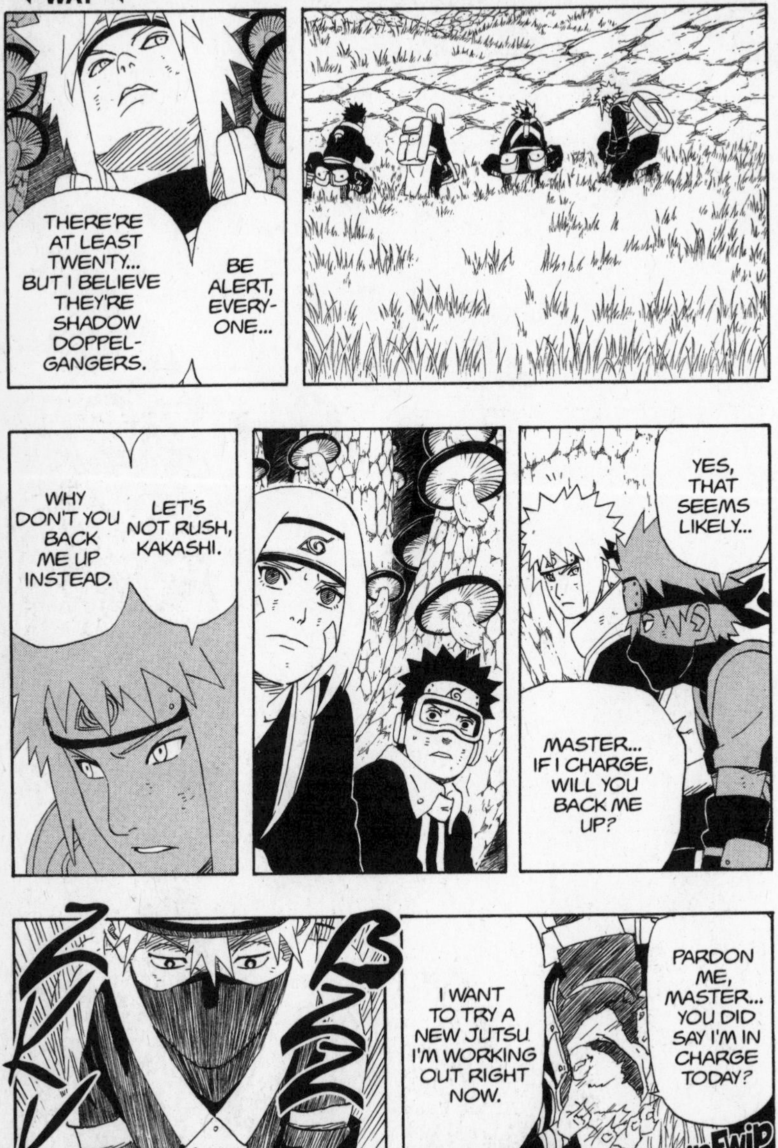
BE ALERT, EVERY-ONE...
THERE'RE AT LEAST TWENTY... BUT I BELIEVE THEY'RE SHADOW DOPPEL-GANGERS.
YES, THAT SEEMS LIKELY...
MASTER... IF I CHARGE, WILL YOU BACK ME UP?
LET'S NOT RUSH, KAKASHI.
WHY DON'T YOU BACK ME UP INSTEAD.
PARDON ME, MASTER... YOU DID SAY I'M IN CHARGE TODAY?
I WANT TO TRY A NEW JUTSU I'M WORKING OUT RIGHT NOW.
FWIP FWIP FWIP

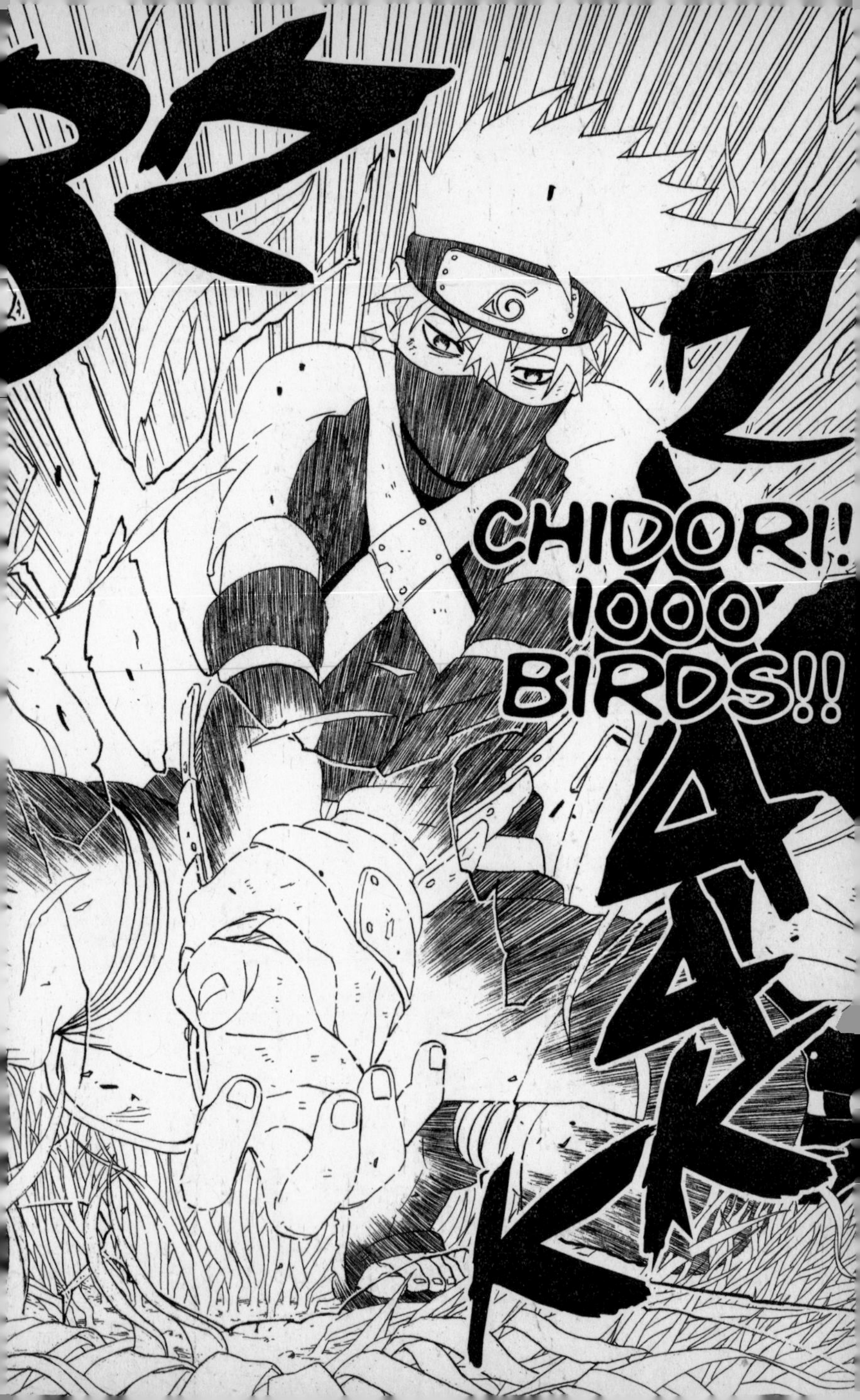
CHIDORI! 1000 BIRDS!!

READ THIS WAY

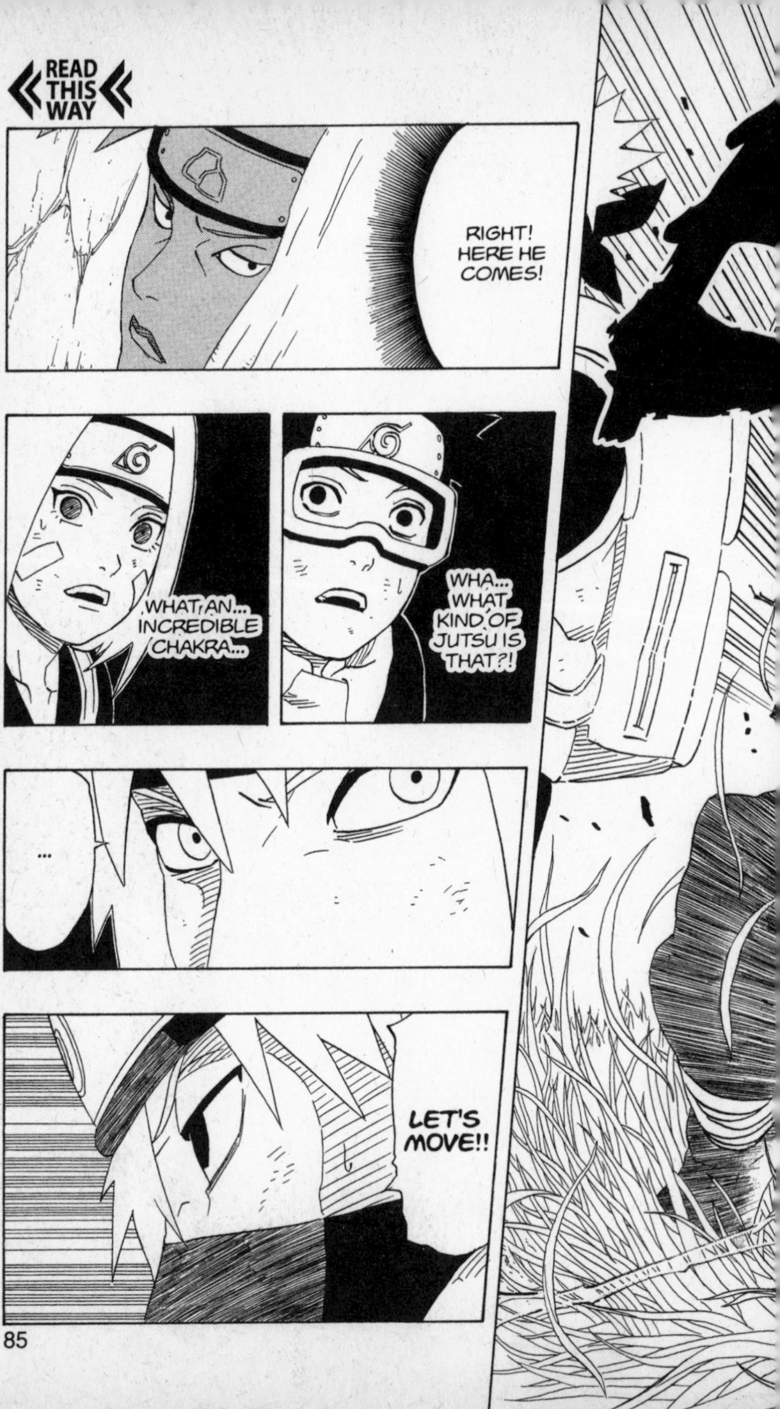

RIGHT! HERE HE COMES!
WHA... WHAT KIND OF JUTSU IS THAT?!
WHAT AN... INCREDIBLE CHAKRA...
...
LET'S MOVE!!

NARUTO™

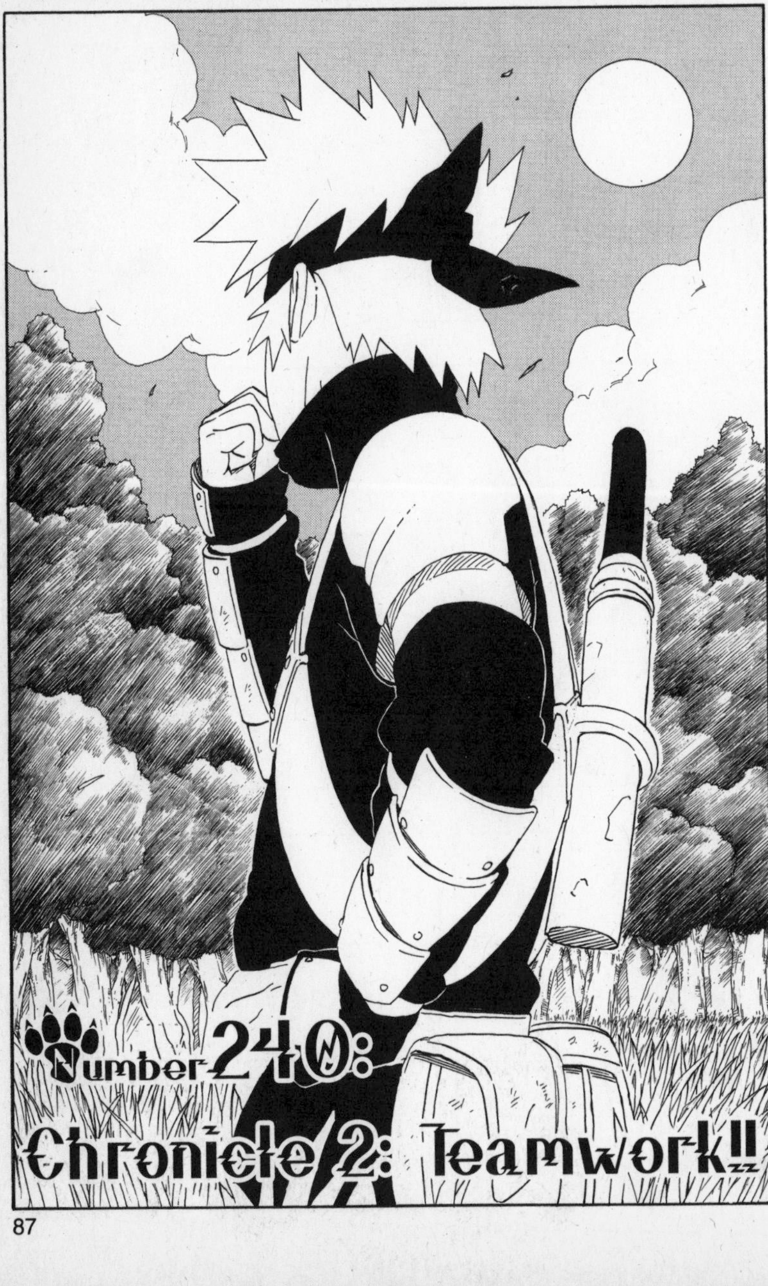
Number 240:
Chronicle 2: Teamwork!!

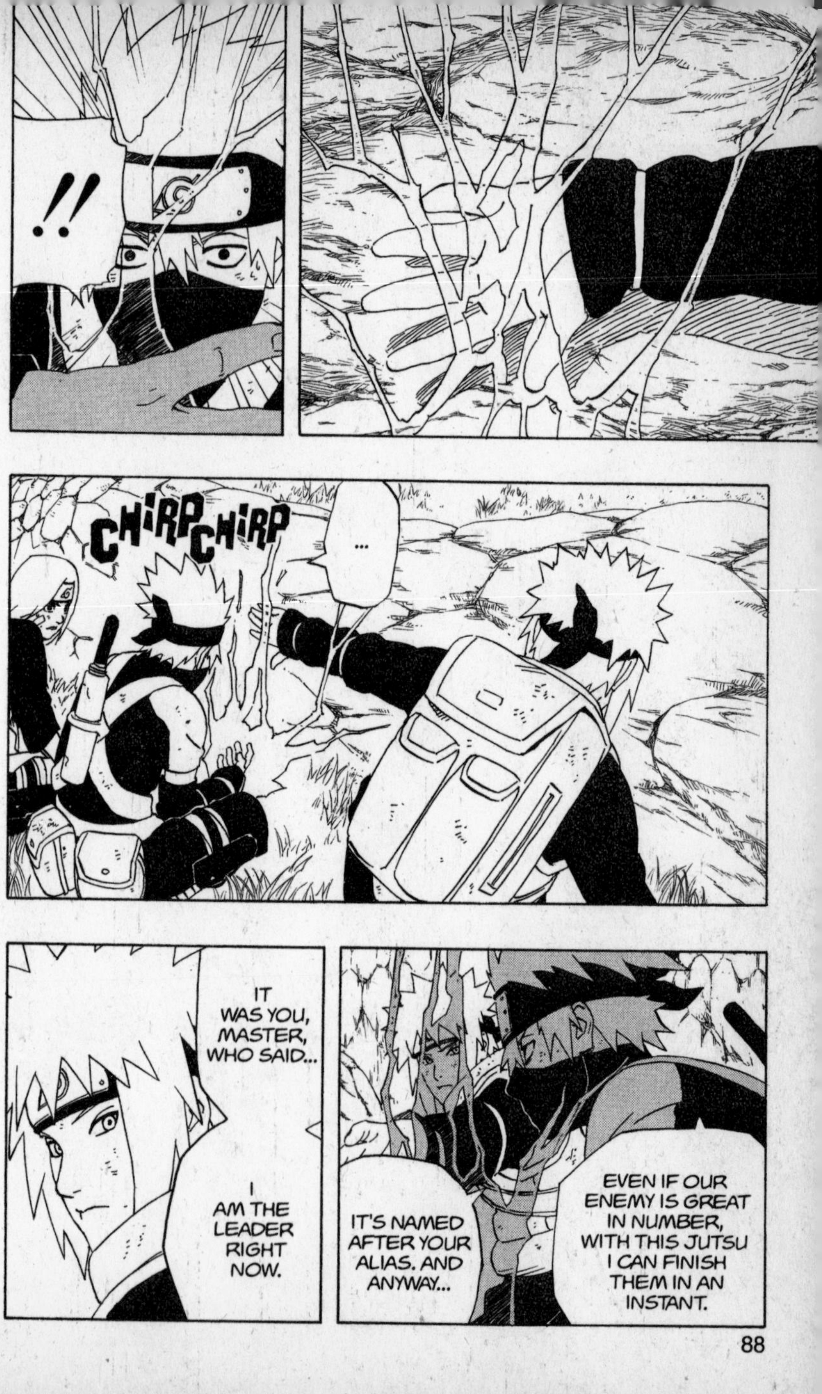
!!
...
CHIRP CHIRP
EVEN IF OUR ENEMY IS GREAT IN NUMBER, WITH THIS JUTSU I CAN FINISH THEM IN AN INSTANT.
IT'S NAMED AFTER YOUR ALIAS. AND ANYWAY...
IT WAS YOU, MASTER, WHO SAID...
I AM THE LEADER RIGHT NOW.

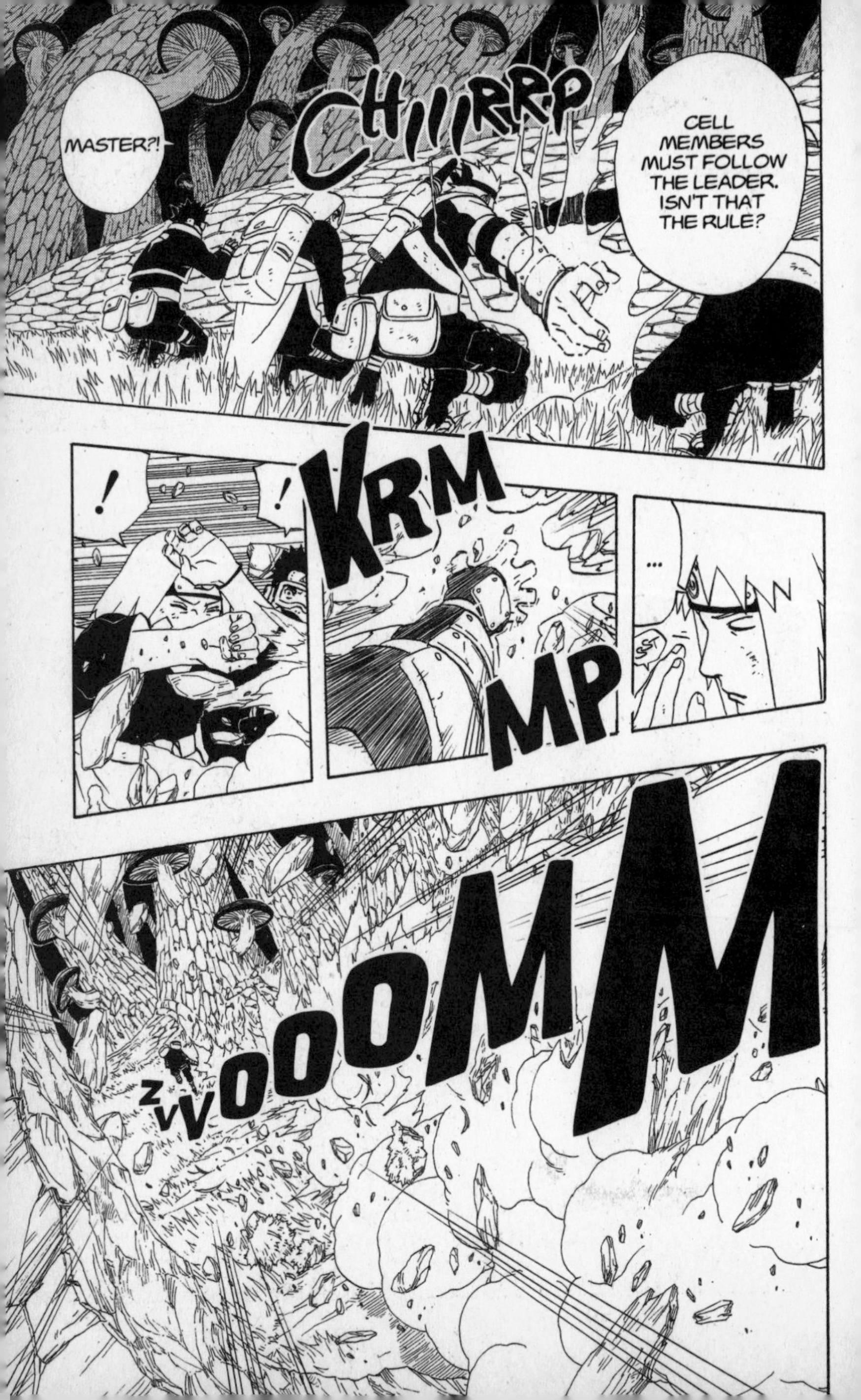
CELL MEMBERS MUST FOLLOW THE LEADER. ISN'T THAT THE RULE?
CHIIRRP
MASTER?!
...
KRM
MP
!
!
ZVVOOOOMM

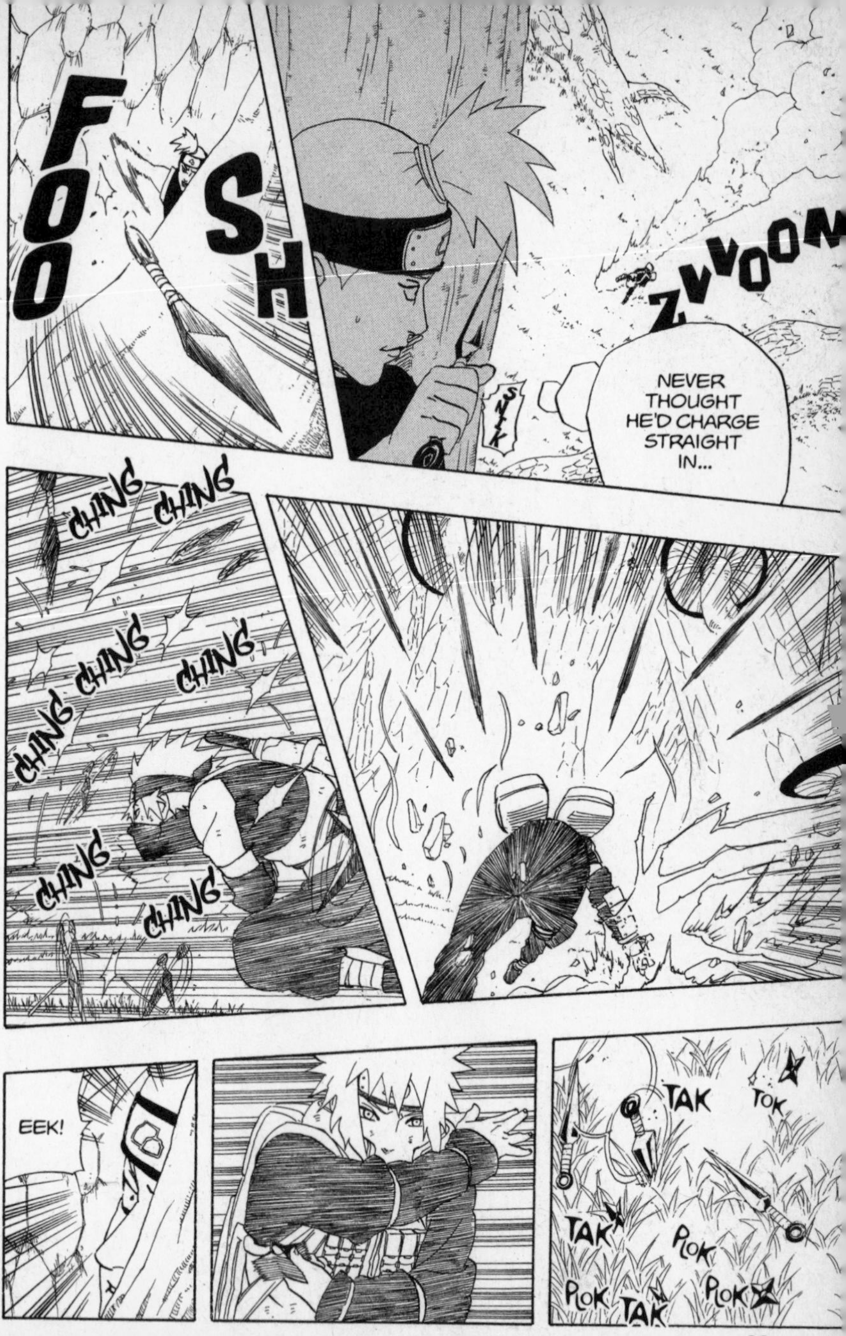
ZVVOOM
NEVER THOUGHT HE'D CHARGE STRAIGHT IN...
SNIK
FOOSH
CHING
CHING
CHING
CHING
CHING
CHING
CHING
CHING
TOK
TAK
TAK
PLOK
PLOK
TAK
PLOK
EEK!

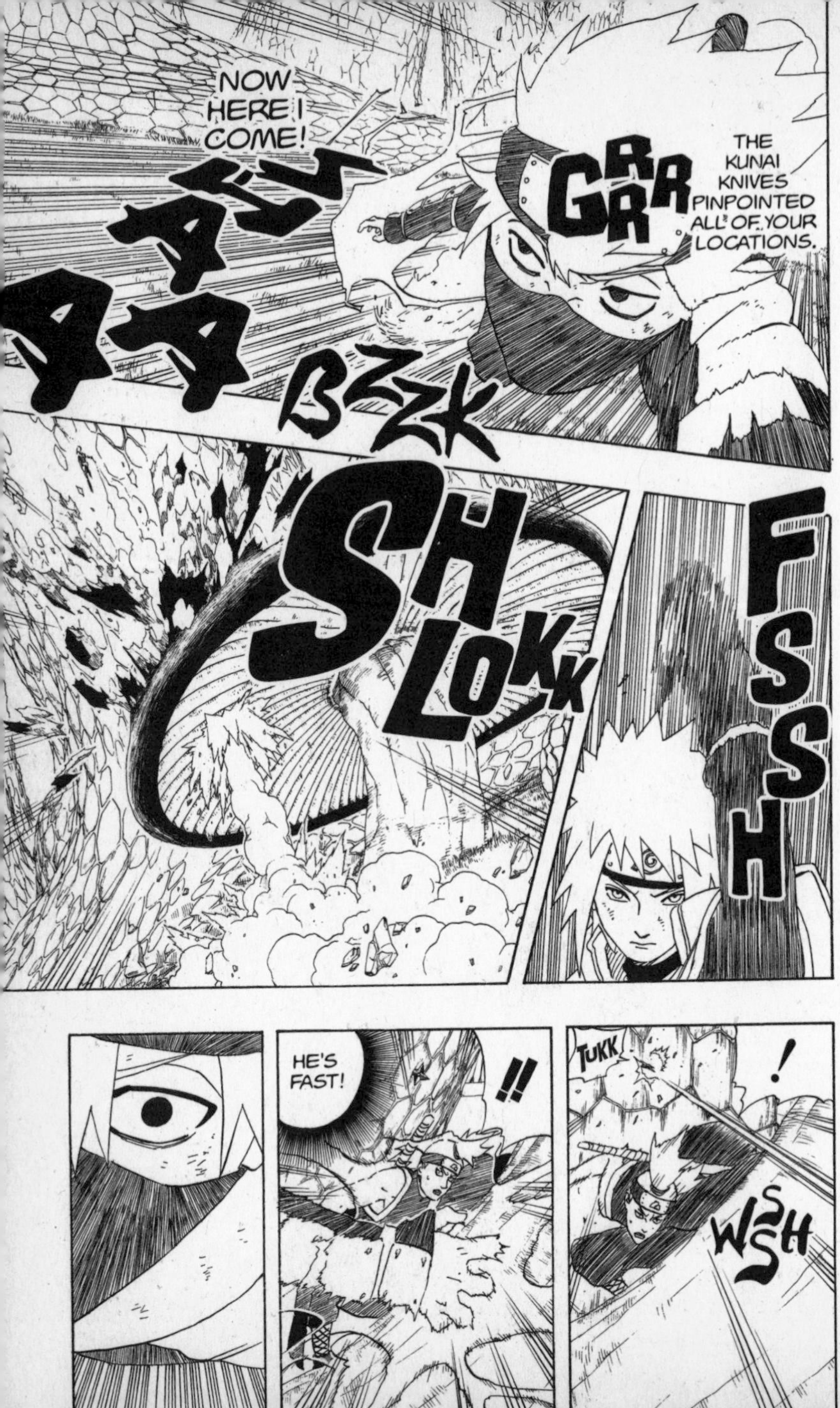
THE KUNAI KNIVES PINPOINTED ALL OF YOUR LOCATIONS.
GRRR
NOW HERE I COME!
BZZK
FSSH
SHLOKK
TUKK
!
WSSH
!!
HE'S FAST!

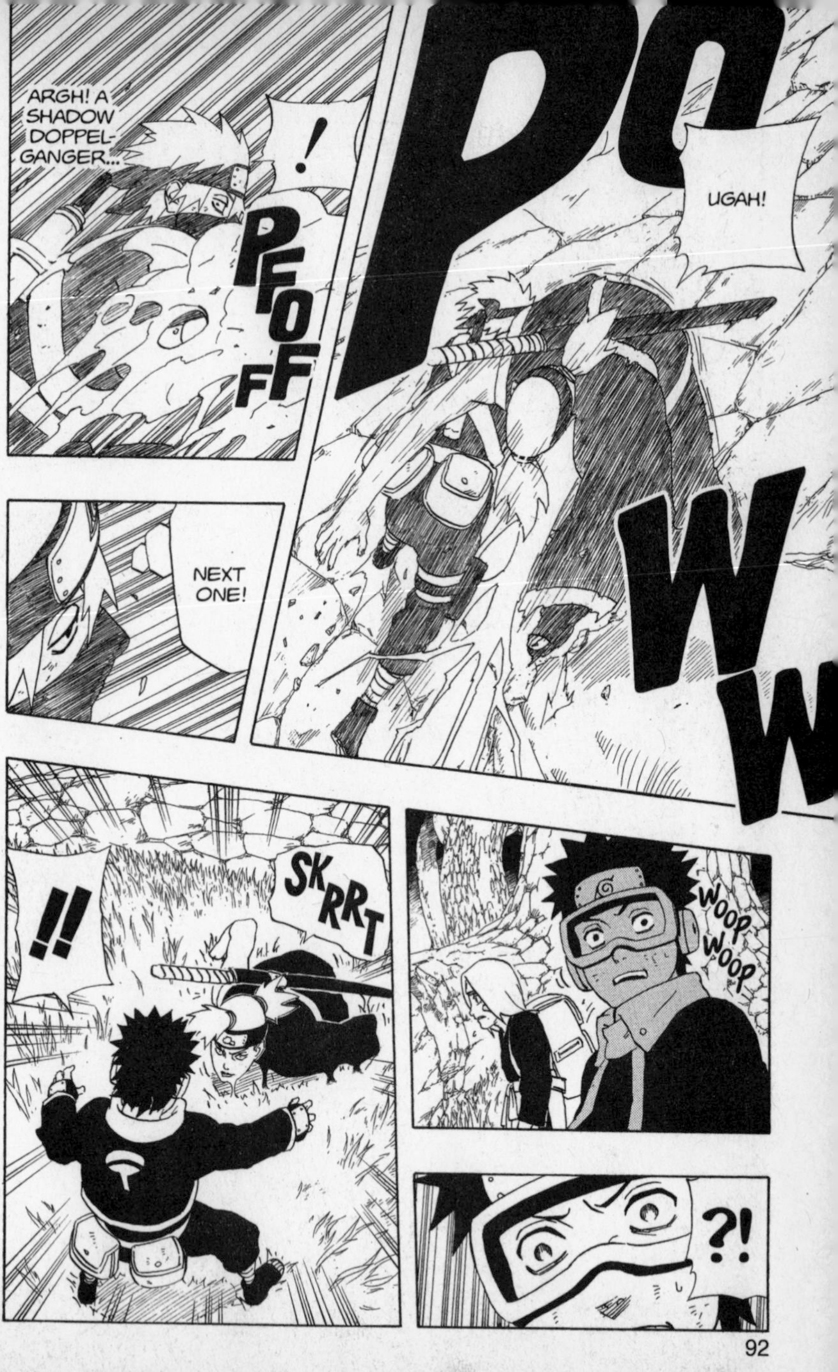

UGAH!
ARGH! A SHADOW DOPPEL-GANGER...
!
PFOOFF
NEXT ONE!
WOOP WOOP
?!
SKRRT
!!

READ THIS WAY

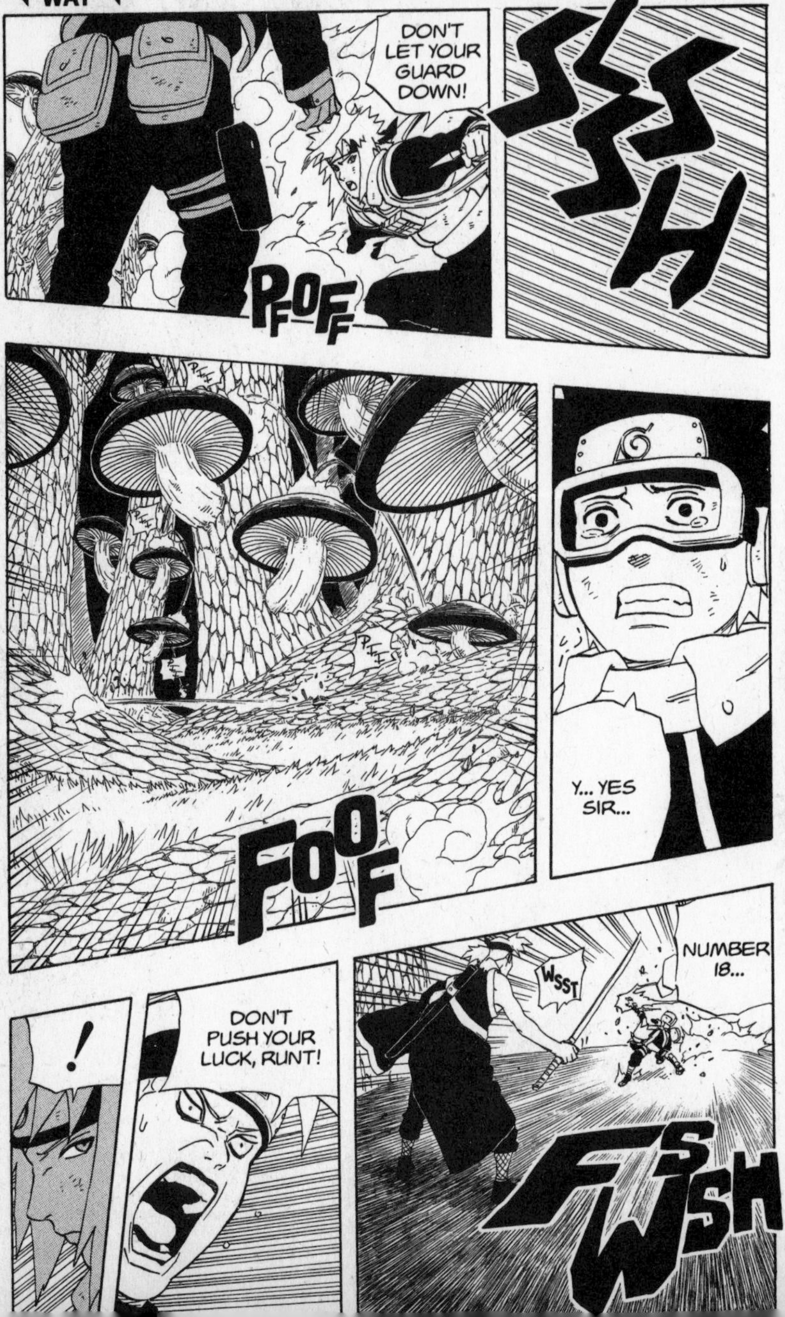
SSSH
DON'T LET YOUR GUARD DOWN!
PFOFF
Y... YES SIR...
FOOF
NUMBER 18...
WSST
FWSSH
DON'T PUSH YOUR LUCK, RUNT!
!

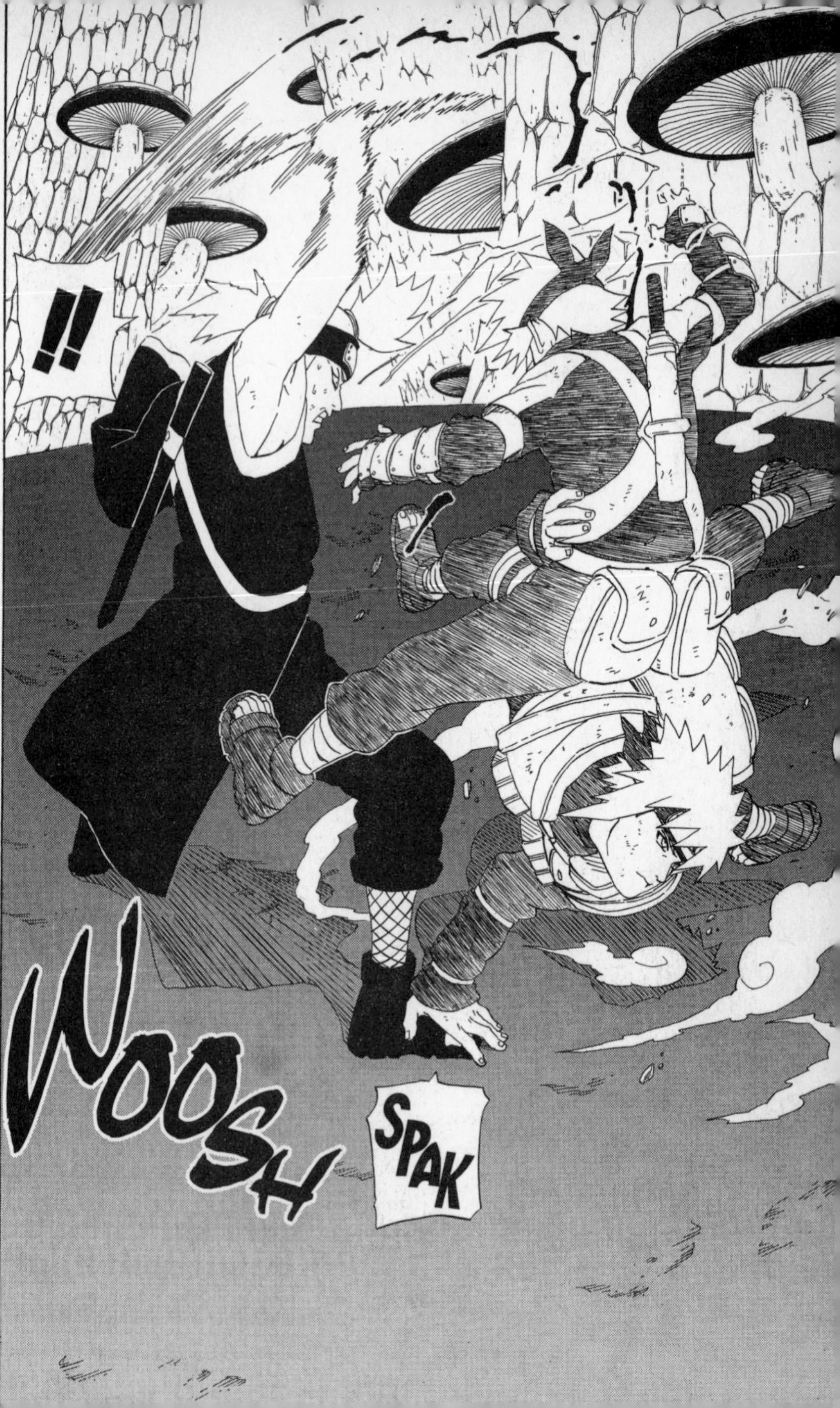
!!
WOOSH
SPAK

READ THIS WAY

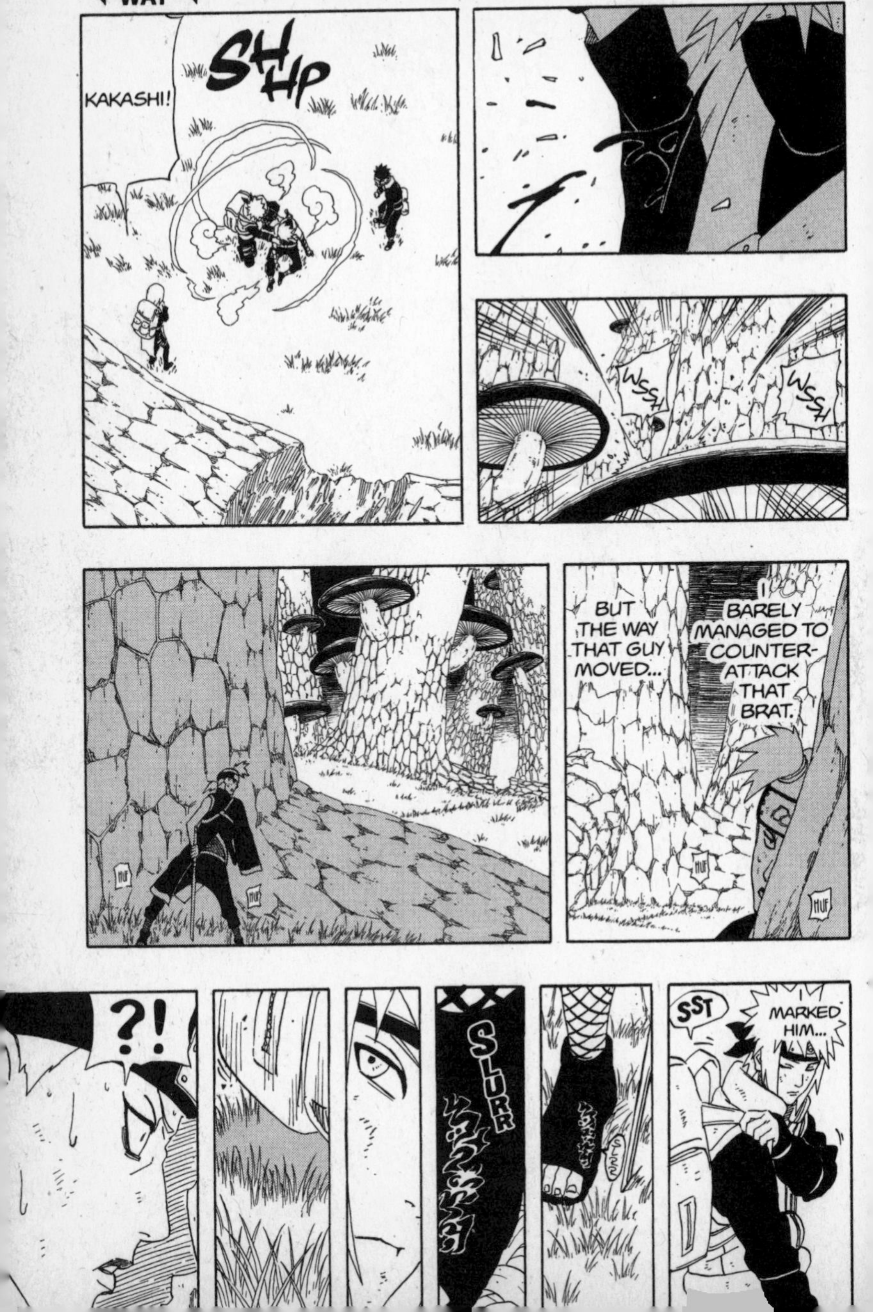
WSSH
WSSH
SHHP
KAKASHI!
I BARELY MANAGED TO COUNTER-ATTACK THAT BRAT.
BUT THE WAY THAT GUY MOVED...
HUF
HUF
HUF
SST
I MARKED HIM...
SLURR
SLURR
?!

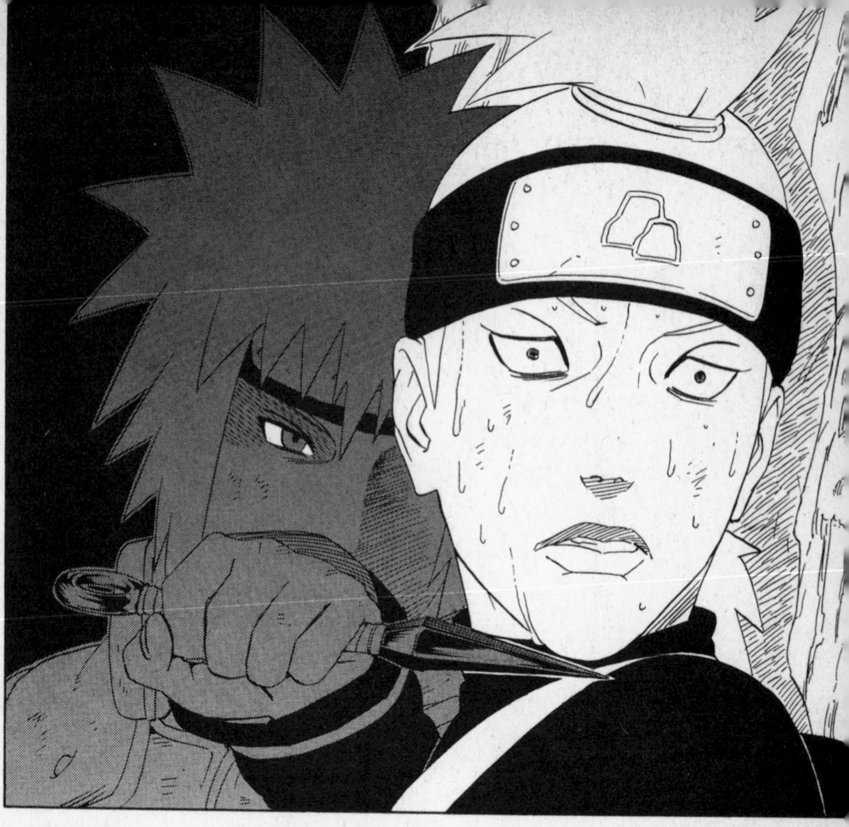
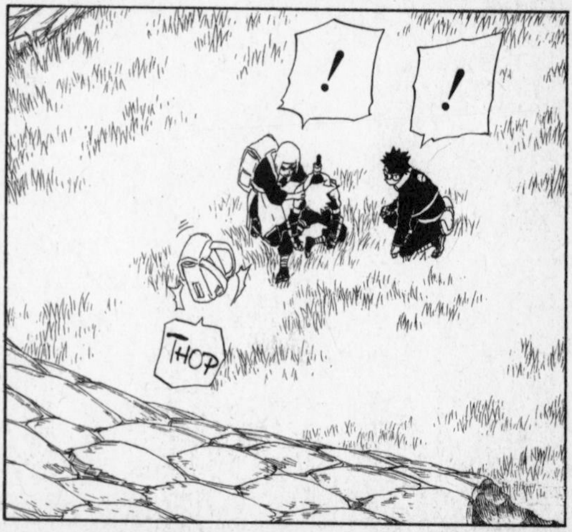
!
!
THOP
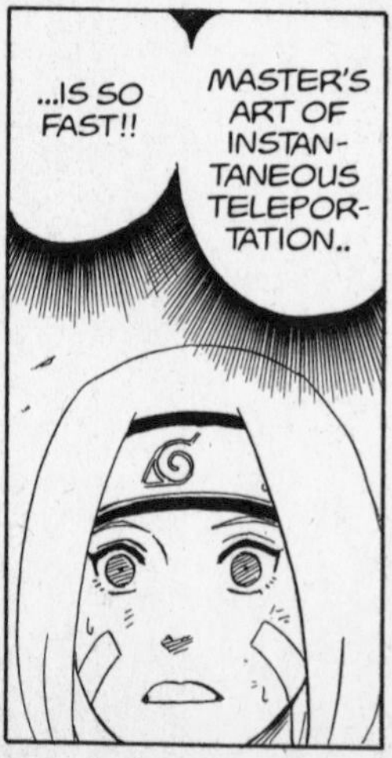
MASTER'S ART OF INSTAN-TANEOUS TELEPOR-TATION..
...IS SO FAST!!

NO...
NO WAY...
YOU CAN'T
BE...

THE
YELLOW
FLASH OF
KONOHA?!

AT
IWAGAKURE...

THEY TOLD
US TO FLEE
THE MOMENT
WE CAUGHT
SIGHT OF YOU.

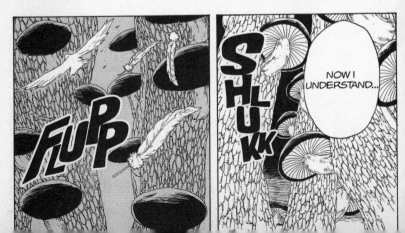

FLUPP

SHLUKK

NOW I
UNDERSTAND...

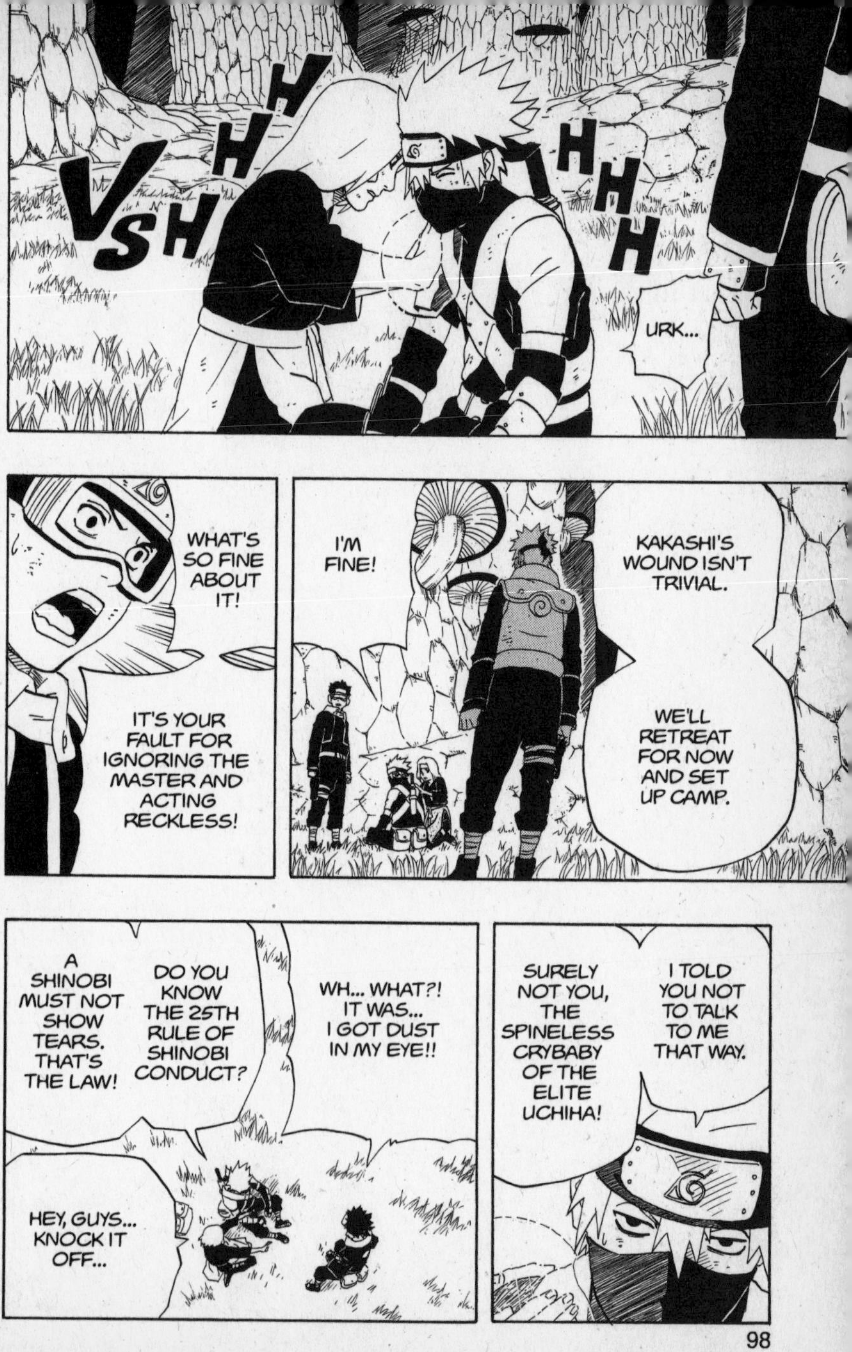
VSHHHHHHHH
URK...
KAKASHI'S WOUND ISN'T TRIVIAL.
WE'LL RETREAT FOR NOW AND SET UP CAMP.
I'M FINE!
WHAT'S SO FINE ABOUT IT!
IT'S YOUR FAULT FOR IGNORING THE MASTER AND ACTING RECKLESS!
I TOLD YOU NOT TO TALK TO ME THAT WAY.
SURELY NOT YOU, THE SPINELESS CRYBABY OF THE ELITE UCHIHA!
WH... WHAT?! IT WAS... I GOT DUST IN MY EYE!!
DO YOU KNOW THE 25TH RULE OF SHINOBI CONDUCT?
A SHINOBI MUST NOT SHOW TEARS. THAT'S THE LAW!
HEY, GUYS... KNOCK IT OFF...

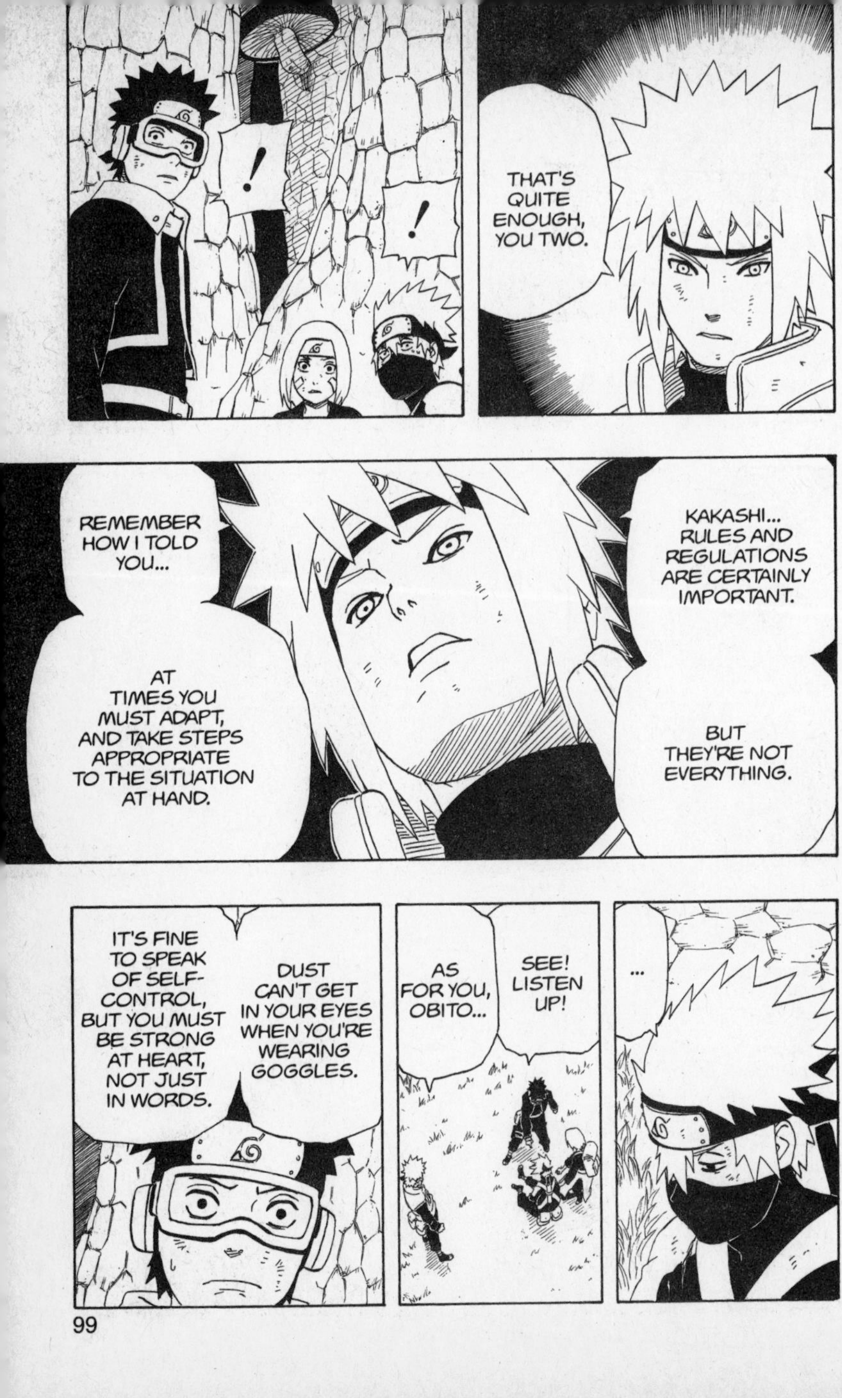
THAT'S QUITE ENOUGH, YOU TWO.
!
!
KAKASHI... RULES AND REGULATIONS ARE CERTAINLY IMPORTANT.
BUT THEY'RE NOT EVERYTHING.
REMEMBER HOW I TOLD YOU...
AT TIMES YOU MUST ADAPT, AND TAKE STEPS APPROPRIATE TO THE SITUATION AT HAND.
...
SEE! LISTEN UP!
AS FOR YOU, OBITO...
DUST CAN'T GET IN YOUR EYES WHEN YOU'RE WEARING GOGGLES.
IT'S FINE TO SPEAK OF SELF-CONTROL, BUT YOU MUST BE STRONG AT HEART, NOT JUST IN WORDS.

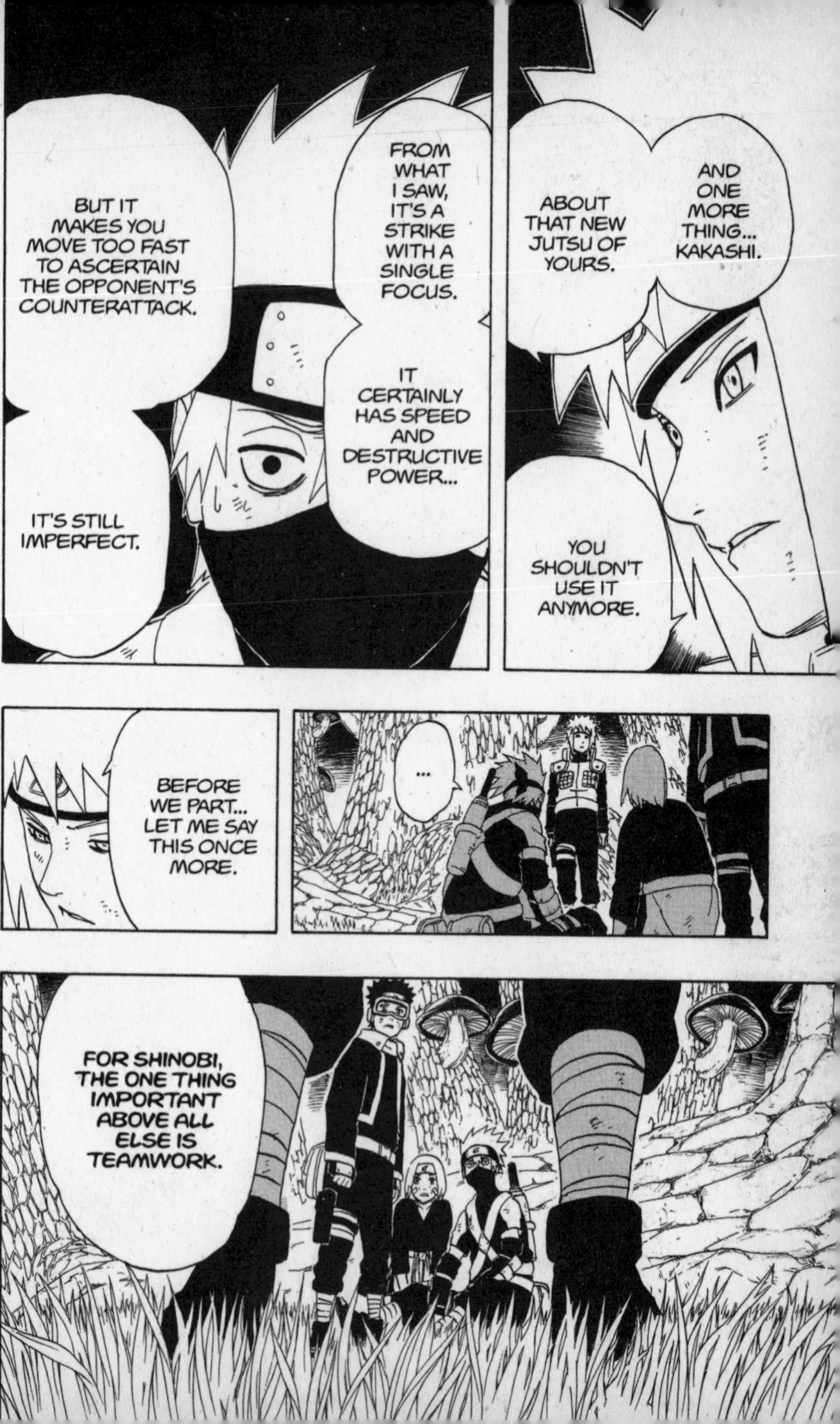
AND ONE MORE THING... KAKASHI.
ABOUT THAT NEW JUTSU OF YOURS.
YOU SHOULDN'T USE IT ANYMORE.
FROM WHAT I SAW, IT'S A STRIKE WITH A SINGLE FOCUS.
IT CERTAINLY HAS SPEED AND DESTRUCTIVE POWER...
BUT IT MAKES YOU MOVE TOO FAST TO ASCERTAIN THE OPPONENT'S COUNTERATTACK.
IT'S STILL IMPERFECT.
...
BEFORE WE PART... LET ME SAY THIS ONCE MORE.
FOR SHINOBI, THE ONE THING IMPORTANT ABOVE ALL ELSE IS TEAMWORK.

READ THIS WAY

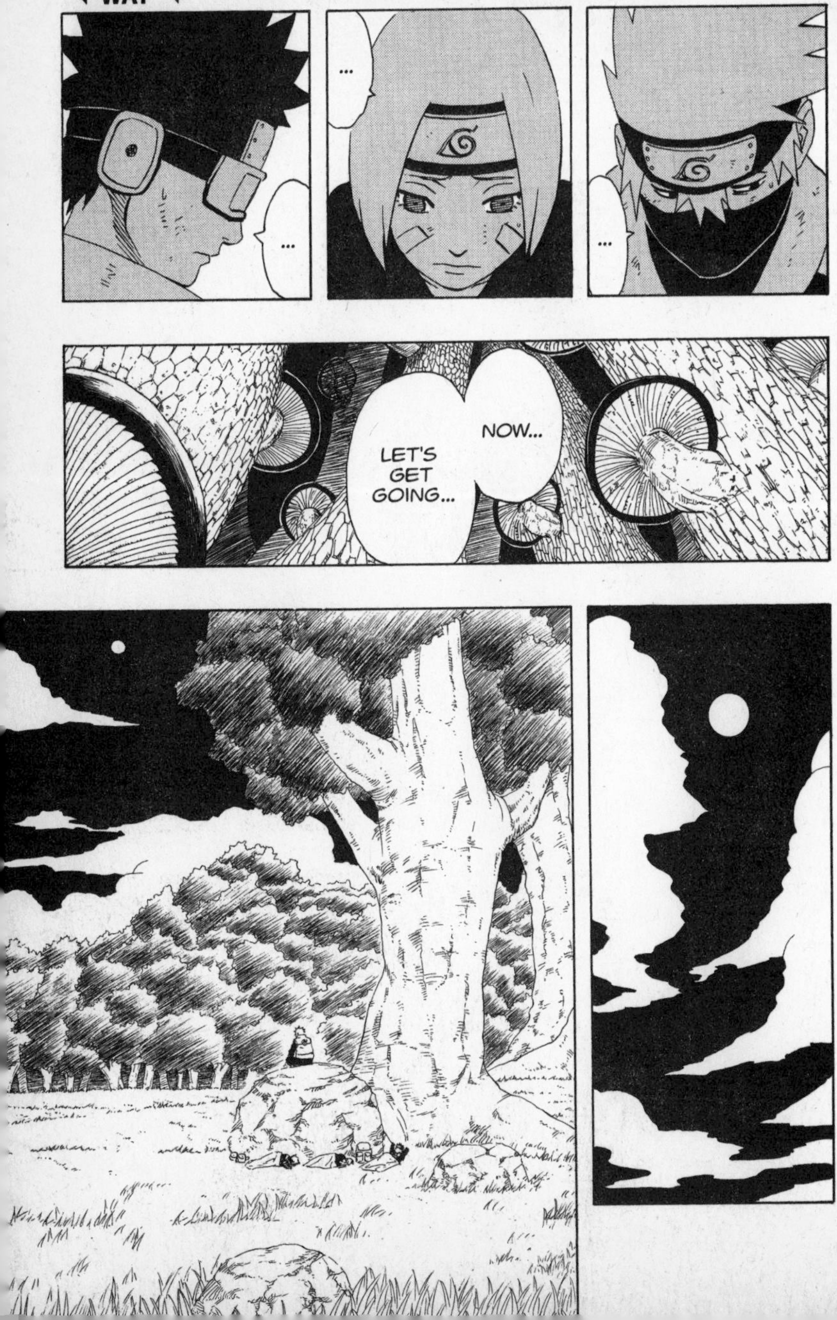
...
...
...
NOW...
LET'S GET GOING...

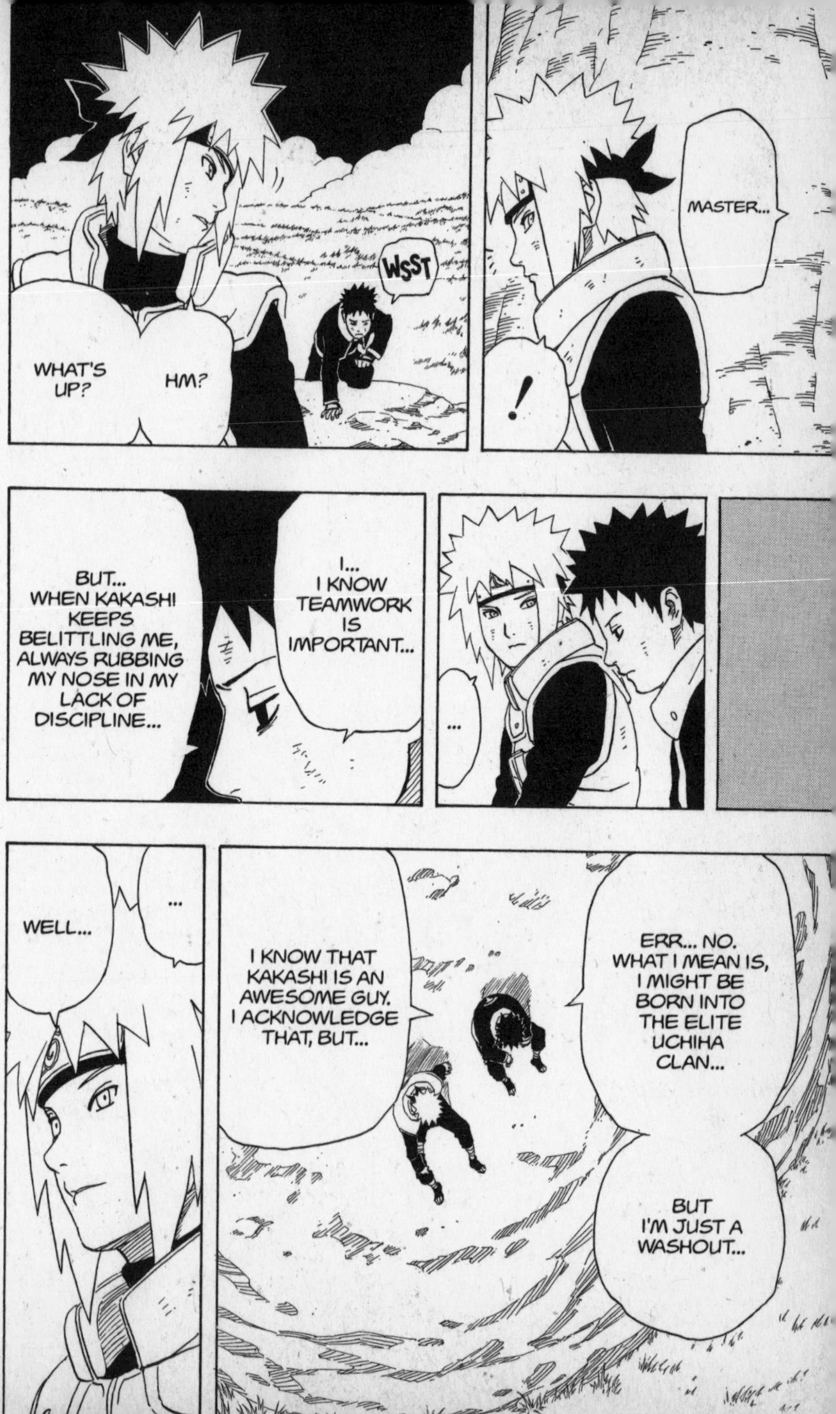
MASTER...
!
WSST
HM?
WHAT'S UP?
...
I... I KNOW TEAMWORK IS IMPORTANT...
BUT... WHEN KAKASHI KEEPS BELITTLING ME, ALWAYS RUBBING MY NOSE IN MY LACK OF DISCIPLINE...
I KNOW THAT KAKASHI IS AN AWESOME GUY. I ACKNOWLEDGE THAT, BUT...
ERR... NO. WHAT I MEAN IS, I MIGHT BE BORN INTO THE ELITE UCHIHA CLAN...
BUT I'M JUST A WASHOUT...
...
WELL...

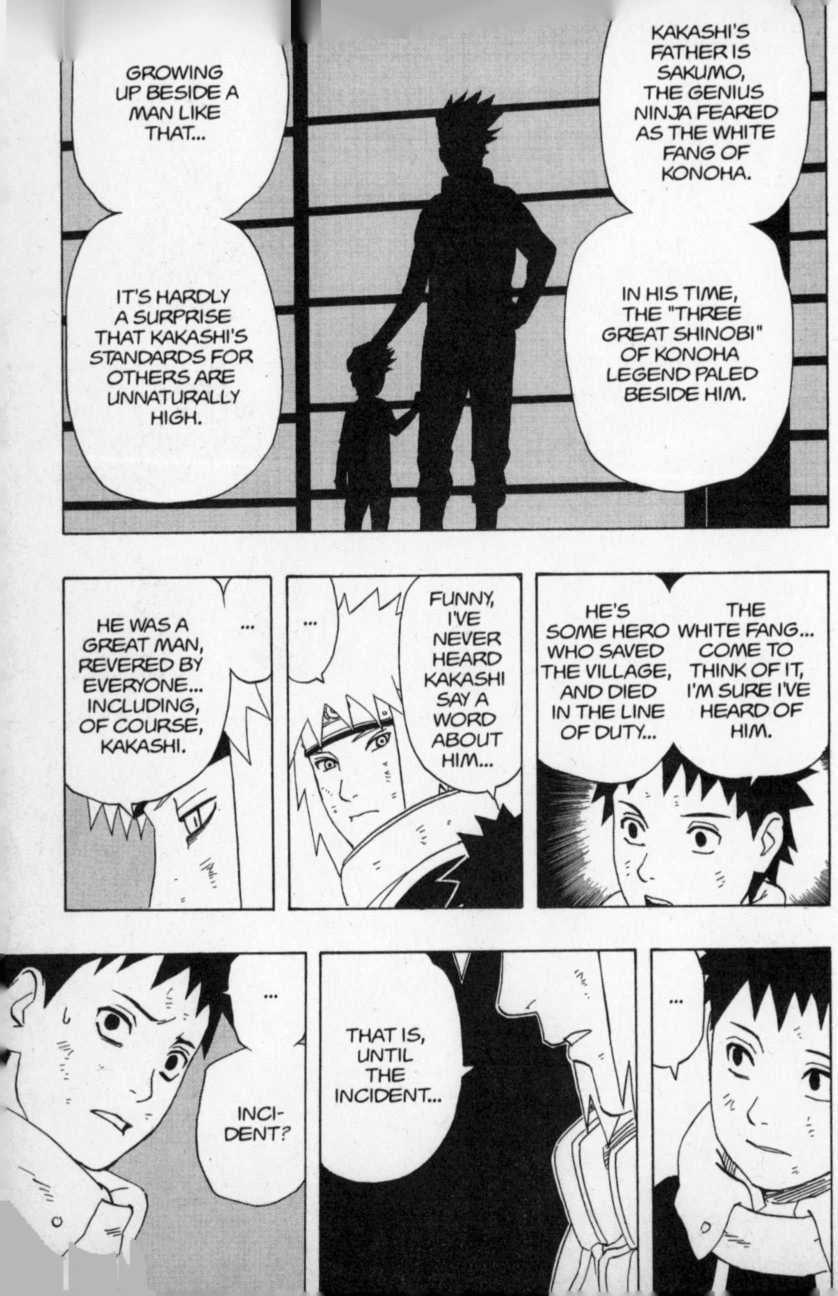
KAKASHI'S FATHER IS SAKUMO, THE GENIUS NINJA FEARED AS THE WHITE FANG OF KONOHA.
IN HIS TIME, THE "THREE GREAT SHINOBI" OF KONOHA LEGEND PALED BESIDE HIM.
GROWING UP BESIDE A MAN LIKE THAT...
IT'S HARDLY A SURPRISE THAT KAKASHI'S STANDARDS FOR OTHERS ARE UNNATURALLY HIGH.
THE WHITE FANG... COME TO THINK OF IT, I'M SURE I'VE HEARD OF HIM.
HE'S SOME HERO WHO SAVED THE VILLAGE, AND DIED IN THE LINE OF DUTY...
FUNNY, I'VE NEVER HEARD KAKASHI SAY A WORD ABOUT HIM...
...
...
HE WAS A GREAT MAN, REVERED BY EVERYONE... INCLUDING, OF COURSE, KAKASHI.
...
THAT IS, UNTIL THE INCIDENT...
...
INCI-DENT?

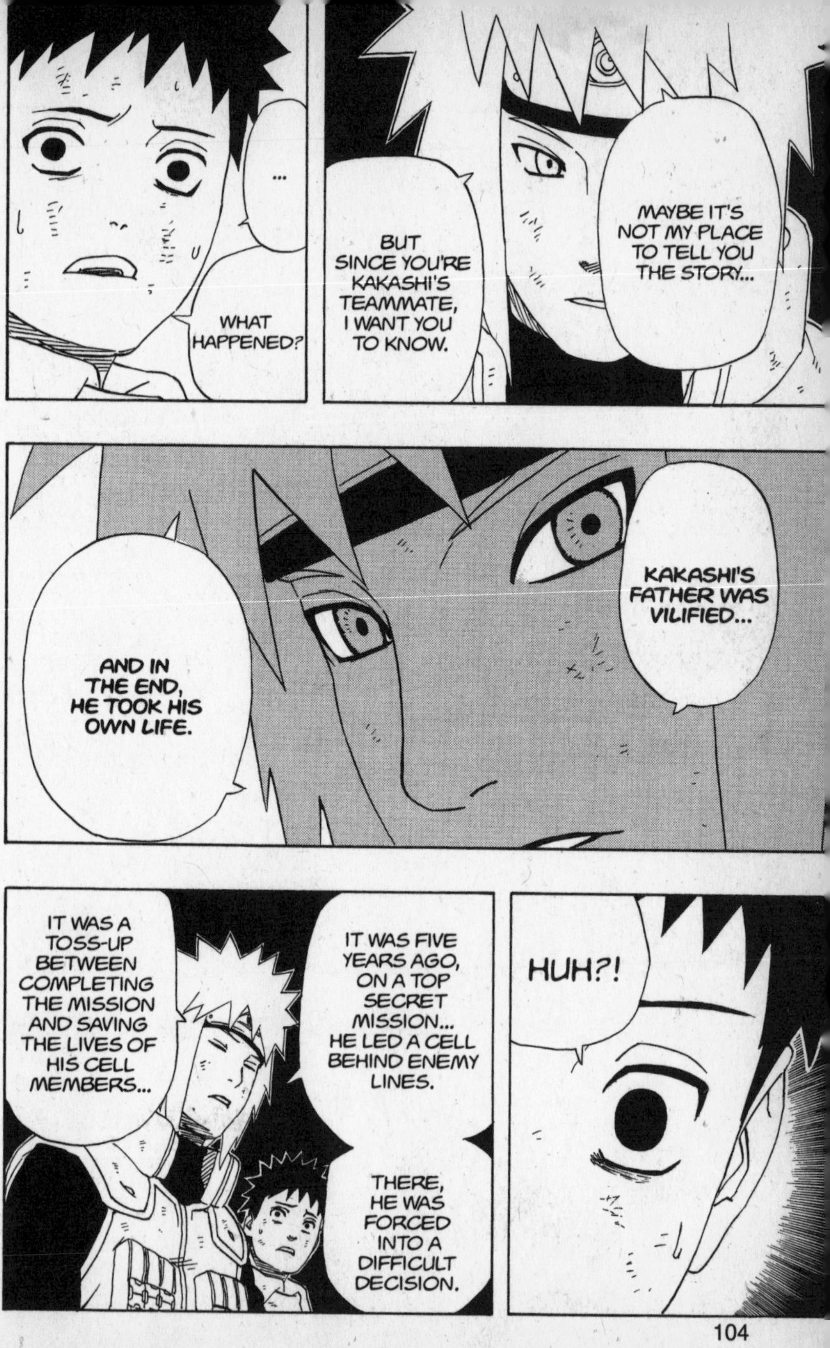
MAYBE IT'S NOT MY PLACE TO TELL YOU THE STORY...
BUT SINCE YOU'RE KAKASHI'S TEAMMATE, I WANT YOU TO KNOW.
...
WHAT HAPPENED?
KAKASHI'S FATHER WAS VILIFIED...
AND IN THE END, HE TOOK HIS OWN LIFE.
HUH?!
IT WAS FIVE YEARS AGO, ON A TOP SECRET MISSION... HE LED A CELL BEHIND ENEMY LINES.
THERE, HE WAS FORCED INTO A DIFFICULT DECISION.
IT WAS A TOSS-UP BETWEEN COMPLETING THE MISSION AND SAVING THE LIVES OF HIS CELL MEMBERS...

READ THIS WAY

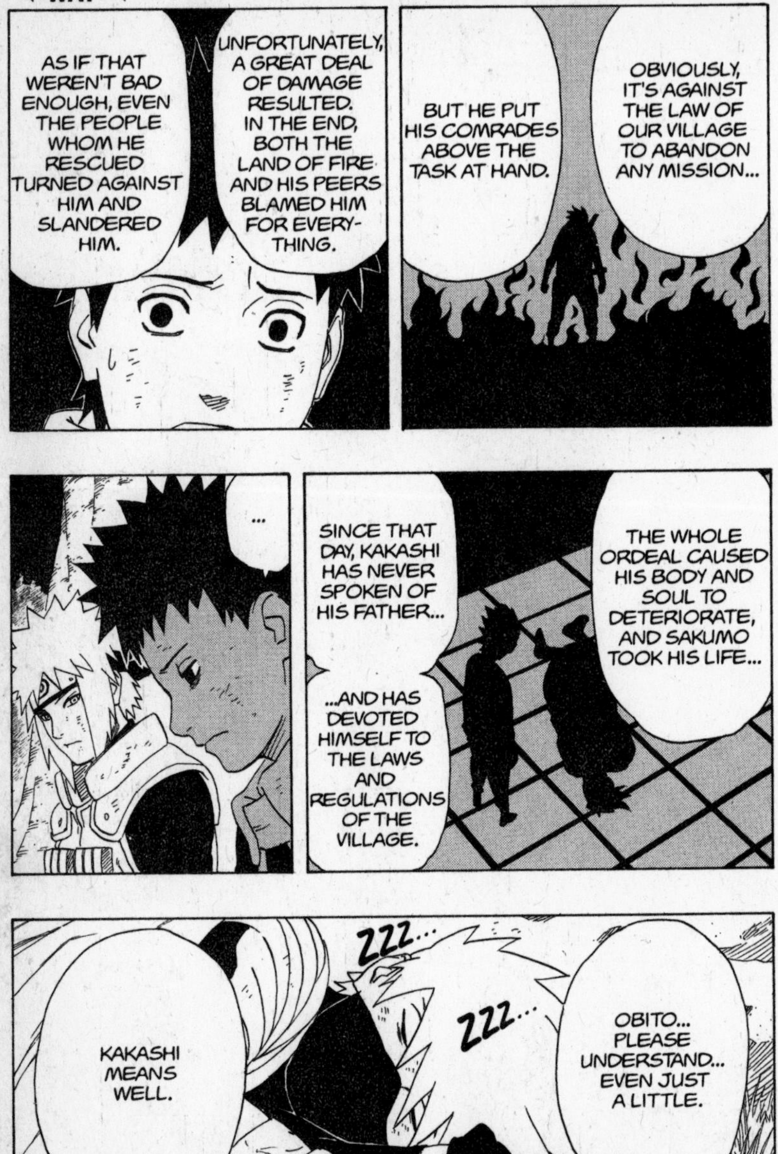

OBVIOUSLY, IT'S AGAINST THE LAW OF OUR VILLAGE TO ABANDON ANY MISSION...
BUT HE PUT HIS COMRADES ABOVE THE TASK AT HAND.
UNFORTUNATELY, A GREAT DEAL OF DAMAGE RESULTED. IN THE END, BOTH THE LAND OF FIRE AND HIS PEERS BLAMED HIM FOR EVERY-THING.
AS IF THAT WEREN'T BAD ENOUGH, EVEN THE PEOPLE WHOM HE RESCUED TURNED AGAINST HIM AND SLANDERED HIM.
THE WHOLE ORDEAL CAUSED HIS BODY AND SOUL TO DETERIORATE, AND SAKUMO TOOK HIS LIFE...
SINCE THAT DAY, KAKASHI HAS NEVER SPOKEN OF HIS FATHER...
...AND HAS DEVOTED HIMSELF TO THE LAWS AND REGULATIONS OF THE VILLAGE.
...
OBITO... PLEASE UNDERSTAND... EVEN JUST A LITTLE.
ZZZ...
ZZZ...
KAKASHI MEANS WELL.

NARUTO™

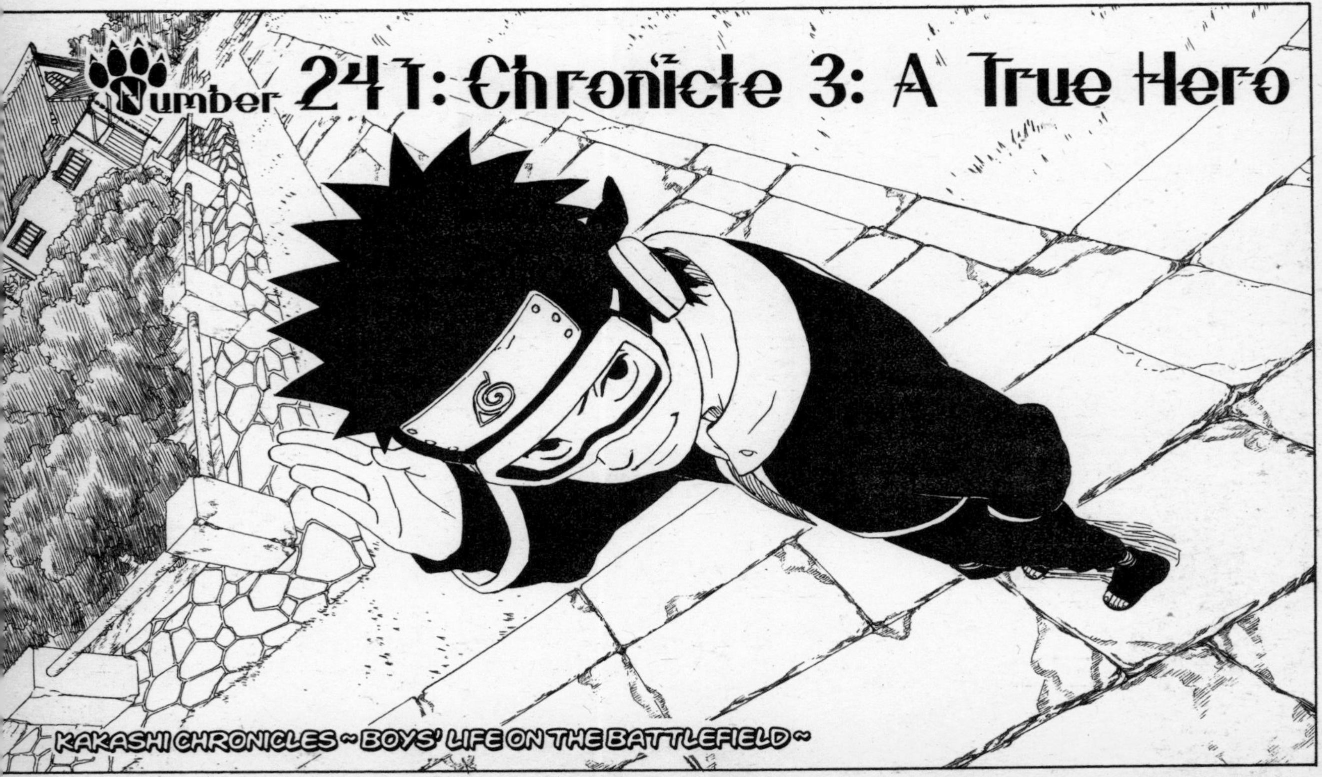
Number 241: Chronicle 3: A True Hero
Kakashi Chronicles ~ Boys' Life on the Battlefield ~

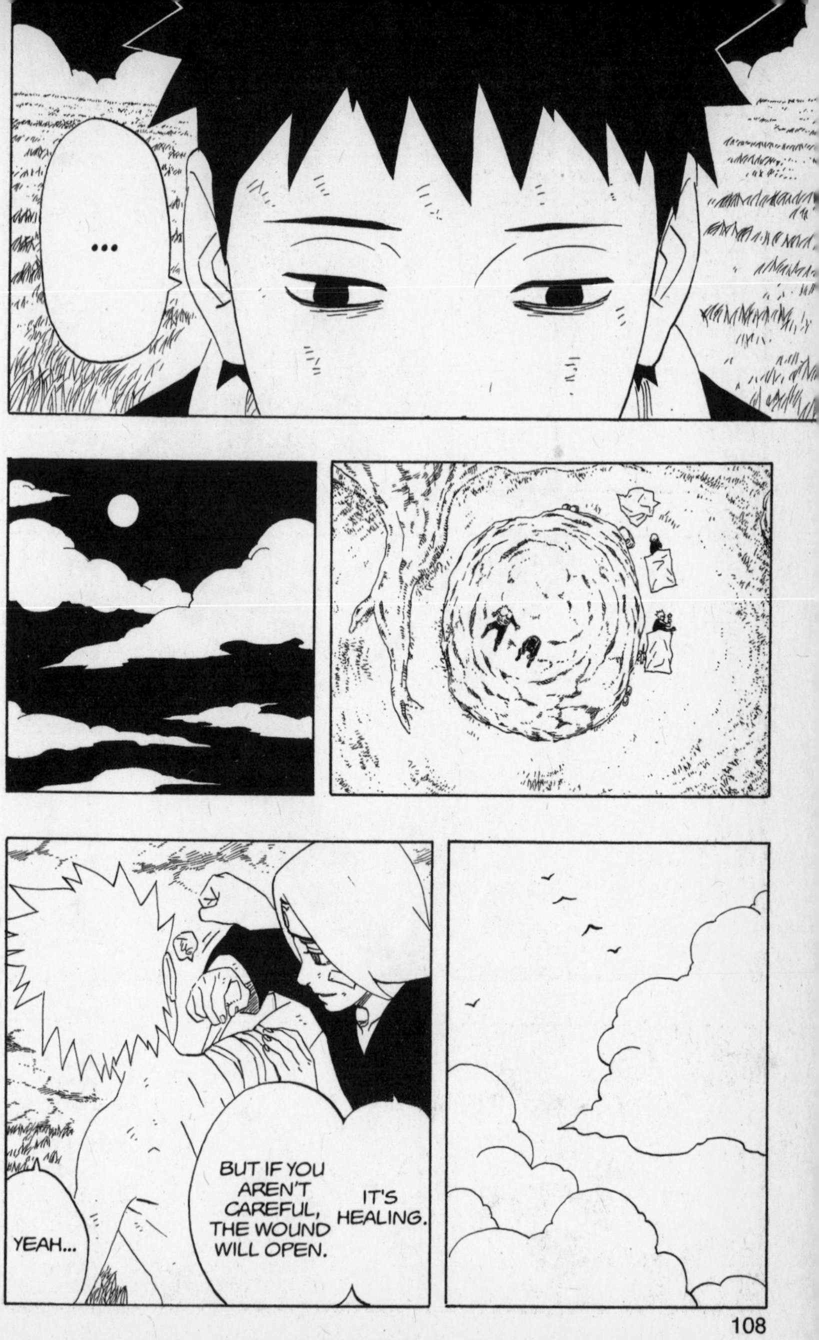
...
IT'S HEALING.
BUT IF YOU AREN'T CAREFUL, THE WOUND WILL OPEN.
YEAH...

READ THIS WAY

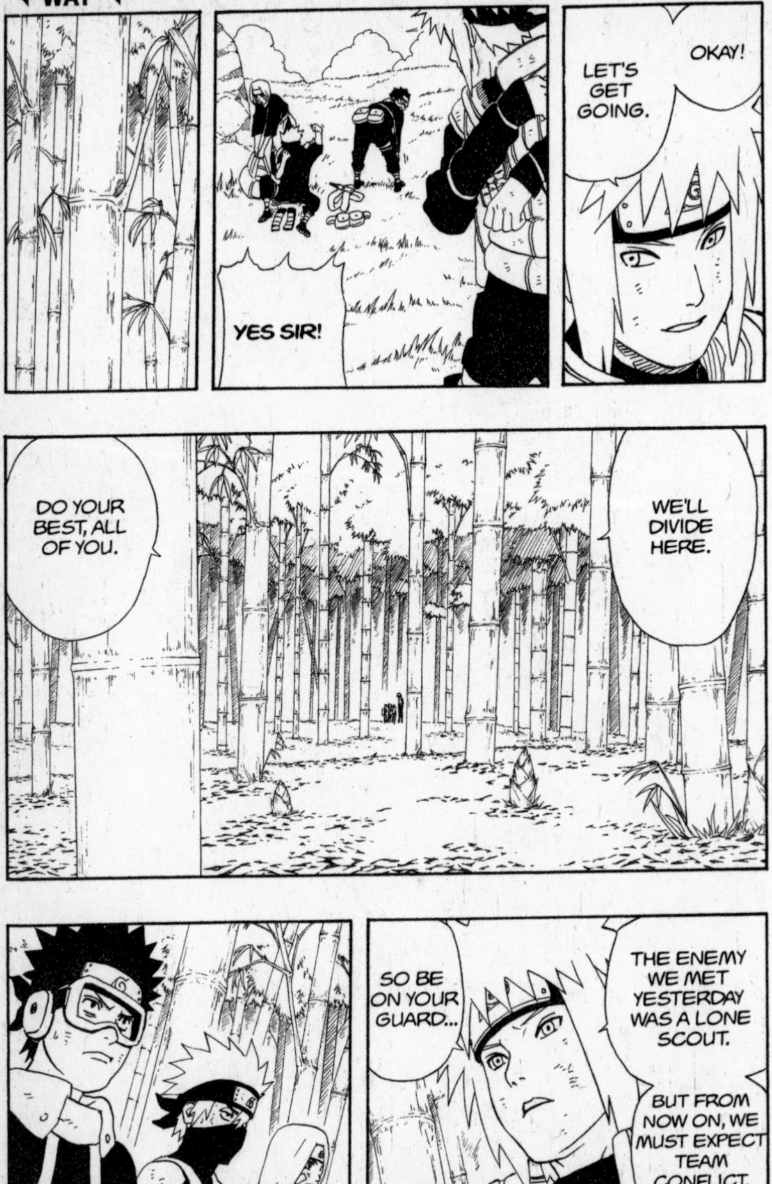
OKAY!
LET'S GET GOING.
YES SIR!
WE'LL DIVIDE HERE.
DO YOUR BEST, ALL OF YOU.
THE ENEMY WE MET YESTERDAY WAS A LONE SCOUT.
BUT FROM NOW ON, WE MUST EXPECT TEAM CONFLICT.
SO BE ON YOUR GUARD...

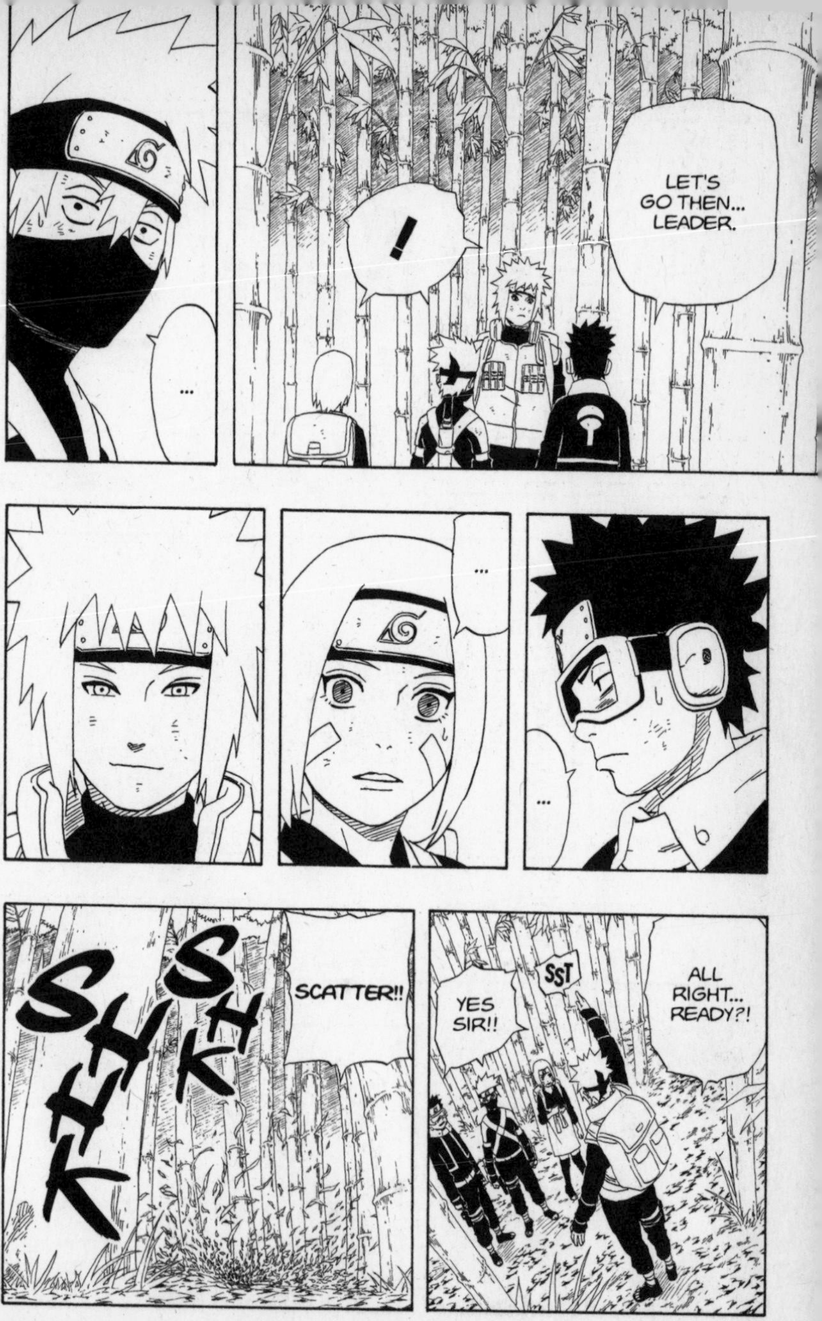
LET'S GO THEN... LEADER.
!
...
...
...
ALL RIGHT... READY?!
SST
YES SIR!!
SCATTER!!
SHK
SHHK

READ THIS WAY

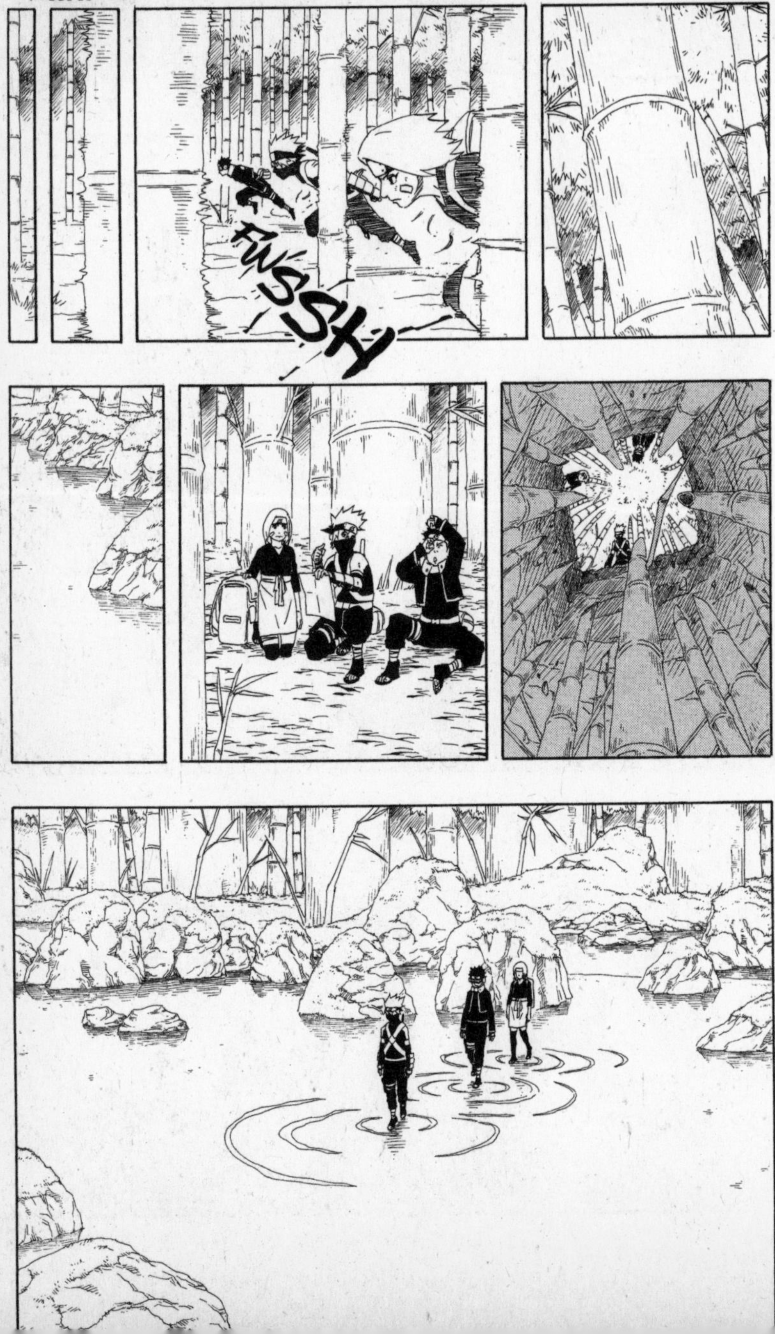
FWSSH

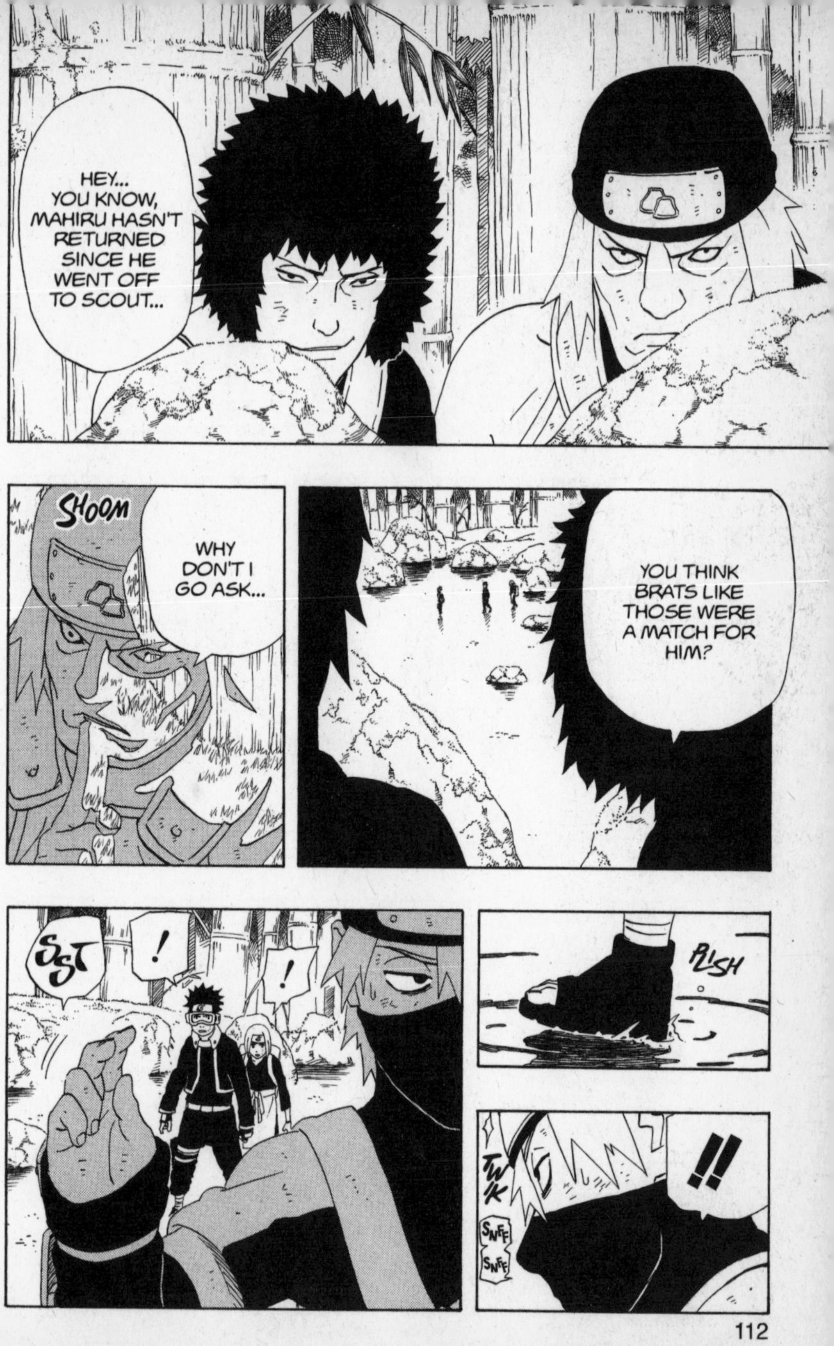
HEY... YOU KNOW, MAHIRU HASN'T RETURNED SINCE HE WENT OFF TO SCOUT...
YOU THINK BRATS LIKE THOSE WERE A MATCH FOR HIM?
SHOOM
WHY DON'T I GO ASK...
PLISH
TWIK
!!
SNFF
SNFF
SST
!
!

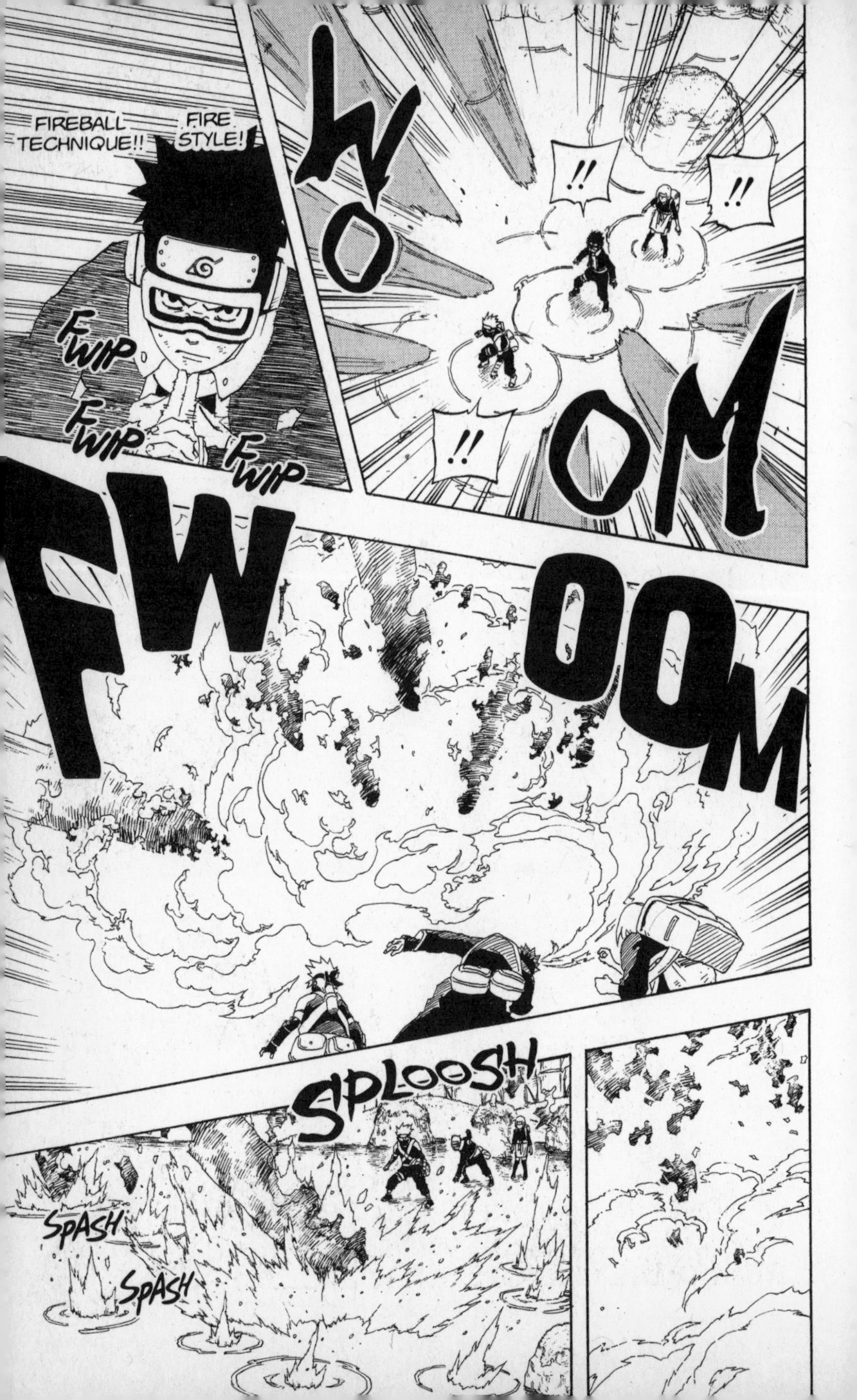
!!
!!
WOOM
!!
FIRE STYLE!
FIREBALL TECHNIQUE!!
FWIP
FWIP
FWIP
FWOOM
SPLOOSH
SPASH
SPASH

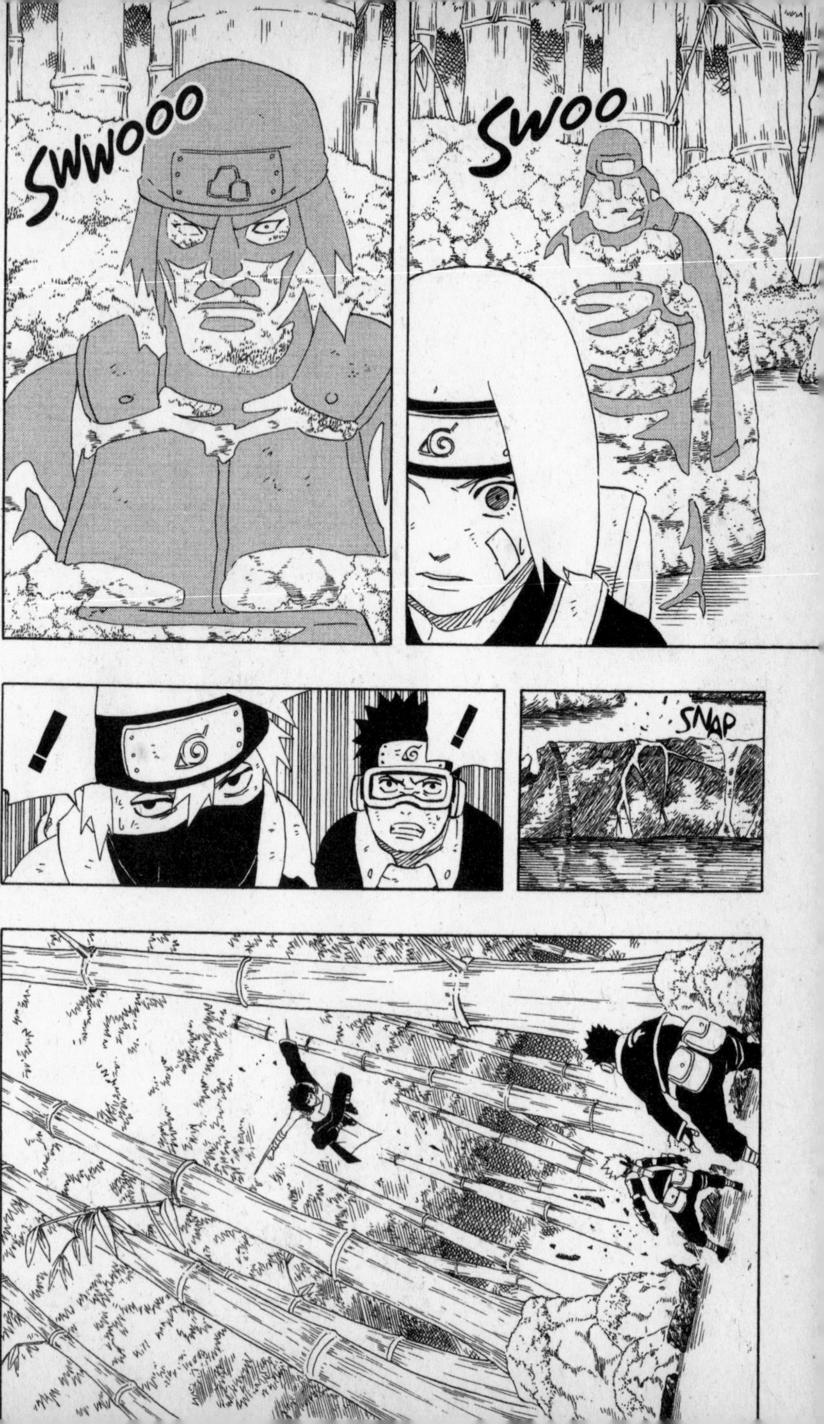
SWOO
SWWOOO
SNAP
!
!

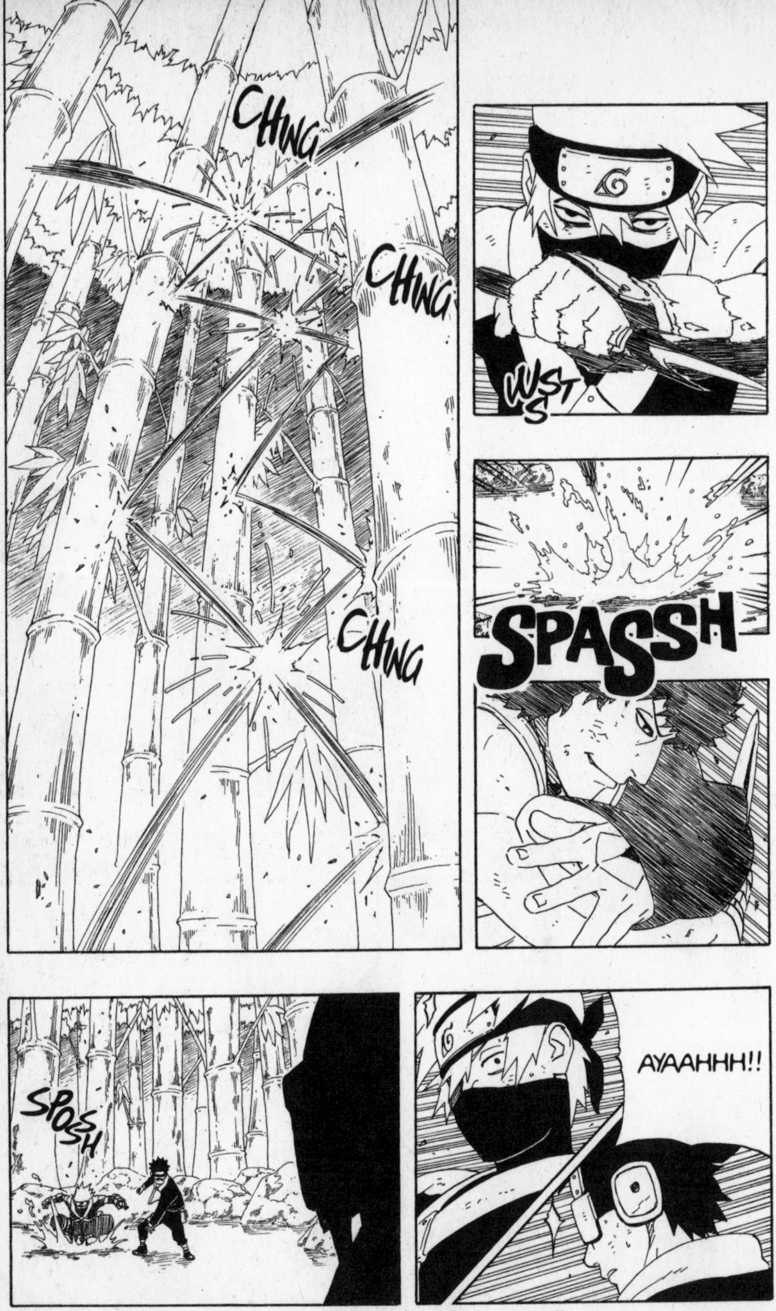
WSTS
SPASSH
CHING
CHING
CHING
AYAAHHH!!
SPOSSH

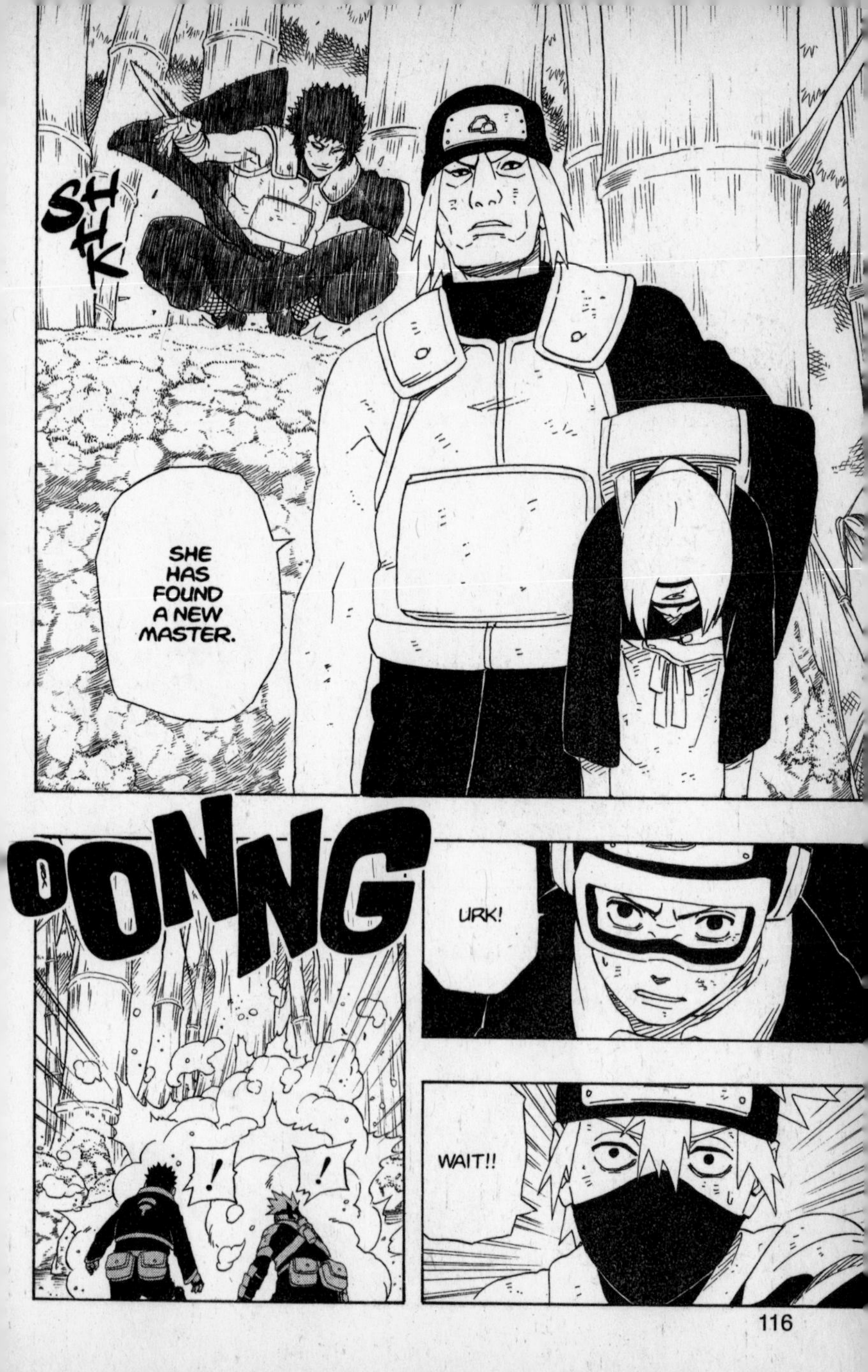
SHHK
SHE HAS FOUND A NEW MASTER.
URK!
WAIT!!
DONNG
!
!

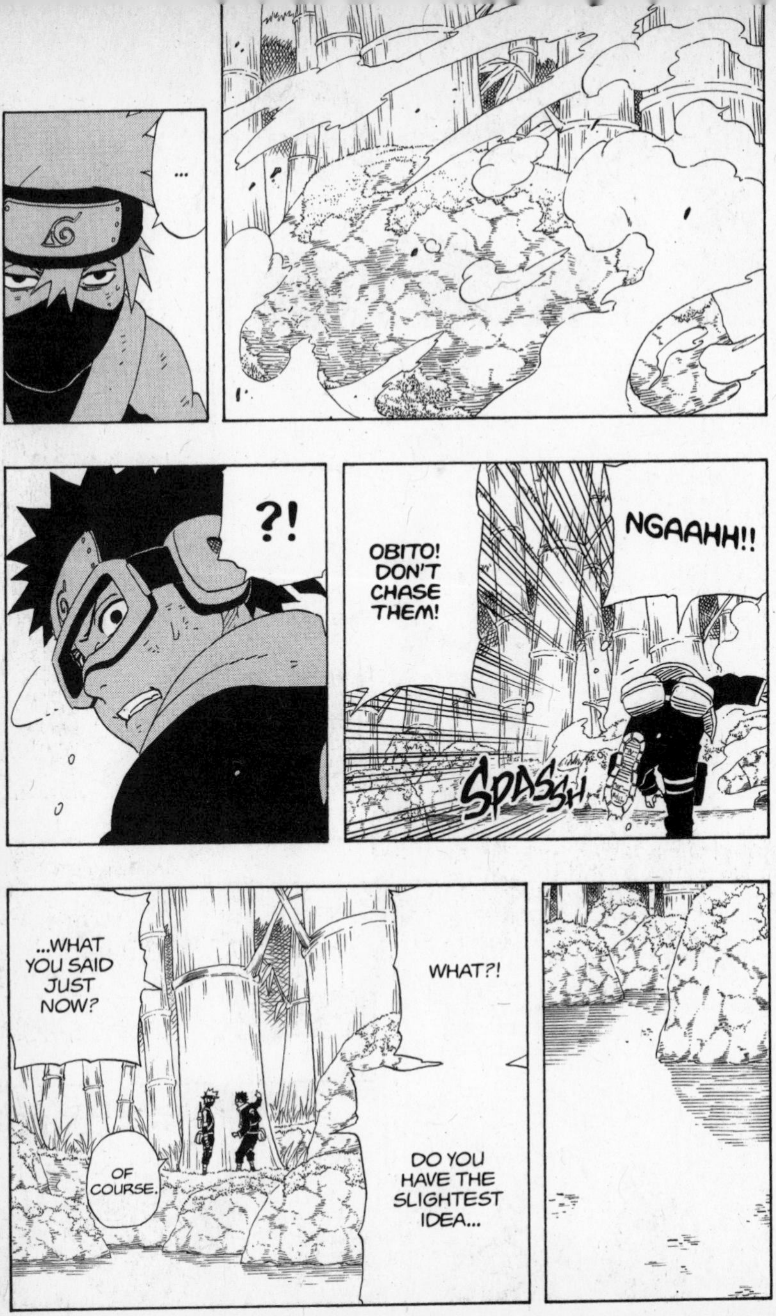
...
NGAAHH!!
OBITO! DON'T CHASE THEM!
SPASSH
?!
DO YOU HAVE THE SLIGHTEST IDEA...
...WHAT YOU SAID JUST NOW?
OF COURSE.
WHAT?!

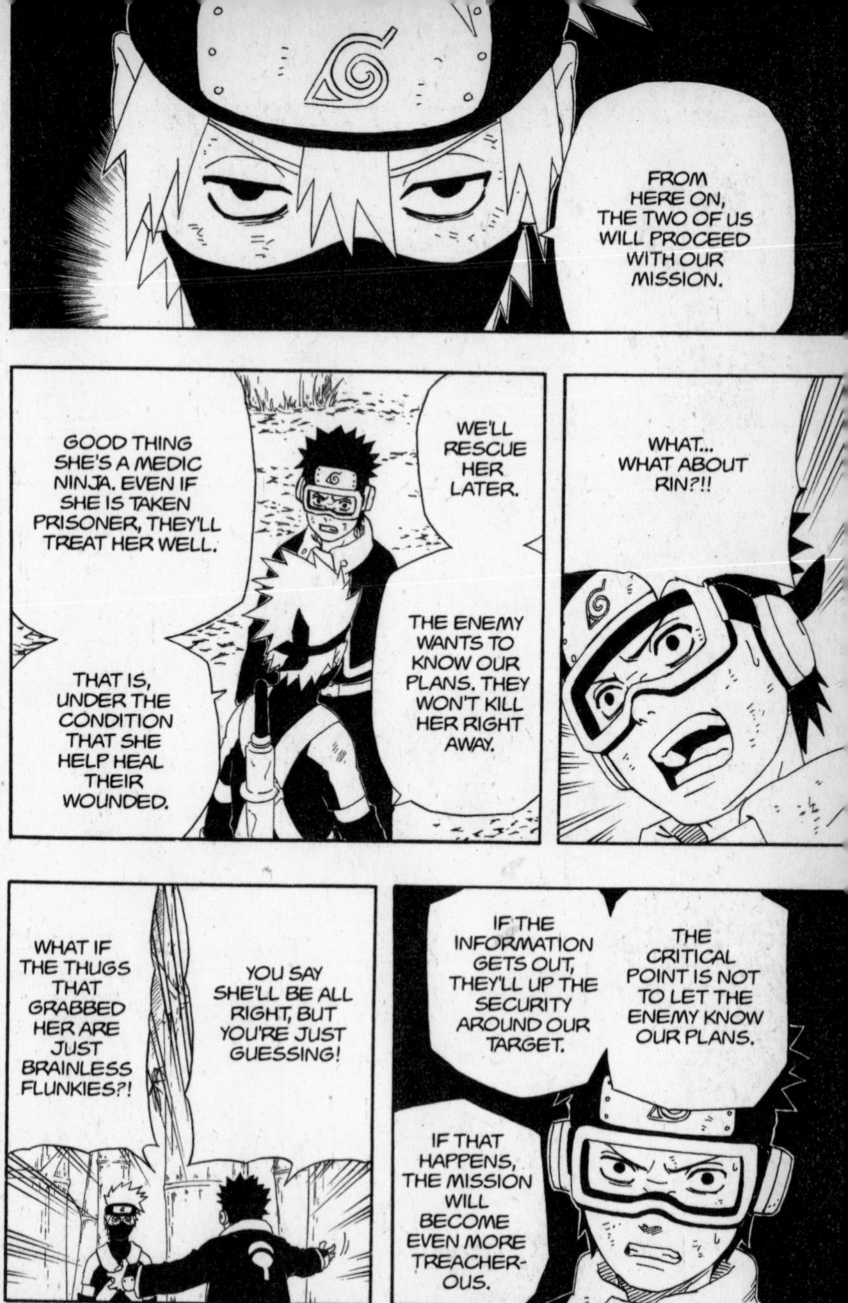
FROM HERE ON, THE TWO OF US WILL PROCEED WITH OUR MISSION.
WHAT... WHAT ABOUT RIN?!!
WE'LL RESCUE HER LATER.
THE ENEMY WANTS TO KNOW OUR PLANS. THEY WON'T KILL HER RIGHT AWAY.
GOOD THING SHE'S A MEDIC NINJA. EVEN IF SHE IS TAKEN PRISONER, THEY'LL TREAT HER WELL.
THAT IS, UNDER THE CONDITION THAT SHE HELP HEAL THEIR WOUNDED.
THE CRITICAL POINT IS NOT TO LET THE ENEMY KNOW OUR PLANS.
IF THE INFORMATION GETS OUT, THEY'LL UP THE SECURITY AROUND OUR TARGET.
IF THAT HAPPENS, THE MISSION WILL BECOME EVEN MORE TREACHER-OUS.
YOU SAY SHE'LL BE ALL RIGHT, BUT YOU'RE JUST GUESSING!
WHAT IF THE THUGS THAT GRABBED HER ARE JUST BRAINLESS FLUNKIES?!

READ THIS WAY

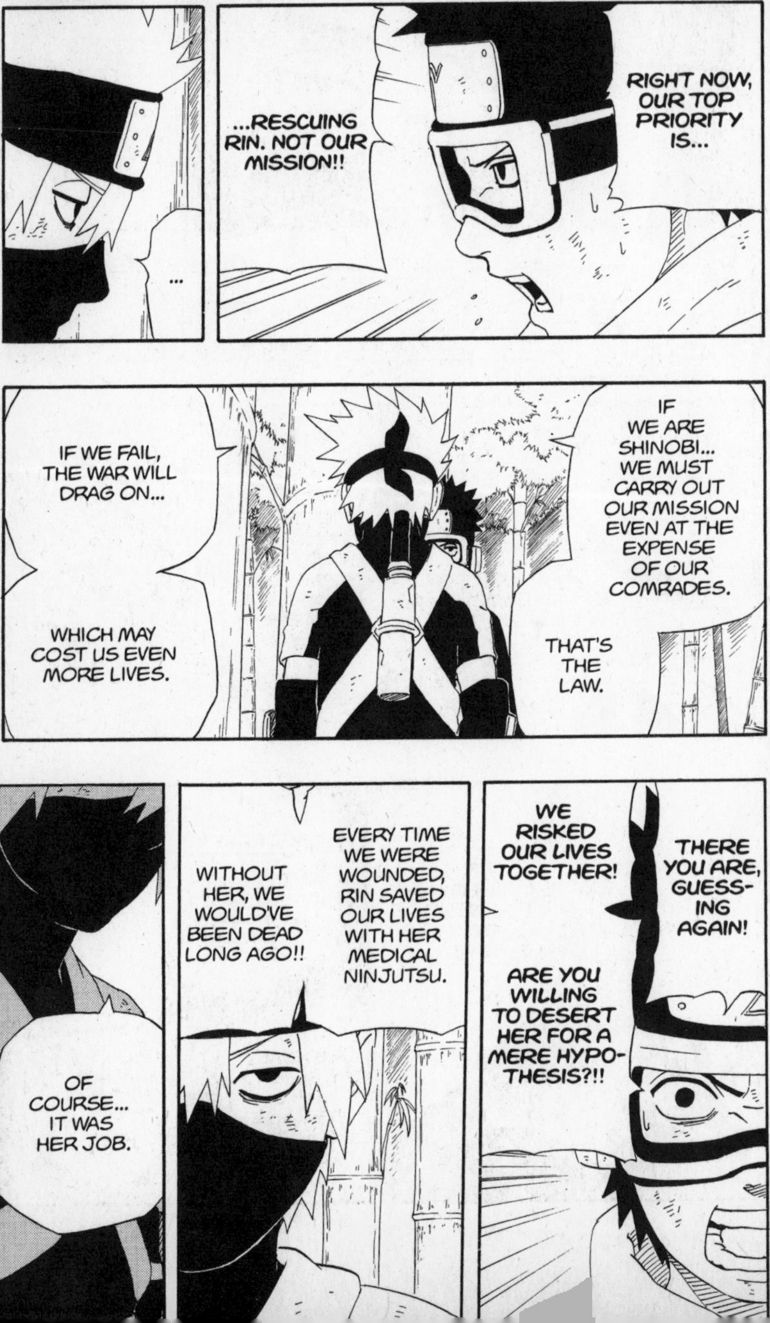
RIGHT NOW, OUR TOP PRIORITY IS...
...RESCUING RIN. NOT OUR MISSION!!
...
IF WE ARE SHINOBI... WE MUST CARRY OUT OUR MISSION EVEN AT THE EXPENSE OF OUR COMRADES.
THAT'S THE LAW.
IF WE FAIL, THE WAR WILL DRAG ON...
WHICH MAY COST US EVEN MORE LIVES.
THERE YOU ARE, GUESSING AGAIN!
WE RISKED OUR LIVES TOGETHER!
ARE YOU WILLING TO DESERT HER FOR A MERE HYPOTHESIS?!!
EVERY TIME WE WERE WOUNDED, RIN SAVED OUR LIVES WITH HER MEDICAL NINJUTSU.
WITHOUT HER, WE WOULD'VE BEEN DEAD LONG AGO!!
OF COURSE... IT WAS HER JOB.

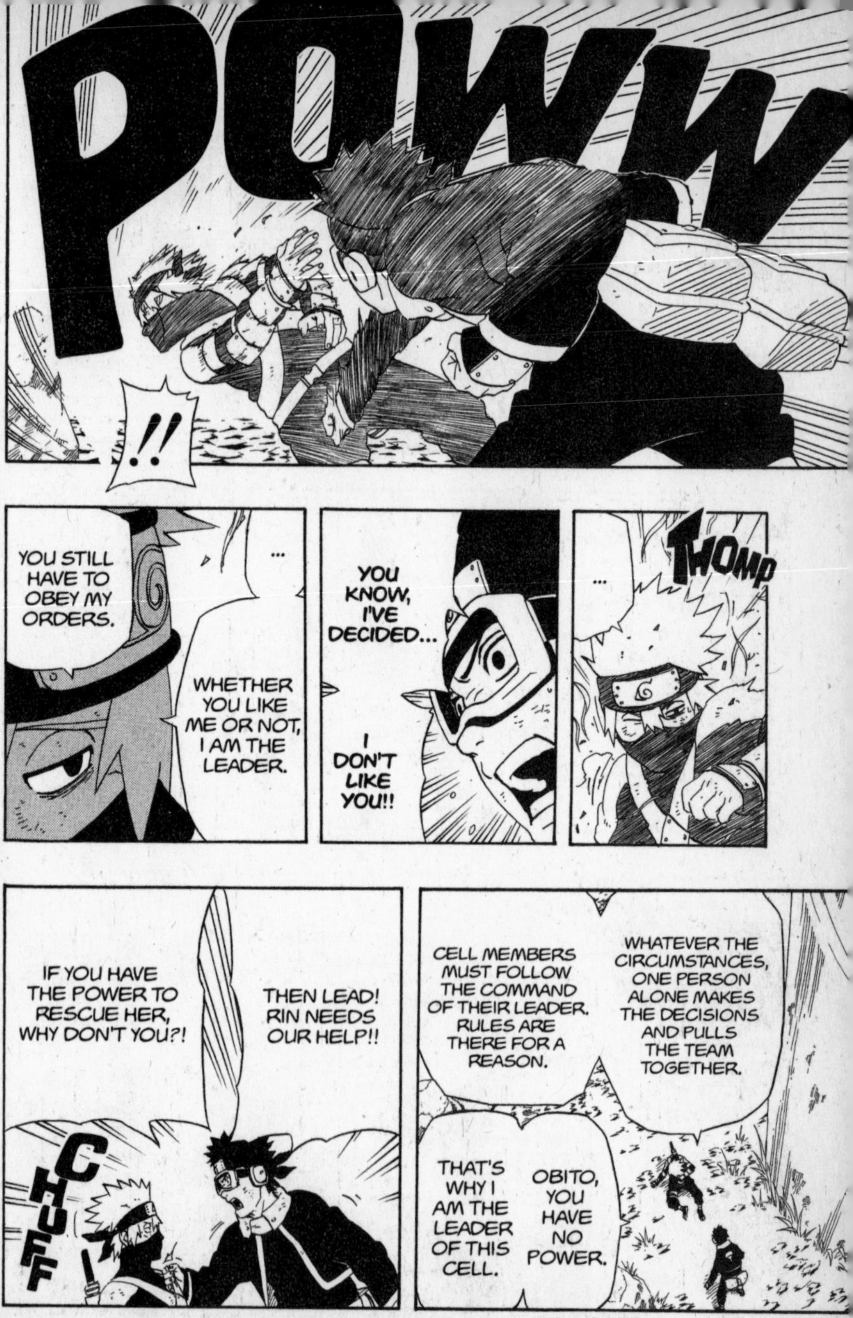
POWW
!!
...
THOMP
YOU KNOW, I'VE DECIDED...
I DON'T LIKE YOU!!
...
WHETHER YOU LIKE ME OR NOT, I AM THE LEADER.
YOU STILL HAVE TO OBEY MY ORDERS.
WHATEVER THE CIRCUMSTANCES, ONE PERSON ALONE MAKES THE DECISIONS AND PULLS THE TEAM TOGETHER.
CELL MEMBERS MUST FOLLOW THE COMMAND OF THEIR LEADER. RULES ARE THERE FOR A REASON.
OBITO, YOU HAVE NO POWER.
THAT'S WHY I AM THE LEADER OF THIS CELL.
THEN LEAD! RIN NEEDS OUR HELP!!
IF YOU HAVE THE POWER TO RESCUE HER, WHY DON'T YOU?!
CHUFF

READ THIS WAY

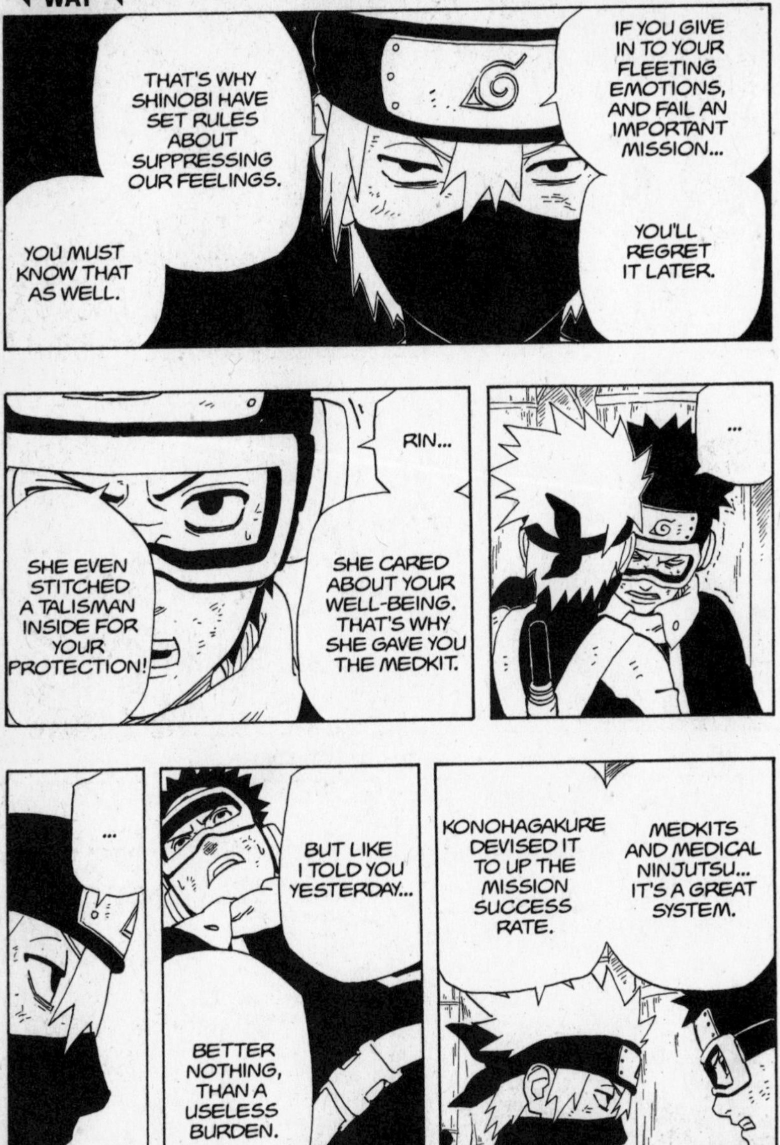
IF YOU GIVE IN TO YOUR FLEETING EMOTIONS, AND FAIL AN IMPORTANT MISSION...
YOU'LL REGRET IT LATER.
THAT'S WHY SHINOBI HAVE SET RULES ABOUT SUPPRESSING OUR FEELINGS.
YOU MUST KNOW THAT AS WELL.
...
RIN...
SHE CARED ABOUT YOUR WELL-BEING. THAT'S WHY SHE GAVE YOU THE MEDKIT.
SHE EVEN STITCHED A TALISMAN INSIDE FOR YOUR PROTECTION!
MEDKITS AND MEDICAL NINJUTSU... IT'S A GREAT SYSTEM.
KONOHAGAKURE DEVISED IT TO UP THE MISSION SUCCESS RATE.
BUT LIKE I TOLD YOU YESTERDAY...
BETTER NOTHING, THAN A USELESS BURDEN.
...

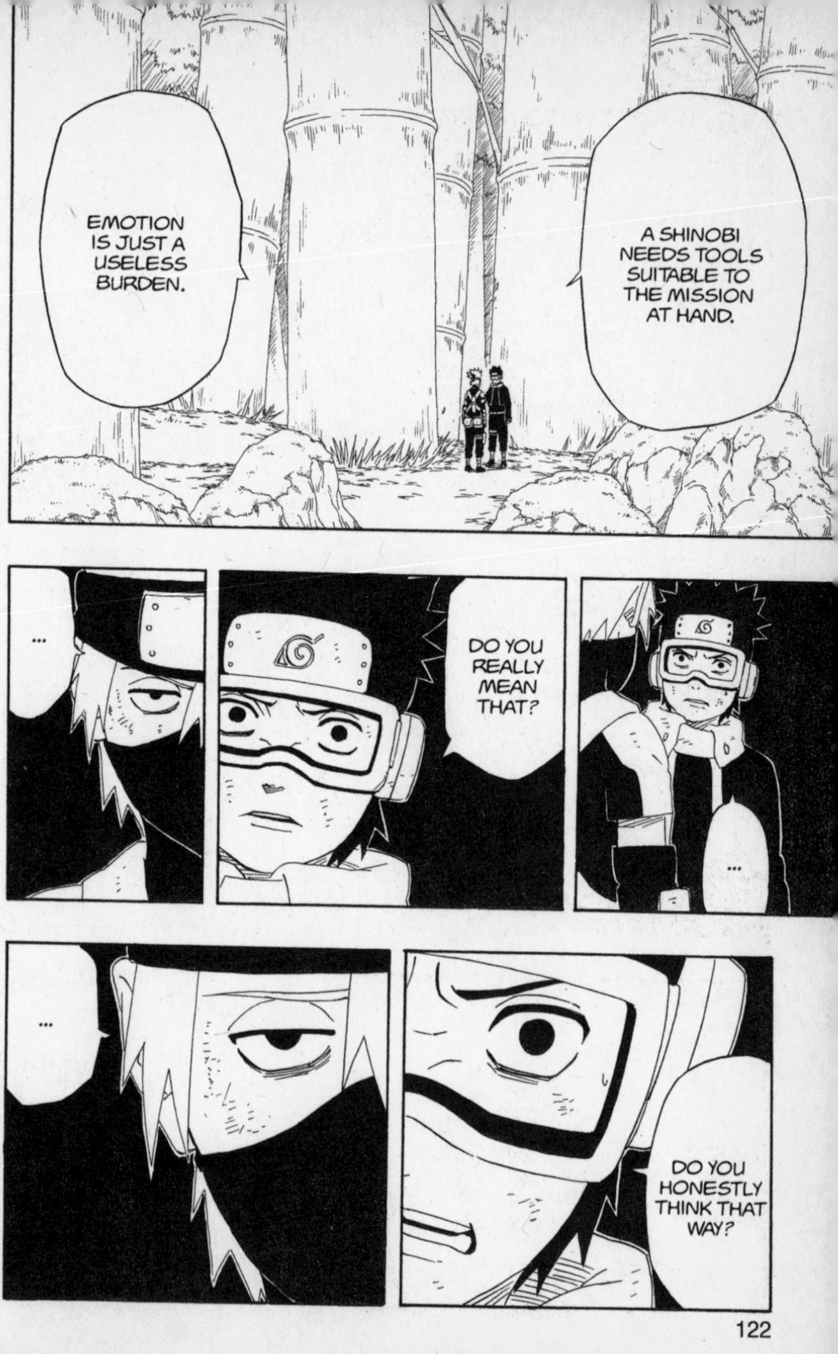
A SHINOBI NEEDS TOOLS SUITABLE TO THE MISSION AT HAND.
EMOTION IS JUST A USELESS BURDEN.
...
DO YOU REALLY MEAN THAT?
...
DO YOU HONESTLY THINK THAT WAY?
...

READ THIS WAY

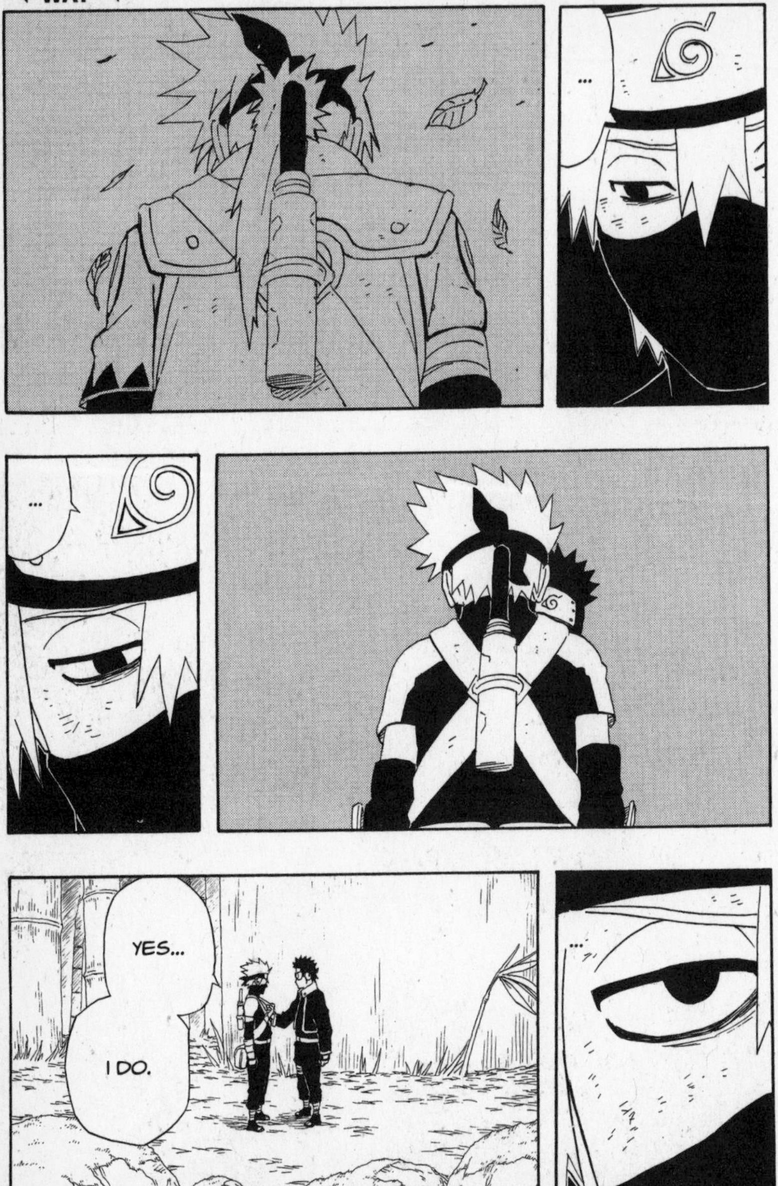
...
...
...
YES...
I DO.

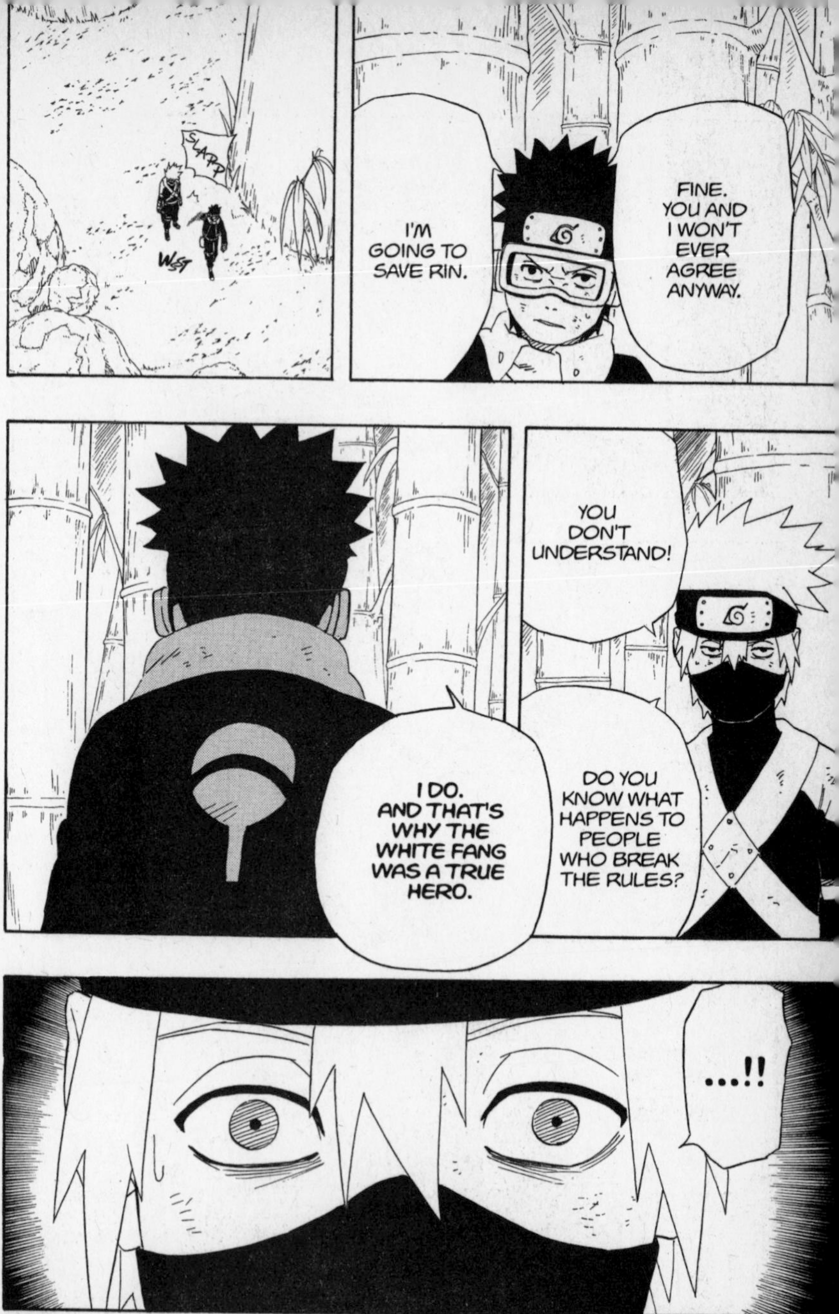
FINE. YOU AND I WON'T EVER AGREE ANYWAY.
I'M GOING TO SAVE RIN.
SLAPP
YOU DON'T UNDERSTAND!
DO YOU KNOW WHAT HAPPENS TO PEOPLE WHO BREAK THE RULES?
I DO. AND THAT'S WHY THE WHITE FANG WAS A TRUE HERO.
...!!

READ THIS WAY

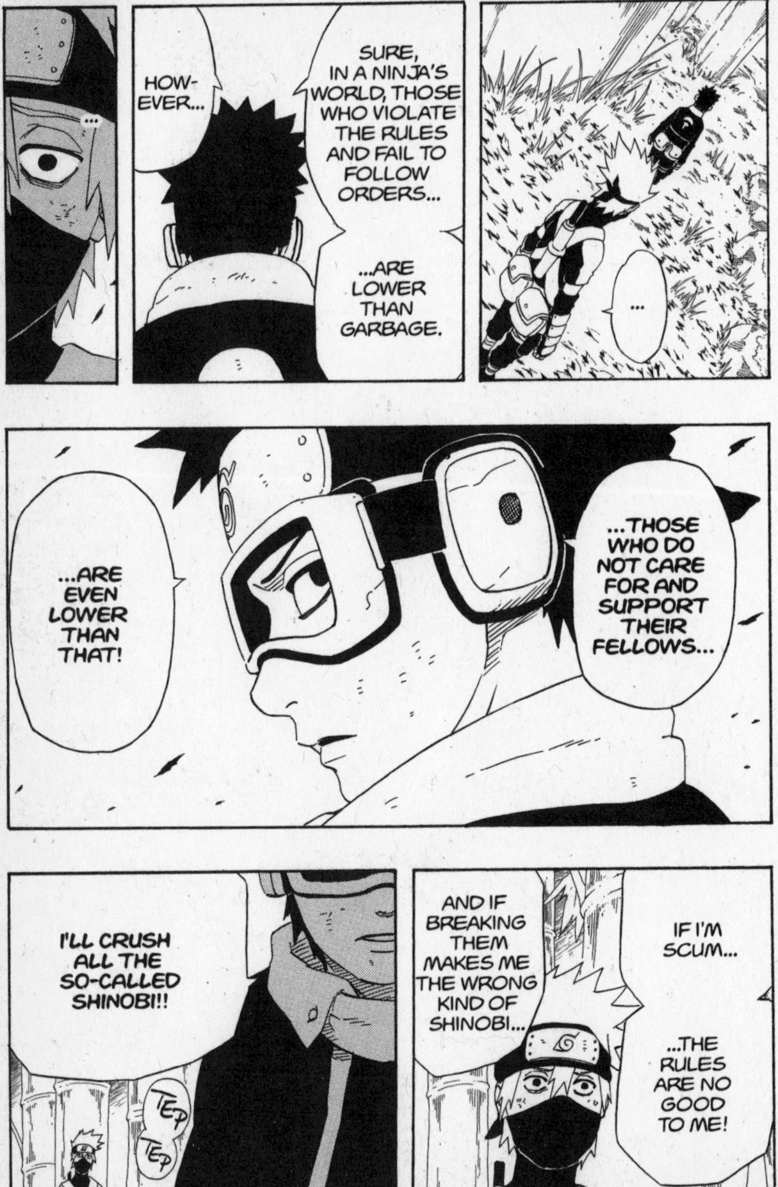
...
SURE, IN A NINJA'S WORLD, THOSE WHO VIOLATE THE RULES AND FAIL TO FOLLOW ORDERS...
...ARE LOWER THAN GARBAGE.
HOW-EVER...
...
...THOSE WHO DO NOT CARE FOR AND SUPPORT THEIR FELLOWS...
...ARE EVEN LOWER THAN THAT!
IF I'M SCUM...
...THE RULES ARE NO GOOD TO ME!
AND IF BREAKING THEM MAKES ME THE WRONG KIND OF SHINOBI...
I'LL CRUSH ALL THE SO-CALLED SHINOBI!!
TEP
TEP

NARUTO™

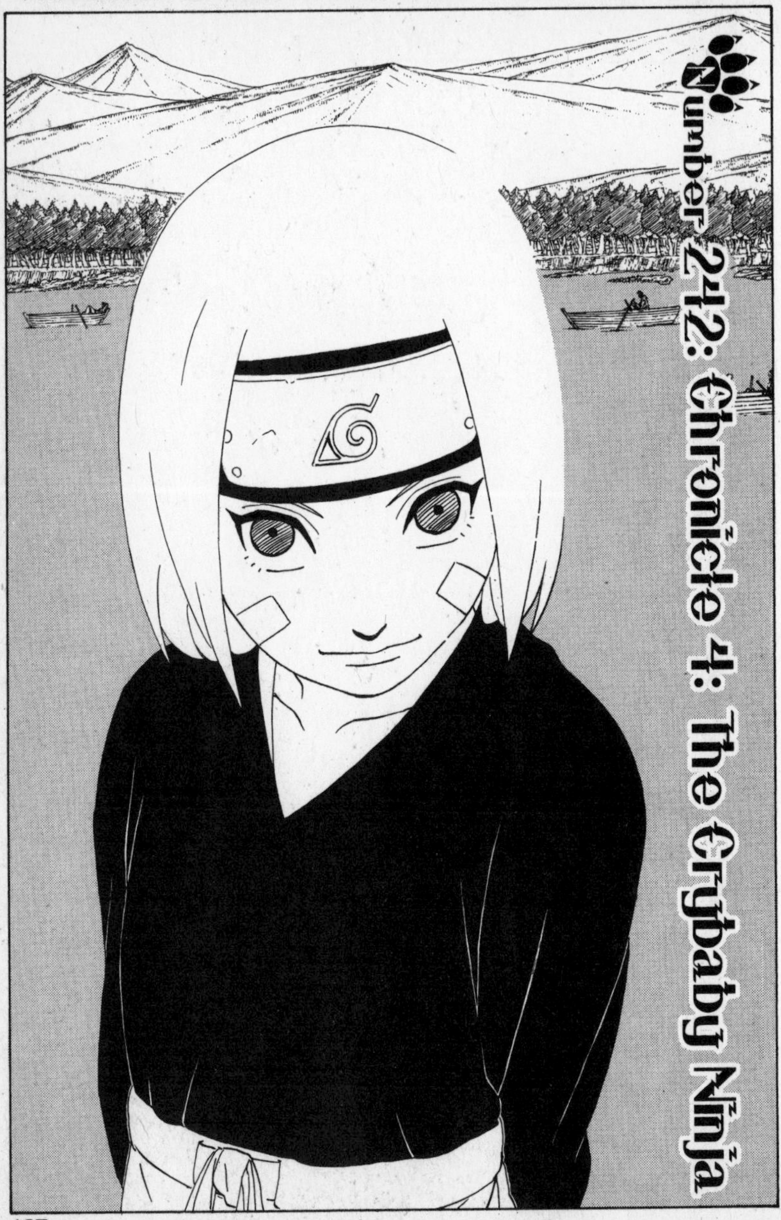
Number 242: Chronicle 4: The Crybaby Ninja

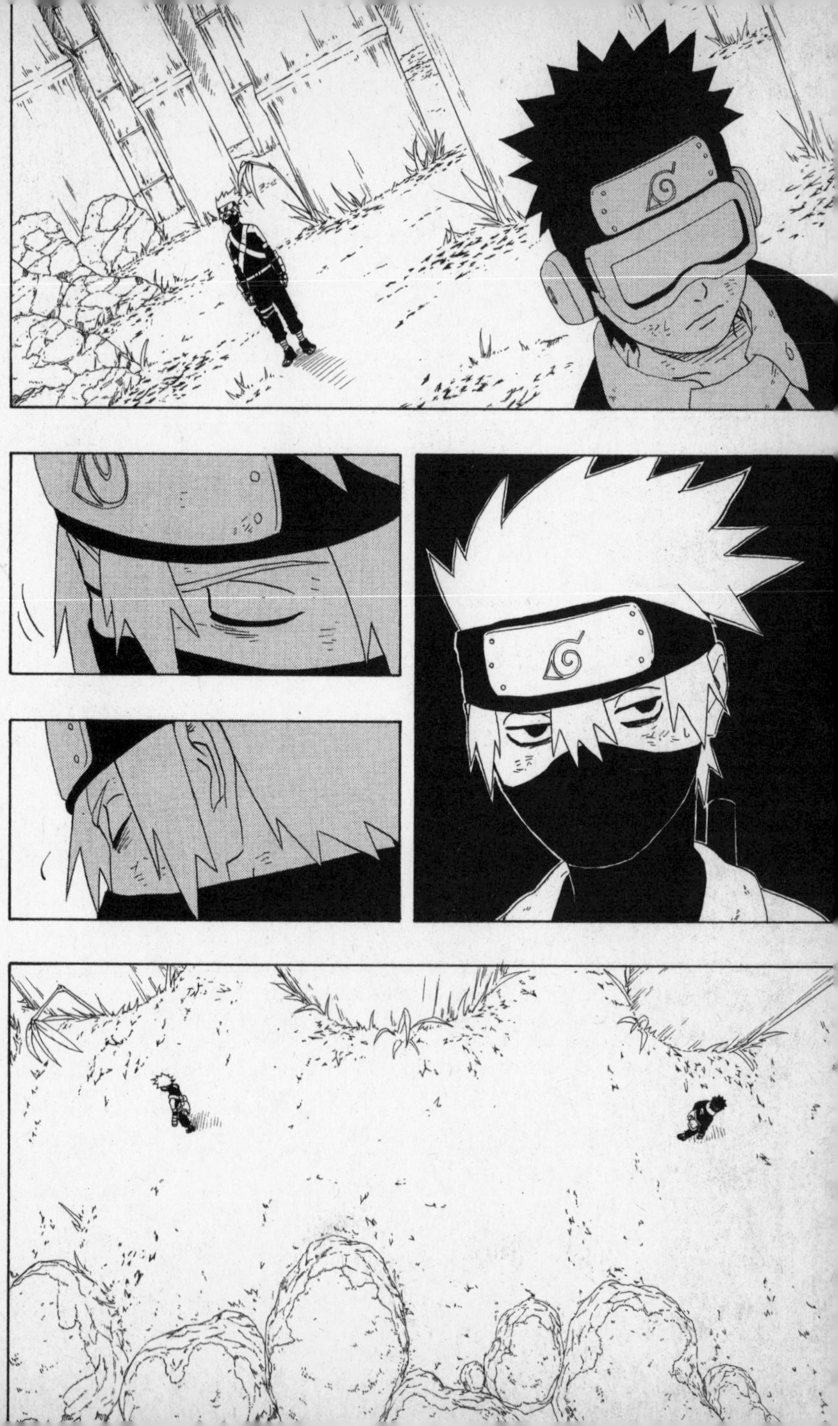

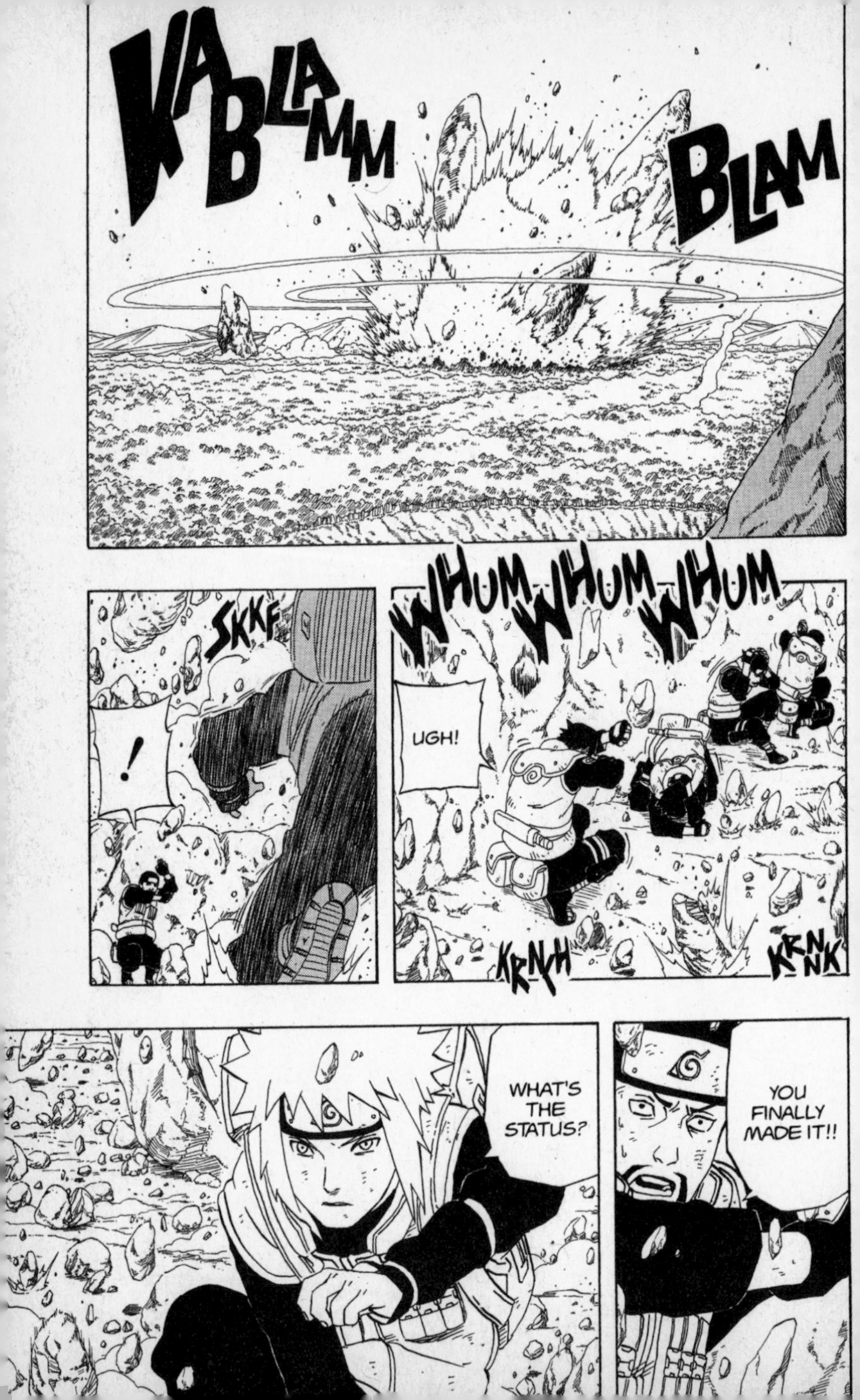
BLAM
KABLAMM
WHUM WHUM WHUM
UGH!
KRNK
KRNCH
SKKF
!
YOU FINALLY MADE IT!!
WHAT'S THE STATUS?

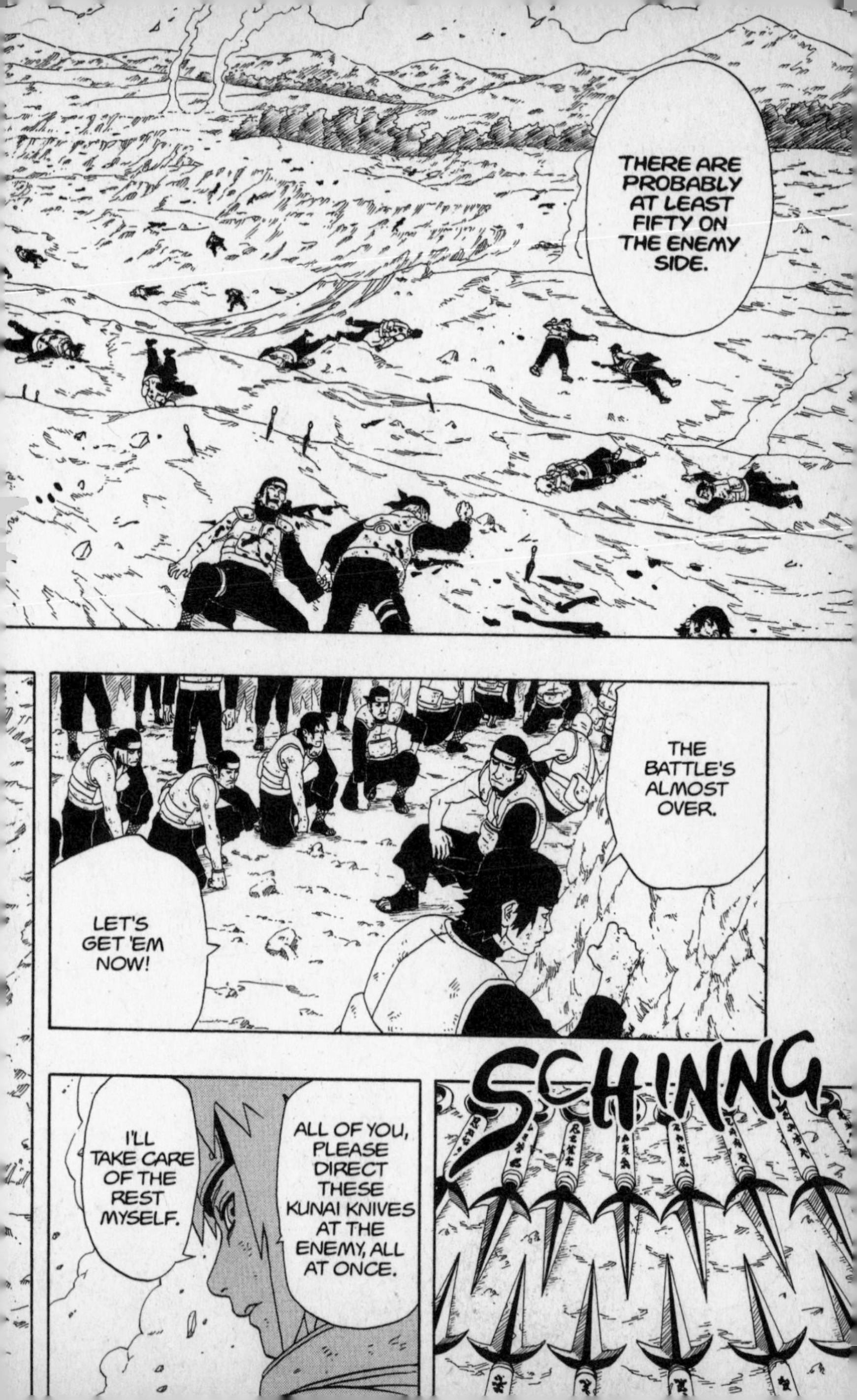
THERE ARE PROBABLY AT LEAST FIFTY ON THE ENEMY SIDE.
THE BATTLE'S ALMOST OVER.
LET'S GET 'EM NOW!
SCHINNG
ALL OF YOU, PLEASE DIRECT THESE KUNAI KNIVES AT THE ENEMY, ALL AT ONCE.
I'LL TAKE CARE OF THE REST MYSELF.

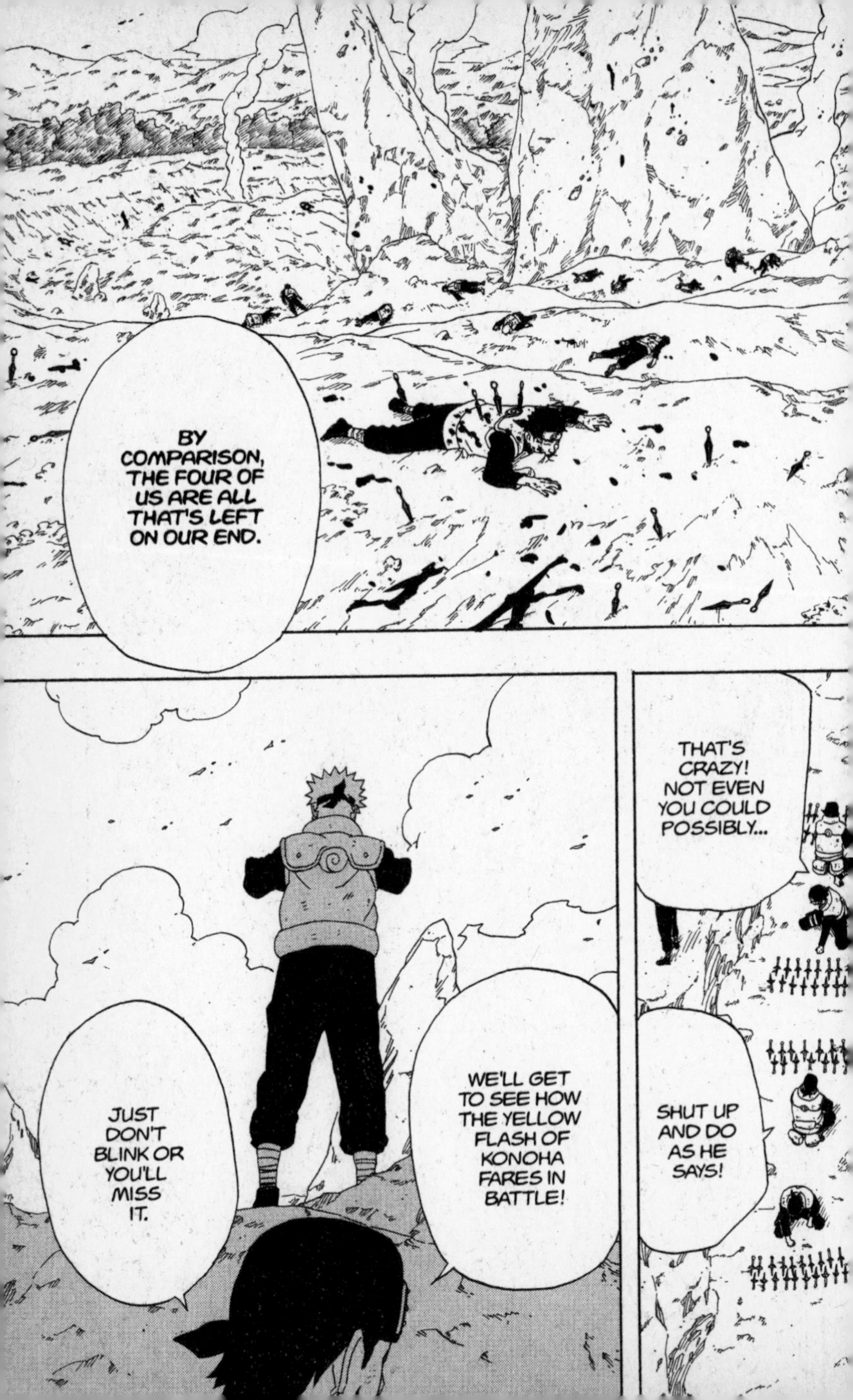
BY COMPARISON, THE FOUR OF US ARE ALL THAT'S LEFT ON OUR END.
THAT'S CRAZY! NOT EVEN YOU COULD POSSIBLY...
SHUT UP AND DO AS HE SAYS!
WE'LL GET TO SEE HOW THE YELLOW FLASH OF KONOHA FARES IN BATTLE!
JUST DON'T BLINK OR YOU'LL MISS IT.

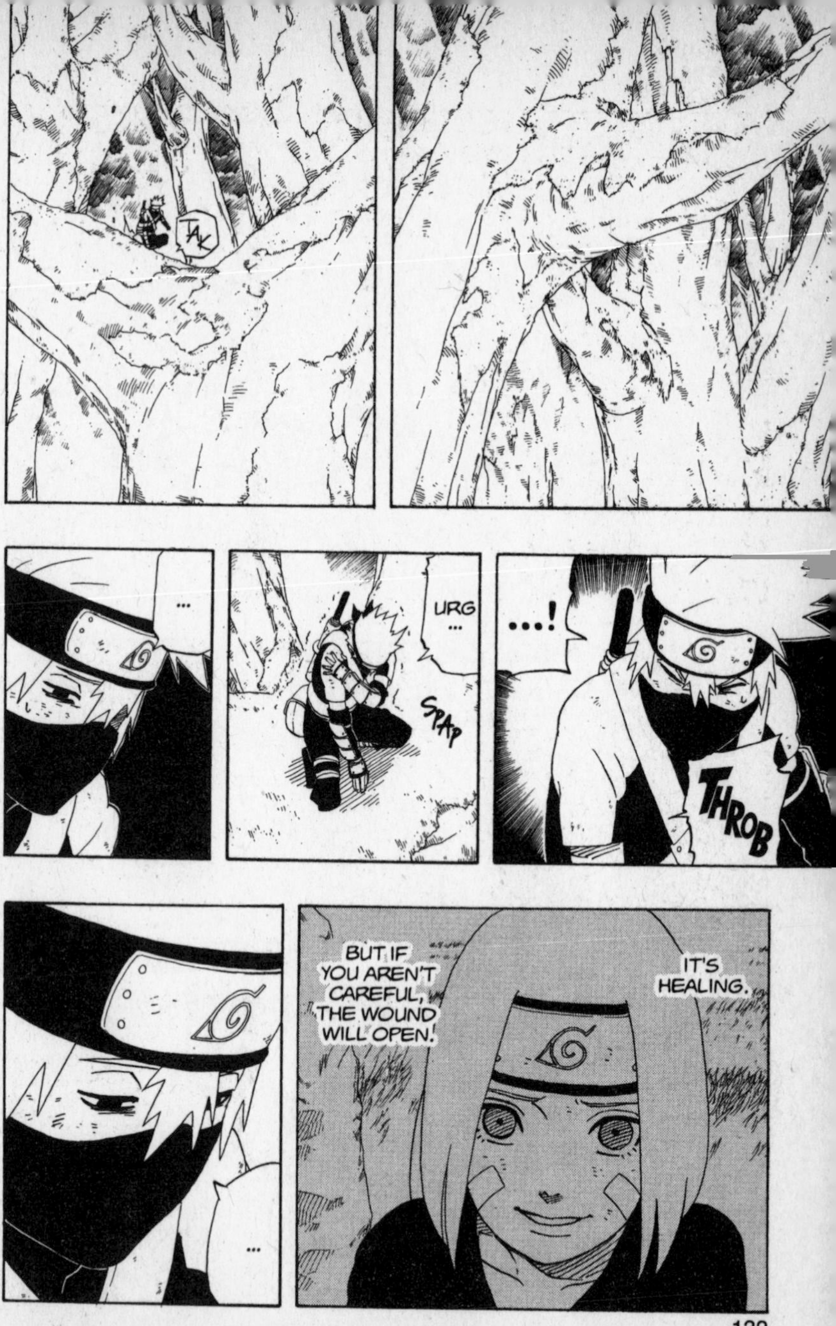
TAK
...!
THROB
URG ...
SPAP
...
IT'S HEALING.
BUT IF YOU AREN'T CAREFUL, THE WOUND WILL OPEN.
...

READ THIS WAY

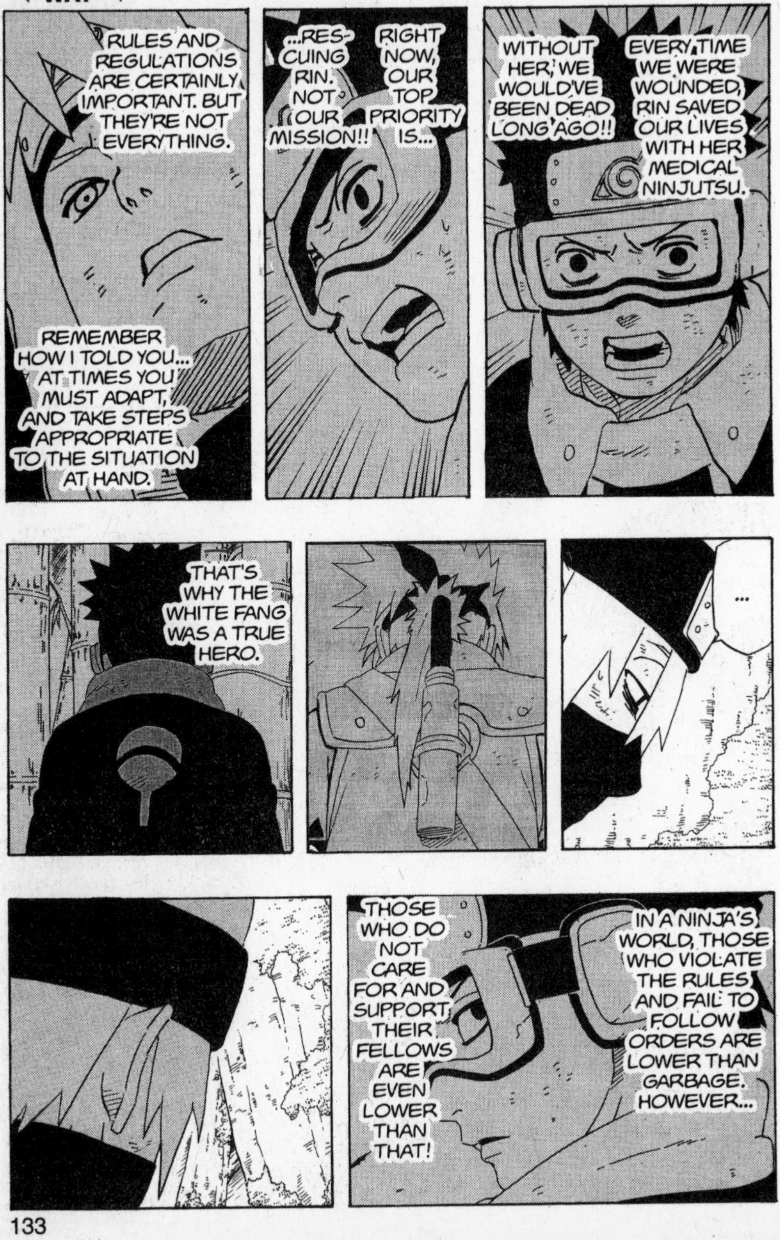
EVERY TIME WE WERE WOUNDED, RIN SAVED OUR LIVES WITH HER MEDICAL NINJUTSU.
WITHOUT HER, WE WOULD'VE BEEN DEAD LONG AGO!!
RIGHT NOW, OUR TOP PRIORITY IS...
...RES-CUING RIN. NOT OUR MISSION!!
RULES AND REGULATIONS ARE CERTAINLY IMPORTANT. BUT THEY'RE NOT EVERYTHING.
REMEMBER HOW I TOLD YOU... AT TIMES YOU MUST ADAPT, AND TAKE STEPS APPROPRIATE TO THE SITUATION AT HAND.
...
THAT'S WHY THE WHITE FANG WAS A TRUE HERO.
IN A NINJA'S WORLD, THOSE WHO VIOLATE THE RULES AND FAIL TO FOLLOW ORDERS ARE LOWER THAN GARBAGE. HOWEVER...
THOSE WHO DO NOT CARE FOR AND SUPPORT THEIR FELLOWS ARE EVEN LOWER THAN THAT!

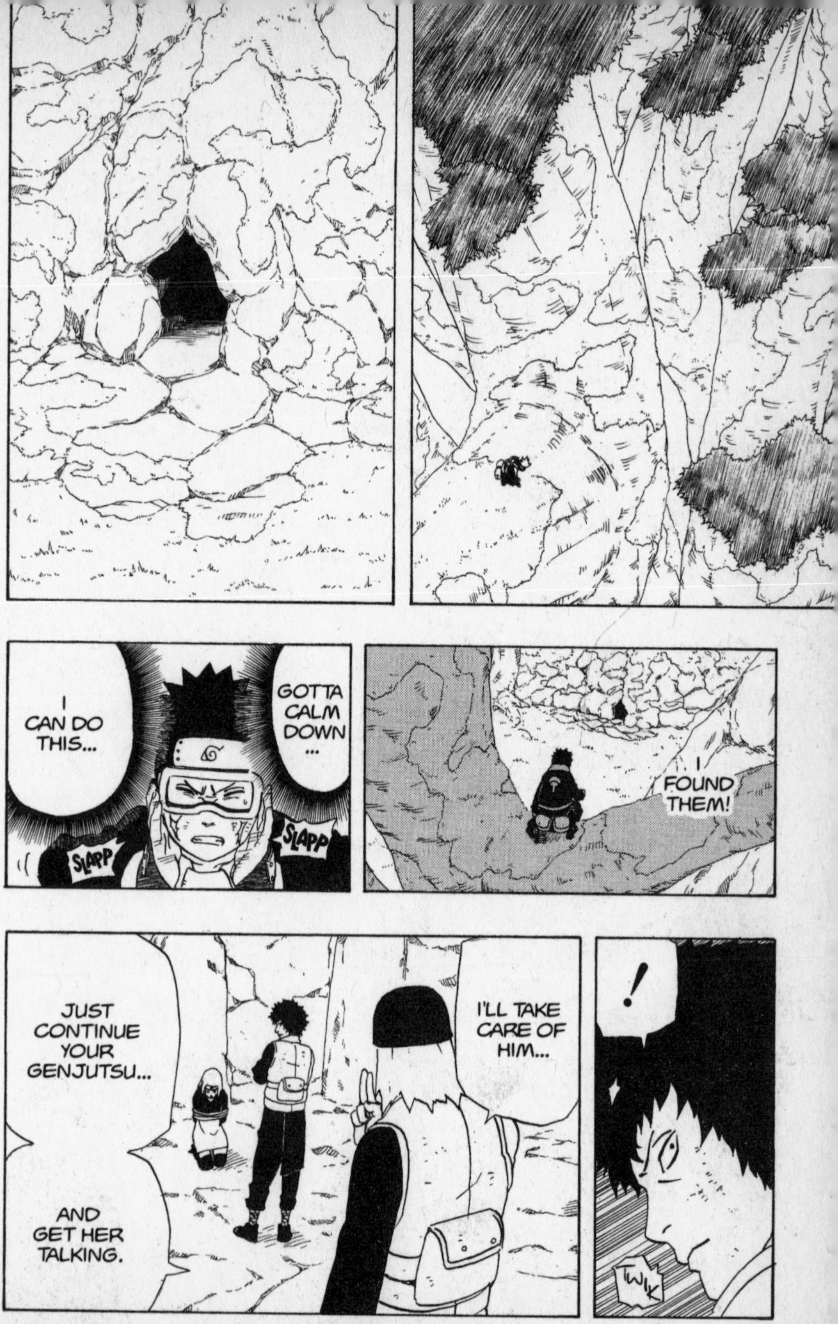
I FOUND THEM!
GOTTA CALM DOWN...
I CAN DO THIS...
SLAPP
SLAPP
!
TWIK
I'LL TAKE CARE OF HIM...
JUST CONTINUE YOUR GENJUTSU...
AND GET HER TALKING.

READ THIS WAY

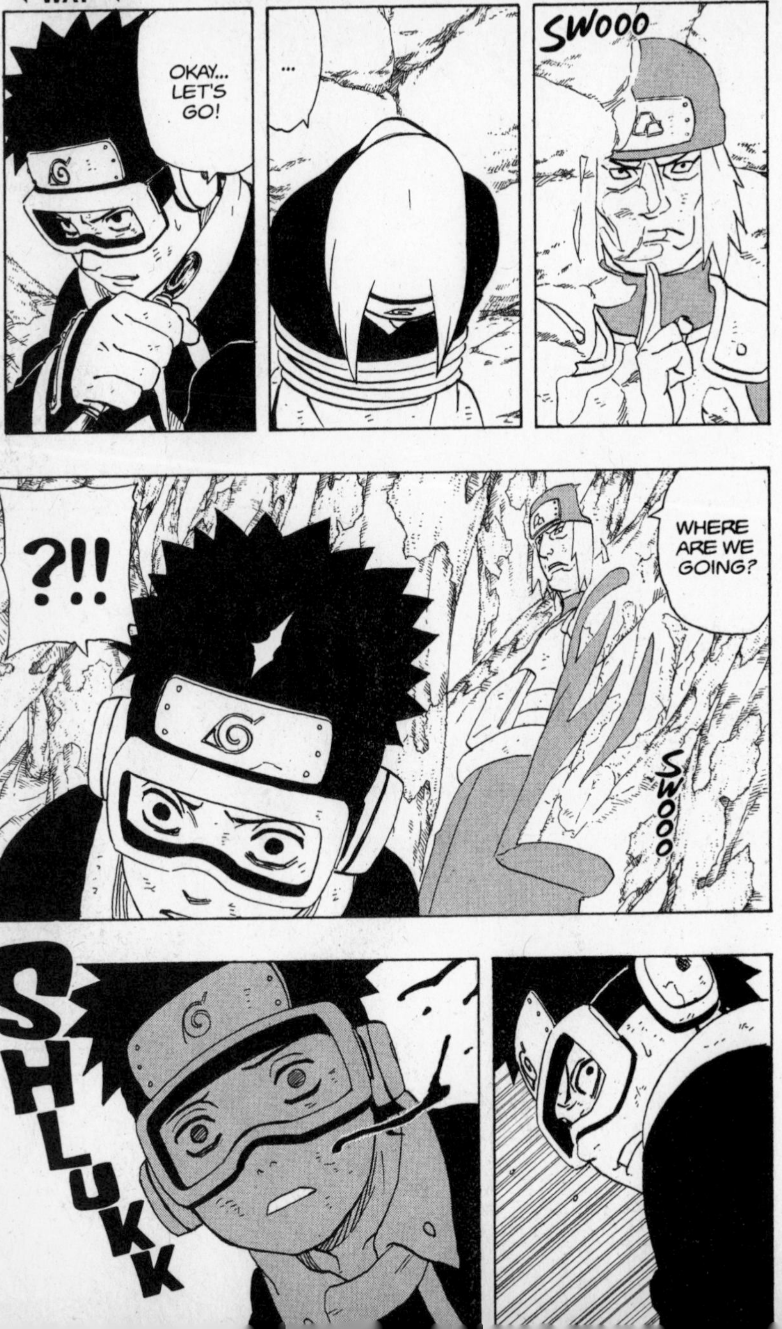
SWOOO
...
OKAY... LET'S GO!
WHERE ARE WE GOING?
SWOOO
?!!
SHLUKK

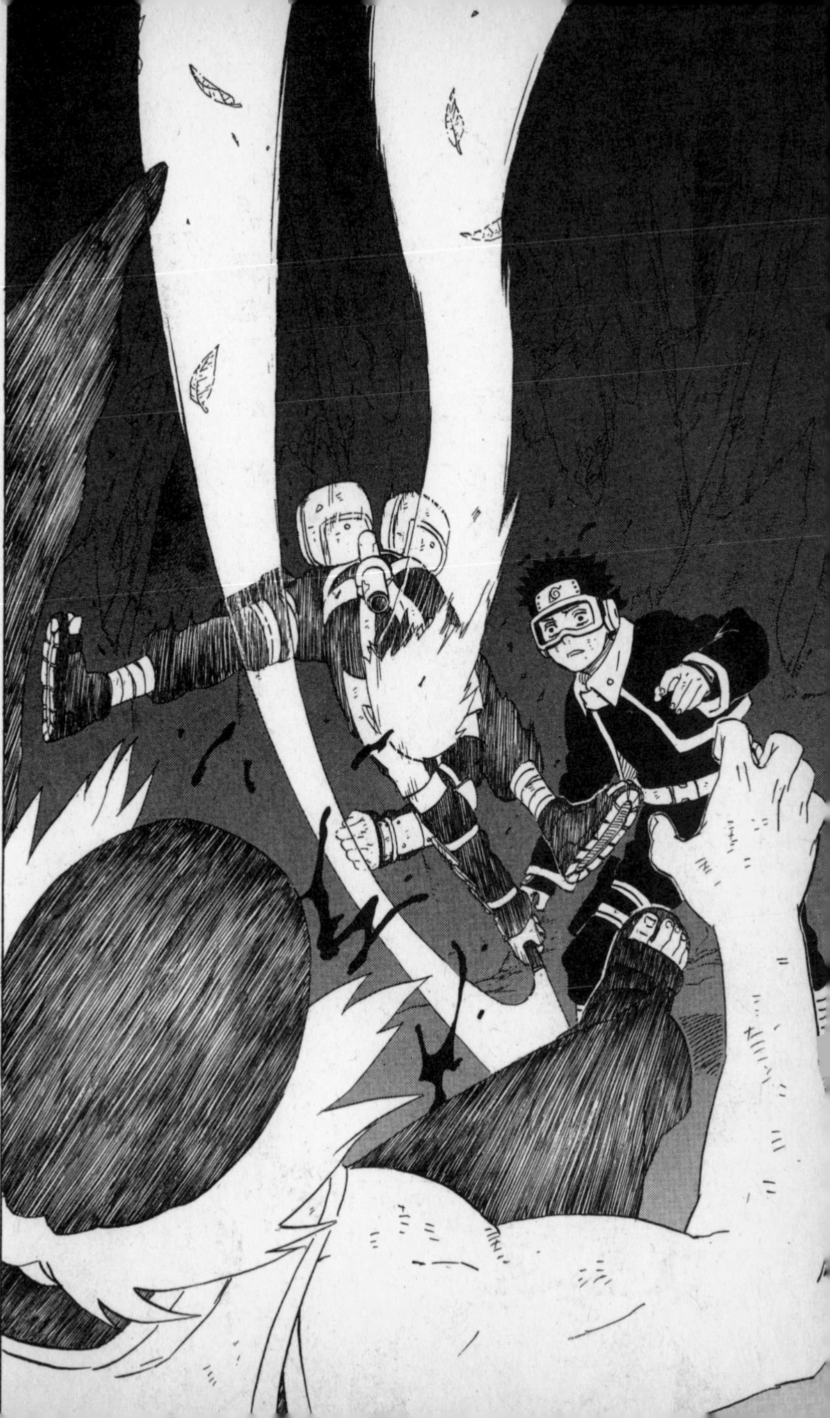

READ THIS WAY

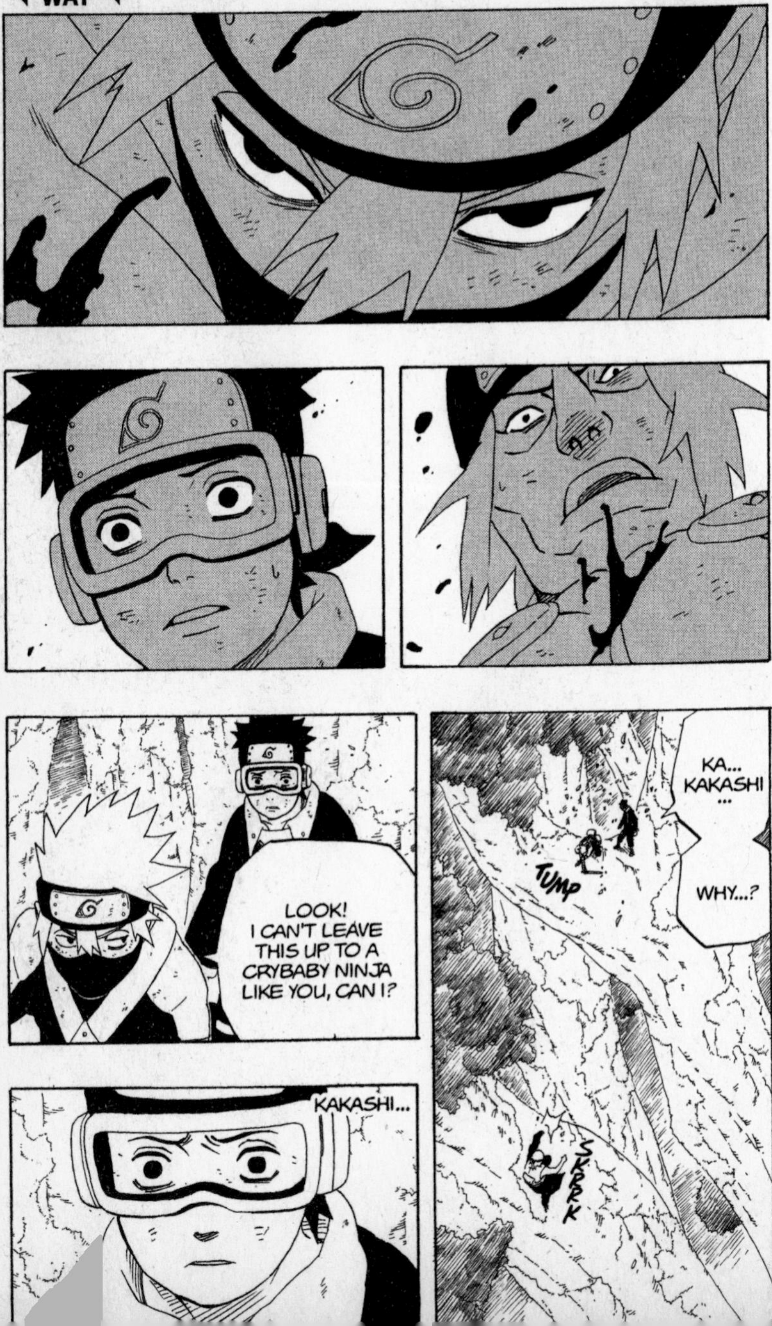
KA... KAKASHI ...
WHY...?
TUMP
SKRRK
LOOK! I CAN'T LEAVE THIS UP TO A CRYBABY NINJA LIKE YOU, CAN I?
KAKASHI...

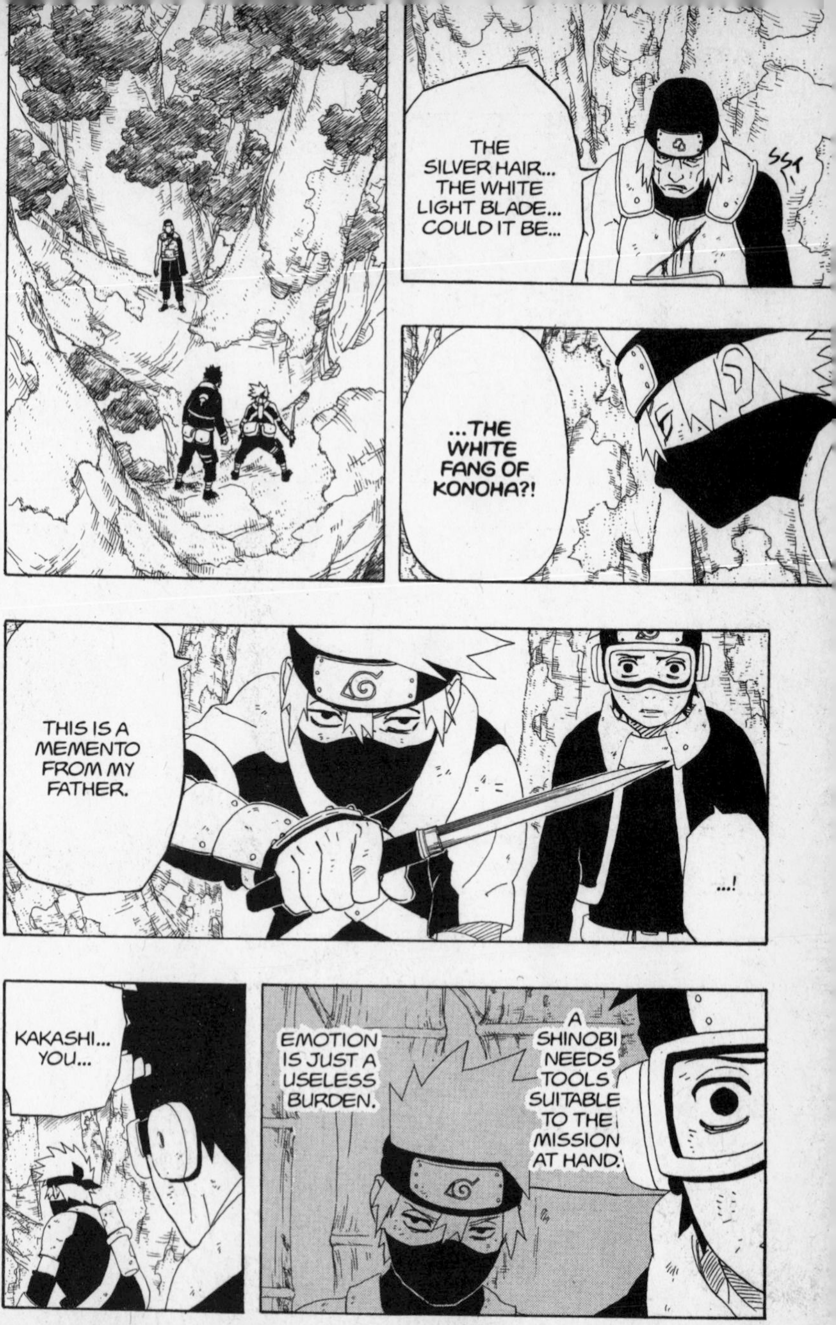
THE SILVER HAIR... THE WHITE LIGHT BLADE... COULD IT BE...
...THE WHITE FANG OF KONOHA?!
THIS IS A MEMENTO FROM MY FATHER.
...!
A SHINOBI NEEDS TOOLS SUITABLE TO THE MISSION AT HAND.
EMOTION IS JUST A USELESS BURDEN.
KAKASHI... YOU...

READ THIS WAY

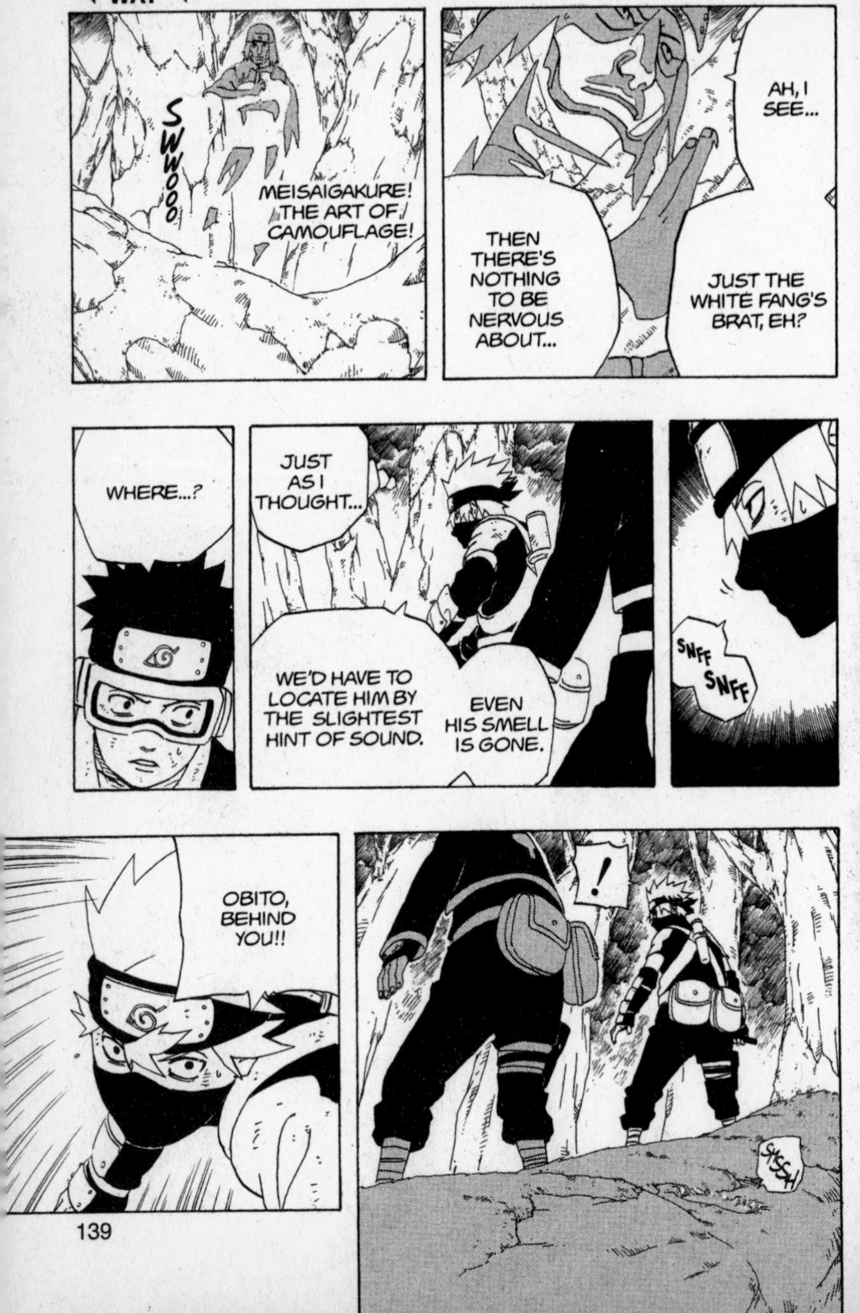
AH, I SEE...
JUST THE WHITE FANG'S BRAT, EH?
THEN THERE'S NOTHING TO BE NERVOUS ABOUT...
MEISAIGAKURE! THE ART OF CAMOUFLAGE!
SWWOOO
SNFF SNFF
JUST AS I THOUGHT...
EVEN HIS SMELL IS GONE.
WE'D HAVE TO LOCATE HIM BY THE SLIGHTEST HINT OF SOUND.
WHERE...?
!
SHSSH
OBITO, BEHIND YOU!!

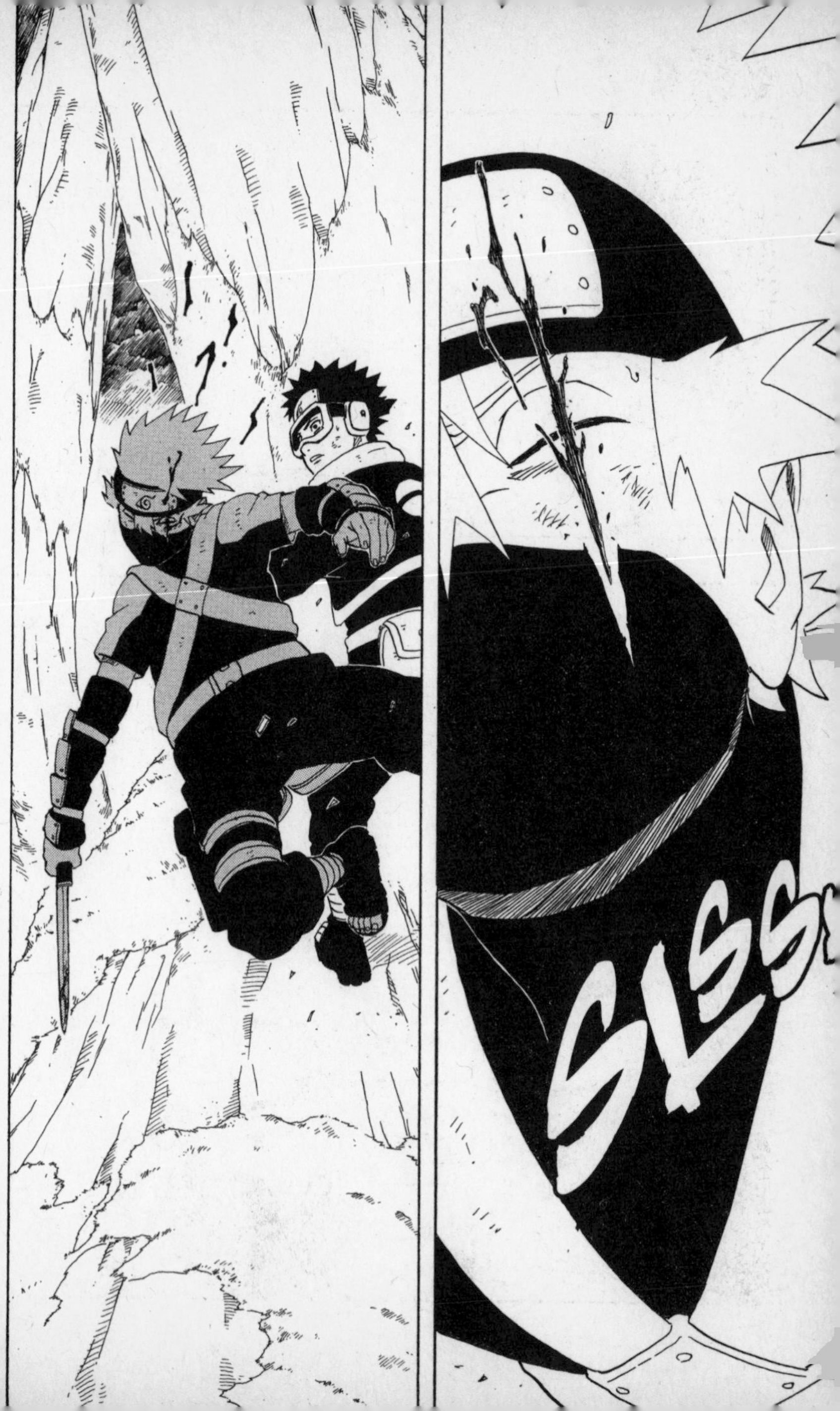
SLSS

READ THIS WAY

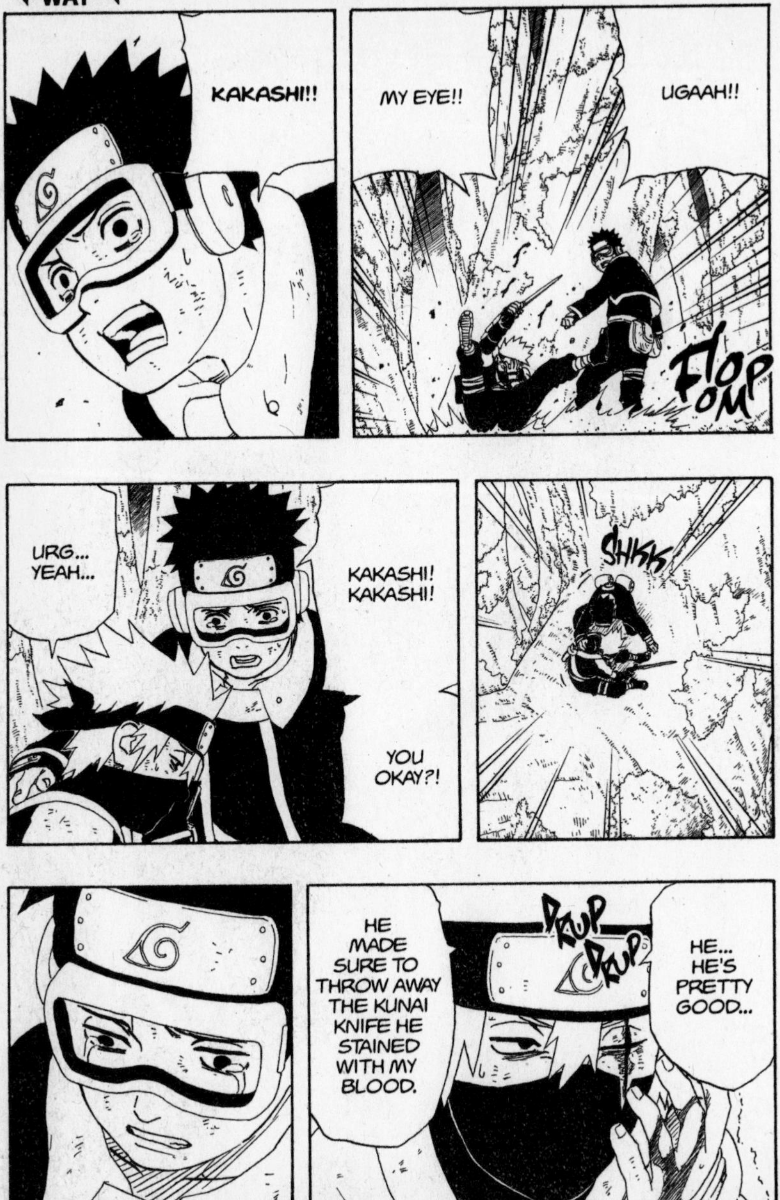
UGAAH!!
MY EYE!!
KAKASHI!!
SHKK
KAKASHI! KAKASHI!
YOU OKAY?!
URG... YEAH...
HE... HE'S PRETTY GOOD...
DRUP DRUP
HE MADE SURE TO THROW AWAY THE KUNAI KNIFE HE STAINED WITH MY BLOOD.

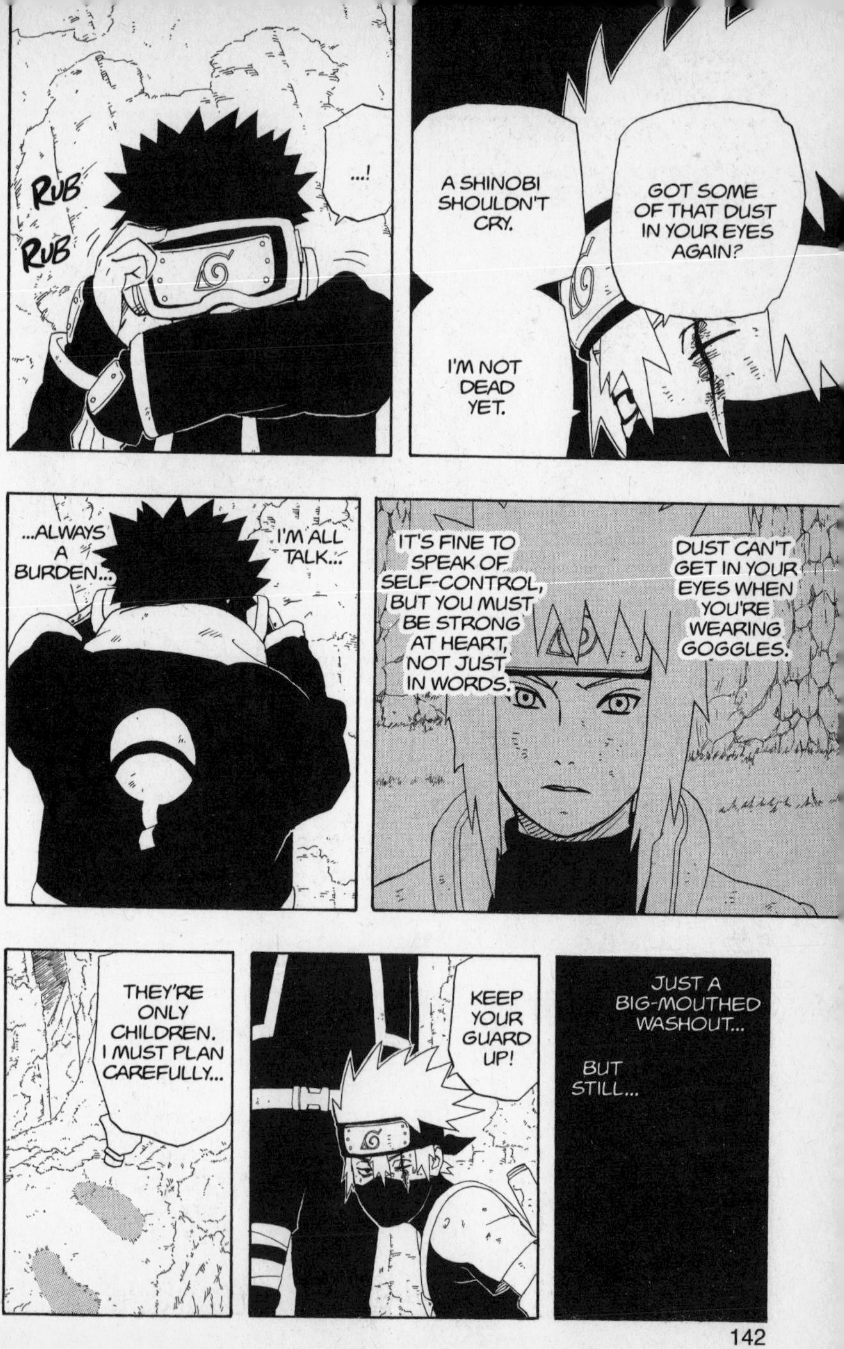
GOT SOME OF THAT DUST IN YOUR EYES AGAIN?
A SHINOBI SHOULDN'T CRY.
I'M NOT DEAD YET.
...!
RUB
RUB
DUST CAN'T GET IN YOUR EYES WHEN YOU'RE WEARING GOGGLES.
IT'S FINE TO SPEAK OF SELF-CONTROL, BUT YOU MUST BE STRONG AT HEART, NOT JUST IN WORDS.
I'M ALL TALK...
...ALWAYS A BURDEN...
JUST A BIG-MOUTHED WASHOUT...
BUT STILL...
KEEP YOUR GUARD UP!
THEY'RE ONLY CHILDREN. I MUST PLAN CAREFULLY...

READ THIS WAY

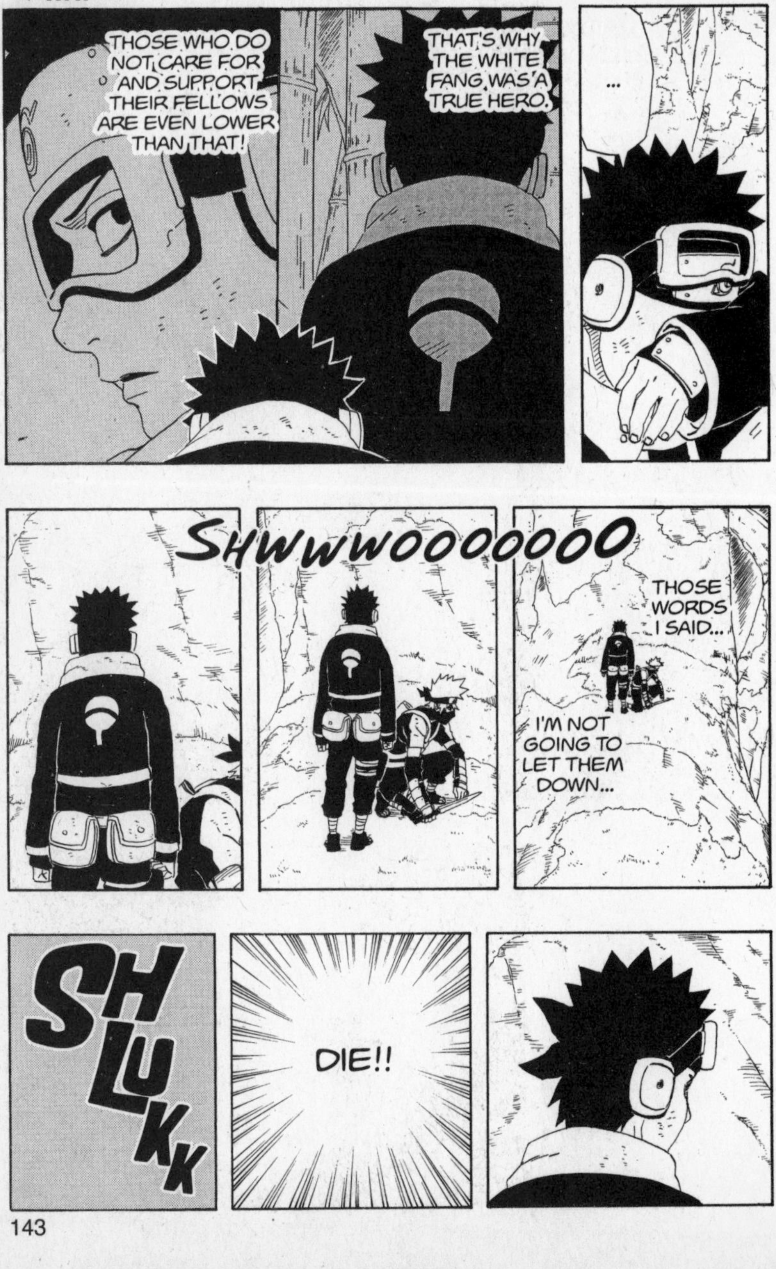
...
THAT'S WHY THE WHITE FANG WAS A TRUE HERO.
THOSE WHO DO NOT CARE FOR AND SUPPORT THEIR FELLOWS ARE EVEN LOWER THAN THAT!
THOSE WORDS I SAID...
I'M NOT GOING TO LET THEM DOWN...
SHWWWOOOOOOO
DIE!!
SHLUKK

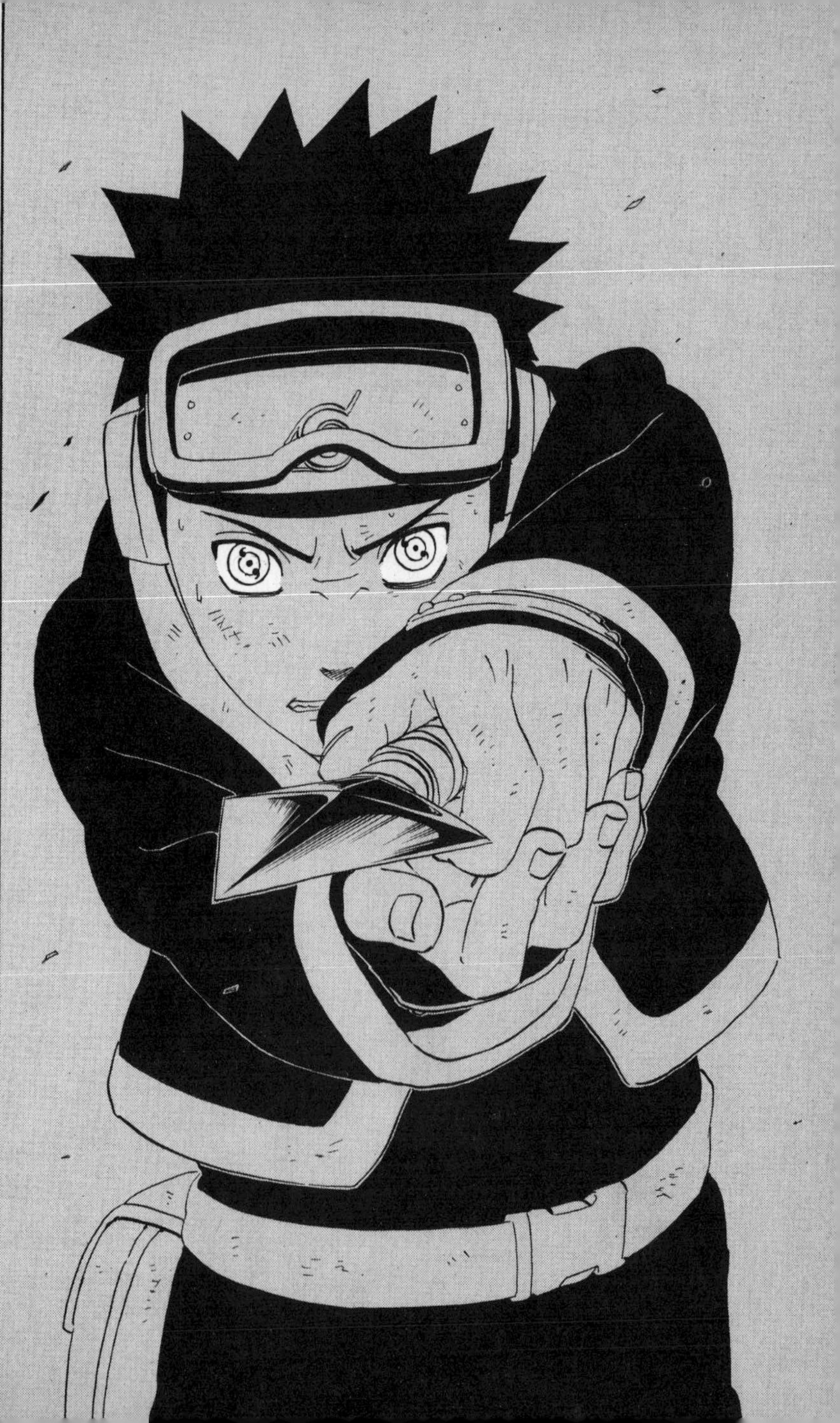

READ THIS WAY

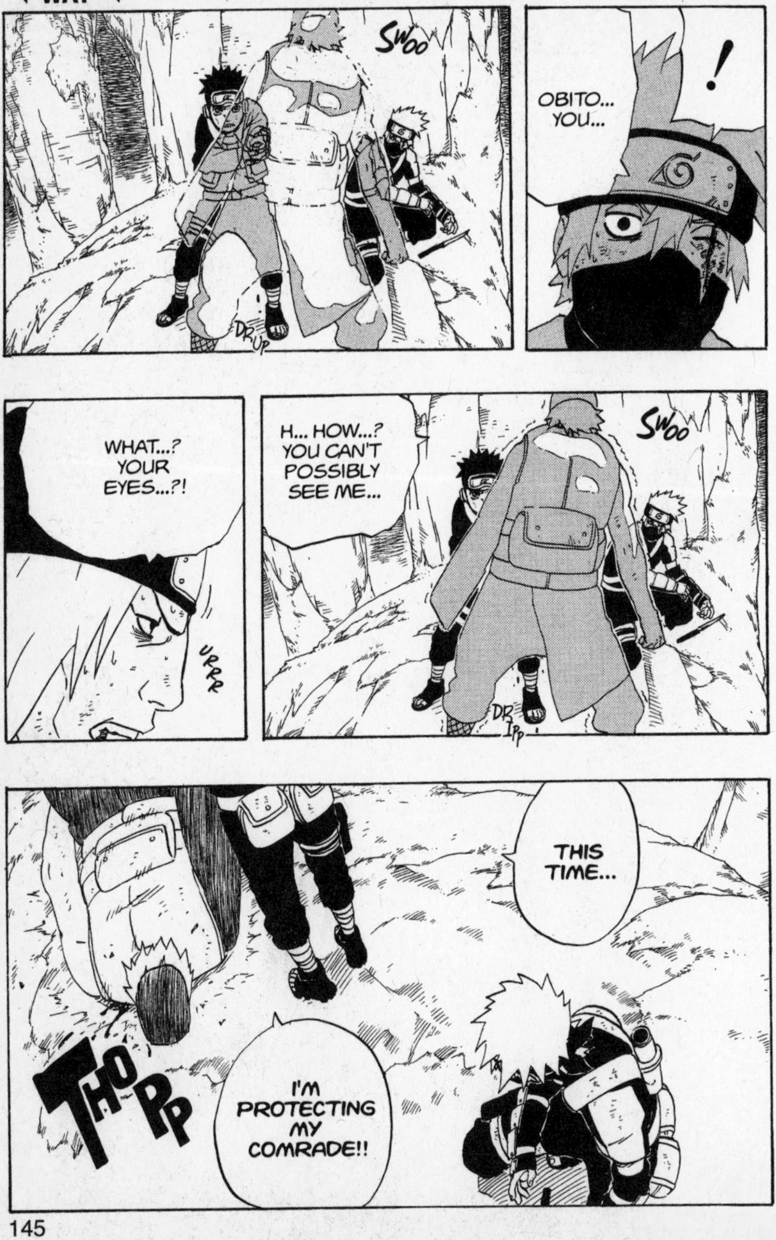
!
OBITO... YOU...
SWOO
DRUP
H... HOW...? YOU CAN'T POSSIBLY SEE ME...
SWOO
DRIPP
WHAT...? YOUR EYES...?!
URRR
THIS TIME...
I'M PROTECTING MY COMRADE!!
THOPP

NARUTO™

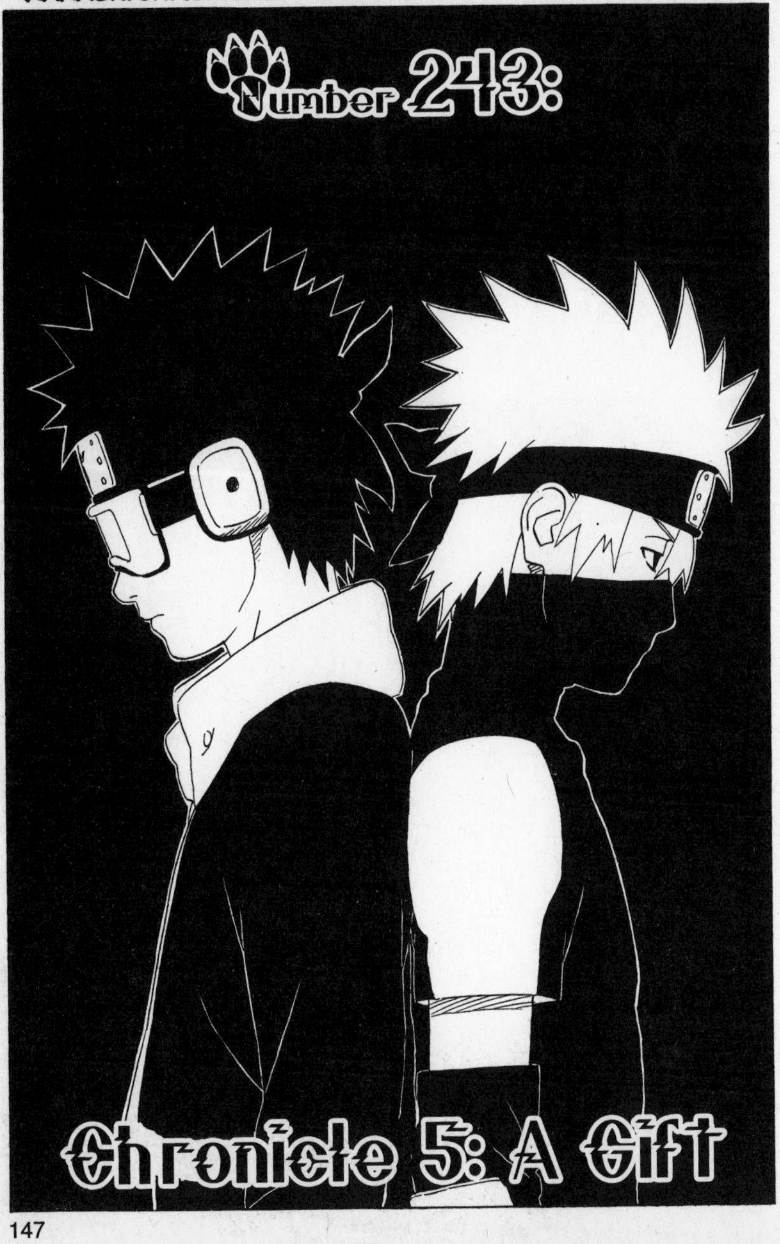
Number 243:
Chronicle 5: A Gift

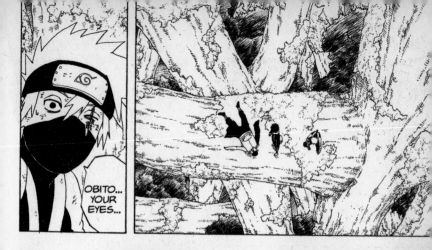

OBITO...
YOUR EYES...

I CAN SEE CHAKRA!

YEAH...

SHARINGAN...

YEAH...

MY EYE IS GONE, OBITO...

SHFF SHFF SHFF

KAKASHI?!!

...

UGH!

...!!

THROBB

148

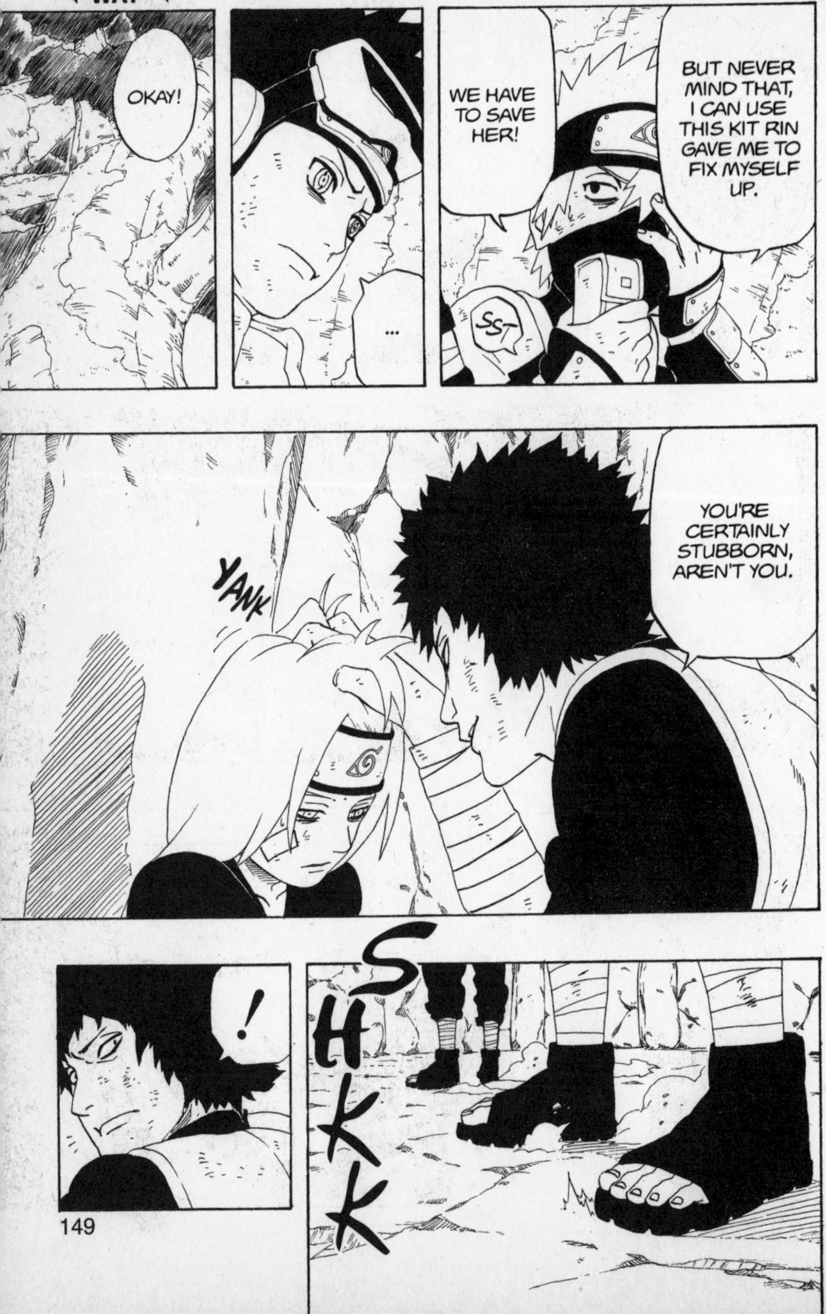
BUT NEVER MIND THAT, I CAN USE THIS KIT RIN GAVE ME TO FIX MYSELF UP.
WE HAVE TO SAVE HER!
SST
...
OKAY!
YOU'RE CERTAINLY STUBBORN, AREN'T YOU.
YANK
SHKKK
!

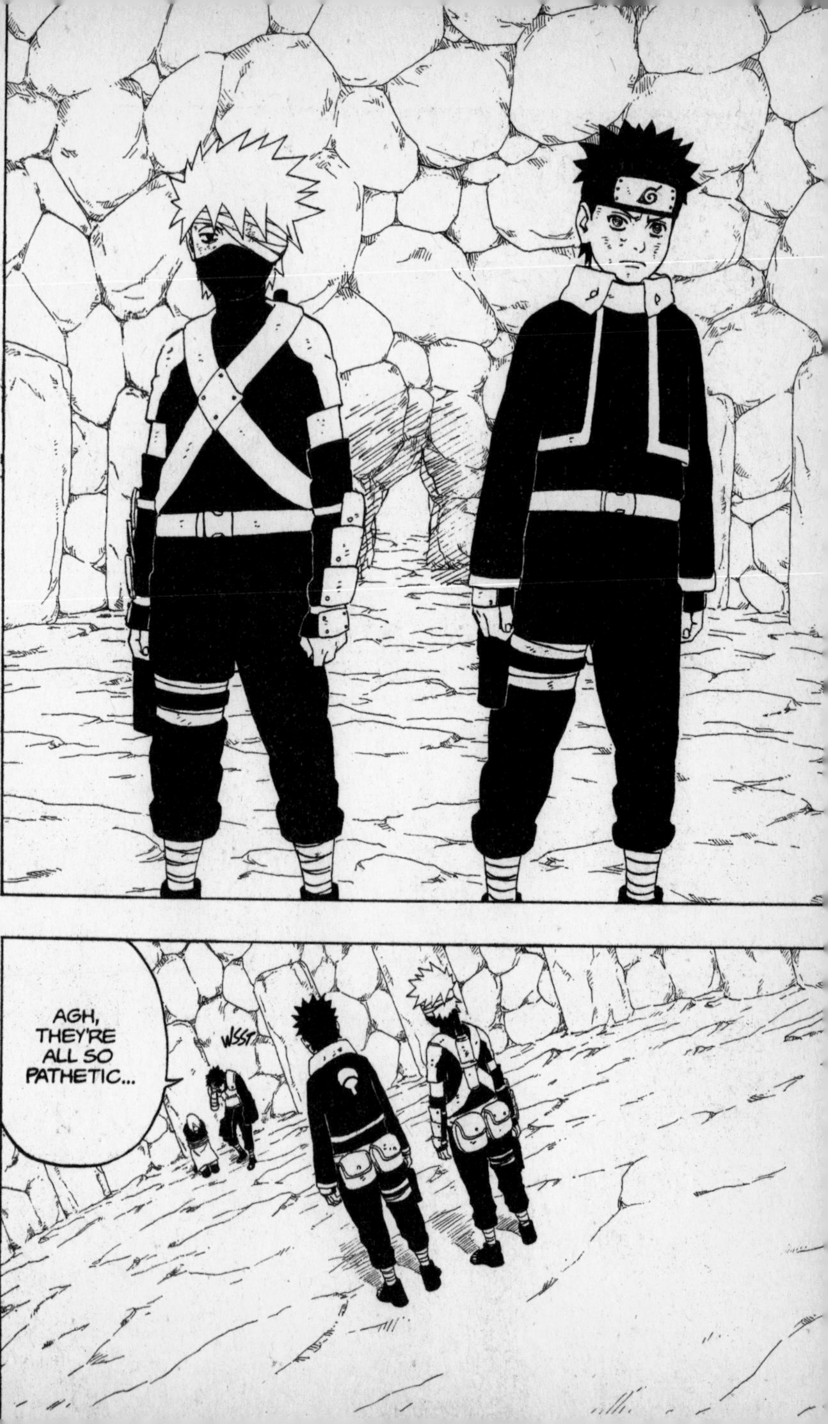
WSST
AGH, THEY'RE ALL SO PATHETIC...

READ THIS WAY

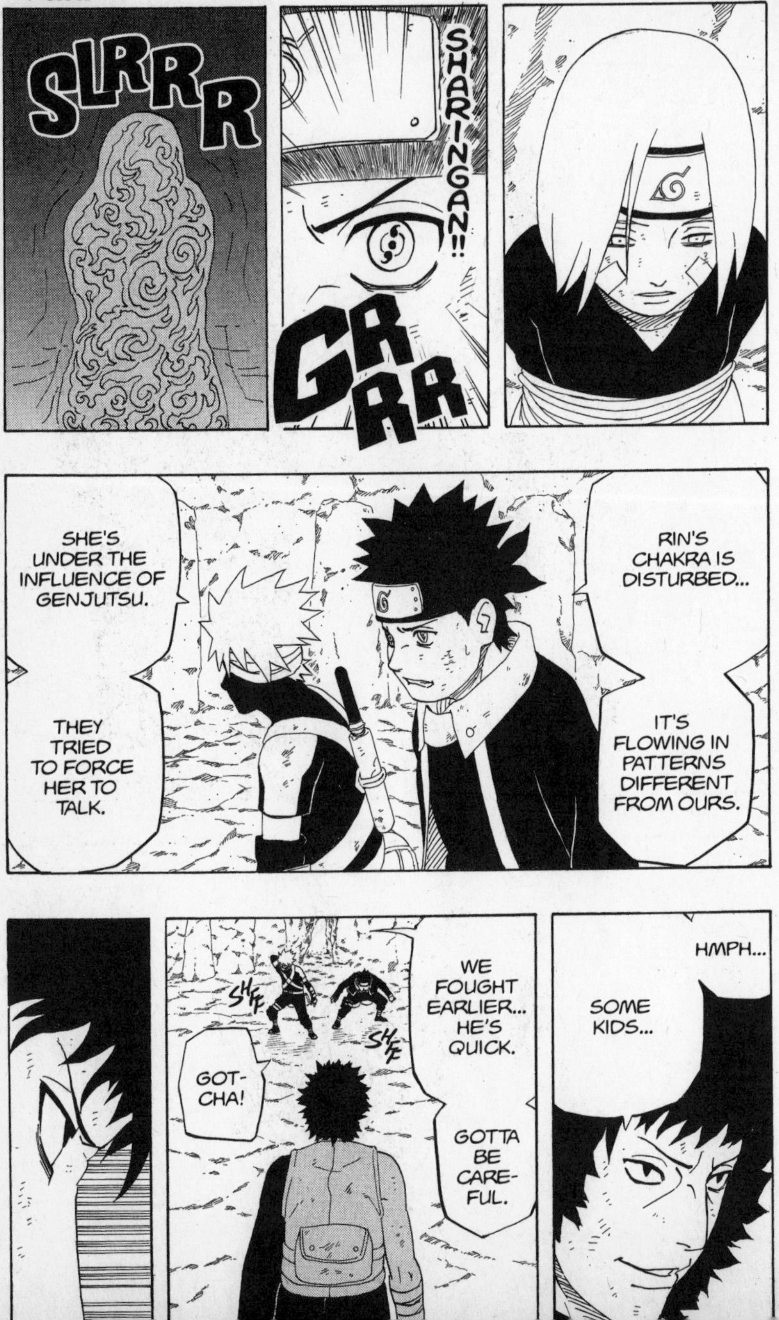
SHARINGAN!!
GRRR
SLRRR
RIN'S CHAKRA IS DISTURBED...
IT'S FLOWING IN PATTERNS DIFFERENT FROM OURS.
SHE'S UNDER THE INFLUENCE OF GENJUTSU.
THEY TRIED TO FORCE HER TO TALK.
HMPH...
SOME KIDS...
WE FOUGHT EARLIER... HE'S QUICK.
GOTTA BE CARE-FUL.
SHFF
SHFF
GOT-CHA!

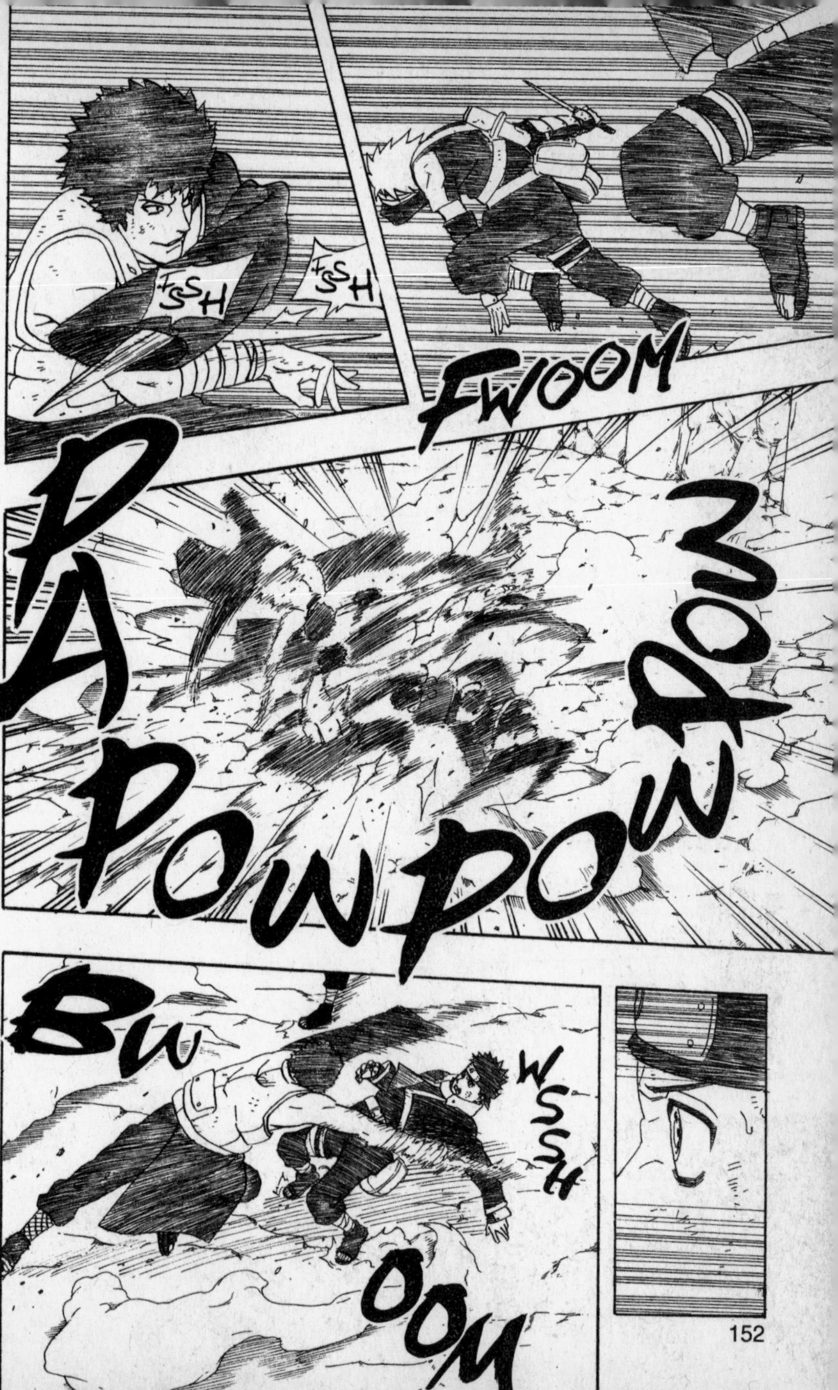
FWOOM
FSSH
FSSH
PA
POW
POW
POW
WSSH
BU
OOM

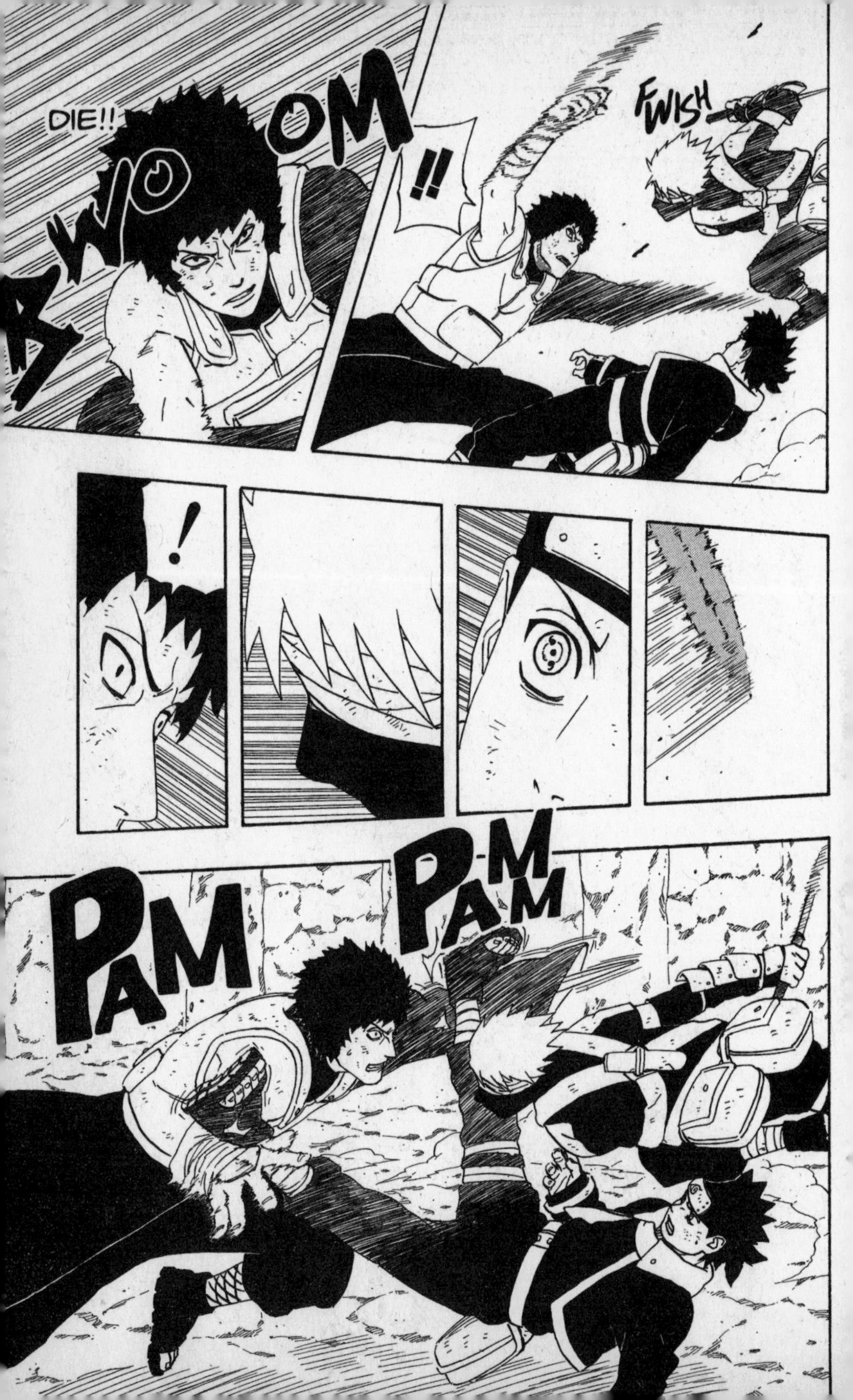
FWISH
!!
DIE!!
BWOOM
!
PAMM
PAM

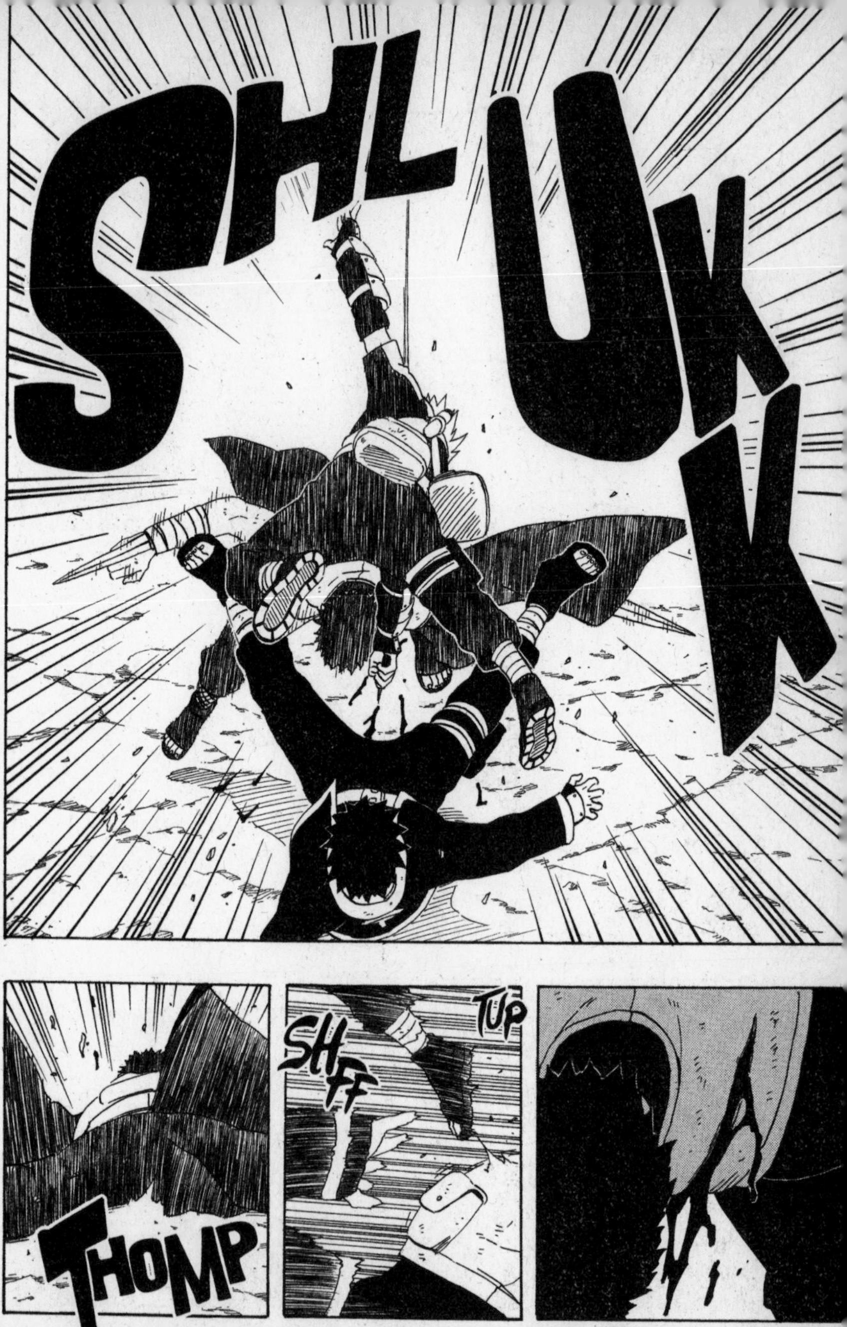
SHLUKK
TUP
SHFF
THOMP

READ THIS WAY

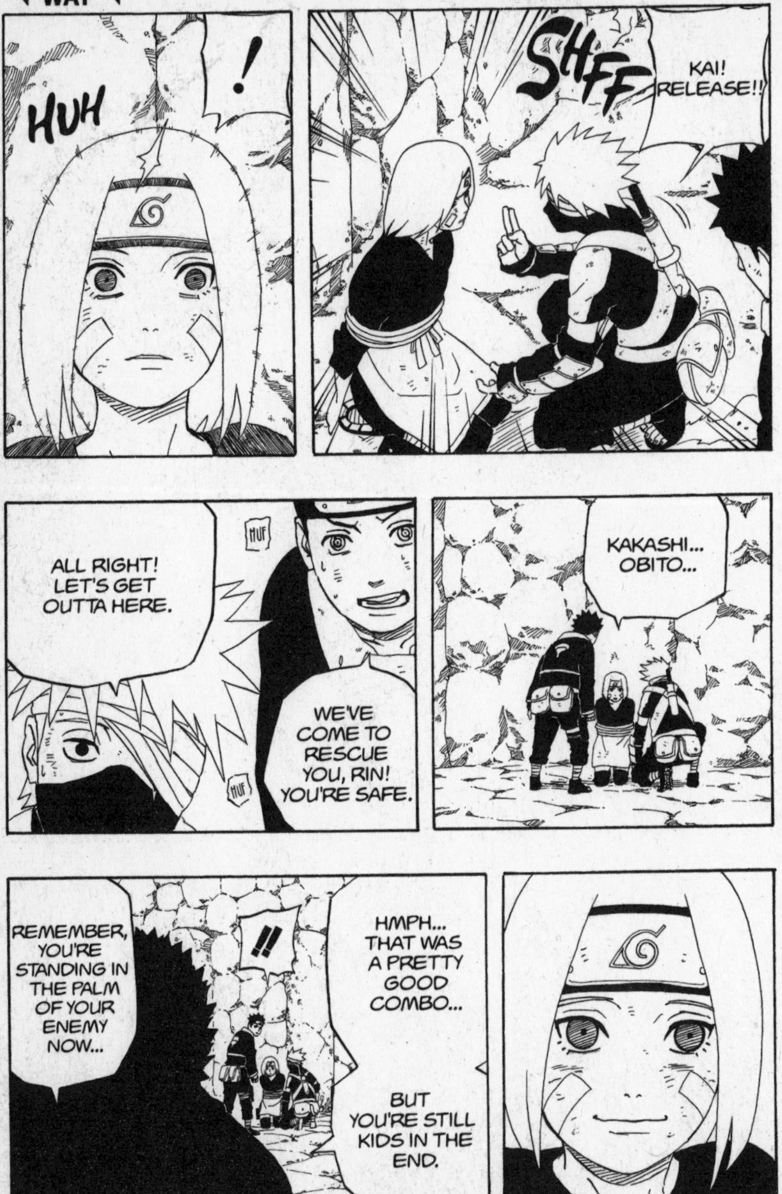
SHFF
KAI! RELEASE!!
!
HUH
KAKASHI... OBITO...
HUF
ALL RIGHT! LET'S GET OUTTA HERE.
WE'VE COME TO RESCUE YOU, RIN! YOU'RE SAFE.
HUF
HMPH... THAT WAS A PRETTY GOOD COMBO...
BUT YOU'RE STILL KIDS IN THE END.
!!
REMEMBER, YOU'RE STANDING IN THE PALM OF YOUR ENEMY NOW...

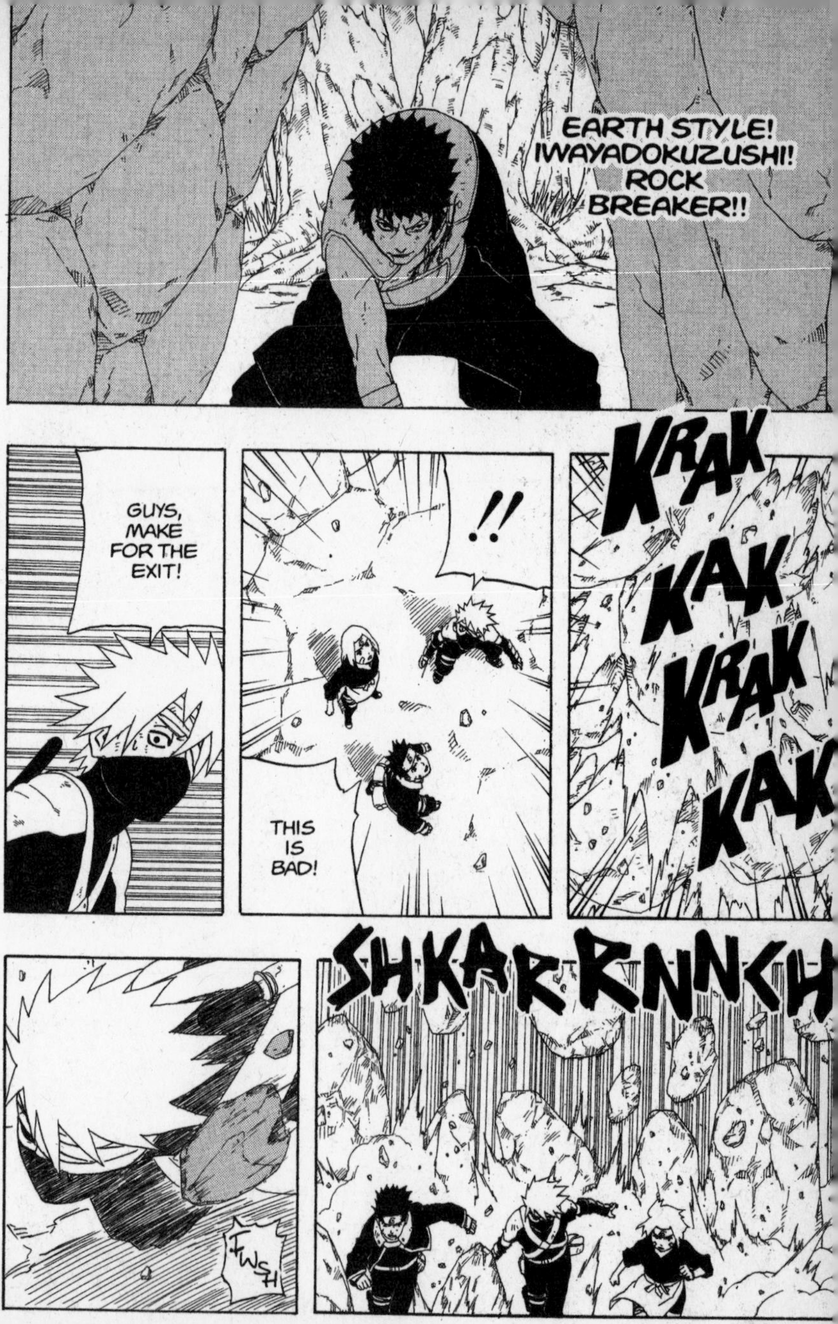
EARTH STYLE! IWAYADOKUZUSHI! ROCK BREAKER!!
KRAK
KAK
KRAK
KAK
!!
THIS IS BAD!
GUYS, MAKE FOR THE EXIT!
SHKARRNNCH
FWSH

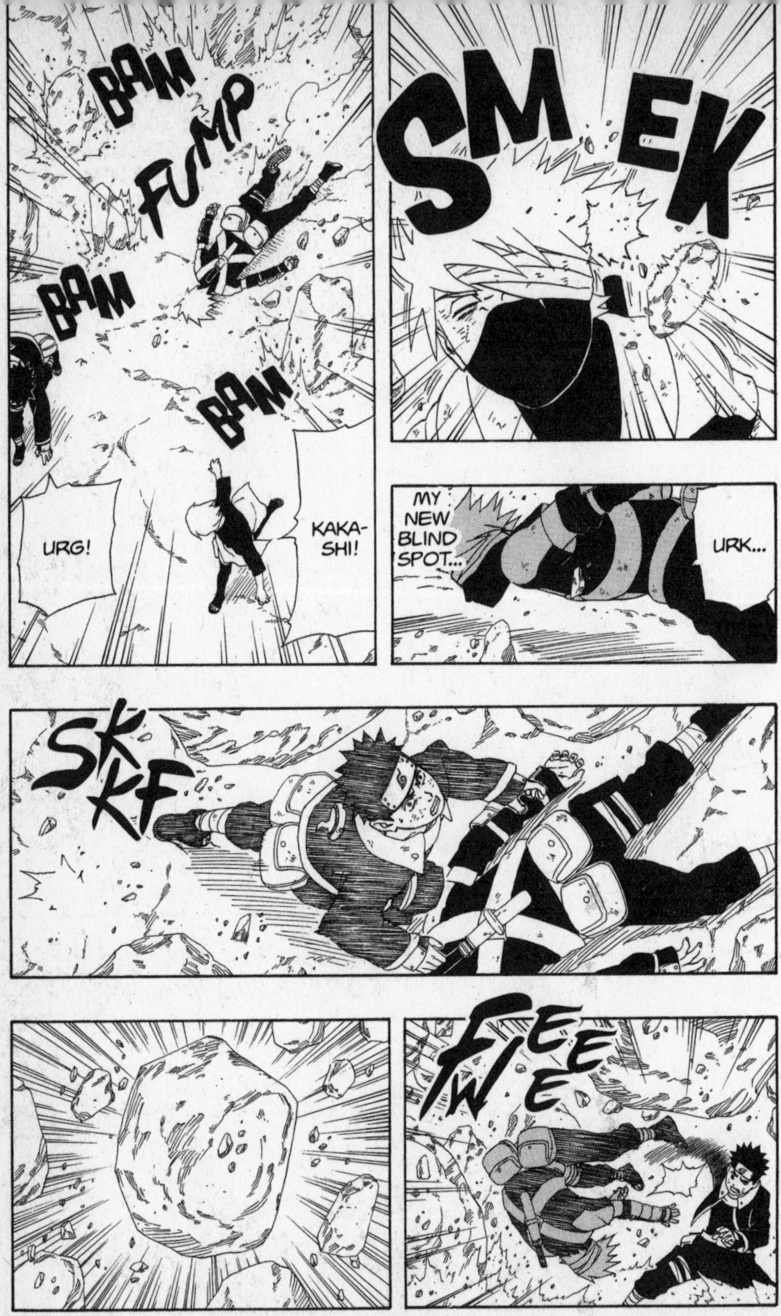
SMEK
URK...
MY NEW BLIND SPOT...
BAM
FUMP
BAM
BAM
KAKA-SHI!
URG!
SKKF
FWEEE

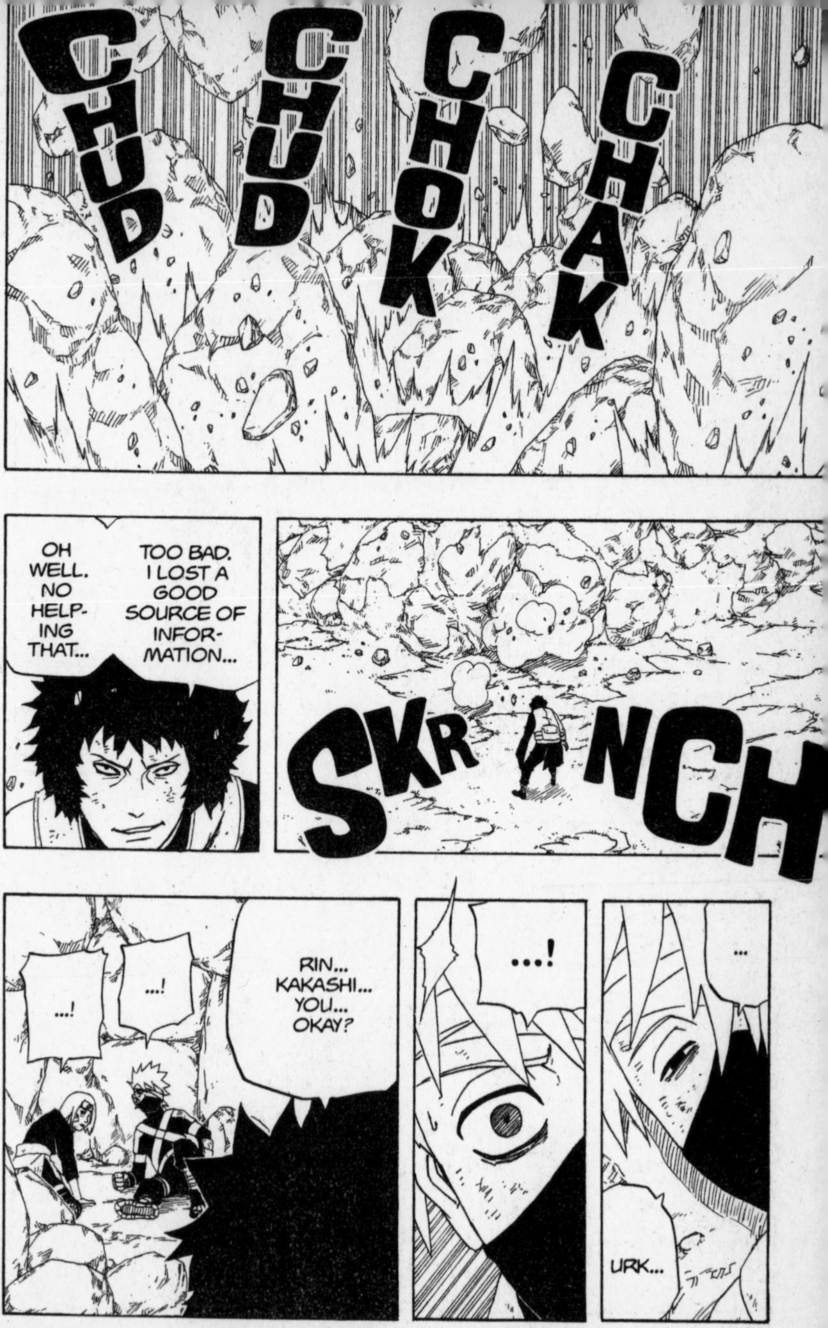
CHAK
CHOK
CHUD
CHUD
SKRNCH
TOO BAD. I LOST A GOOD SOURCE OF INFOR-MATION...
OH WELL. NO HELP-ING THAT...
...
URK...
...!
RIN... KAKASHI... YOU... OKAY?
...!
...!

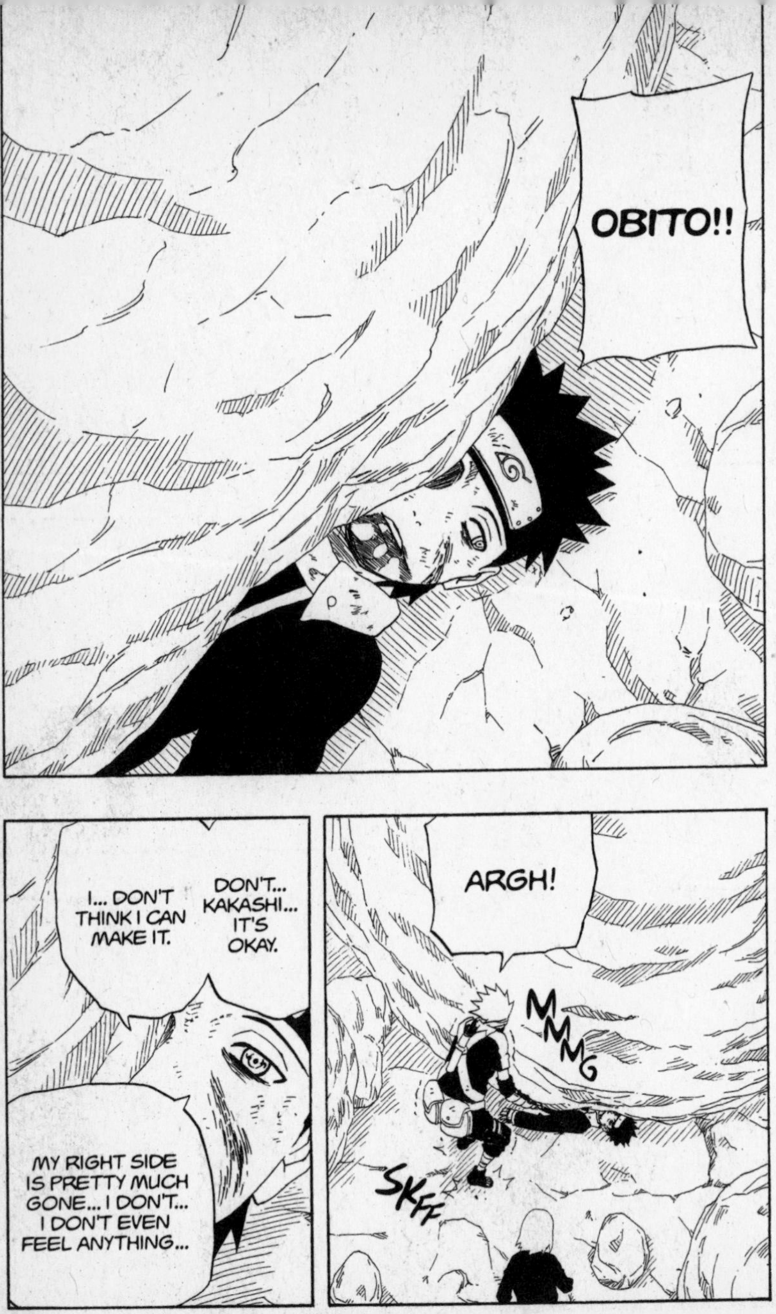
OBITO!!
ARGH!
MMMG
SKFF
DON'T... KAKASHI... IT'S OKAY.
I... DON'T THINK I CAN MAKE IT.
MY RIGHT SIDE IS PRETTY MUCH GONE... I DON'T... I DON'T EVEN FEEL ANYTHING...

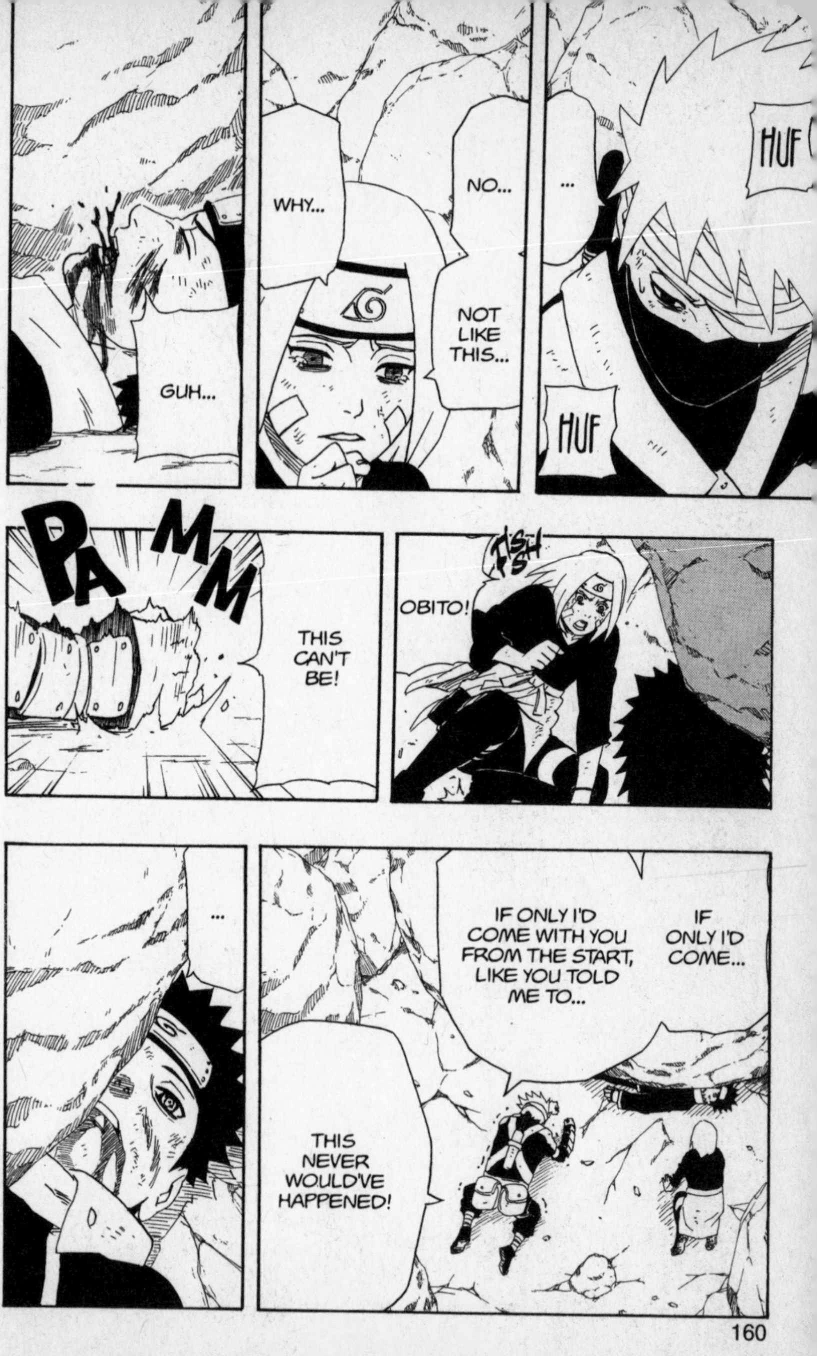
HUF
...
HUF
NO...
WHY...
NOT LIKE THIS...
GUH...
OBITO!
PAMM
THIS CAN'T BE!
IF ONLY I'D COME...
IF ONLY I'D COME WITH YOU FROM THE START, LIKE YOU TOLD ME TO...
THIS NEVER WOULD'VE HAPPENED!
...

READ THIS WAY

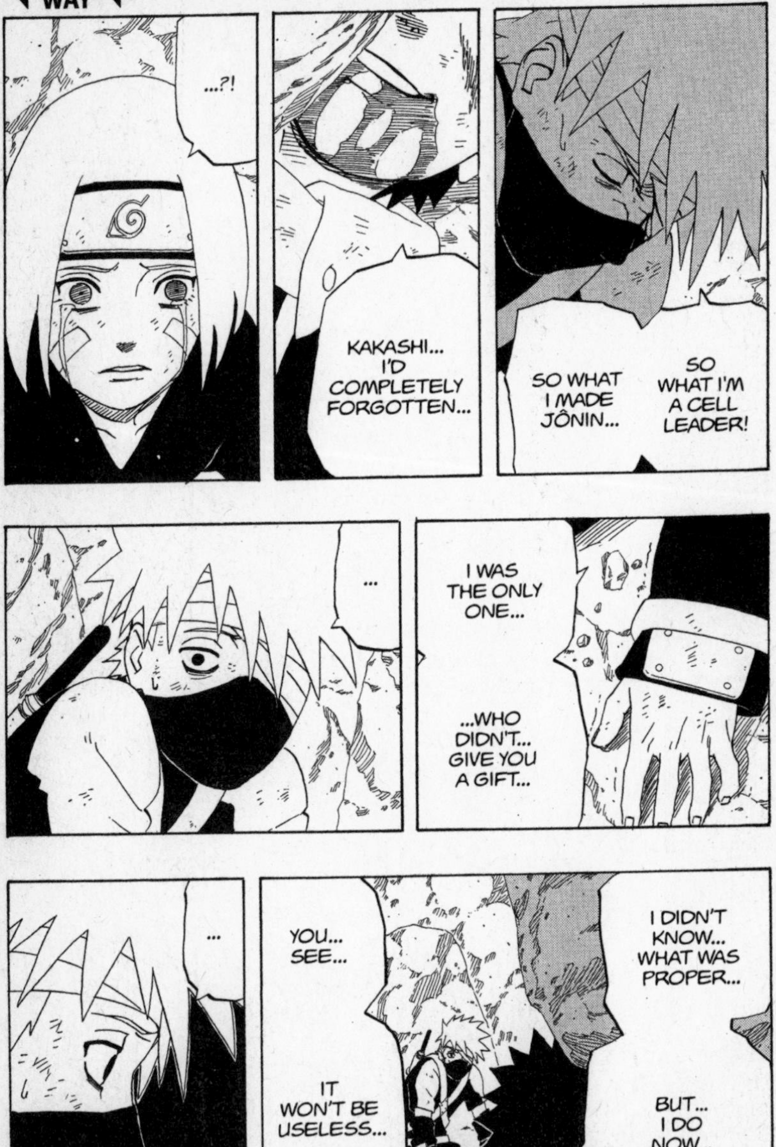

SO WHAT I'M A CELL LEADER!
SO WHAT I MADE JÔNIN...
KAKASHI... I'D COMPLETELY FORGOTTEN...
...?!
I WAS THE ONLY ONE...
...WHO DIDN'T... GIVE YOU A GIFT...
...
I DIDN'T KNOW... WHAT WAS PROPER...
YOU... SEE...
BUT... I DO NOW...
IT WON'T BE USELESS...
...

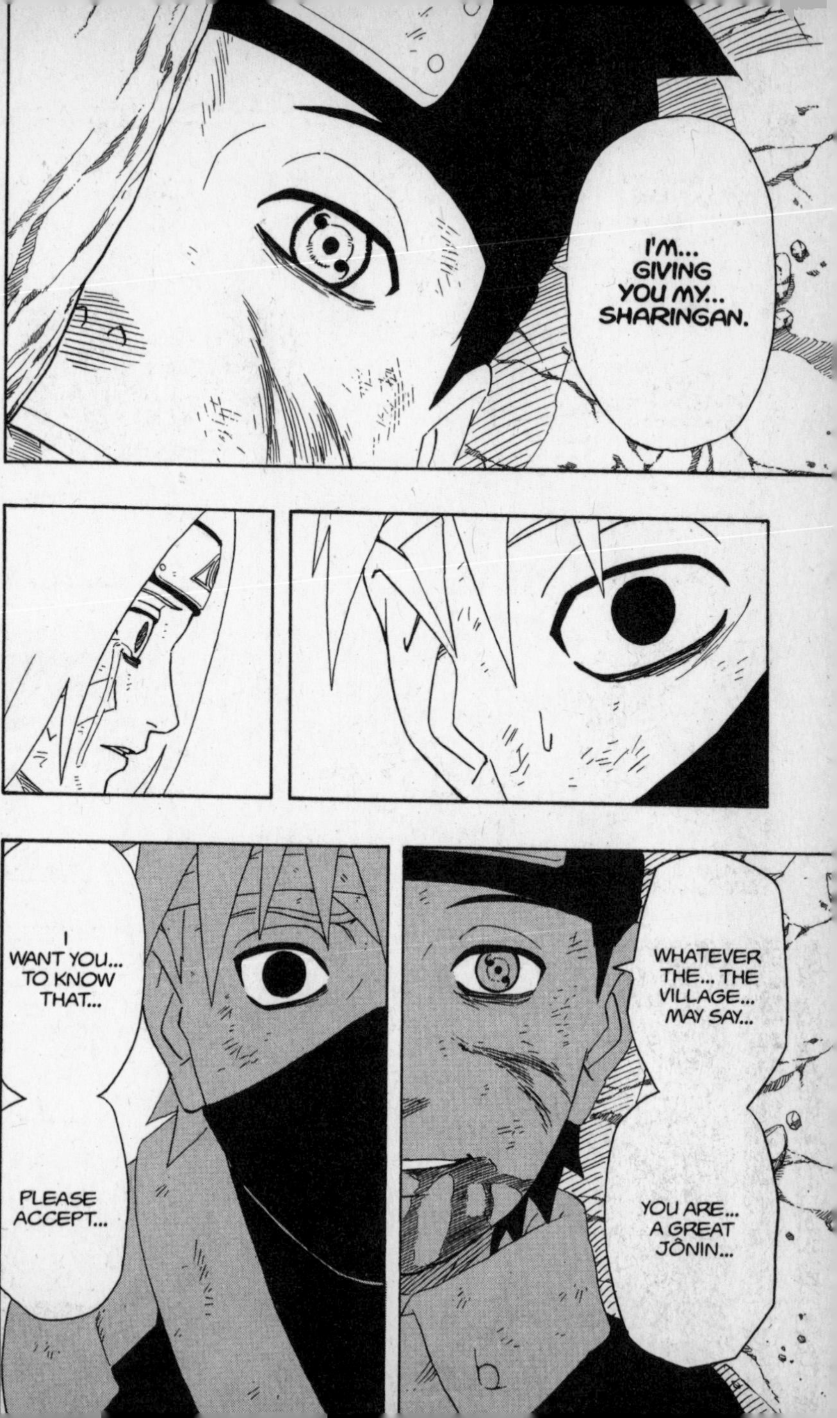
I'M... GIVING YOU MY... SHARINGAN.
WHATEVER THE... THE VILLAGE... MAY SAY...
YOU ARE... A GREAT JÔNIN...
I WANT YOU... TO KNOW THAT...
PLEASE ACCEPT...

READ THIS WAY

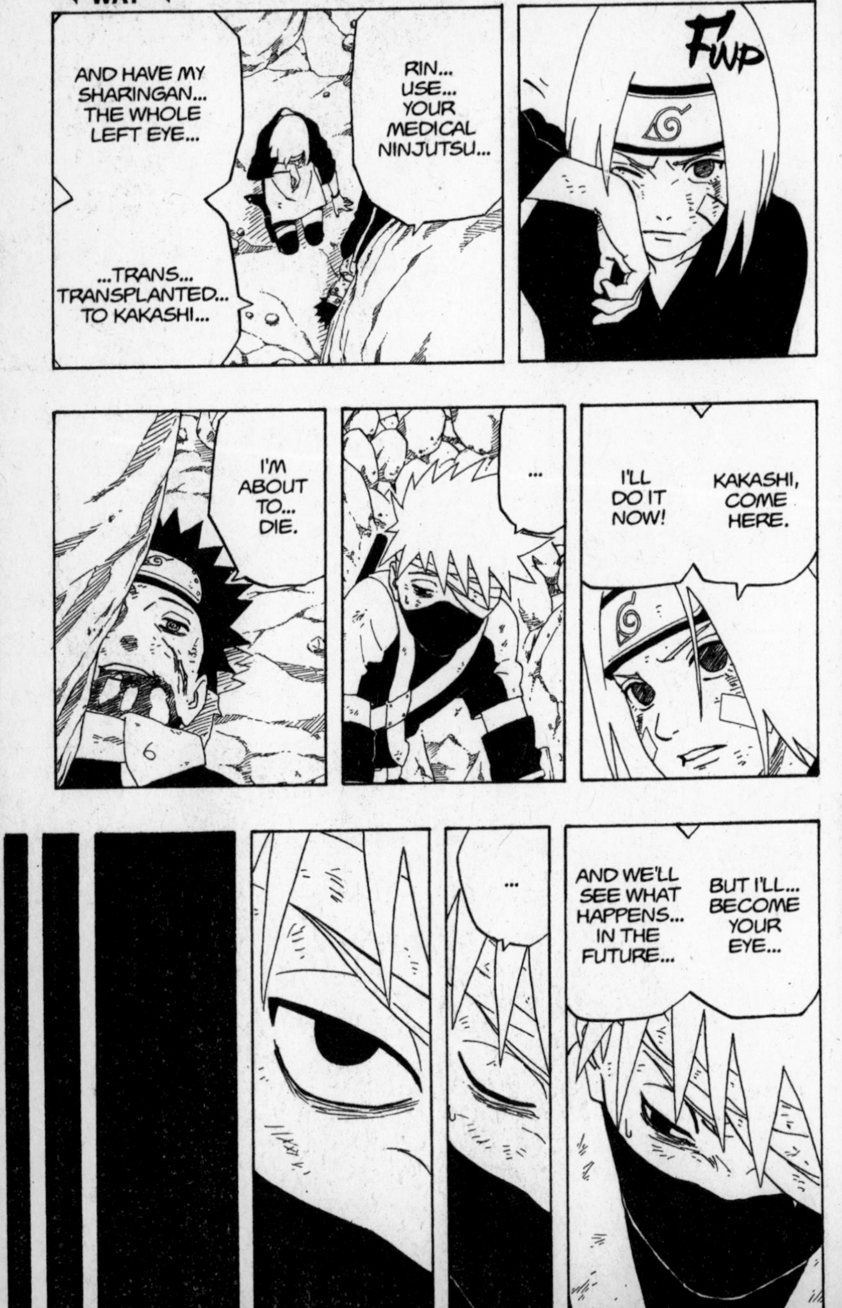
FWP
RIN... USE... YOUR MEDICAL NINJUTSU...
AND HAVE MY SHARINGAN... THE WHOLE LEFT EYE...
...TRANS... TRANSPLANTED... TO KAKASHI...
KAKASHI, COME HERE.
I'LL DO IT NOW!
...
I'M ABOUT TO... DIE.
BUT I'LL... BECOME YOUR EYE...
AND WE'LL SEE WHAT HAPPENS... IN THE FUTURE...
...

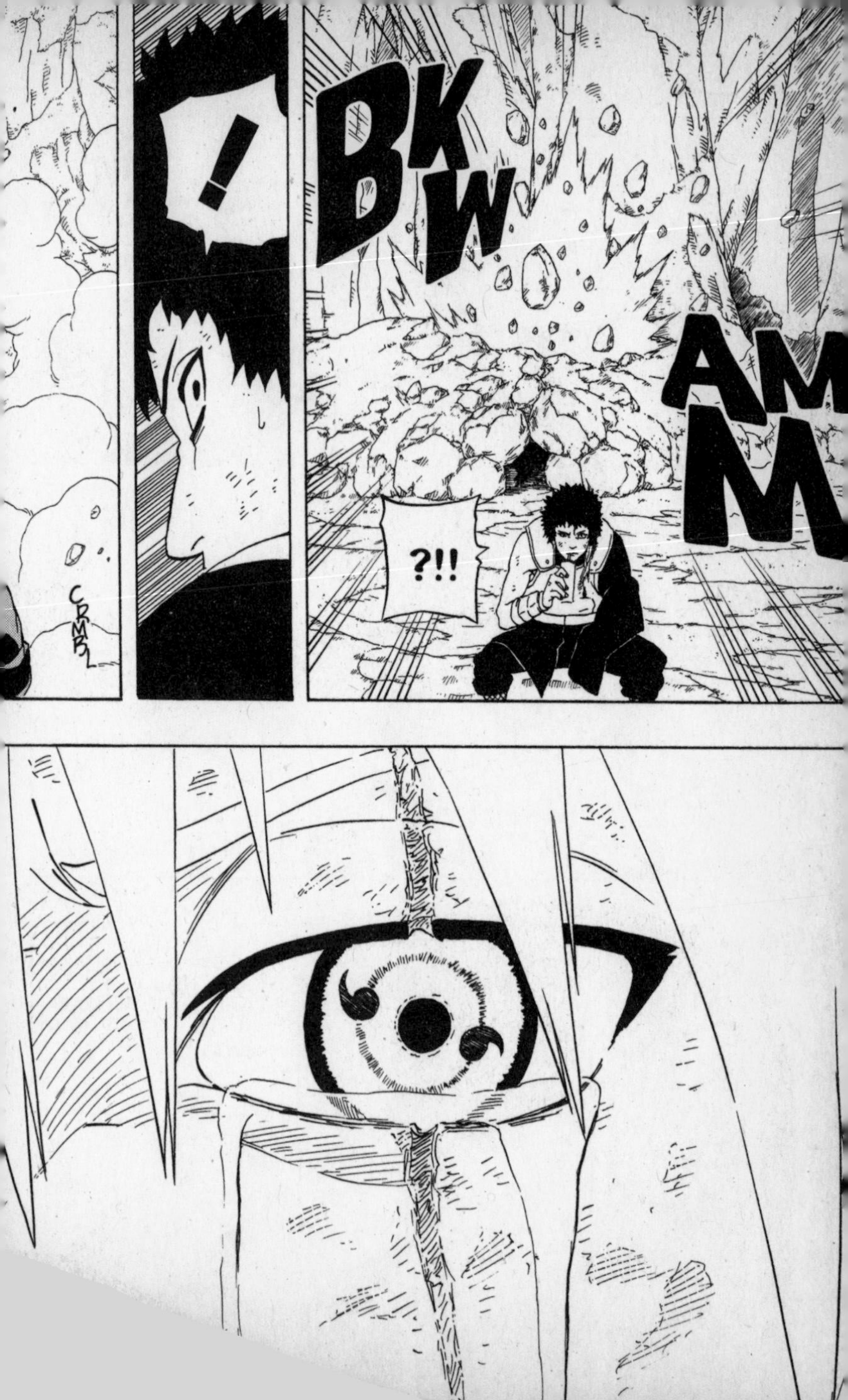
BKWAMM
?!!
!
CRMBL

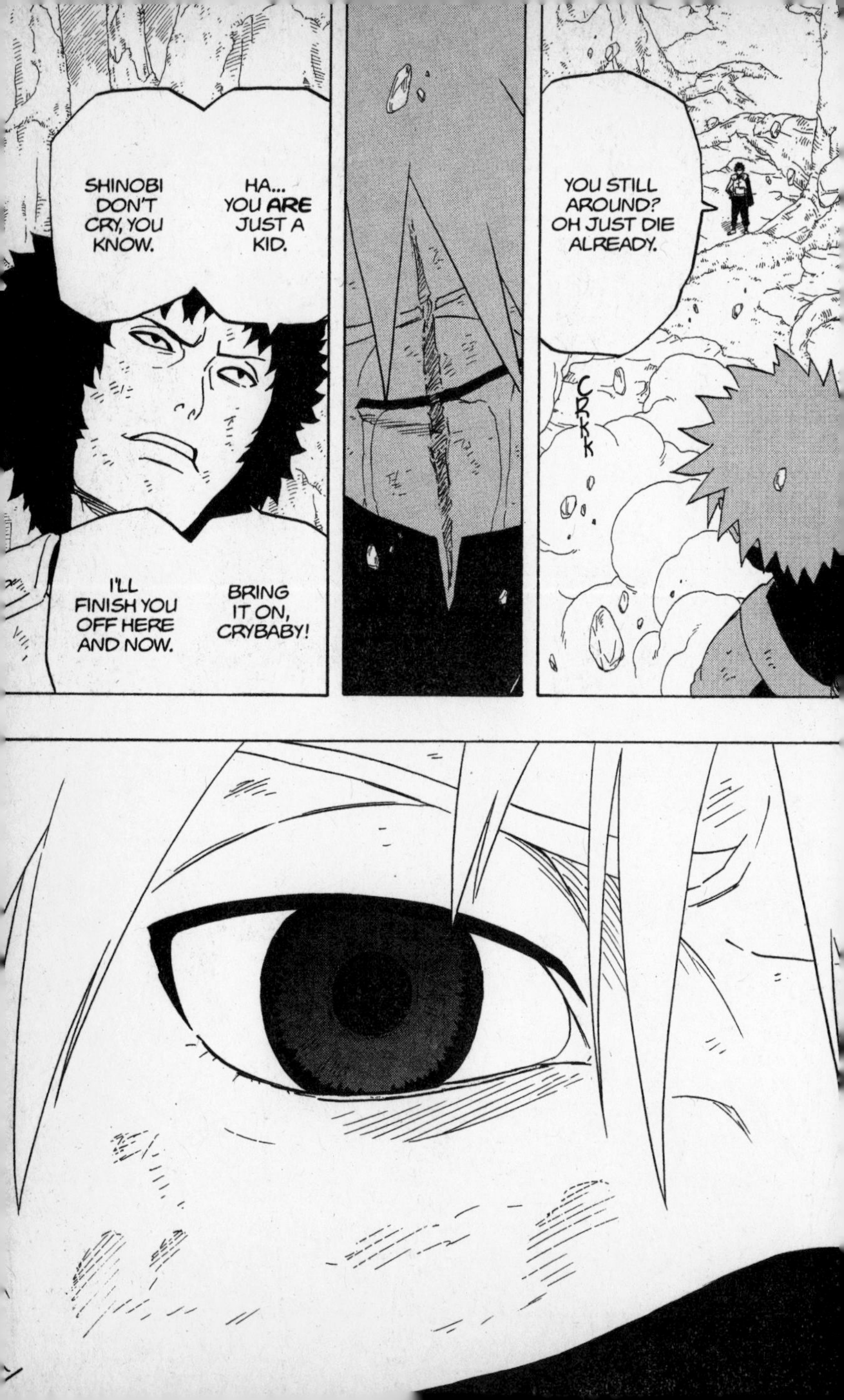
YOU STILL AROUND? OH JUST DIE ALREADY.
CRKK
HA... YOU ARE JUST A KID.
SHINOBI DON'T CRY, YOU KNOW.
BRING IT ON, CRYBABY!
I'LL FINISH YOU OFF HERE AND NOW.

NARUTO™

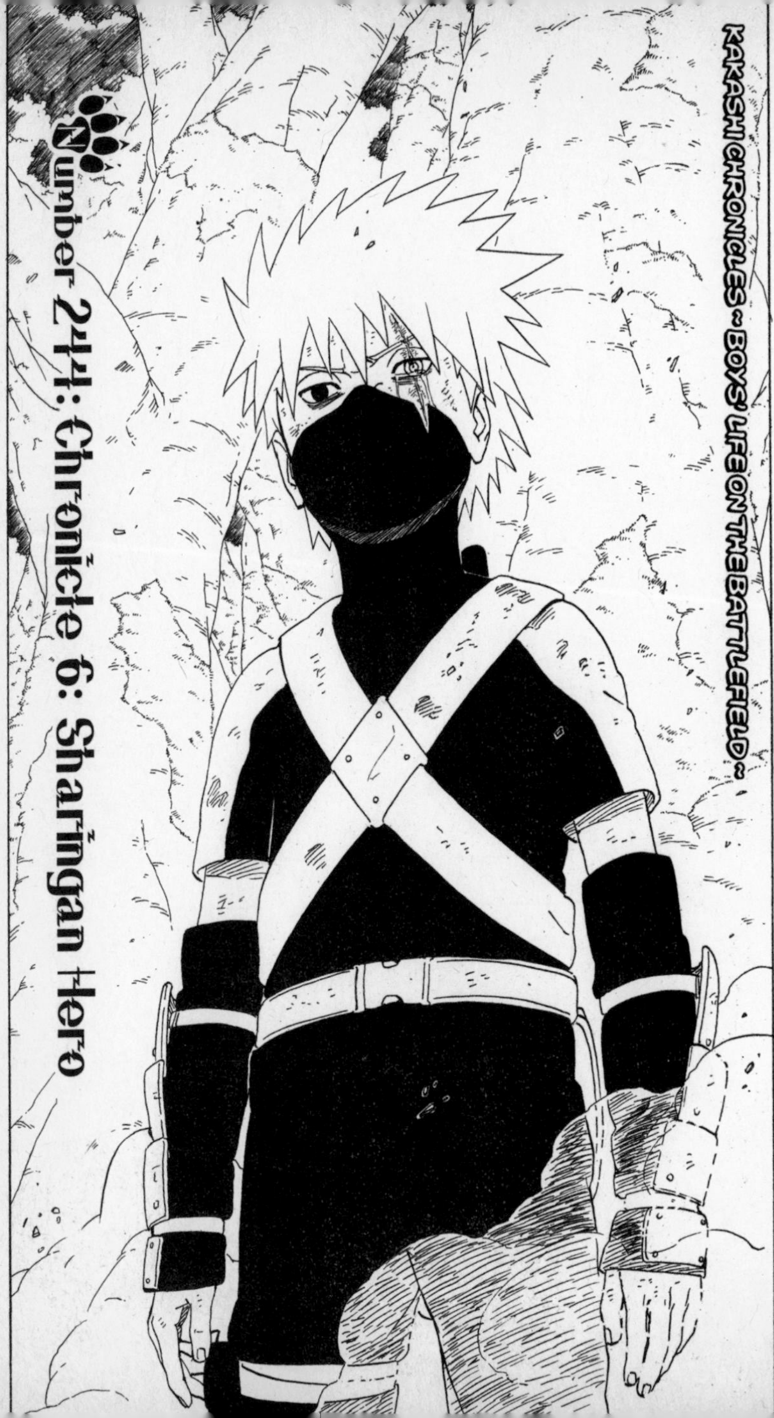
KAKASHI CHRONICLES ~BOYS' LIFE ON THE BATTLEFIELD~
Number 244: Chronicle 6: Sharingan Hero

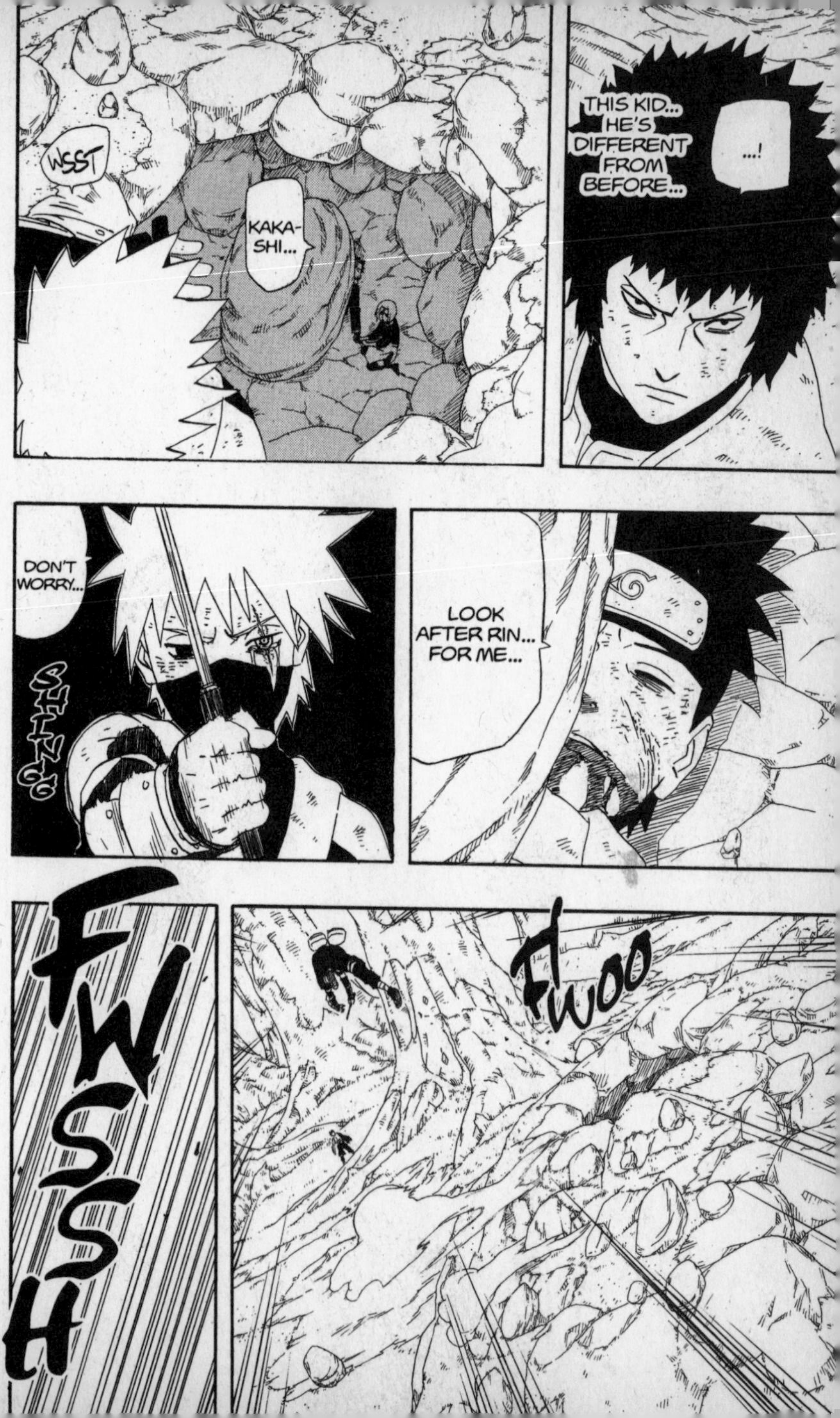
...!
THIS KID... HE'S DIFFERENT FROM BEFORE...
KAKA-SHI...
WSST
LOOK AFTER RIN... FOR ME...
DON'T WORRY...
SHING
FWOO
FWSSH

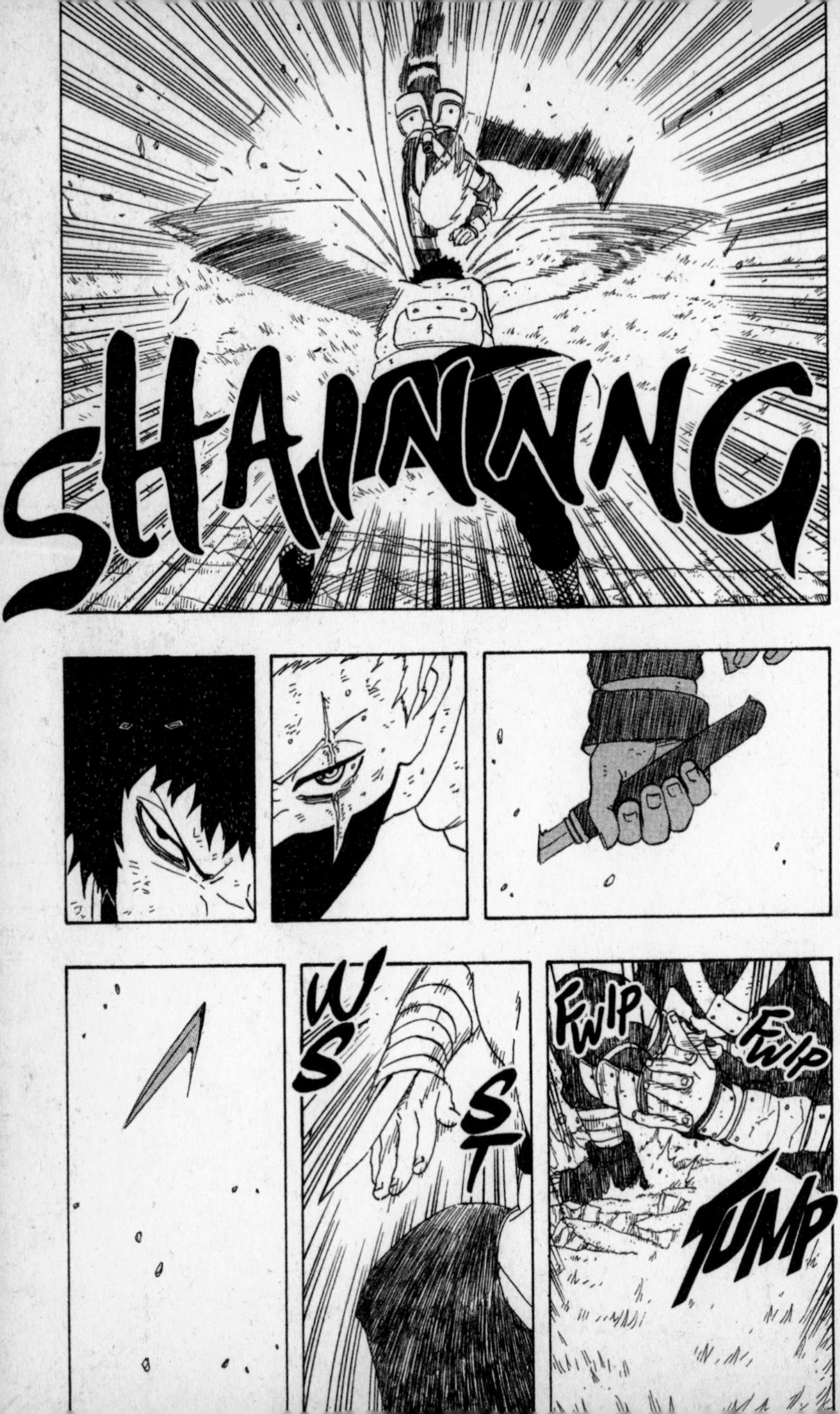
SHAINNNG
FWIP
FWIP
TUMP
WSST

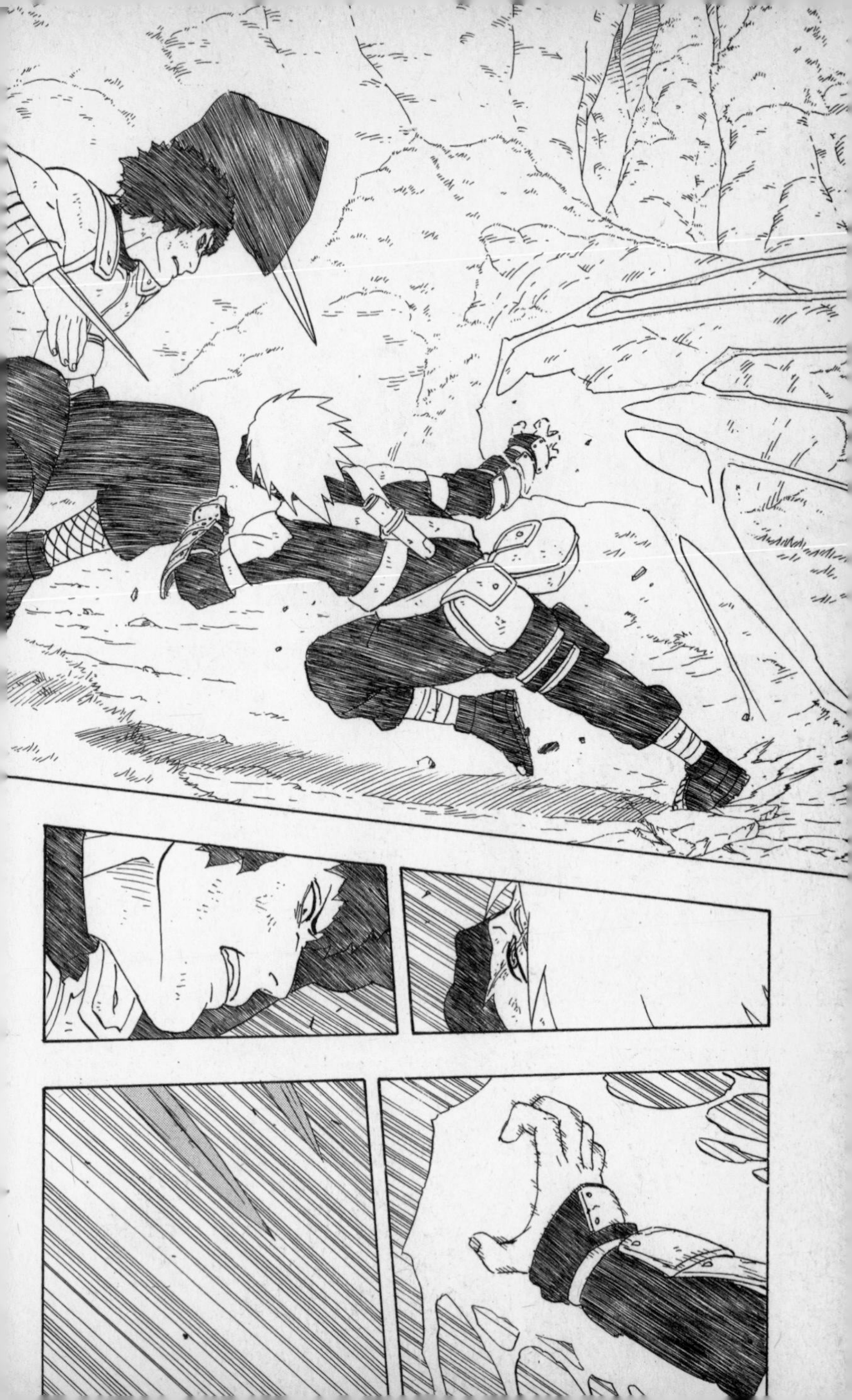

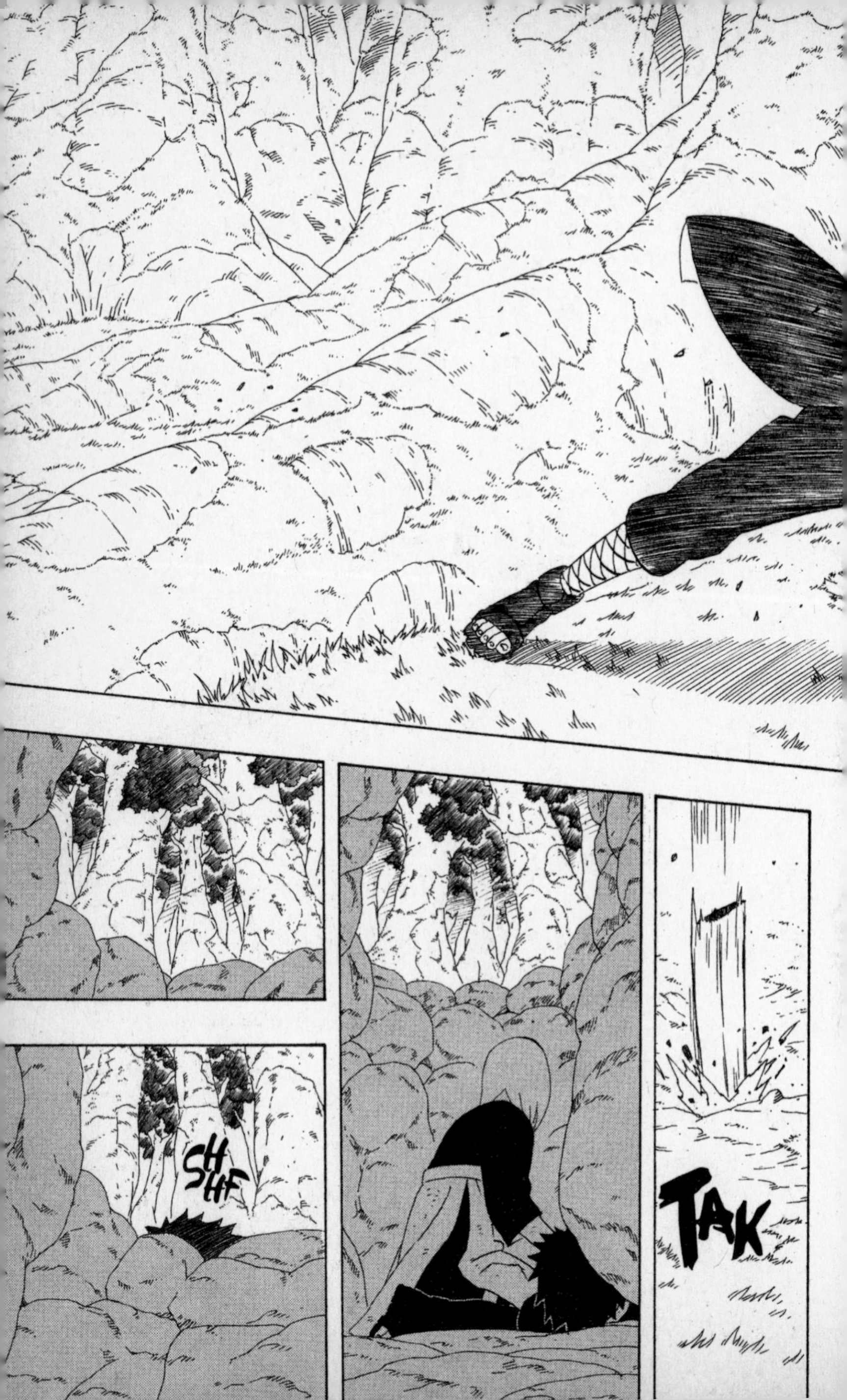
TAK
SHF
SHF

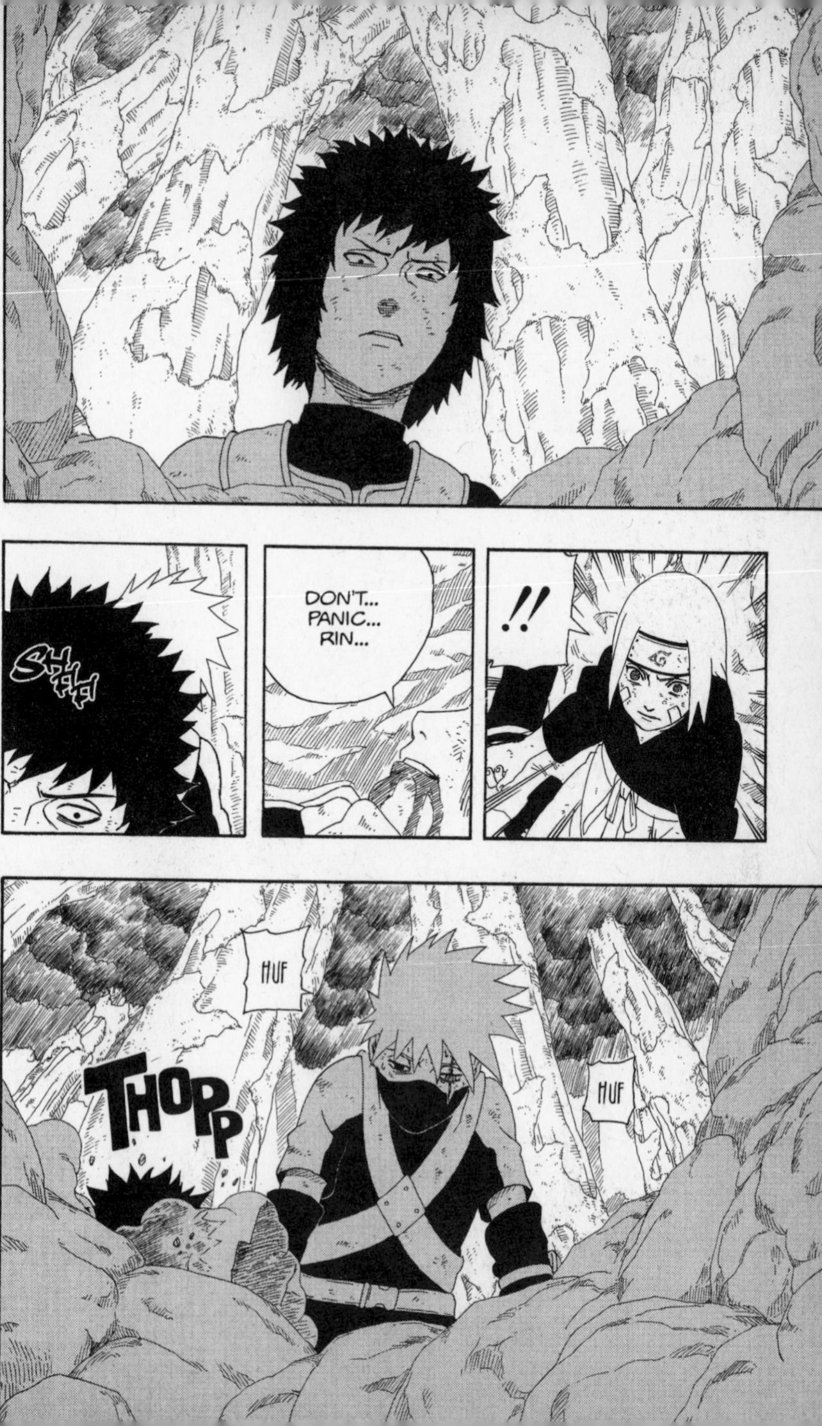
!!
DON'T... PANIC... RIN...
HUF
HUF
THOPP

READ THIS WAY

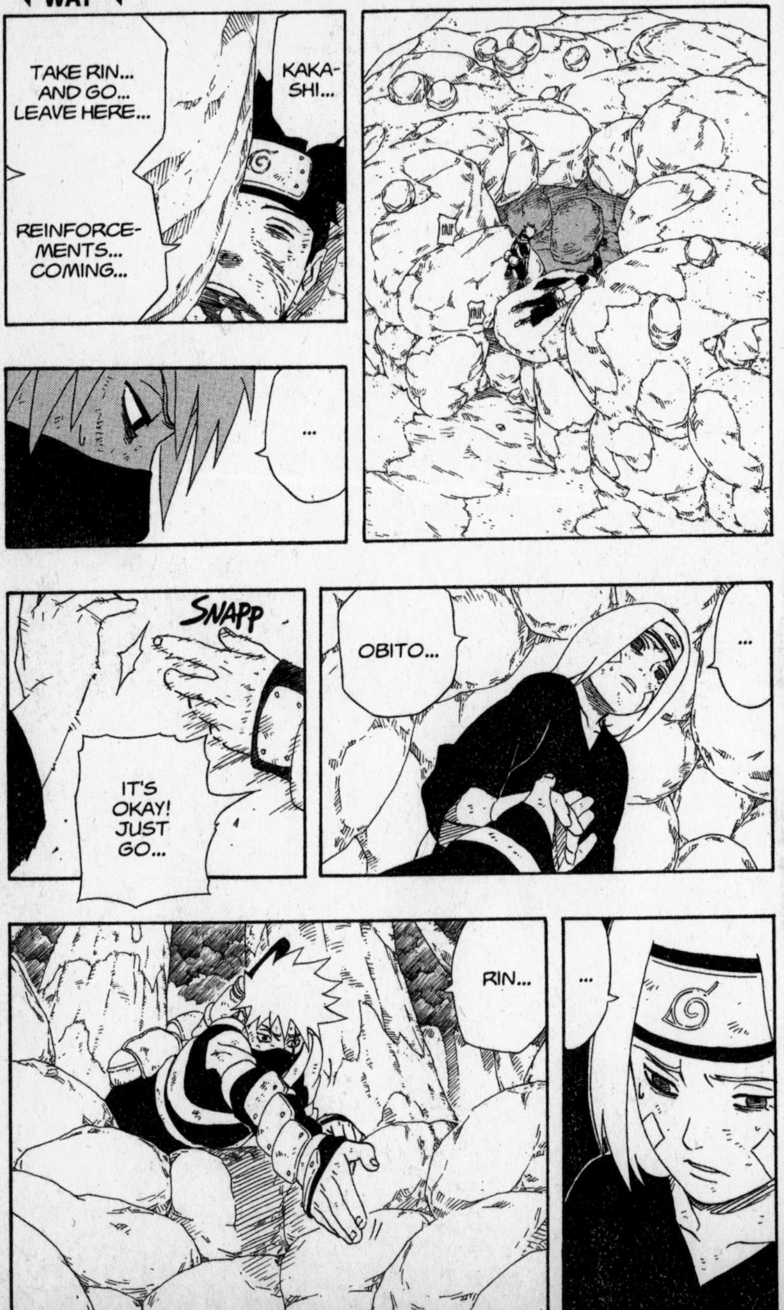
HUF
HUF
KAKA-SHI...
TAKE RIN... AND GO... LEAVE HERE...
REINFORCE-MENTS... COMING...
...
...
OBITO...
SNAPP
IT'S OKAY! JUST GO...
...
RIN...

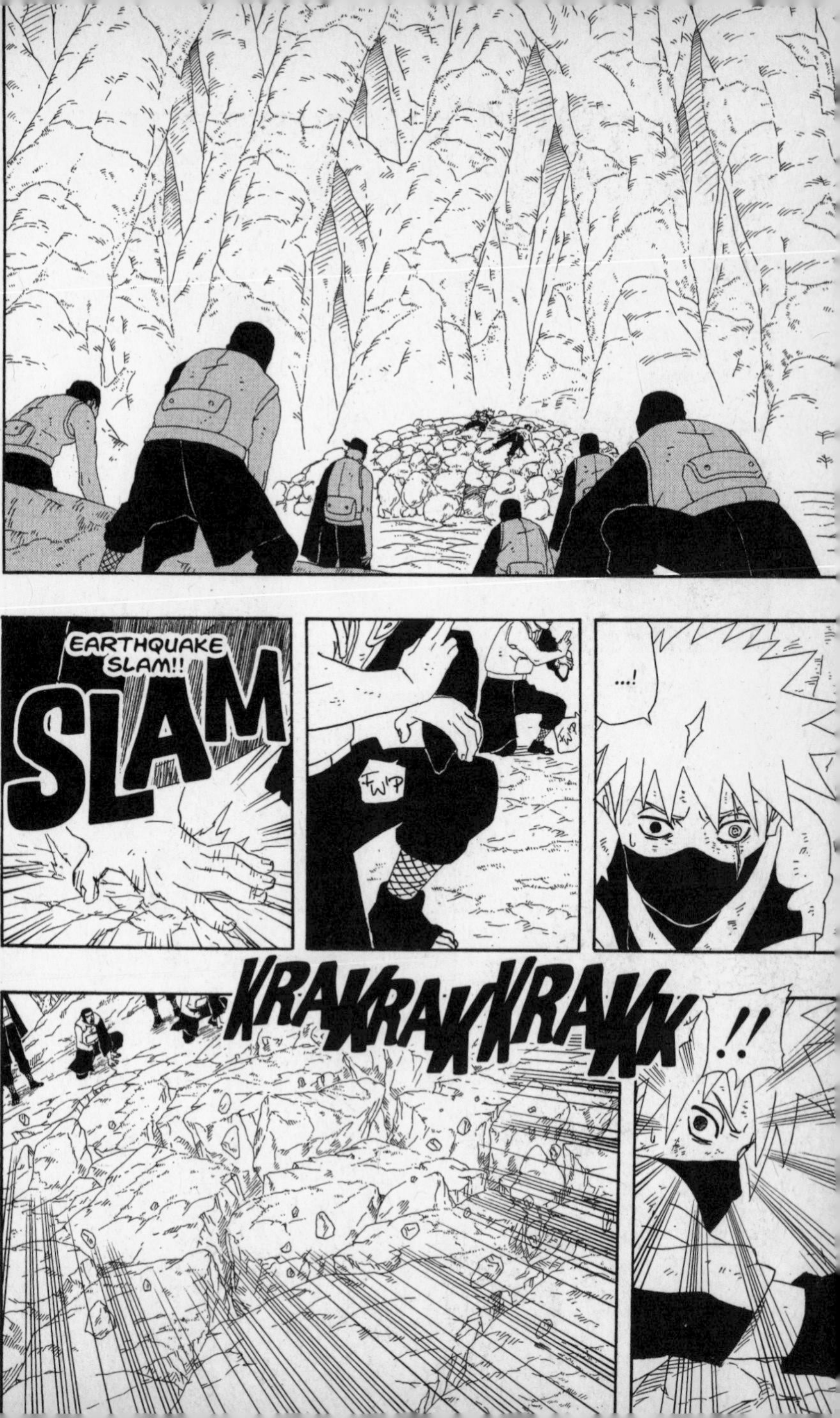
...!
FWP
FWP
EARTHQUAKE SLAM!!
SLAM
!!
KRAKKRAKKRAKK

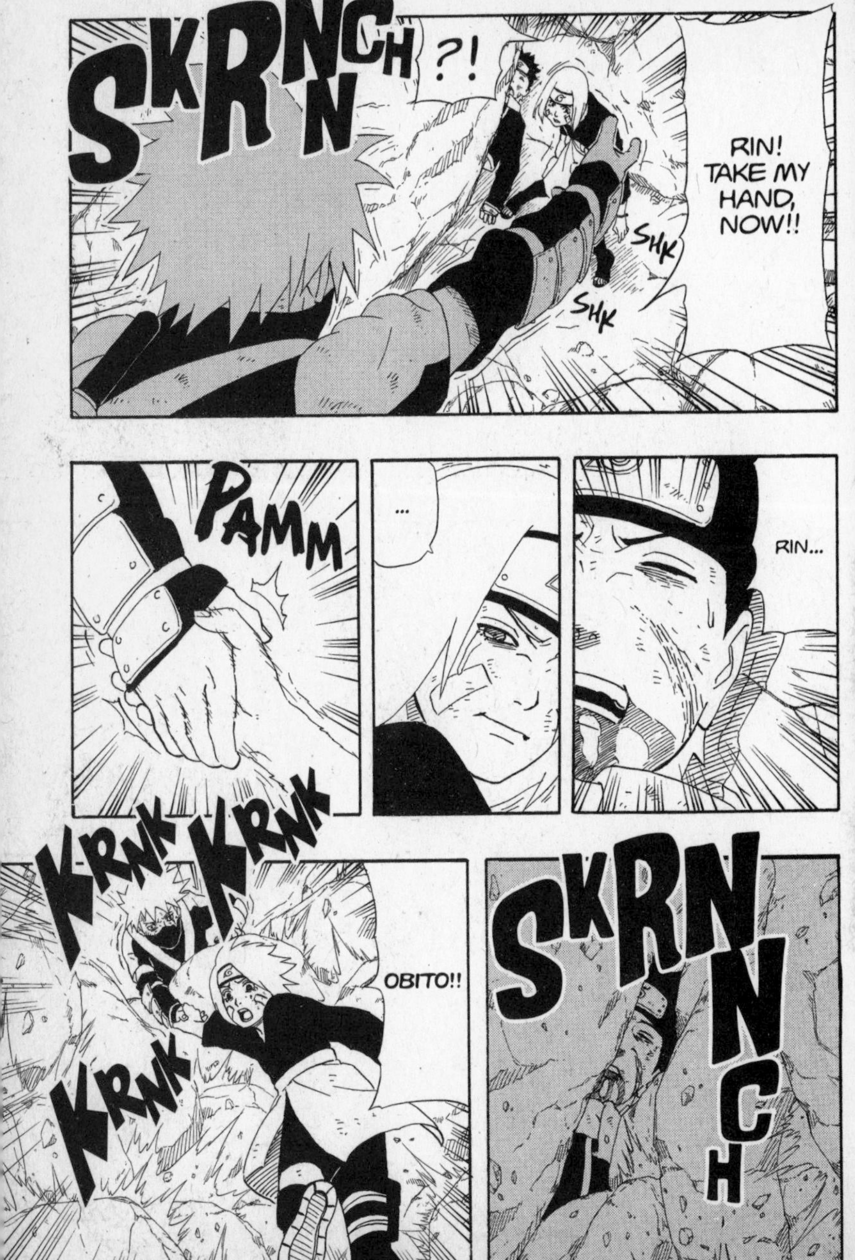
?!
RIN! TAKE MY HAND, NOW!!
SHK
SHK
SKRNCH
RIN...
...
PAMM
SKRNCH
OBITO!!
KRNK
KRNK
KRNK

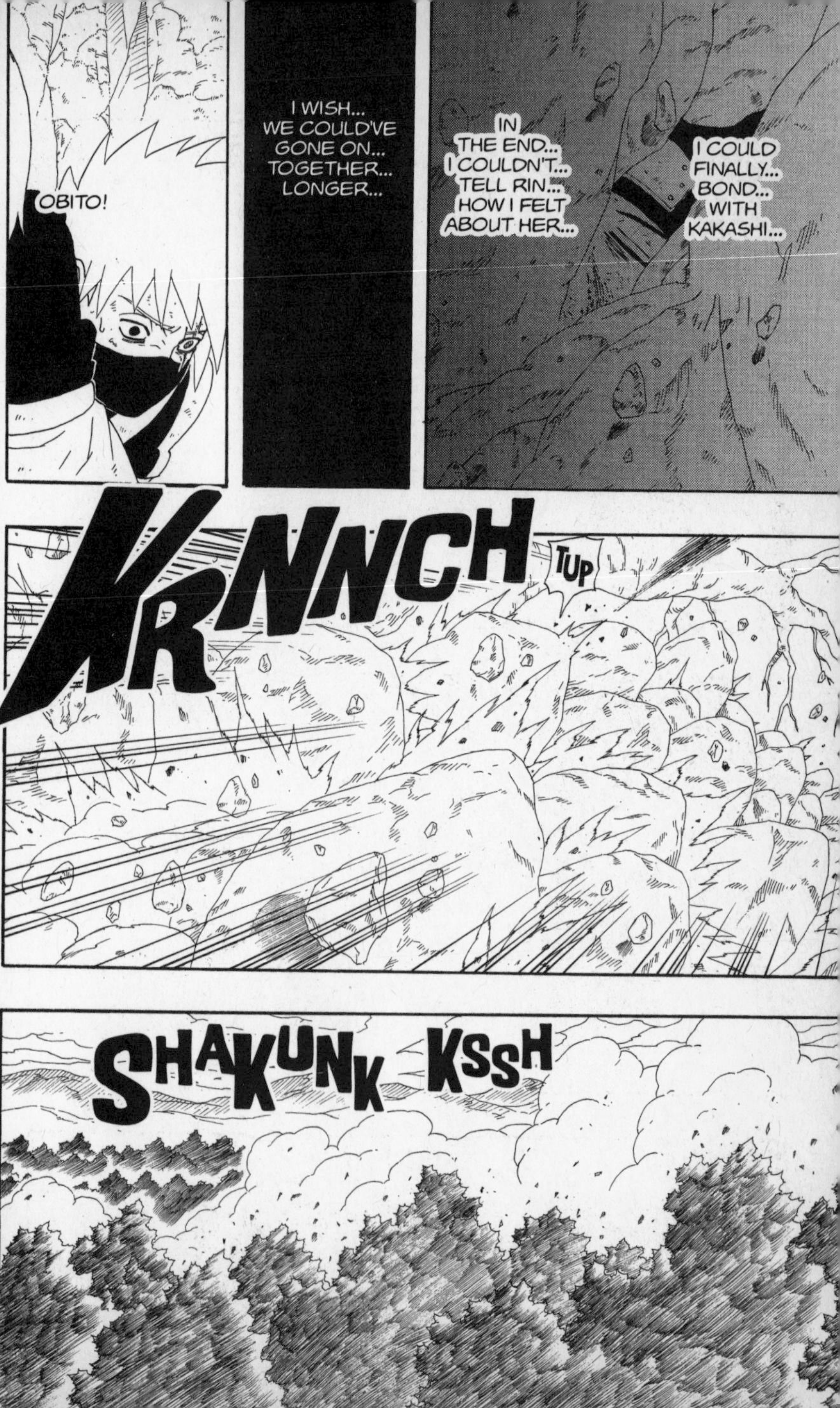
I COULD FINALLY... BOND... WITH KAKASHI...
IN THE END... I COULDN'T... TELL RIN... HOW I FELT ABOUT HER...
I WISH... WE COULD'VE GONE ON... TOGETHER... LONGER...
OBITO!
KRNNCH
TUP
SHAKUNK
KSSH

READ THIS WAY

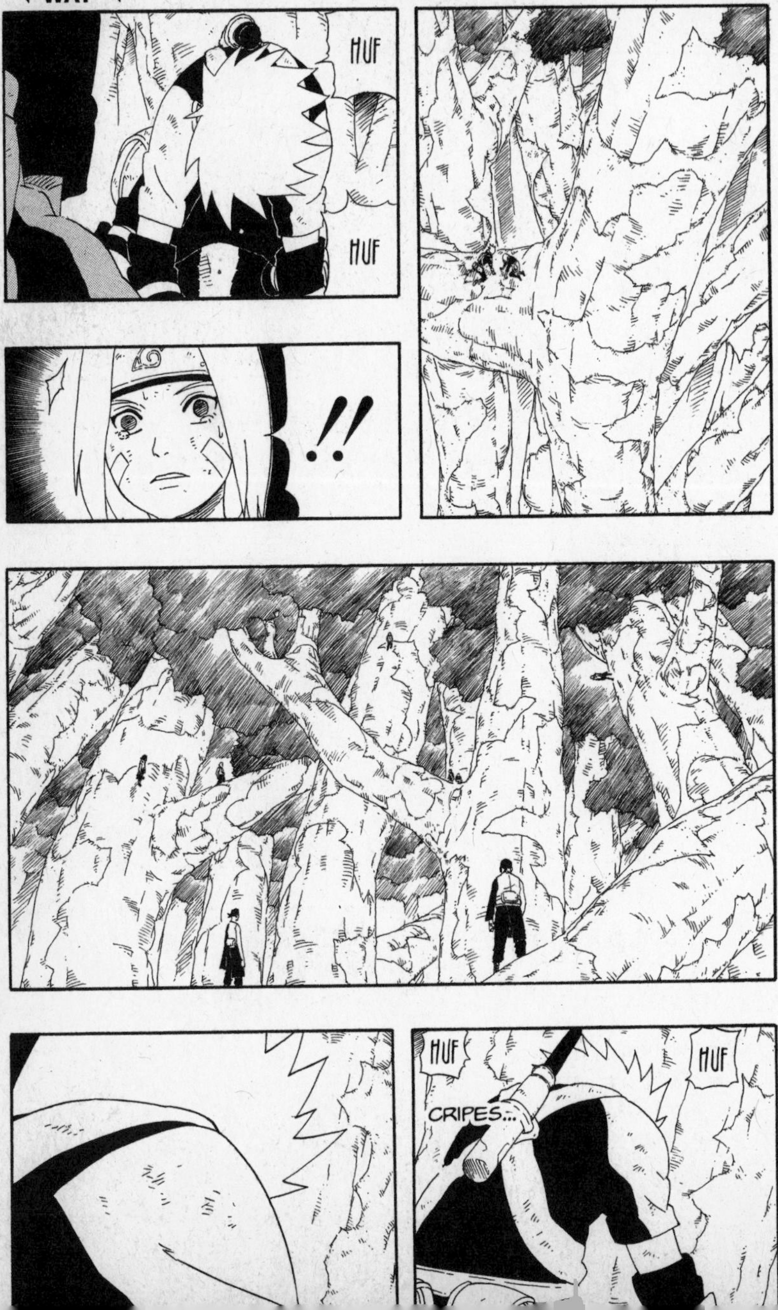
HUF
HUF
!!
HUF
HUF
CRIPES...

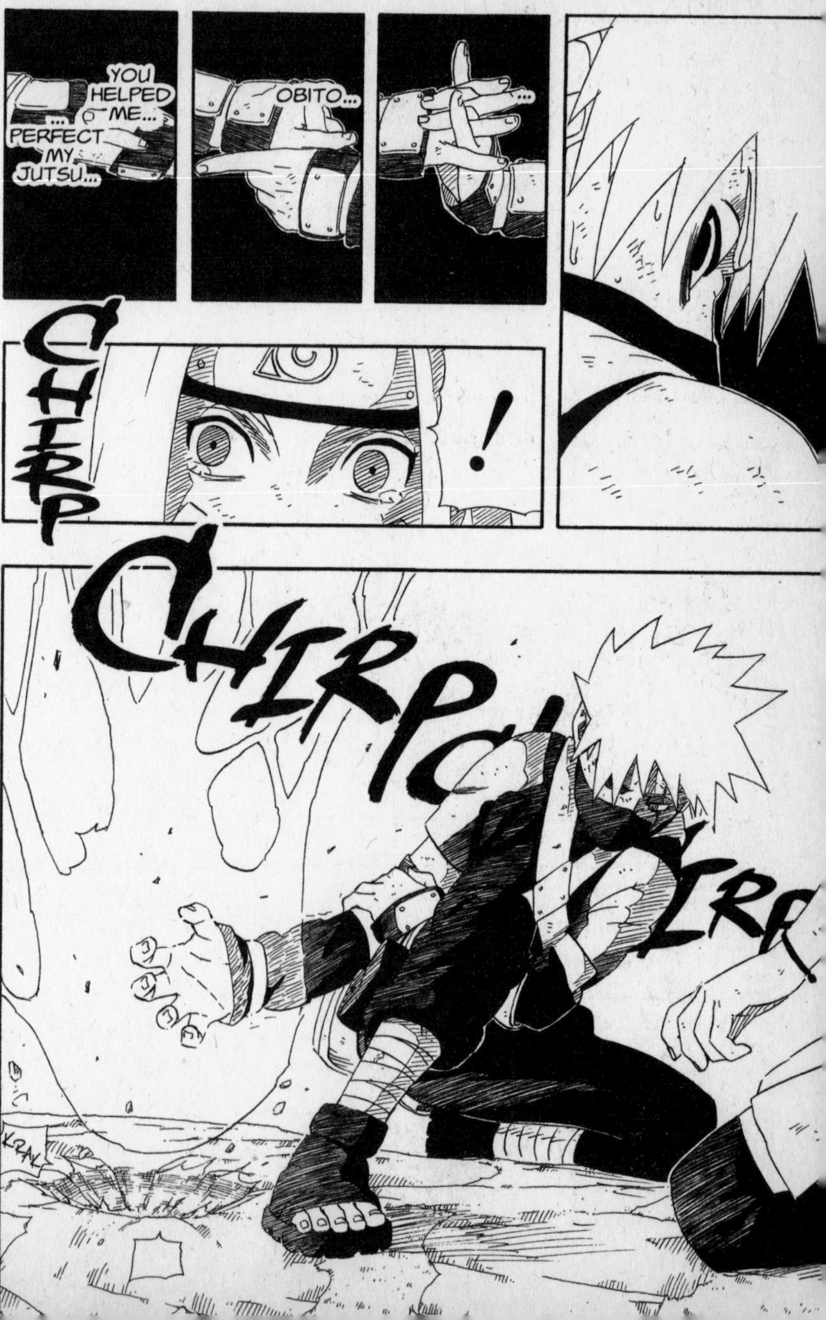
...
OBITO...
YOU HELPED ME...
... PERFECT MY JUTSU...
!
CHIRP
CHIRP
KRAK

READ THIS WAY

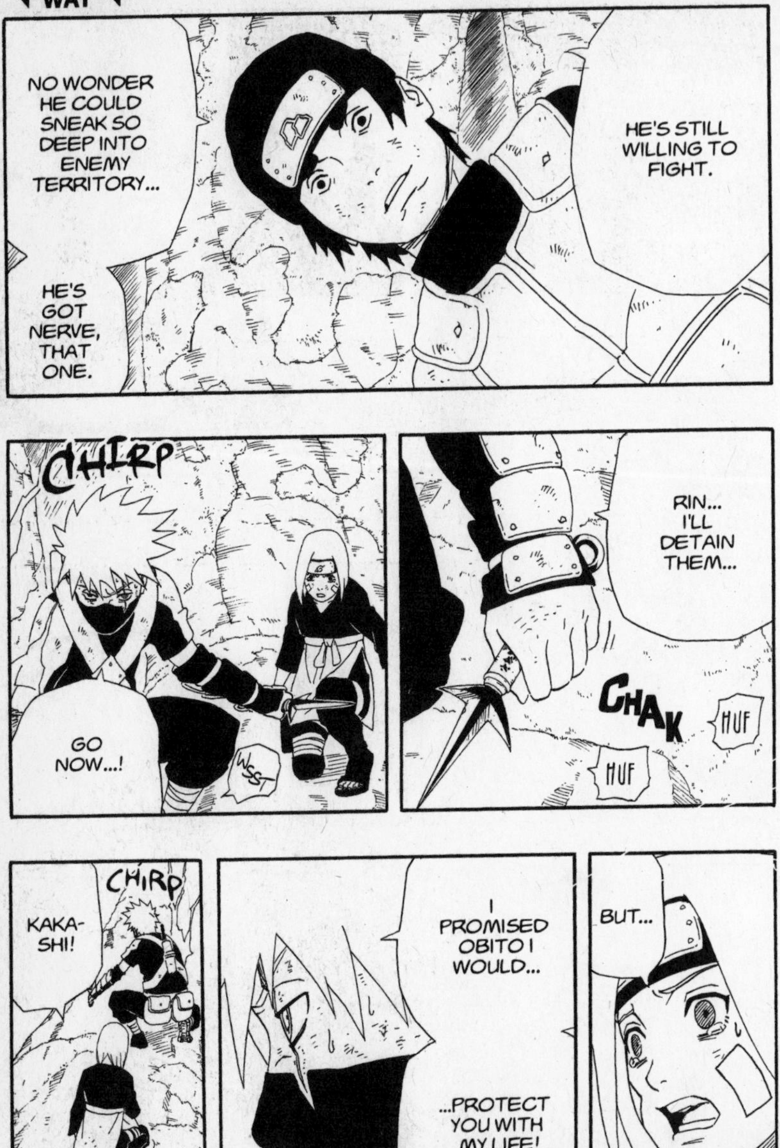

HE'S STILL WILLING TO FIGHT.
NO WONDER HE COULD SNEAK SO DEEP INTO ENEMY TERRITORY...
HE'S GOT NERVE, THAT ONE.
RIN... I'LL DETAIN THEM...
CHAK
HUF
HUF
CHIRP
GO NOW...!
WSST
BUT...
I PROMISED OBITO I WOULD...
...PROTECT YOU WITH MY LIFE!
CHIRP
KAKA-SHI!

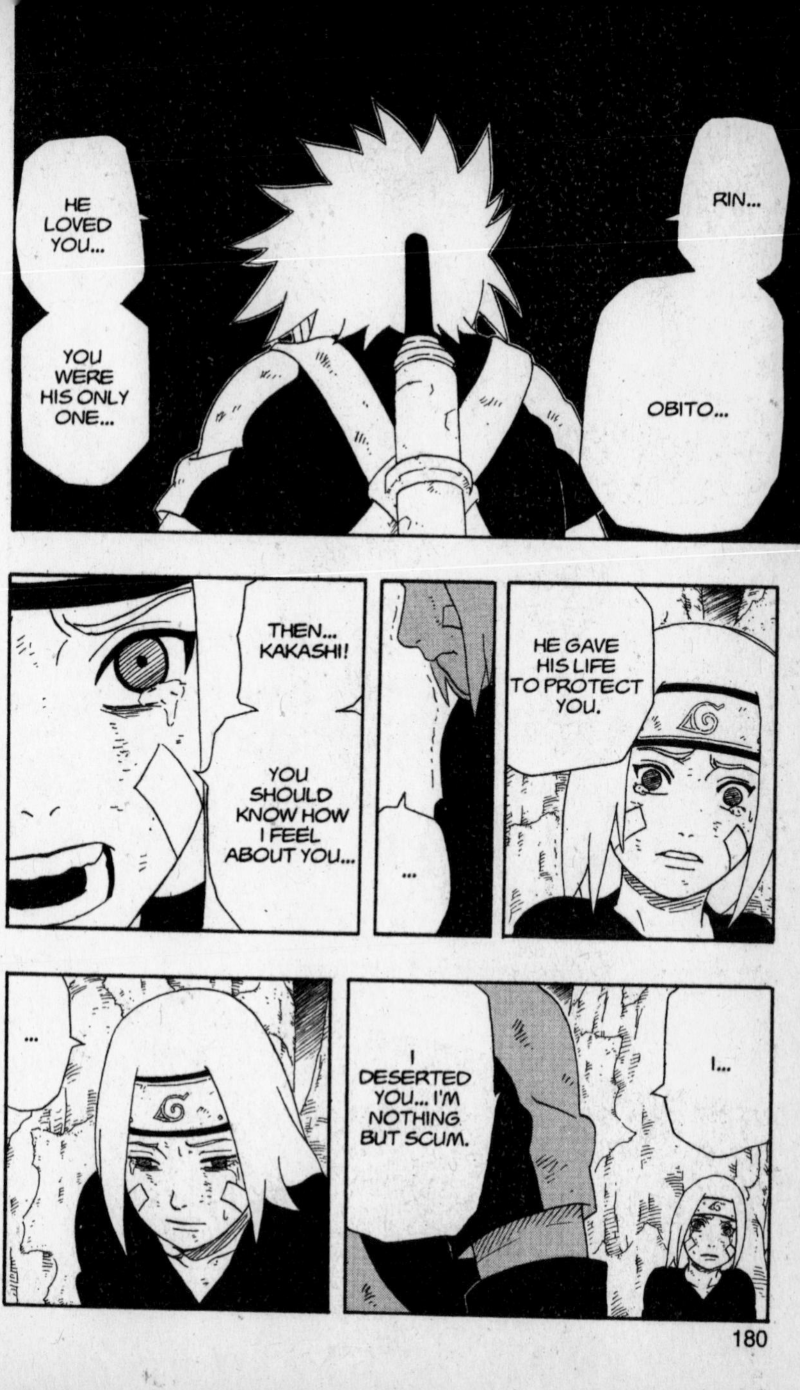
RIN...
OBITO...
HE LOVED YOU...
YOU WERE HIS ONLY ONE...
HE GAVE HIS LIFE TO PROTECT YOU.
...
THEN... KAKASHI!
YOU SHOULD KNOW HOW I FEEL ABOUT YOU...
I...
I DESERTED YOU... I'M NOTHING BUT SCUM.
...

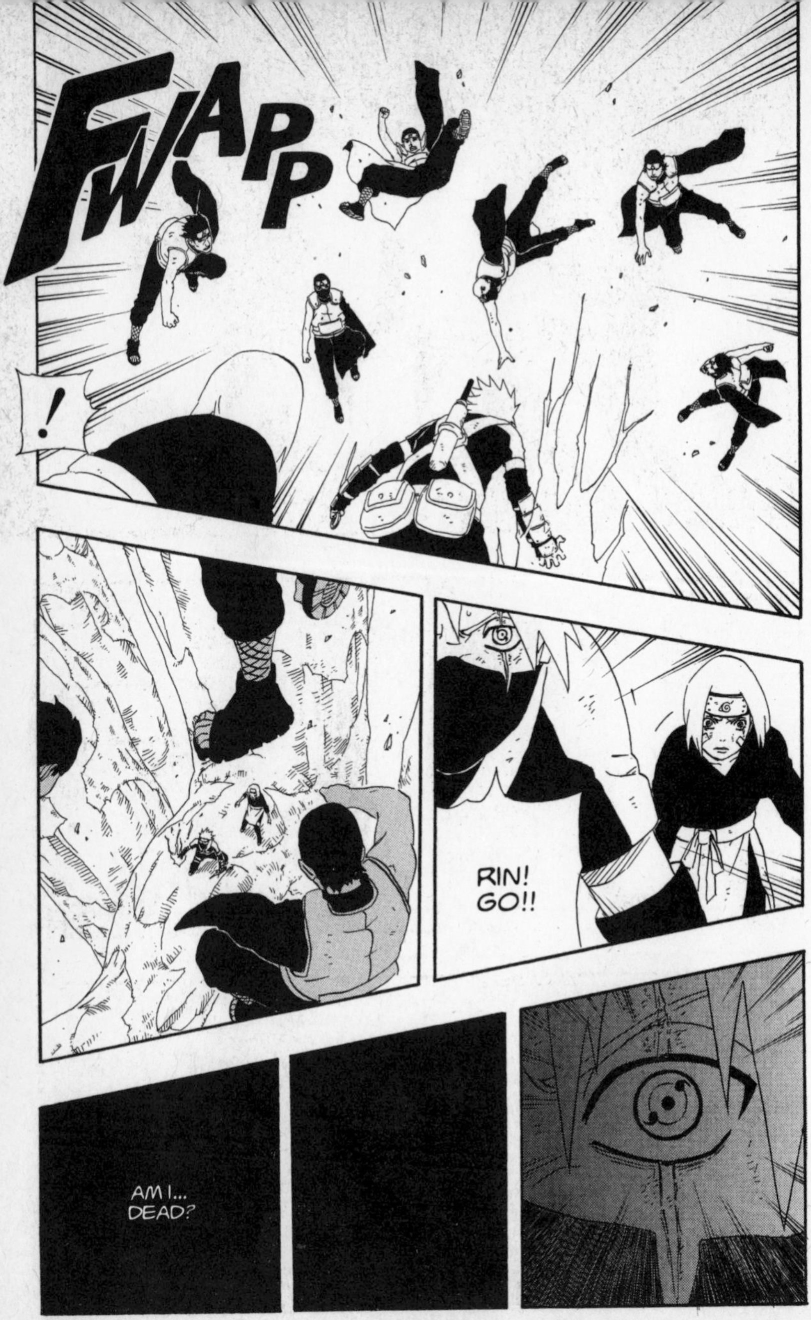
FWAPP
!
RIN! GO!!
AM I... DEAD?

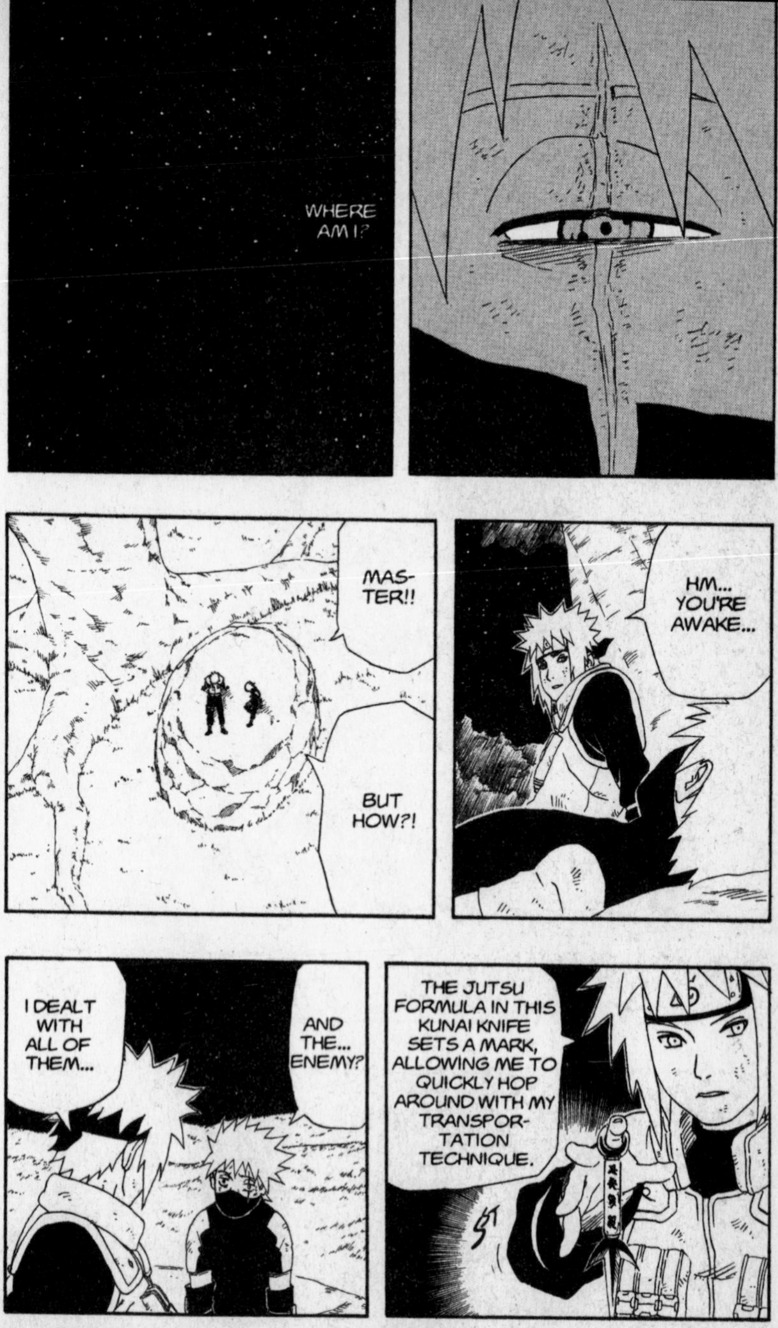
WHERE AM I?
HM... YOU'RE AWAKE...
MASTER!!
BUT HOW?!
THE JUTSU FORMULA IN THIS KUNAI KNIFE SETS A MARK, ALLOWING ME TO QUICKLY HOP AROUND WITH MY TRANSPORTATION TECHNIQUE.
AND THE... ENEMY?
I DEALT WITH ALL OF THEM...

READ THIS WAY

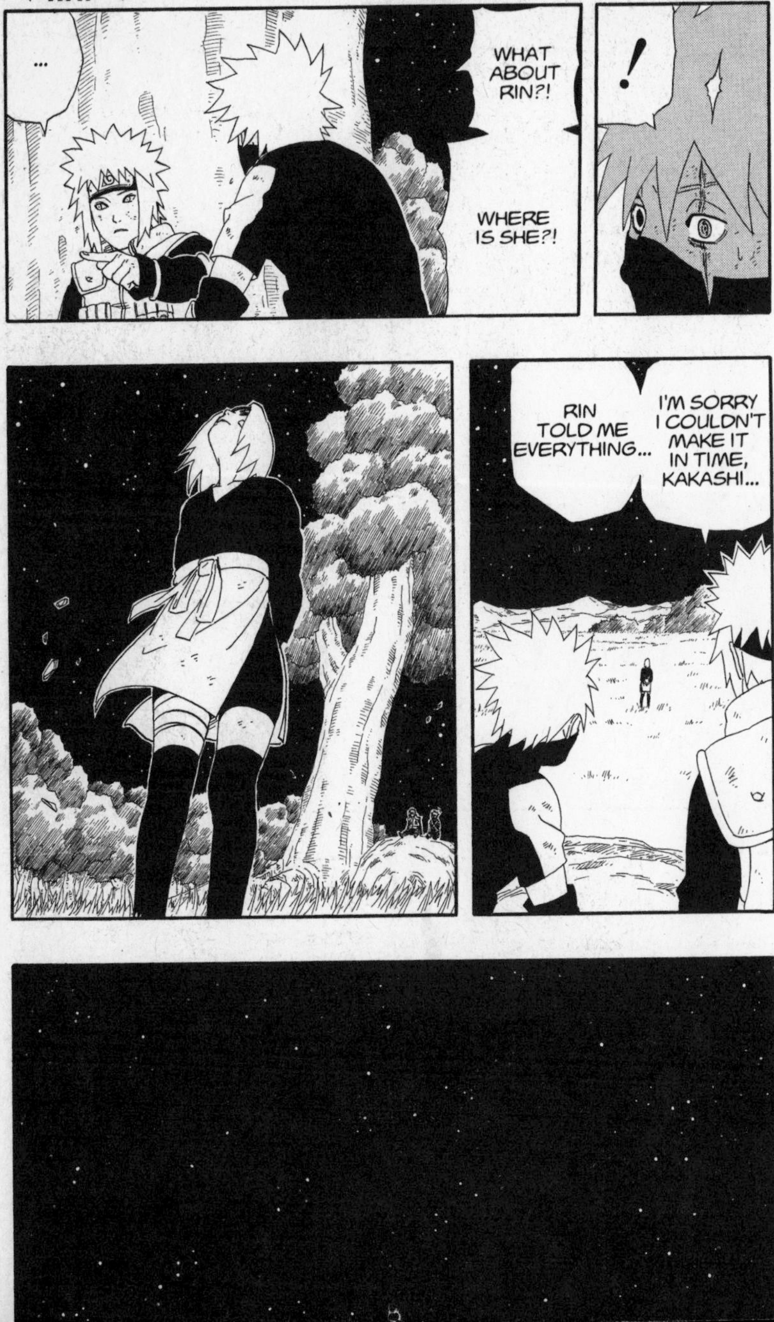
!
WHAT ABOUT RIN?!
WHERE IS SHE?!
...
I'M SORRY I COULDN'T MAKE IT IN TIME, KAKASHI...
RIN TOLD ME EVERYTHING...

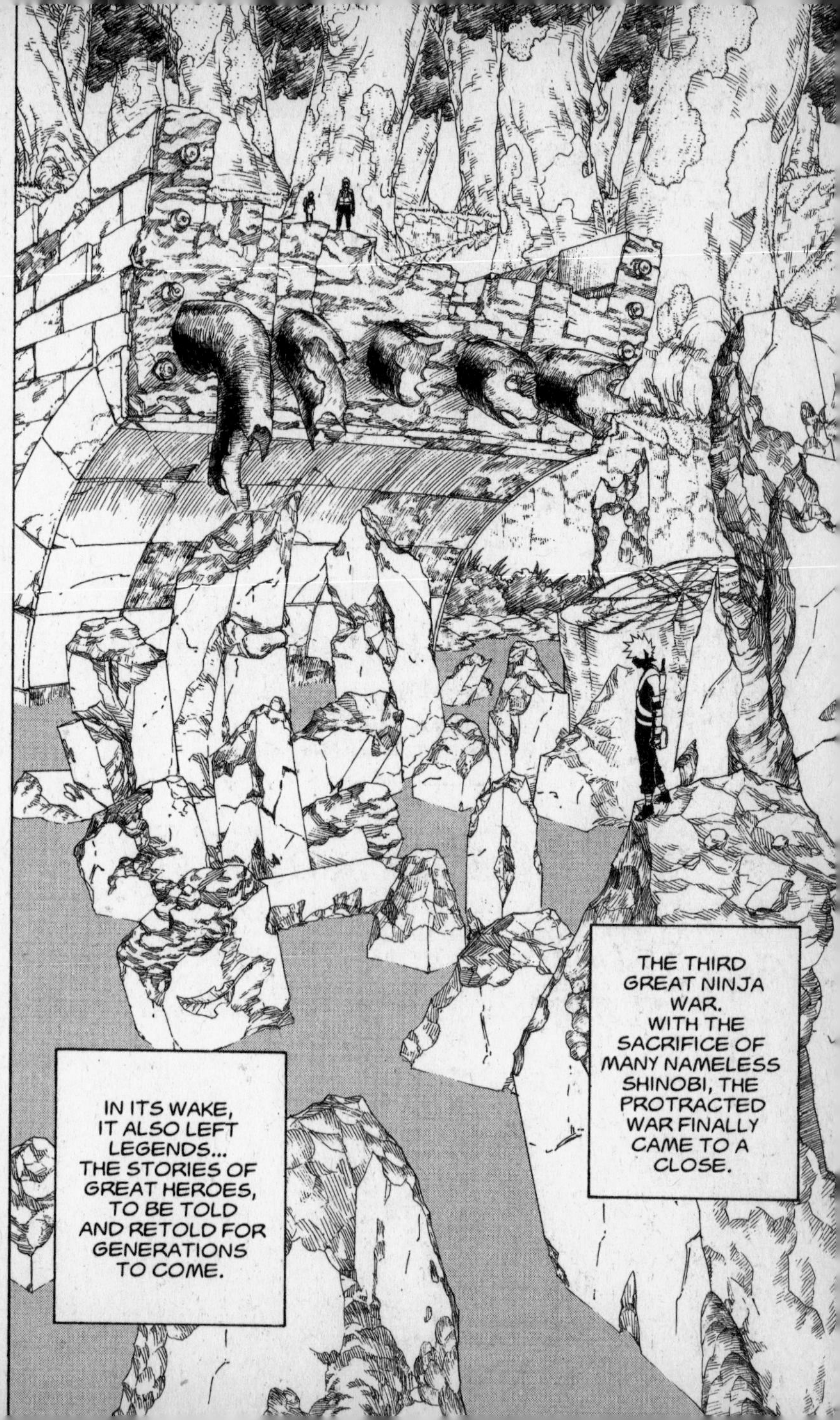
THE THIRD GREAT NINJA WAR. WITH THE SACRIFICE OF MANY NAMELESS SHINOBI, THE PROTRACTED WAR FINALLY CAME TO A CLOSE.
IN ITS WAKE, IT ALSO LEFT LEGENDS... THE STORIES OF GREAT HEROES, TO BE TOLD AND RETOLD FOR GENERATIONS TO COME.

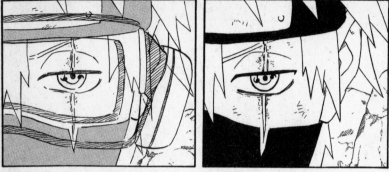

THE BATTLE OF KANNABI BRIDGE.

THAT DAY, TWO HEROES WERE BORN IN KONOHA-GAKURE, EACH WITH HIS OWN SHARINGAN.

ONE FOUND HIS NAME ENGRAVED ON THE MEMORIAL STONE...

THE OTHER CAME TO BE KNOWN AS KAKASHI OF THE SHARINGAN. IN TIME, THE TALES OF HIS BRAVERY SPANNED ALL BORDERS, AND BEYOND.

185

KAKASHI CHRONICLES / THE END

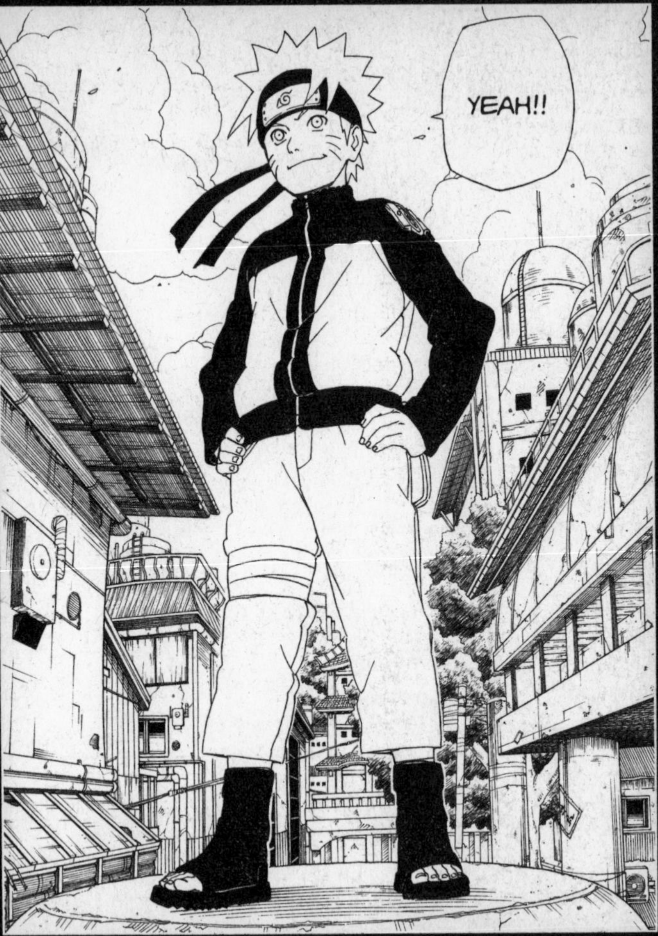
YEAH!!

IN THE NEXT VOLUME...

HOMECOMING

Naruto returns! It's been two years since Naruto left to train with Jiraiya. Now he reunites with his old friends to find out he's still not the most accomplished of his former teammates. But when one of them is kidnapped, it's up to Naruto to prove he's got the stuff to save him!

AVAILABLE MARCH 2008!

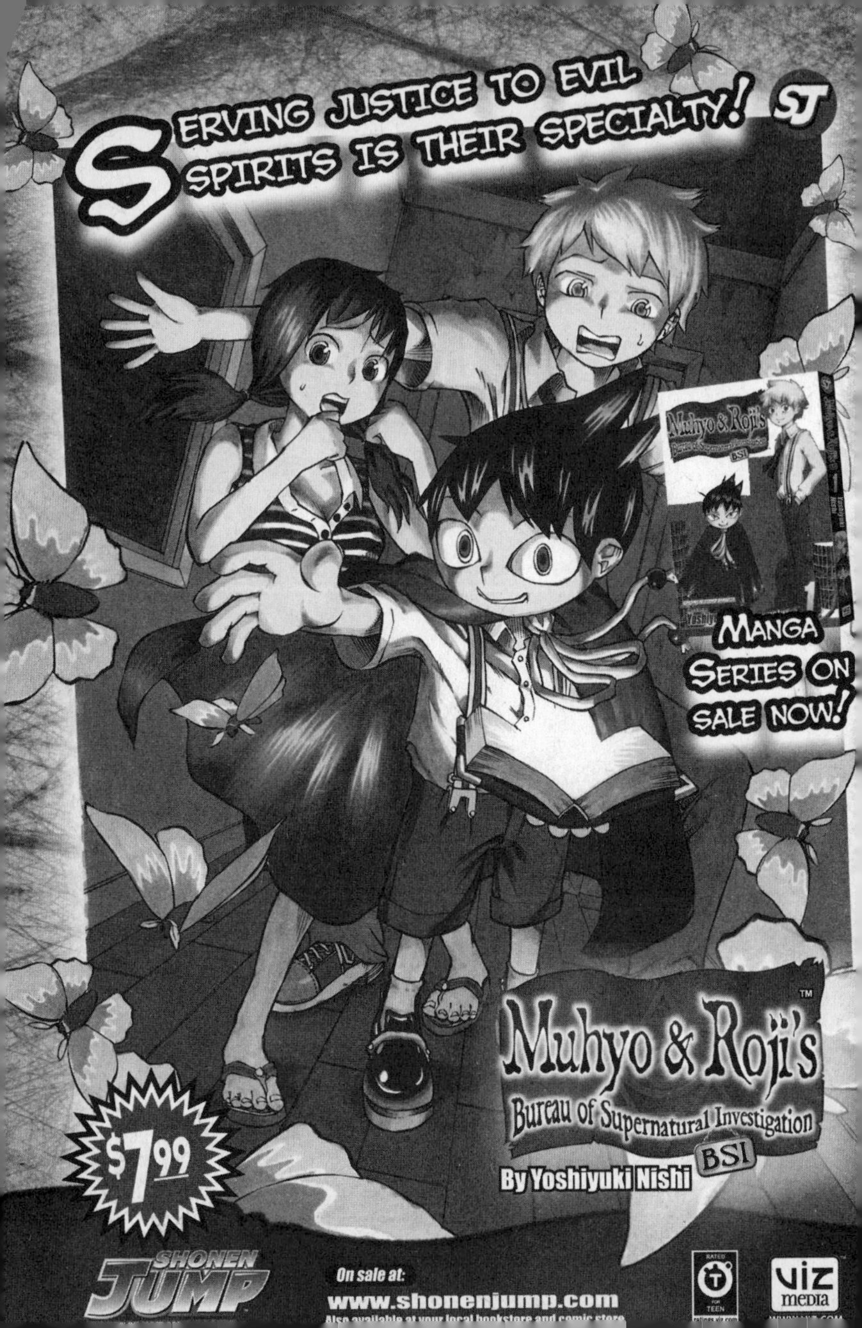
SERVING JUSTICE TO EVIL SPIRITS IS THEIR SPECIALTY!
SJ
MANGA SERIES ON SALE NOW!
Muhyo & Roji's™
Bureau of Supernatural Investigation
BSI
By Yoshiyuki Nishi
$7.99
SHONEN JUMP
On sale at:
www.shonenjump.com
RATED T FOR TEEN
VIZ media

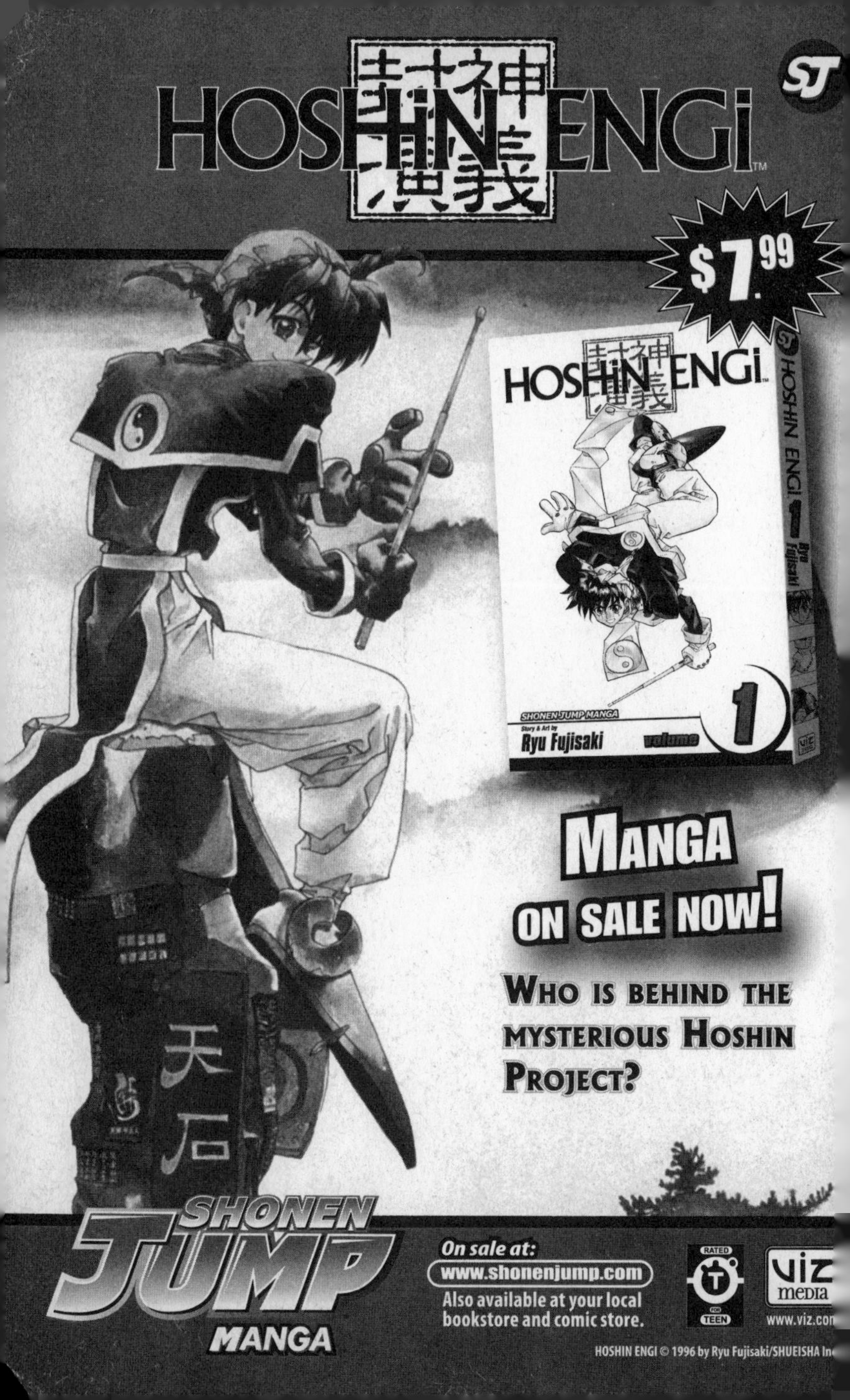

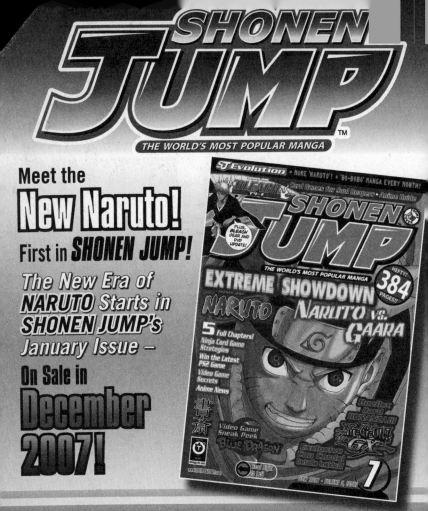